WHAT PEOPLE ARE SAYING ABOUT GEORGE WOOD, BRIT EATON, AND *THE UNCOVERY DEVOTIONAL*...

My friend George Wood has given us a tremendous resource to meet the needs of our hearts. *The Uncovery Devotional: Rethinking Recovery One Day at a Time* offers a unique approach to recovery, particularly for individuals struggling with addiction, mental health issues, and suicidal thoughts. It aims to provide daily opportunities for personal growth, healing, and transformation by addressing the underlying traumas that contribute to these struggles. The Uncovery program emphasizes a Christ-centered perspective and believes that recovery is not just a process or a one-time event but a lifelong journey toward a new and transformed life. One of the distinguishing aspects of *The Uncovery Devotional* is its reimagining of the traditional twelve-step process. George Wood has brilliantly focused each month on a specific theme related to one of the twelve steps, offering a fresh perspective and allowing for a deeper exploration of that particular step.

—*Brian Simmons*
Passion & Fire Ministries
The Passion Translation Project

This is far more than a devotional. This is a Christic, new covenant manifesto. This is an accessible, personal, challenging, and empowering manual for approaching the Bible, understanding your identity, and engaging with God. I can't stress strongly enough the importance of this book. Its reach is well beyond the targeted audience that the Uncovery was created for. The themes in this book reflect the journey God has taken me on in the past twenty years, and they are laid out with so much wisdom and order that it's like looking at a journal of my own walk with the Holy Spirit. The revelation of union and the finished work of the cross changes everything, if you believe it. By the end of this journey, you just might. Thank you, George and Brit, for creating a priceless resource that will still be here to guide my great-great-grandchildren long after I have gone home.

—*Bill Vanderbush*
President, Faith Mountain Ministries

This 365-day devotional is exactly what this generation needs. It provides guidance and a step-by-step process on *how* to walk in freedom. Every one of us is in some form of recovery, and this book is like having a spiritual father guide your heart in truth and freedom. No matter where you are in your spiritual journey, this book will take you by the hand and lead you to greater freedom.

—*Joey Papa*
The Failed Christian Podcast and JoeyTalks

Continuing the journey from the first book, *The Uncovery*, this one is incredibly raw and real. This life-changing devotional dares to challenge conventional recovery approaches, presenting 365 days of unflinching honesty and profound insights. A must-read for those seeking true transformation and hope, it fearlessly tackles the struggles of life head-on, potentially saving lives along the way. This compelling journey of faith and recovery is light for anyone seeking genuine healing and a deeper connection with God.

—*Brian "Head" Welch*
Co-founder, Grammy Award-winning band Korn
New York Times best-selling author

The Uncovery Devotional goes beyond traditional Christ-centered recovery programs, providing daily opportunities to heal from trauma and struggle at a deeper level. This devotional will guide readers towards a brand new life, empowering them to uncover their God-given strength and embrace a holistic approach to recovery, all while pointing them to Christ, our ultimate Healer. I'm honored to endorse this book!

—*Jordan Raynor*
Author, *The Word Before Work* and *Redeeming Your Time*

I've known George Wood for most of my life. We grew up together in the same small town in Upstate New York. We played high school football together, attended the same parties, and lived similar lifestyles in our younger days. I've followed George's career from afar and have been amazed at the transformation that has taken place in his life. George's redemption story is an incredible example of the power of God's unfailing and unrelenting love. These daily devotions will challenge, inspire, and mentor you as you grow in and through the love of our Lord and Savior Jesus Christ.

—*Herb Hand*
Co-offensive coordinator, University of Central Florida Knights

As you seek to transform your life from being marred by addiction, trauma, or suicidal thoughts, you need to intentionally make choices that build a life worth staying sober, restored, and alive for. This devotional helps accomplish that. Each day's message challenges you to see yourself for more than your struggles and addictions, giving a call to action for you to step into the promised-land life that is yours for the taking. One that is filled with endless amounts of grace, hope, renewal, and love found in Jesus Christ. Don't believe the lies of the devil; recovery is possible, it's for you, and it starts now!

—*Terry Skaggs, MA, LMFT*
Host, *Testimonies with Terry Podcast*

"I failed...again." The story of my life. Throughout a destructive street lifestyle of selling drugs, robbing, and using, I know the cycle of addiction all too well. Yet while incarcerated for over twelve years, my life was forever changed. I encountered Jesus, began walking in my purpose, and am now helping others do the same. A daily principle that I soon adopted at the beginning of my faith walk was daily Bible reading. Here, my dawg, friend, and fellow soldier in Christ, George Wood, along with his coauthor Brit Eaton, present us with a great tool for daily Bible devotion. "Rethinking recovery" is a useful tool that will biblically challenge, encourage, and hold you accountable to the commands and promises of God.

—*E.i. the King*
Christian hip-hop artist

George is a good pastor, and along with his coauthor Brit Eaton, their daily liturgy has done something truly good for those seeking salvation and freedom from the bondage of addiction. In every daily reading, George and Brit point to Jesus, the One who has walked through the darkness, and the only one who can truly lead us out. No doubt, this book will be a daily guide for spiritual formation of many so desperately seeking it.

—*Tommy Phillips*
Pastor, Watermark Church; Christian folk artist

There is an ever-growing chasm that the enemy of our souls uses to separate us from healing, hope, and truly holding the ever-pursuing love of our God. On one side, he uses trauma to lure us into cycles of sin, addiction, and breakdowns in mental health to bury beloved sons and daughters in hopelessness and shame. On the other side, he uses judgment, fear, and ego to distract and distance the very people God is calling near as ambassadors of His restoring love to live stuck in their own bubble. *Here's the truth*: somewhere, we relate deeply to both of those chasms, all the time. We all need healing, and we've all been called to carry the Healer. In this crucial place, *The Uncovery Devotional* is a gift! Paced with short, power-packed daily devotions that deal with the whole person (body, soul, and spirit), this is an ideal resource for both those actively walking through recovery and the well-meaning people in their lives who desire to walk with them, but often don't know what to do. It is rare to find resources that speak authoritatively in both a robust theology of God's true heart for creation *and* a grounded and well-researched psychology that understands the nature of trauma and addiction, but it is exactly what George and Brit have delivered here. Read this book alongside a friend or a few who will share the journey with you, and wrestle honestly with what you find in these pages. If you do, it won't just change your life. It will transform the very community around you!

—*Chuck Ammons*
Lead pastor, Overflow Church

The Uncovery Devotional is a powerful encouragement and help for individuals walking the path of recovery. This profound devotional is a beacon of hope, offering a transformative journey toward greater freedom, health, and spiritual renewal in Jesus Christ. It is not merely a collection of words; it is a lifeline for those in recovery, reminding them that they are not alone in their struggles. Readers will discover a wealth of wisdom, deep insights, and scriptural truths that gently guide them towards a life of healing and wholeness. George and Brit skillfully weave together personal experiences, biblical teachings, practical applications, and deep insights, creating a tapestry of inspiration that resonates with the heart and soul.

—*Kristi and Bill Gaultiere*
Founders, Soul Shepherding Institute
Authors, *Journey of the Soul*

George and his words are inspiring because his life is inspiring. George is all-in. He'd have it no other way because Jesus would have it no other way. My time around George always challenges me to rethink any ways I'm holding back, to let go, and fall deeper in love with my Creator and Sustainer.

—*Gary Taylor*
Lead pastor, BayMarin Church

This is an excellent companion resource for a very important book (*The Uncovery*) and a subtle reminder that in recovery, every day counts.

—*Brian Sanders*
Author, *6 Seasons of Calling*; founder, Underground Network

The Uncovery Devotional is a profound exploration of the powerful linkage between trauma, addiction, and faith. In this captivating devotional, George Wood and his coauthor Brit Eaton skillfully weave together Scripture and quote-worthy ideas to shed light on the intricate connections between these three crucial aspects of human experience. Through their previous book, *The Uncovery*, readers embark on a transformative journey, delving into the depths of trauma's impact on the psyche and its profound influence on addiction. In addition to its insightful exploration of trauma and addiction, *The Uncovery Devotional* embraces the pivotal role of faith in the healing process. The authors adeptly explore how faith can serve as a guiding light, leading individuals toward understanding, forgiveness, and a path to recovery. By intertwining personal faith journeys and the triumphs of those who have found solace and strength in their beliefs, the book offers a compelling testament to the transformative power of faith in healing from trauma and addiction. Whether you are someone who has experienced trauma or addiction, healing is a daily journey, and *The Uncovery Devotional* will guide you step by step for the entire year!

—*Evan Owens*
Executive director, Reboot Recovery

If you, like me, finished *The Uncovery* with both conviction and a longing to lean in, this book is the next step. It's a daily companion to reorient the soul and rewire the neural pathways toward a Jesus-drenched and transformative journey toward healing.

—*Lucas Pulley*
Executive director, Underground Network

Recovery is not a once-in-a-while activity. It is the center of a lifestyle that allows for growth and renewal every day. *The Uncovery Devotional* is an important addition to the ways a recovery lifestyle can be experienced. George Wood and Brit Eaton have developed a focused book of daily readings to help make and maintain this essential spiritual discipline. They go beyond what our first thoughts might be about recovery and faith and lead us into rethinking how recovery can grow. This is a worthy addition to the spiritual disciplines of recovery.

—*Barry Lehman*
Author, *Mastering Recovery*; retired pastor
Licensed alcohol and drug counselor, Mayo Clinic

In their book *The Uncovery*, my friends George Wood and Brit Eaton issued a wake-up call to believers to step beyond the cozy confines of cultural Christianity and cooperate with the Holy Spirit to cultivate communities of healing and restoration through the power of Jesus. In the follow-up devotional that you now hold in your hands, they have taken this important message even further. Readers are invited to connect with God through His Word, and then invite Him to uncover and heal the places of hurt and pain that too often stay hidden in our hearts. The daily readings each have a Scripture, a real-world reflection, and a prayer that create a place of focus and provide an opportunity for connection with God and with our own hearts. I encourage you to make *The Uncovery Devotional* a part of your daily connection with God, welcoming His Spirit to heal and bring hope to every hurting place in your heart.

—*Brad McKoy*
Author, *Culture of the Few*

We know choosing to live a life that embodies the power of community to heal is not a one-day choice. It is an everyday choice. While *The Uncovery* is a great introduction, *The Uncovery Devotional* is a better example of what the work looks like—a daily decision to pursue healing. This devotional book is full of wisdom, principles, and practical application that we see lived out in our Timothy Initiative community. It is a tool for anyone pursuing their own recovery or for people walking with someone in recovery.

—*Lindsay Carr*
Executive director, the Timothy Initiative
www.timothyinitiative.org

A 365-DAY DEVOTIONAL

THE
UNCOVERY
DEVOTIONAL

RETHINKING RECOVERY
ONE DAY AT A TIME

GEORGE A. WOOD & BRIT EATON

WHITAKER
HOUSE

THE UNCOVERY DEVOTIONAL
Rethinking Recovery One Day at a Time

www.georgeawood.com
www.youtube.com/@GeorgeWoodSoberTruth
briteaton.com
sobertruthproject.org

ISBN: 979-8-88769-051-3 • eBook ISBN: 979-8-88769-052-0

Printed in the United States of America
© 2023 by George A. Wood and Brit Eaton

Whitaker House • 1030 Hunt Valley Circle • New Kensington, PA 15068
www.whitakerhouse.com

Library of Congress Cataloging-in-Publication Data
Names: Wood, George A., 1969– author. | Eaton, Brit, 1980– author.
Title: The uncovery devotional : rethinking recovery one day at a time /
   George A. Wood and Brit Eaton.
Description: New Kensington, PA : Whitaker House, [2023] | Summary:
   "Suggests that everyone is recovering from something, whether it be an
   addiction, a painful incident from the past, or a daily challenge just
   to get by, and offers short, year-long devotional readings, Scriptures,
   and prayers"— Provided by publisher.
Identifiers: LCCN 2023016977 (print) | LCCN 2023016978 (ebook) | ISBN
   9798887690513 | ISBN 9798887690520 (eBook)
Subjects: LCSH: Recovering addicts—Prayers and devotions. | Devotional
   calendars. | Substance abuse—Religious aspects—Christianity. | Mental
   illness—Religious aspects—Christianity. | Suicide—Religious
   aspects—Christianity. | Hope—Religious aspects—Christianity. | BISAC:
   RELIGION / Christian Living / Devotional | RELIGION / Christian Living /
   Inspirational
Classification: LCC BV4596.A24 W66 2023 (print) | LCC BV4596.A24 (ebook)
   | DDC 248.8/629—dc23/eng/20230705
LC record available at https://lccn.loc.gov/2023016977
LC ebook record available at https://lccn.loc.gov/2023016978

1 2 3 4 5 6 7 8 9 10 11 ⊔⊔ 30 29 28 27 26 25 24 23

We need to stop just pulling people out of the river.
We need to go upstream and find out why they're falling in.

—Archbishop Desmond Tutu

DEDICATION

From George:

This devotional is dedicated to my extraordinary family members, who truly embody the essence of power, greatness, and wonder.

First and foremost, I want to express my heartfelt dedication to my son, River. I am in awe of your unwavering dedication to pursuing your dreams, regardless of the immense effort it takes. Your passion is contagious, and it inspires me to never give up on my own aspirations.

Next, I want to acknowledge my incredible wife, Julie. Your tireless work for those less fortunate is nothing short of remarkable. Because of your self-lessness, families are kept together, children find hope, and generations are forever changed. Your dedication to making a difference in the world is an inspiration to us all.

And finally, I want to recognize Finn, who fearlessly defies societal expectations to embrace his true self. Your courage in being unapologetically who you were created to be is nothing short of extraordinary. Your authenticity reminds me to always stay true to myself and encourages me to support others in doing the same.

To each one of you, my family, you inspire me each and every day to be the best father, husband, and leader I can be. Your love, support, and unwavering belief in me are the driving forces behind my desire to continuously improve. I am forever grateful for the love and strength you bring into my life.

From Brit:

To my husband, Mike: Thank you for living out true covenant with me.

To my daughter, Bella: Your pure, childlike faith inspires me every day.

To my spiritual momma, Deb: Thank you for inviting me deeper into the Father's heart.

CONTENTS

FOREWORD

Now faith is the substance of things hoped for,
the evidence of things not seen.
—Hebrews 11:1 (NKJV)

Faith isn't opposed to evidence, and it isn't the opposite of reason, but it does sometimes call us to go beyond the evidence to things that might be hard to see.

A large multisite study compared outcomes between different evidence-based methodologies for addressing addiction. Although the results were inconclusive, the researchers noticed something interesting: individual counselors had very different results even if they were using the same approach. The difference in outcomes was driven by the empathy rating the counselors were given. The more empathetic they were, the better the results, with some of the least empathetic counselors actively causing harm.

It wasn't just the technical skill or know-how of the practitioners; it also mattered how they treated those they were trying to help. Without love, all of the knowledge and expertise in the world didn't improve the counseling.

George Wood leads with love. The compassion in his work shines through. He's rooted in the basics, the things you need to know, but what makes him special is the how and the why. If we could ensure that every therapist, counselor, outreach worker, pastor, or minister had a fraction of the empathy that George lives out every day, we'd be on the fast track to ending the overdose crisis and addressing our epidemic of addiction.

That kind of care doesn't come from an intellectual interest but from lived experience. George is no stranger to loss and trauma. There are a lot of good reasons for the man to be bitter and jaded…but he isn't.

For a long time, George has made a lot of small choices every day to be who he is today. He's had to make those choices when no one was looking, he's had to make them when they were hard, and he's had to make them when it would have been far easier to do otherwise, and no one would have even noticed.

He's built a lot of wisdom through struggles, great and small, the big decisions and the tiny moments. It's why he is able to speak not just with knowledge but with authority. He has lived what he teaches.

Recovery can look different for a lot of folks. But there are two realities we all contend with: we have bodies, and we are more than our bodies.

First, there is the reality of our bodies—the physicality of our being matters. For a journey of healing and wholeness, we need to take into account what we eat, if we get enough sleep, how our brains work, and a whole variety of things we can put into our bodies that can hurt or heal.

But we are more than the sum of our physical parts and biological processes. We are creatures who make meaning and discover purpose. These things are the realm of faith, religion, and spirituality. It's not just the *how to* but also the *why*.

When I first started learning more about the causes of addiction and all the different ways to approach and treat it, I wanted to know who was right and who was wrong. (And there certainly are some folks out there who have it all wrong.) But more often than not, I run into people who are just holding a different piece of the puzzle or a new mirror for reflection. Every story about addiction and recovery is as unique as our fingerprints.

I hope you'll spend some time looking into the mirror that George Wood and coauthor Brit Eaton are holding up. In fact, I hope you spend the whole next year doing that with the book you are holding right now. George shares not just knowledge but wisdom, not just information but discernment.

If you are a Christian, this book will be a blessing. If you've been hurt by Christians in the past because of hypocrisy and judgment, I'd like you to meet George and Brit, who live their faith differently. If you aren't sure, that's okay. This book can be an encouragement for anyone with an open heart, no matter where your journey is taking you.

This book will speak to those who have struggled with alcohol or other drugs and know both the struggles and the joy of finding freedom. It can also be a comfort and encouragement to those who are walking alongside others in the midst of a struggle with addictions of all sorts. But ultimately, this book can provide wisdom, insight, and encouragement to anyone on a journey of change and discovery.

Each of us needs healthy relationships to be the best of who we were created to be. I hope you have those, or can soon find them, in your local community. As you are on the journey, George and Brit extend hands of friendship in the form of these daily reflections.

When it comes to addressing addiction, mental health issues, suicidal thoughts, and trauma, we need all the professional support we can get. We need the best research and new scientific approaches, treatments, and therapies.

But we are always also more than our bodies. We need food for our souls and nourishment for our spirits. We need eyes to see beyond the daily challenges we face, toward a life of flourishing even when it seems out of reach. This is the journey of faith we are invited to.

Take a year to walk with someone who can testify to a lifesaving faith, a hope that will not quit, and a love that never ends.

—*Timothy McMahan King*
Author, *Addiction Nation*

INTRODUCTION

The old has gone, the new is here!
—2 Corinthians 5:17

Real recovery isn't a process, nor is it a one-time event. It's a lifelong journey toward a promised-land life of transformation. But sometimes that journey takes more than twelve steps, thirty days, or even a year, or two, or twenty. Where traditional Christ-centered recovery programs leave one wanting more, this yearlong devotional provides people who struggle with addiction, mental health problems, and suicidal thoughts with daily opportunities to go deeper—to uncover and heal from the trauma that causes the struggle in the first place. It's what we call the *Uncovery*, a Holy Spirit-led exploration that removes labels and honors the whole individual.

Wild opportunities for hope, healing, and transformation exist for you in the Christian recovery space because you're not working to recover an old, broken life—you're going after a brand new one. In the days to come, you'll experience a new take on twelve steps focused on *rethinking recovery*. For example, in March, we expand on the concept of making a fearless moral inventory with a month's worth of entries on reflection. Similarly, December embodies the best of the pay-it-forward spirit with a month focused on resolution.

By picking up this devotional, you've made a conscious choice to do recovery differently. And in the months that follow, you'll do more than get sober—you'll discover the truth about who you really are. Are you ready?

January

REPRESSION

For I know that good itself does not dwell in me, that is,
in my sinful nature. For I have the desire to do what is good,
but I cannot carry it out.
—Romans 7:18

January 1: GOTTA START SOMEWHERE

Because of the LORD's great love we are not consumed,
for his compassions never fail. They are new every morning;
great is your faithfulness.
—Lamentations 3:22–23

New Year's resolutions are a little overrated. There's beauty in the idea of a fresh start, a clean slate, and a new day of mercies from our good Father God. But New Year's resolutions, not unlike initial salvation and initial sobriety, rarely take root right away. Even when your heart says *yes*, it takes your body, mind, spirit, and will some time to catch up.

Resolving to do anything looks a lot like recovery. There's a moment of deliverance, followed by a lifelong journey of transformation that leads you into a promised-land life that you actually want to stay sober for. You'll have good days and bad days, successes and failures. The only way out, by the grace of God, is through it all.

New Year's resolutions, like salvation and sobriety, are not the final destination. They're the first step on a journey to discovering who you really are: a beloved child of God. It's who you've always been and always will be in God's eyes, by grace alone. To get where you want to go, you've gotta start somewhere. Start here. Start now.

God, You are good and faithful to me. You never get tired of showing mercy to me, and I want to honor You with my choices. Show me how to do that and help me walk it out. Amen.

January 2: MENTAL HEALTH CHECK

My grace is sufficient for you, for my power is made perfect in weakness.
—2 Corinthians 12:9

How are you today? No, *really*—how are you? We repeat the question because the standard greeting has lost all meaning. Typically, when we ask after someone's well-being, we expect a surface-level response of "good," "fine," or "very well, thanks." And those being asked are ready to provide one of those pat answers, perhaps unwilling or unable to tell it like it really is.

Coming in hot off the heels of the holiday season—after spending time with family and friends, surviving family and friends, or deeply feeling their absence—you may feel melancholy at best and struggling at worst. That's why January is Mental Wellness Month, a season to check in with yourself and the people you love and see how everyone is *really* doing.

One in four adults suffers from a diagnosable mental health disorder. Countless more endure silence and frustration. It's time to break the cycle, starting with you and the people you love most. There is no shame in struggling. But there is hope in Jesus. When you own your struggles, and thereby own your part in destigmatizing mental health problems, you'll help people see the truth—that recovery is for everyone.

God, it's hard to admit my weaknesses. But today, I will choose to find my strength in You. Renew my mind in Your Spirit and help me seek wise counsel as I heal. Amen.

January 3: JUST THREE THINGS

May the grace of the Lord Jesus Christ, and the love of God, and the fellowship of the Holy Spirit be with you all.
—2 Corinthians 13:14

If you've run in Christian circles for any length of time, you've likely heard at least a sermon or two on the concept of identity, for better or worse. We've approached it from every human angle, every dogmatic doctrine, every bit of broken theology imaginable—and we've missed the beautiful simplicity of it all.

We can't possibly know *who* we are without first knowing *whose* we are. When counseling people who struggle with addiction, mental health problems, and suicidal thoughts, we often share these three principles to lay a foundation for physical and spiritual healing:

1. Jesus paid it all.

2. You're one with the Father.

3. The Holy Spirit is always working.

To some, this may seem basic, but anything else is extra. The beauty of the simple gospel is this: you're already forgiven.

If you're struggling to believe any of these core truths, you're in luck—we'll unpack each of these Trinity-focused principles over the next three days. For now, suspend disbelief for a moment and let the beauty of these truths wash over you.

God, I want to believe that Jesus took care of my sins on the cross, that You love me and I'm united with You, and that the Holy Spirit can guide and direct me. Help my unbelief. Amen.

January 4: JESUS PAID IT ALL

You see, at just the right time, when we were still powerless,
Christ died for the ungodly.
—Romans 5:6

One thing stands true about the love and grace of God: from a human perspective, it's nothing short of *reckless*. God didn't wait for us to follow the Law to the letter. He didn't wait until we sacrificed enough offerings to *get right* with Him. He didn't even wait for us to repent and turn to Him. He knew that left to our own devices, we would destroy one another and be separated from Him forever. And He wasn't having it!

Our good Father God put on flesh, lived a perfect, sinless life to show us what we are capable of in Him, and died a criminal's death in our place— while we were still sinners. All so we could be with Him—a perfect and holy God—after we'd been washed clean by the blood of Jesus, a perfect and holy sacrifice. This scandal of grace gets to us every time.

Jesus paid it all for you, and there's literally nothing you could ever do to earn it or repay Him. It's finished! That's the kind of mercy and grace that lead people to repentance—and it's available to you today.

God, are You really this good? Please reveal Yourself and show me how much You love me. Thank You for paying it all for me on the cross. Remind me how forgiven I really am. Amen.

January 5: ONE WITH THE FATHER

I have given them the glory that you gave me, that they may be one as we
are one—I in them and you in me—
so that they may be brought to complete unity.
—John 17:22–23

Walk into a room, or into some well-meaning church, and start shouting, "I'm one with God!" People are going to look at you a little sideways. Let's be honest—it does sound a little crazy, even for a Christian. But the words Jesus prayed over you in the garden of Gethsemane shortly before He was crucified prove it, once and for all. His sacrifice brought you back into a beloved child relationship with a good Father God who has known you since before the foundations of the earth.

But here's the thing: You and God aren't just family—you're *one*. If you claim Jesus as Savior, you're what's known as "in Christ." Jesus is in you, and you're in Him. But here's where it gets wild—Jesus and God the Father are *one*. They have been since before time began. If Christ is in you, and God is in Christ, you are *one* with God the Father by proxy through the power of the Holy Spirit. Why? So we would know God sent Jesus and loves us as His children.

The unity implications of this passage in John are bigger than you might think. Jesus didn't just die for you—he died for all, even the people we hate. But that's a passage for another day. For now, spend some time enjoying full, unrestricted access to a good Father God who thinks you're to die for!

God, You are so amazing! I struggle to wrap my mind around being one with You, but my heart receives it. Help me to know and love You even more. Amen.

January 6: THE HOLY SPIRIT'S ALWAYS WORKING

Now the Lord is the Spirit, and where the Spirit of the Lord is,
there is freedom.
—2 Corinthians 3:17

Recovery is natural. Our bodies and minds are uniquely created to regenerate and heal as part of God's grand design. Scabs on your skin can fall off and the scars fade away, your broken bones can repair themselves, and your brain can create new neural connections to repair years of trauma—all under the right natural conditions, of course. And yet *the Uncovery* presents a new facet of whole-life restoration we often fail to acknowledge and partner with: the supernatural power of the Holy Spirit at work.

It's a wonder that the Holy Spirit is so often overlooked compared to the other Persons of the Trinity. We believe in God as Creator, a good Father, and righteous Judge. We believe in Jesus, the Father's only Son, who saved us all and put us back into right relationship with the Father. But the Holy Spirit, fully God and fully eternal like the rest of the Trinity, made this supernatural transfer of grace possible as our permanent Helper, giving us power, love, and self-discipline—things we simply can't muster in our own strength.

Without the loving conviction of the Holy Spirit, real recovery is not possible. Your coulda, shoulda, woulda excuses will rule over you unless your heart and mind are aligned with God's. The Holy Spirit is the Person of the Trinity who works with you to make a promised-land life possible, and the Spirit's power is available to you right now. Have you received the Holy Spirit? Would you like to?

God, I want to know every part of who You are. I accept You as Father, and I accept Jesus as my Savior and Lord. Fill me with Your Holy Spirit now and be my strength in weakness. Amen.

January 7: RECOVERY IS FOR EVERYONE

If we claim to be without sin, we deceive ourselves and the truth is not in us. If we confess our sins, he is faithful and just and will forgive us our sins and purify us from all unrighteousness.
—1 John 1:8–9

Recovery is one of the most powerful evangelistic tools that we, the church, have in our toolbelts. Problem is, we treat people who are struggling the same way we treat people who are sinning, with contempt and judgment. It's no wonder so many of us suffer in silence; the shame and stigmas that come with addiction, mental health problems, and suicidal thoughts are too heavy to bear.

But recovery is for *everyone*, just as the gospel is for *everyone*. When Jesus died on the cross, He defeated sin once and *for all*. When any of us believe we're not in need of recovery, we're essentially saying we're not in need of a Savior. We're rejecting God's gift of grace and His invitation to repent, which, by the way, simply means to change your mind.

Real recovery is saying *yes* to God's gift of grace, turning away from your old ways of life, getting to know God as a good Father, and keeping your eyes locked on Jesus on a journey of discovery that leads to a promised-land life. This radical grace gift isn't reserved for elitist saints or puritanical perfectionists; it's for broken men and women just like us. Recovery is the gospel.

God, I confess I've partnered with the stigmas and shame surrounding people in recovery. Restore the joy of Your salvation in me and remind me that we are all in need of a Savior. Amen.

January 8: IRON SHARPENS IRON

I myself am convinced, my brothers and sisters,
that you yourselves are full of goodness, filled with knowledge and compe-
tent to instruct one another.
—Romans 15:14

Imagine a world where people in recovery could feel understood, encouraged, and empowered to build promised-land lives worth living. Imagine having— *or being*—someone to lean on, not only in the darkest valleys but on the mountaintop and everywhere in between. Someone who will not only answer a call for accountability or vouch for you in times of growth, but one who will commit to discipling you and serving as a spiritual father, mother, or mentor through your recovery. Sounds *amazing*, doesn't it?

Perhaps you've been blessed to have—*or be*—a mentor in the recovery space. Countless others haven't experienced it yet. While sponsors and accountability partners are a clear asset to those who struggle, real, lasting mentorship can only come from a place of authentic community, not Friday-night programming or man-made assignments.

January is National Mentoring Month, a time where people unite in celebration of the power of community to heal trauma and drive meaningful change in people's lives. Mentorship is one of the most powerful pay-it-forward parts of recovery. Once you taste the sweetness of being healed and whole, you will naturally want to help others experience the same. Wherever you are on your recovery journey, pray about finding—*or being*—a mentor to someone in need.

God, You created humans for relationship with You and with one another. Place mentors in my life to be the iron that sharpens iron in the recovery space and use me as You see fit. Amen.

January 9: REALITIES OF TRAUMA

I sought the LORD, and he answered me;
he delivered me from all my fears.
—Psalm 34:4

Not everyone who experiences trauma will suffer from addiction, mental health problems, or suicidal thoughts. But everyone who suffers from these afflictions has experienced trauma of some kind. Deep wounds like abandonment or abuse strengthen some and cripple others. Loss, bullying, sickness, and even natural disasters can mean life or death. This is one of the most important reasons why one-size-fits-all recovery programming rarely works.

Trauma is more than just something that happens *to* you. It is also what happens *inside* you. Different circumstances impact different people in different ways for different reasons, which is why none of us have room to judge what triggers trauma inside another person.

The hard part is this: even when you do nothing to contribute to the trauma that led you down a path of destruction, at some point, you may become a willing participant in the aftermath. When that trauma is repressed, it becomes a breeding ground for sickness, sin, and suffering. Only by walking out *the Uncovery*—unearthing and carefully exploring these experiences through Spirit-led, trauma-informed ministry—can we find deeper healing and deliverance from the broken life that made us need recovery in the first place.

God, I'm sick and tired of being sick and tired. In Your infinite wisdom and perfect timing, show me any trauma in my life that You'd like to address and deliver me from it in Jesus's name. Amen.

January 10: TRANSFORMATIVE CREATIVITY

So God created mankind in his own image, in the image of God he created them; male and female he created them.
—Genesis 1:27

When God created humans, He created them in His image. The richness of this truth is often lost in translation. The Creator made us creators just like Him, capable of ruling over and subduing the earth. He trusted Adam to name the animals, Eve to be a perfect and balanced match for her creative mate, and gave them both rights to reign, naked and unashamed.

You may not think yourself a creative type. But artists, musicians, writers, and designers aren't the only ones who get to lean into the Father's innate gift of creativity. Thinkers and dreamers, adventurers and innovators, makers and producers, visionaries and workers of all kinds are included; people like you who can tap into new ways of thinking and being.

When it comes to recovery, you'll need to tap into your creative side to imagine a life that's worth living and staying sober for. Thankfully, kingdom creativity is a skill that can be honed and strengthened in the natural. Give yourself permission to dream with God about what a transformed life could look like. Share the desires of your heart. Draw up the blueprints and lay the foundation, with the Creator of the universe as your lead architect. The Father longs to co-create with you. Will you meet Him?

God, I believe You created me in Your image and called me "good." Show me Your best vision for my life and help me find creative and joy-filled ways to live that life abundantly. Amen.

January 11: TRANSFORMATIVE PERSEVERANCE

I can do all things through Christ who strengthens me.
—Philippians 4:13 (NKJV)

You can do hard things. No, really—you can. No matter how long it takes, no matter how impossible it seems, you can do *all things* through Christ who strengthens you. This transformative perseverance is a key concept in the apostle Paul's writings, and it's been proven throughout Scripture and in the lives of believers for generations. When we partner with God's will, we can accomplish things we never ever could on our own.

Now let's explore what this powerful passage of truth *isn't* saying. It does not say, "I can do anything and everything I want, and Christ will strengthen me." This "if you can dream it, you can do it" mentality leads to disappointment and destruction every time. Worldly perseverance will tell you to pull yourself up by your bootstraps and try harder so that you'll be successful. Kingdom perseverance means holding fast and leaning on the Father's strength, *especially* in times of suffering.

Staying steadfast in the everyday as you walk out your recovery journey is no small task. The tough times are tough, but the boring times can be absolutely brutal. Our very human desire to be titillated can be our downfall, unless we choose to elevate our existence and focus on what's true, noble, just, pure, lovely, good, virtuous, and praiseworthy. (See Philippians 4:8.) You can do anything you want…when what you want is what God wants. He wants you healed, whole, and transformed. And in His strength, you will be.

God, I confess I don't always know what's best for me. I think I know what I want, but I know You know better. Check my motives and show me Your way to find healing and hope. Amen.

January 12: TRANSFORMATIVE IMAGINATION

Do not conform to the pattern of this world, but be transformed by the renewing of your mind. Then you will be able to test and approve what God's will is—his good, pleasing and perfect will.
—Romans 12:2

Imagination and identity go hand in hand. The word *imagination* is derived from two Latin words: *imago*, which means "image," and *imagnari*, which means "picture to oneself." The images in our heads have the power to determine our steps; our imagination tells us what we will do even before we do it.

Imagination is a gift from God, meant to help you not only envision the life He has for you but to believe it's even possible. However, trauma can hijack your imagination, forcing it to hold on to harmful images, destructive ideas, and a future that's steeped in death. For example, when your brain catalogs pornographic images, your imagination can turn to them for release in a heartbeat when times get tough—before you ever touch magazines or technology. This is why you need a healthy, God-driven imagination to experience transformation that really lasts.

The good news is, your brain can actually heal from trauma over time, thanks to God's incredible gift of neuroplasticity. Through healthier habits, new positive experiences, Christ-centered therapy, and Holy Spirit intervention, you can literally and figuratively renew your mind and restore your identity.

God, You know every thought I've ever had. And somehow You still love me. Purify my imagination and heal me from past trauma so I can align my thoughts with Yours. Amen.

January 13: TRANSFORMATIVE RESILIENCE

"In your anger do not sin": Do not let the sun go down while you are still angry, and do not give the devil a foothold.
—Ephesians 4:26–27

Whether you're twenty days or twenty years into your journey, you've likely discovered the truth: recovery is *hard work*. Difficulties, disappointments, setbacks, relapses, and other struggles are pretty much inevitable, no matter how strong of a support system you have in place. Take heart. You may slip and fall countless times on the road to recovery, but it's not about how many times you fall—it's about how willing you are to get back up and try again.

Resilience isn't a gift; it's a learned behavior developed over years of handling difficulty. Resilience may be part of why God allows His people to endure hardship this side of heaven. While it's not in God's character to inflict pain, He may use pain inflicted by others and ourselves for our good and His glory. Your ability to bounce back will help you learn to adapt to transformative, life-changing situations when they come your way.

Keep in mind, resilience isn't a lack of emotional response. When stress, adversity, or even trauma strike, it's perfectly normal to feel anger, grief, and every type of emotional pain. This shows you're still *alive* and still *human*, both prerequisites for real recovery! The emotions you feel may even help to uncover repressed trauma, so welcome your feelings when they come. And when it's time, surrender those emotions to God. Instead of asking, "Why?" ask Him,

"What's next?" The bounce-back elasticity of resilience will keep you on the narrow path, free from the temptation to sin out of blind emotion. This is the essence of self-control, and it's available to you today.

God, sometimes I feel so out of control when things don't go how I want them to. I want to be more resilient so I can find Your peace even in the storm. Help me be more like You. Amen.

January 14: A PROMISED-LAND LIFE

Be strong and courageous, for you shall cause this people to inherit the land that I swore to their fathers to give them.
—Joshua 1:6 (ESV)

If you've spent any time in the Old Testament, you know that God set aside a promised land for the Israelites. It was ready and waiting for them after their miraculous delivery from four hundred years of generational slavery in Egypt. But instead of following God's lead, they wandered the wilderness for *forty years* before finally entering the promised land.

Have you ever done this? Have you ever known there was a better life waiting for you, but you just couldn't—or wouldn't—step into it? If so, chances are it's because you couldn't visualize what a promised-land life really looks like. And when you can't see the potential for a transformed life, you inevitably go back to what you know.

Even in the most forward-thinking recovery organizations, sobriety or deliverance from a bad habit is often glorified over transformation or a promised-land life. Getting to the good life God has for you requires potential for a life worth living—and worth fighting for. If you lack the means or the ability to build such a life on your own—or even imagine such a life is possible—it's okay. You were never meant to do recovery on your own. Ask a trusted mentor or friend to help you see the potential for your future.

God, things feel so heavy sometimes, I don't know how to see past today. Open my heart and mind to the promised-land life You have for me and give me strength to go for it. Amen.

*"I have the right to do anything," you say—but not everything is beneficial. "I
have the right to do anything"—but I will not be mastered by anything.*
—1 Corinthians 6:12

What comes to mind when you hear the word *addiction?* Drugs and alcohol?
A homeless guy strung out on the street corner? A specific person—a friend,
family member, coworker, or maybe even yourself?

Our views of the world are shaped by our culture and communities. And
healthy as those communities may have been, they were, at best, limited. We
only know what we know—until we learn something that challenges everything we thought we knew. When it comes to addiction, even those who have
had firsthand experience likely still have more to learn.

Addictions don't always look like we think they should. They can be chemical or behavioral, chosen or thrust upon us. Alcohol, drugs, sex, food, codependency, gambling, gaming, social media, shopping, offense, exercise, politics—the list of things one can become addicted to goes on and on. While
struggling with sugar cravings might not seem as destructive as heroin or
porn, the neurological premise is the same.

Here's the tricky part: Not all things you can become addicted to are
inherently bad. Food, for example, is necessary even if you have an addiction
or eating disorder. What's more, not everyone who dabbles in a potentially
addictive thing will become addicted. This isn't about addiction genes or generational curses; it's almost always about trauma. Trauma in your past doesn't
excuse addictive behavior, but uncovering and dealing with past trauma can
unlock insights to help you better understand why you became addicted in the
first place. This is where real recovery begins.

*God, without You, I'm powerless over my struggles. Help me to uncover and
understand the real reasons why I do the things I do—and help me find healing
that transforms my life. Amen.*

January 16: THE TRUTH ABOUT TRAUMA

Therefore, as God's chosen people, holy and dearly loved, clothe
yourselves with compassion, kindness, humility, gentleness and patience.
—Colossians 3:12

Addictions, mental health problems, and suicidal thoughts don't discriminate. People from all walks of life can experience trauma, and the inability or unwillingness to deal with that trauma and find healing can manifest in a multitude of ways. For those of us who struggle, this truth presents an opportunity for deeper levels of healing. For those of us who are called to love and lead people who struggle, this truth presents an opportunity for deeper levels of compassion.

Jesus understood this well. When He encountered someone suffering from sin and in need of good news, He went to great lengths to show them that He intimately understood their circumstances. From curious Zacchaeus atop a sycamore tree (see Luke 19:1–6) to the woman caught in the act of adultery (see John 8:3–11), Jesus was moved with compassion. He was committed to setting them free from sin *and* from the deep wounds that drove them to sin in the first place. This is the essence of trauma-informed care and ministry.

Trauma doesn't excuse sin, but understanding it can help shed light on our struggles. Deeper understanding drives deeper compassion, allowing you to care for and minister to others and yourself in the kind, humble, and gentle ways of Jesus. Open your heart and mind today to the truth that recovery is for everyone. And know that the grace of God put on display in and through Jesus has the power to set you free and heal your wounds.

God, I admit I am tempted to label and judge myself and others by our surface struggles. Show me the impacts of trauma and move me with compassion to love and lead like Jesus did. Amen.

January 17: ADAPT AND OVERCOME

In all these things we are more than conquerors
through him who loved us.
—Romans 8:37

Change is inevitable. And yet change in our lives, even good change, has the potential to create chaos in our hearts and minds if we are unwilling or unable to adapt. When one's whole world changes and the dissonance of the unfamiliar sets in, the stress can put recovery at risk. We see this in times of major life transition for people in recovery—changes in housing, having a baby, getting married, starting a new job, getting sober, and even getting saved! When we dig in our heels, we're usually afraid of losing something we value, failing in a new environment, or both.

None of us are immune to the stress of change—but admittedly, some of us handle it better than others. That's why adaptability is a critical soft skill to hone and build during recovery. Yes, you can actually learn to handle change and even see change as an opportunity. Talk with and learn from others who have been through a similar season. Look for silver-lining possibilities that can only come from God. He never changes, but He's always working on us!

Change may be inevitable, but it can also be a catalyst for breakthrough and victory. The better you can handle change, the better your chances for continual growth and transformation. What changes are you wrestling with right now? What are you afraid of? Take it to the Father and ask Him to help you see opportunity that comes with change.

God, change is so hard. When change is beyond my control, please give me wisdom and peace to lean into it and embrace it as the only true pathway to transformation. Amen.

January 18: CONTINUAL COURAGE

Have I not commanded you? Be strong and courageous.
Do not be afraid; do not be discouraged, for the LORD your God
will be with you wherever you go.
—Joshua 1:9

God said, *"Be strong and courageous"* twenty-five times in Scripture, but four of those times, He said it to Joshua—once before He led the Israelites into the promised land (Deuteronomy 31:23) and three times after they'd reached it (Joshua 1:6, 7, 9).

You may wonder why the Israelites still needed so much encouragement if they had made it to the promised land. Shouldn't they be home free? Far from it. There was all-out *war* happening in the land. God knew Joshua and his people needed to be continually reminded of who He was as Father and who they were in Him on their collective identity journey.

Each time the Father speaks strength and courage over His people, He offers an invitation to tap into His own strength and courage—strength that is made perfect in our weakness and courage that transcends human logic. This certainly didn't relieve the Israelites of their duties in preparation for battle, but it did remind them that their hope for a promised-land life was really coming from God, who promised to go before them. This same God goes before you too—and will be with you every step on your way to a promised-land life worth living and worth fighting for.

God, life is hard. I thought sobriety would make life easier, but I'm still fighting so many battles. Help me remember that You always go before me and that in You, I've already won. Amen.

January 19: UNCOMPROMISING VIGILANCE

Watch and pray so that you will not fall into temptation.
The spirit is willing, but the flesh is weak.
—Matthew 26:41

"I didn't see it coming." We say these words all too often when we relapse back into broken ways of thinking, acting, and being. And while some things can take us by complete surprise, if we're honest, we'll admit that we "didn't see it coming" because we weren't looking for it in the first place. When we stumble, it's because we've compromised boundaries, allowing distractions to hinder our situational awareness.

It's like texting and driving—you can really only do one or the other at a time. When you keep your eyes on Jesus and the journey in front of you, walking out your recovery is simpler because you can dodge clear pitfalls, roadblocks, or hazards along the way. Look elsewhere for hope, healing, or direction, and you'll inevitably trip and fall over what would have been in plain sight with your eyes forward.

The good news is, there is grace to cover you when you stumble. God doesn't expect you to walk out recovery perfectly. But when you walk it out laser-focused on Him, you'll do it much better than you could on your own.

So ask yourself honestly: Am I compromising my boundaries? Am I allowing distractions to hinder my view of Jesus? Could I be more vigilant as I move forward into the life God has for me? If you answered *yes* or even *maybe*, take it to the Father and let Him captivate your attention with His goodness, love, and grace.

God, I admit there are times when I let my guard down and make myself vulnerable to old habits and thoughts. Forgive me. Send Your Spirit to help me stay vigilant on my journey. Amen.

January 20: MOVING FORWARD

There is a time for everything,
and a season for every activity under the heavens.
—Ecclesiastes 3:1

In recovery, it can be easy to overstay our welcome. We're not talking about staying past midnight at our sponsor's place or crashing for years in Mom's basement, although these can certainly come into play. We're talking about staying in seasons of life, even good ones, for longer than God has planned.

Sometimes we overstay because we like what's known, even though sticking to what we know doesn't help us grow. Sometimes we overstay because of fear, worried we might miss out or fall flat if we step into something new. Sometimes we overstay because we're not paying attention to God's gentle or not-so-gentle nudge in the right direction. This is where complacency becomes our enemy, and our recovery journey comes to a screeching halt.

Being aware of what's around you and knowing when it's time to make a move are characteristics of a transformed life. As you grow and mature mentally and spiritually, you'll become more aware of when God says it's time to move on—from friends you've outgrown, from a job you're no longer passionate about, or from systems and structures, powers and principalities that no longer serve you well…even if they once did. When God says it's time to move, be sensitive to His leading. So ask yourself, "Is God asking me to take one small step or maybe even a giant leap that I haven't said yes to yet?" If He brings something to mind, it's time to make a move.

God, I want to walk with You. Don't let me get too far ahead of You and don't let me lag behind. Help me go where You go, stay where You stay, and move where You move. Amen.

January 21: SOBRIETY VS. TRANSFORMATION

Then the man and his wife heard the sound of the LORD God as he was walking in the garden in the cool of the day, and they hid from the LORD God among the trees of the garden.
—Genesis 3:8

"Where are you?...Who told you that you were naked?...What is this you have done?" (Genesis 3:9, 11, 13). When God asked these three questions of Adam and Eve immediately after the fall in in Genesis, He may have been inviting them into what we might now call a *growth mindset*, which assumes people can and do change, where failure isn't seen as fatal, but as an opportunity to stretch, grow, and make a course correction.

But Adam and Eve responded to God's questions with a fixed mindset, which assumes that people never change. They hid. They covered their nakedness. And when God called them to a place of higher accountability, Adam blamed Eve, Eve blamed the serpent, and the serpent sat there silent and satisfied.

As you work your way toward a promised-land life, you will likely stumble and fall at least once or twice. When you do, you'll likely blow it at least once or twice in the way you respond. It's the nature of true recovery.

The hard truth is, when you value *sobriety* (a fixed mindset) over the refinement that brings *transformation* (a growth mindset), you go on sinning by faith—because you believe it's who you are. But when you choose to love unconditionally, celebrate the small victories, learn from your failures, and continually affirm a true, God-given identity in people, you'll see lives transformed, including your own.

God, forgive me for the times I refused to own my part in relapse and grow through my failures. Give me the courage to testify to Your goodness so others can experience transformation. Amen.

January 22: HEALING WITH WISDOM

He heals the brokenhearted and binds up their wounds.
—Psalm 147:3

The recovery space is broad and wide, spanning both sacred and secular organizations with wildly varying methodologies. This brings so many questions to the table, questions we may *think* we already know the answers to but are worthy of deeper exploration.

Are addiction, mental health problems, and suicidal thoughts sin or sickness? Your answer will impact how you go to the source for healing. Are people in recovery being healed or cured? The sources you go to for help may give you language, but the transformative power available to you will transcend earthly wisdom. Is it really okay to have Jesus and a therapist too? Oh, my goodness gracious, *yes*. Hard stop. You will find competing answers to these questions, even within the walls of the church.

God created us for community and knew we would need the wisdom of those who have gone before us to help shed light on opportunities for healing, deliverance, and transformation. If you don't have a counselor, get one. If you don't think you need one, keep in mind that *recovery is for everyone*. True healing can be found when you're willing to face past trauma head-on. Are you willing?

God, I admit, I have tried to take my healing into my own hands. Forgive me and put people into my life who can help me find levels of freedom I never could have imagined. Amen.

January 23: CONFESSIONS OF A BELOVED CHILD

Therefore confess your sins to each other and
pray for each other so that you may be healed.
The prayer of a righteous person is powerful and effective.
—James 5:16

Take a deep breath. It's time to deal with a tough recovery issue. The hardest part of moving toward a promised-land life is owning up to and confessing anything that's actively keeping you from it. While we would never recommend some legalistic, box-checking approach that keeps you obsessed with making sure your proverbial slate is wiped clean, having a healthy level of self-awareness is key to finding real recovery.

Here's the beauty of confession: Once we've named a sin, spoken it aloud, received God's forgiveness, and asked for accountability with a trusted friend, mentor, or counselor, we're instantly free from the power that sin had over us. We have access to that freedom even before we ask for it. That's the reckless part about grace.

Confession humbles you and reminds you of the grace you have already been given. It allows you to continue to choose God's way every day—not because you have to but because you want to. What sins are you carrying that you need to deal with? God is waiting with open arms to receive your confession and remind you just how loved you are.

God, I confess I don't always take my struggles and sins to You or my trusted mentors. Remind me that You are loving and gracious, quick to forgive, and ready to restore me. Forgive me. Amen.

January 24: A SINLESS LIFE

Be perfect, therefore, as your heavenly Father is perfect.
—Matthew 5:48

"Be perfect." Two of the most stirring and challenging words in Scripture were laid down by Jesus, the grace-filled Son of God and Son of Man. Since He was, in fact, the only human to ever walk out a perfect, sinless life, this seems an especially high call. But is it even realistic? And if not, why would Jesus say it?

Context is incredibly important here. In Matthew 5, Jesus was summing up a teaching on the fulfillment of the law of Moses. Verse 48 connects back to a specific command in the Old Testament: *"You shall be holy, for I the LORD your God am holy"* (Leviticus 19:2 NKJV). This law wouldn't be fulfilled through humankind's attempt to be perfect. It could only be fulfilled in the person of Christ through His perfect sacrifice for our sins.

Thanks to Jesus's sacrifice on the cross, we *"are not under the law, but under grace"* (Romans 6:14). Now this isn't some kind of "greasy grace" that gives you free reign to sin all you want. You haven't been set free *to* sin; you've been set free *from* sin. Your obedience to God's commands comes from a place of love, not fear. Sin has no authority or jurisdiction over you anymore. If you receive this truth in its fullness, you'll realize that a perfect, sinless life is actually possible with Christ.

God, I receive the grace Jesus died for me to have. I know this means You now see me as holy, perfect, and blameless in Christ. Help me to live up to the person He died for me to be. Amen.

January 25: BODY AND MIND

May your whole spirit, soul and body be kept blameless
at the coming of our Lord Jesus Christ.
—1 Thessalonians 5:23

Are you feeling weary? Heavy? Struggling not to struggle?

Repressed trauma, whether physical, emotional, or spiritual, takes a real toll on the body. Initial responses to trauma manifest physically in ways we understand—exhaustion, nightmares, even routine aches and pains. But long-term repressed trauma is linked to chronic illness, especially in people with post-traumatic stress disorder (PTSD). We're not just talking about addiction and mental health problems; repressed trauma can lead to type 2 diabetes, arthritis, heart disease, and even cancer.

Connecting the dots between the mind and the body is no small task in recovery. You may understand truth conceptually, but struggle to embrace it and apply it practically. Even when you know what to do, you often don't do it, won't do it, or can't do it, at least not yet. This isn't because you're bad; it's because you're carrying trauma and in need of healing.

The good news is, healing from repressed trauma is real and available. It's hard heart work for sure. That's why you'll need the help of a good Father God, a trusted counselor, and a supportive and authentic community to help you uncover it, deal with it, heal from it, and be freed from it for good. God has a promised-land life that's waiting for you on the other side of your trauma. Are you ready to be set free?

God, help me find the courage to uncover repressed trauma and move toward healing. Place people in my path, even today, who can help me take steps toward a promised-land life. Amen.

January 26: A NEW THING

Forget the former things; do not dwell on the past. See, I am doing a new thing! Now it springs up; do you not perceive it?
—Isaiah 43:18–19

The past may be in the past, but when we carry trauma, the past is a regular, unwelcome visitor who lives rent-free in our minds. As time goes on, traumatized minds can stay stuck, seeing past trauma as a present threat, even when we have no logical reason to dwell on it anymore. This can trigger anxiety, depression, anger, and apathy, which can lead to addiction, mental health problems, and thoughts of suicide. These are *not* characteristics of a promised-land life!

For some, practicing mindfulness works wonders. Meditating on the truth of the Father's love, the finished work of Jesus on the cross, and the power of the Holy Spirit living in you leaves little room for the past to rule you in the present. For others, deeper trauma healing, even clinical therapy, may be necessary to move past trauma from your short-term memory to your long-term memory, removing the immediate threat. There is no shame in this! It's why God our Healer created people to be healers too.

The Father wants you to know that your past has not only been forgiven and redeemed, it has been erased and rewritten in Him. (See Colossians 2:14.) Believing and agreeing with this truth as you pursue healing through counseling, therapy, and the power of authentic community will make all the difference.

God, I believe You are doing a new thing, but my past continues to weigh me down. Help me see Your hand in my healing and deliver me from trauma that keeps me from Your goodness. Amen.

January 27: A NEW CREATION

*See, I will create new heavens and a new earth. The former things will
not be remembered, nor will they come to mind.*
—Isaiah 65:17

Imagine new heavens and a new earth, with no memory of this one. Many
believers cling to the idea that the problem of pain in our present world will
all be okay if we can just get to heaven. But Jesus didn't die on a cross and rise
from the dead just so we can catch a break in heaven. He died so that we can
have a full, abundant life here and now.

In Matthew 6, when Jesus teaches His disciples to pray, He models a powerful, declarative phrase: *"On earth as it is in heaven"* (verse 10). God's kingdom
will come and God's will *will* be done when we choose to declare it to be so
now, not later, in Jesus's name.

The Holy Spirit gives you authority to tap into that heavenly realm today.
It's a place where the pains of the past are distant memories that only come
to mind when recalling God's faithfulness. God's new creation, the one you
may be longing for and clinging to, starts now, in you. *"Therefore, if anyone
is in Christ, the new creation has come: The old has gone, the new is here!"*
(2 Corinthians 5:17). Let the joy of this reality move you to embrace this
life—a promised-land life that's worth living.

*God, thank You for giving me an abundant life. Help me see Your new creation
in me. Your Kingdom come and Your will be done, on earth as it is in heaven. In
Jesus's name, amen.*

January 28: RENEWING THE MIND

Then you will know the truth, and the truth will set you free.
—John 8:32

In Jesus's day, Jewish descendants of Abraham weren't slaves anymore. Sure,
their ancestors had been slaves for generations in Egypt once upon a time,
but in their foggy minds, they had *"never been slaves of anyone"* (verse 33).

41

And when Jesus dropped this truth bomb on them, the people who had once believed Him started plotting to kill Him.

> Jesus replied, "Very truly I tell you, everyone who sins is a slave to sin. Now a slave has no permanent place in the family, but a son belongs to it forever. So if the Son sets you free, you will be free indeed."
>
> (John 8:34–36)

The words Jesus spoke were meant to be good news, but people fixated on that first part about being slaves to sin, which made them furious. They fueled that fire with offense over Jesus saying He was the Son of God. The invitation was laced with grace, hope, and even an offer of *sonship*, but their minds weren't ready to receive it.

How is your mind today? Can you see the good news for what it is? Is offense keeping you stuck and keeping the people you love at arm's length? Allow yourself to be transformed by *"the renewing of your mind"* (Romans 12:2) so you can see and partner with God's perfect will for your life.

God, without You, I'd be a slave to sin. Thank You for setting me free. Help me to shake off that old slavery mindset and embrace new ways of thinking, acting, and being in You. Amen.

January 29: NATURE AND NURTURE

Can a mother forget the baby at her breast and have no compassion on the child she has borne? Though she may forget, I will not forget you!
—Isaiah 49:15

Through years of loving and leading people through struggles with addiction, mental health, and suicidal thoughts, I (George) have been blessed beyond words to have the counsel and support of members of the scientific community. I learn so much from them about the nature of God in how He created us.

My favorite scientific discovery is one that is *really* good news for Christ-centered recovery: *There is no addiction gene.* Epigenetic studies have proven that addiction is a product of early-childhood environmental factors, not genetic predisposition. A lack of prenatal and postnatal nurturing can cause certain genes to go dormant, making excessive consumption and addiction more likely. However, through trauma-informed care, these dormant genes can be awakened once again to combat addictive tendencies! How cool is that?

In medical communities, people are no longer labeled *generational addicts* because of their family of origin—and we, the church, would benefit from realizing this too. This calls for compassion and grace for each person's unique recovery journey, yours included. So if you've ever received a label like *addict*, *alcoholic*, or *crazy* attached to your family history, lay it down now at the feet of Jesus and embrace your true identity: *Beloved child of God.*

God, thank You for freeing me from generational curses and not holding my family's sins against me. Help me combat systemic issues and find generational health and wholeness. Amen.

January 30: THE FINE LINE

When anxiety was great within me, your consolation brought me joy.
—Psalm 94:19

Addictions don't always look the same. In fact, sometimes what we call addictions aren't addictions at all. A true addiction comes from a need to find pleasure or avoid pain, but a compulsion is an insatiable urge to do something out of fear or anxiety. Both addictions and compulsive behaviors are serious and derived from trauma, and both will put people in need of recovery.

Getting to the root causes of our behaviors can help those who struggle receive proper diagnoses and treatment that leads to healing. This is the essence of trauma-informed care and ministry. Jesus was moved with compassion to set people free from bondage inflicted by trauma. He healed outward sickness as well as deep inner wounds with the gift of Himself.

Maybe you or someone you love is dealing with an addiction to drugs, alcohol, pornography, or power. Maybe you or someone you love is dealing with compulsive behaviors like shopping, hoarding, bulimia, or gambling. Wherever you fall on the fine line between the two struggles, there is healing for you today in the person of Jesus and in the trauma-informed care of His people.

God, I believe You have the power to set me free from addictions and compulsive behaviors of all kinds. Relieve my anxious heart. Remind me who I am in You and deliver me. Amen.

Two are better than one, because they have a good return for their labor:
if either of them falls down, one can help the other up. But pity anyone
who falls and has no one to help them up.
—Ecclesiastes 4:9–10

Of all the deadly forces that seek to steal, kill, and destroy in your promised-land life, isolation is hands down the worst culprit. A silent killer, forced or chosen isolation keeps people who struggle from the authentic community that's necessary to find hope, healing, and long-term accountability.

When we say isolation is a killer, we're not being dramatic. Addictions and struggles with mental health go nuclear in isolated environments. Our modern society contributes to this problem; time with friends and family is replaced with social media scrolling, counseling appointments are replaced by search engines and false-prophet influencers, and fleeting suicidal thoughts turn to ideations—and even plans—in a heartbeat.

Wherever you are on your own recovery journey, you need to have someone, somewhere, who loves you like Jesus does, checks in and does life with you, and continually points you back to the Father's love. If you need help, there is *no shame* in asking for it. And if you can give help, *please do so.* You may be a text message, phone call, or check-in away from saving a life today.

God, I know authentic, Christ-centered community is necessary to stay in step with You. Help me avoid the temptation to isolate and help me bless others by connecting. Amen.

February

RELIANCE

*For it is God who works in you to will and to act
in order to fulfill his good purpose.*
—Philippians 2:13

February 1: ESTEEMING YOURSELF

*Very truly I tell you, whoever believes in me will do the works I have
been doing, and they will do even greater things than these, because I am
going to the Father.*
—John 14:12

You don't hear many sermons preached on self-esteem these days. You could probably drop this book right now, grab your smartphone, and find a YouTube video or podcast teaching on sin self-*consciousness* in about fifteen seconds. But self-esteem? That's tricky territory for most Bible teachers. After all, aren't you supposed to be *dying to self* more and more every day?

The funny thing is, dying to self isn't really about death at all. It's about transformative rebirth into a promised-land life that's waiting for you. There is a moment of delivery, for sure, but the emphasis is on the journey ahead. You will not find the confidence you need for this journey by looking inward. You will need something or *someone* greater than yourself.

The world defines self-esteem as confidence in your own abilities. As believers in Jesus, we urge you instead to define self-esteem as having confidence in who God says you are.

Esteeming yourself means realigning your mind and heart with what God says about you—that you are chosen (John 15:16), redeemed (Galatians 3:13), forgiven (1 John 1:9), accepted (Romans 15:7), important (1 Peter 2:9), and loved (Jeremiah 31:3). It means seeing God, your good Father, as your source of strength and power. Healthy, Jesus-centered self-esteem means having confidence that God will show up when and how you need Him to, in His perfect timing.

God, I admit I overestimate my own abilities. I'm slow to lean on You, my source, for the strength I need to walk confidently through life. Remind me who I am and whose I am. Amen.

February 2: LEARNING AND UNLEARNING

*Take my yoke upon you and learn from me,
for I am gentle and humble in heart, and you will find rest for your souls.
For my yoke is easy and my burden is light.*
—Matthew 11:29–30

When it comes to personal, professional, and spiritual growth, learning is key. It's why people pore over self-help books, pursue degrees, certifications, and credentials, and serve up positions, opinions, and "perfected" doctrines, calling them "truth." And when they're convinced they've already found all the answers, they become less open to receiving evidence to the contrary.

While the pursuit of answers is certainly a noble one, we're often not even asking the right questions. Just as important as learning is unlearning—being willing to let go of any man-made "truths" that do not reflect the heart and Word of God. When we have believed lies for generations, it can be quite a blow to the ego to let go and let God help us relearn His truth in His timing. It's painful, but it's necessary.

Jesus never said, "Figure Me out." He said, "Follow Me." The best learning blends theory with practice and encourages us to challenge our greatest assumptions and doubt our doubts.

Today, keep your focus on the beauty and simplicity of the gospel. And when your next opportunity comes to learn, unlearn, or relearn something, start by asking God, "What do You want me to know about that, Father?" He will draw nearer and nearer to you as you draw near to Him.

God, I give You permission to challenge my assumptions about You. Draw me near and show me who You are. Remind me that no matter how good I think You are, You're even better. Amen.

February 3: MARKED BY LOVE

A new command I give you: Love one another. As I have loved you, so you must love one another. By this everyone will know that you are my disciples, if you love one another.
—John 13:34–35

When it comes to helping people recover from addiction, mental health problems, and suicidal thoughts, we, the church, have work to do. Our often antiquated, legalistic mindsets can create stigmatizing and discriminatory barriers to entry for people from all walks of life who are really hurting.

Perhaps you've witnessed it, experienced it, or even participated in it. You aren't the first.

We're not doing it on purpose; it's just so deeply ingrained in our church cultures that we don't always realize it's happening. In an attempt to be the iron that sharpens iron and a shining example of healthy boundaries, some of us have become better known by how we alienate, marginalize, and exclude than by our love. It's not what Jesus intended.

His command? Love one another. Not in some "love ya, bro" superficial way, but in an unconditional, godly, *agape* love kind of way.

Jesus didn't just love you: He loved you to death and back again.

It's not always easy or even possible to love like Jesus did. But when we do, we put the full glory of God's grace on display for the whole world to see. As followers of Jesus, we are meant to wear our love right out there on our sleeves—to be marked by it, like a tattoo on our hearts and a banner over our lives. When we do, hurting people will see Jesus in us, and they'll have a genuine encounter with a good Father God of transformation.

God, help me to put Your love on full display in my life to love people like Jesus does. Mark me with Your love, so people will know You sent me in Jesus's name. Amen.

February 4: FAMILY BUSINESS

When you walk through the fire, you will not be burned;
the flames will not set you ablaze.
—Isaiah 43:2

Deliverance can be tricky. We declare, "I got sober," "I got saved," or "I'm finally free!" But after that initial moment of euphoria, reality sets in. Salvation, sobriety, and any other kind of deliverance is only the first step on a lifelong journey to discovering who we were made to be. Maybe we still feel like a slave at heart.

Telling a lifelong slave that they're not only free, but *family* feels like a stretch at first. It's going to take a whole lot more than platitudes, prayers, and twelve-step programming for them to believe it's true, let alone embrace the new life that comes with it. God as Father? A *good* and *loving* Father at that? Even if they believe it, it can take some time for their hearts to catch up with their heads, especially if their earthly families were not good or loving by comparison.

Thankfully, God isn't just good and loving; He is patient and kind. Your identity in Him is secure—you're His beloved child, a coheir with Jesus, and an ambassador for the kingdom, whether you believe it yet or not. In time, as He reveals His strength made perfect in your weakness (see 2 Corinthians 12:9), you will begin to embrace your role in the family business and help to seek out and save the lost by the power of the Holy Spirit living in you. You can't earn the title. God will commission you and qualify you along the way, sometimes through fire. But He *will* be with you. Keep your eyes on Him, and you will not be burned.

God, life can be overwhelming. You've delivered me, but some days I feel like I still don't know who I am. Will You show me? Will You remind me who I really am? Thank You. Amen.

February 5: UNCONVENTIONAL GRACE

He took the blind man by the hand and led him outside the village.
When he had spit on the man's eyes and put his hands on him,
Jesus asked, "Do you see anything?"
—Mark 8:23

When Jesus walked the earth, healing was high on His priority list. Blind eyes were opened, deaf ears were unstopped, lame people leapt, and the speechless shouted for joy, just as the prophet said they would. (See Isaiah 35:5–6.) He gave some sermons and flipped a few tables, but Jesus loved to heal—and He did it just about everywhere He went. But when Jesus healed, He didn't always do it in the same way. Let's focus in on one of His favorite types of healing—blind eyes.

Sometimes a single touch from Jesus was all it took to heal blind eyes, as in the case of the two blind men in Matthew 9:27–31. Sometimes healing blind eyes required a muddy mix of dirt and Jesus's saliva to make a healing mask, as it did for a man born blind in John 9:1–7. Sometimes it took Jesus spitting on someone's eyes and laying hands on them like it did for the blind man at Bethsaida in Mark 8:22–26.

Jesus's wild variety of healing styles demonstrates that God's grace doesn't always look like you think it should and that progressive deliverance is not only a possibility, but a promise. Apply this truth to recovery, and you may sense God calling you to love in radically grace-laced (and weird!) ways.

God, sometimes I don't understand how You want to heal. Forgive me for when I try to take healing into my own hands. Help me only say what You say and do what You do. Amen.

February 6: FORGIVING THE UNFORGIVABLE

For I will forgive their wickedness and will remember their sins no more.
—Hebrews 8:12

Forgiveness and recovery go hand in hand. Without supernatural strength from God to forgive your offenders, the disease of offense lives on and can keep you soul-sick even in sobriety. Deep down, you probably know that forgiveness is a good thing, both for you and the person who needs your grace. So why is it so hard to do sometimes?

People muster all kinds of reasons to withhold forgiveness. They don't want to forgive, they're not ready to forgive, or perhaps they don't know how. Oftentimes their offender isn't even repentant, which enhances the urge to withhold forgiveness. Even when this feels right from an earthly standpoint, especially in extreme cases of abuse, neglect, assault, and other heinous offenses, forgiveness isn't actually up to us. Judgment rests with God alone, as does the power of unreasonable forgiveness to transform lives.

"God may forgive you, but I never will" is a dangerous sentiment for believers because it essentially calls God a liar and a fool. When God put on flesh and came to the earth as Jesus, He regularly offered forgiveness to unrepentant sinners. A few refused it, but most received it and left the conversation utterly transformed. It will take this kind of supernatural forgiveness to heal deep trauma and set captives and prisoners free.

Jesus only said and did what His Father was saying and doing (see John 5:19)—and God's mode of operation was and is always grace. If God says that our offenders are forgiven, who are we to say otherwise?

Partner with His heart today. Choose to forgive your offender—even if you never tell them you've done so—and watch God move in your life and theirs.

God, forgive me for withholding forgiveness. I only want to do what You do and say what You say. Fill me with Your strength and move me with compassion to forgive. Help me. Amen.

February 7: RETHINKING RECONCILIATION

Paul and Barnabas…had such a sharp disagreement that they parted company.
—Acts 15:35, 39

If you're ready to go deeper into the Uncovery and explore what forgiveness really means, it's important to understand your endgame with forgiveness.

God commands forgiveness throughout Scripture, but we sometimes don't see the happy-ending reconciliation scene we crave. Case in point: the apostle Paul and his buddy Barnabas. They quarreled over mobilizing early church mission teams—and whether or not to extend grace to Mark, one of those team members. They literally parted ways because of this. Seems a little less than Christlike, doesn't it?

But the disagreement didn't come as a surprise to God at all. Neither did this early church split. In fact, the split had to happen so that Paul could commission Silas, who became known as *"a brother…born for adversity"* (Proverbs 17:17 ESV) to both Paul *and* the apostle Peter. Paul and Barnabas ended up covering way more ground for the kingdom separately than they ever could have together. God had grace for their lack of grace and redeemed the situation. Colossians 4:10 indicates that Paul, Barnabas, and Mark were later reconciled.

Restoration doesn't always equal reconciliation this side of eternity. Sometimes too much damage has been done, and separation is necessary for kingdom advancement. You may forgive someone who abused you, but it may not be safe to reconcile. You may forgive someone who betrays you, but it may take time to rebuild trust again, if it's even possible. But God, in His goodness, is able to do far more than you can ask for or imagine.

Reconciliation is possible with two willing parties and the Holy Spirit in the mix. But even when reconciliation isn't possible in the natural, God can still work it all for our good and His glory.

God, Your word says You not only forgive, but You also forget our offenses against You. You continually restore us and bring us back to reconciled union with You. Help me be more like that. Amen.

Blessed is the one who does not condemn himself by what he approves.
—Romans 14:22

One of the toughest parts about the Christ-centered recovery journey is the necessary process of learning, unlearning, and relearning. Whether you were raised in the church or found Jesus quite recently, you have at least some idea in your mind about who He is and who you are in Him. These limiting core beliefs are the lenses through which you will be able to see the world.

The difficulty lies in the fact that we only know what we know when we know it. As we grow in our knowledge and love of God as a good Father, He continues to reveal deeper truths about His character. Many of these truths may challenge your assumptions about who you once thought God was—and they may challenge the deep, incorrect core beliefs you carry.

When we hold to our deeply embedded assumptions, changing our beliefs can be incredibly challenging. It requires not only identifying lies we've believed about God and ourselves, but also admitting we were wrong. Humbling yourself and asking God to reveal His truth, even if it hurts at first, is the way forward. He will help you flip the narrative.

Instead of believing you're just a sinner, accept your new identity as a beloved child of God. Instead of believing the world is out to get you, claim your life's purpose and start living it out—for God and others. Instead of believing God is mad at you, receive His grace in full and give it away to others. Instead of believing things are hopeless, become better acquainted with Hope Himself.

Letting go of limiting core beliefs becomes easier the more you do it. And the more you partner with God as He reveals His truth to you in His timing, the more freedom you find in Him.

God, I've made a lot of assumptions about You. If any of my limiting core beliefs go against who You say You are and who You say I am in You, show me and help me flip the narrative. Amen.

I will call them "my people" who are not my people; and I will call her
"my loved one" who is not my loved one."
—Romans 9:25

Labels are intensely polarizing, especially the ones we place on ourselves and others. Smart or dumb. Good or bad. Clean or dirty. Fast or slow. Affixing a *good* label on a person can be just as damaging as a bad one, because good people are good…until they aren't. And when people cease to walk out a good label as we expect, our brains literally don't know what to do with it.

Good labels are often placed on leaders, which is a huge problem in the recovery space. Words like *brilliant, faithful,* and *beyond reproach* may be highly desirable in a leader, but these expectations leave little room for recovery leaders, who are fellow travelers on a journey, to go deeper into the healing that comes with the Uncovery. They have to work hard to earn the labels we give them—and the energy they spend keeping up appearances comes at the expense of the people they're called to love and lead.

There are certain good leadership traits we should rightly expect from those who ascend the ranks, and leaders must have standards to aspire to by the grace of God. But the pedestals we put our leaders on are so precarious that some of them are falling. Yet even in failure, they are beloved children of God, just like we are.

So when you speak a *good* label over someone, declare it as a truth and a spiritual affirmation of identity, not as a flattering affirmation of self. Brilliant leaders put the brilliance of God on display. Faithful leaders are full of faith in God to help them lead better. Leaders are beyond reproach not because they have anything to prove, but because their life is a testimony in and of itself. Every good label must originate from God Himself.

God, I've dehumanized leaders by attaching unrealistic "good" labels to them. I've clung to my own good labels, feeding my ego and deceiving myself. Help me speak Your truth always. Amen.

February 10: "BAD" LABELS

*In the very place where it was said to them, "You are not my people,"
there they will be called "children of the living God."*
—Romans 9:26

The lie of labeling begins as early as elementary school. You likely knew you were either a good kid or a bad kid. If you were a good kid, you stayed away from the bad ones. If you were a bad kid, you thought you probably always would be.

Labels like *good* and *bad* are used to describe outward behavior. But the reality is, good kids don't always think and do good things. The opposite is also true—bad kids aren't always bad. We weren't born with a label of *good* or *bad*; we were all created in the image of God, and if our behavior indicates something good or something bad, it's a product of our environment. Digging deep into the lives of those we're tempted to call bad reveals a common denominator: trauma.

Trauma is bad. It's not just the bad thing that happens to you; it's what happens inside of you because of what happens to you. Trauma can create limiting core beliefs out of a fixed mindset that threaten your safety, security, and purpose. Those beliefs can reinforce bad labels and bad behavior. Addicts use. Alcoholics drink. Sinners sin.

But people are not bad. People may make bad life decisions that are a product of trauma in early life, but that does not make them bad. For people in recovery, this is critical to understand. You are not your behavior. And when you separate your behavior from your true identity as a beloved child of a good Father God, you start acting out of your true identity, not your label.

God, reveal to me any "bad" labels I've put on myself or others. Strip them away and replace them with Your truth. Show me who I really am in You and show me how You see others. Amen.

February 11: THEOLOGICAL TWEAKING

You will seek me and find me when you seek me with all your heart.
—Jeremiah 29:13

Whether you were raised in the Christian church or not, you likely grew up knowing at least a few things about God. What you came to know in your formative years about His existence, His character, and His level of involvement in your life was probably shaped by others, such as parents, guardians, friends, teachers, and pastors. What they taught you may or may not have been accurate, but it became your truth—your personal theology, your understanding of who God is. Perhaps your initial thoughts and beliefs about God served you well in life.

For some, these initial theologies can create places of deep wounding. When we believe God is anything other than good, faithful, holy, loving, gracious, and in control, we may struggle to trust Him, so we keep Him at arm's length. And when we do, we develop broken theologies that misrepresent the Father based on how we see Him.

The only effective way to check our theology is to align it with Scripture. As believers, we don't read the Bible because we have to; we read it because we want to better understand God, His character, and His plans for our lives. Scripture is alive, and God will use it to invite, challenge, and even lovingly convict you of sin. It's not the only way He speaks, but it's the most foolproof method.

The beauty is, when you dig deep to uncover the truth about who God really is—and allow the Holy Spirit to tweak your theology as needed—you'll not only see God more clearly, you'll see who you are in Him more clearly. You'll see just how loved and forgiven you are, right now. You'll see there's always more to learn about God and His character, and that He will meet you where you are when you earnestly seek His face.

God, I don't want to just know about You—I want to know You personally. Please reveal any part of my personal theology that doesn't reflect Your heart. Show me who You really are. Amen.

February 12: TRUE RELIGION

Formerly, when you did not know God,
you were slaves to those who by nature are not gods.
—Galatians 4:8

Life's too short to pretend we're not religious. We all worship someone or something. But the things we worship often aren't God—they're not even a reflection of His character.

This creates a huge problem for organized religion, especially the Christian church. What started as collective worship of a good Father God has gotten caught up in a *religious spirit* that distracts us from the Father and instead focuses on a works-based theology that keeps us checking boxes instead of chasing after Jesus. Religion itself becomes an idol instead of a pathway to the heart of God.

This reality makes Christ-centered recovery an unsafe space all too often. Legalism and lockstep programming are a lethal combination that can hinder deep healing. One size rarely fits all, and we need to embrace the creativity and diversity Jesus leveraged during His ministry. He rarely said or did the same things to heal and forgive, but He always said and did what His Father was saying or doing. He went off script so much that He frustrated His own disciples. But this God-given ability and willingness to pivot to meet people right where they were made all the difference.

True religion is more than a system of beliefs. True religion is genuine and proper worship of God the Father, the Son, and the Holy Spirit—not a religious spirit, false deity, or demon. Knowing who God is requires you to also recognize who He is not.

God, You are worthy of all my worship. If anything or anyone stands in the way of You being first in my life, realign my heart. Help me see You and choose You always. You are better than any substitute. Amen.

February 13: LETTING GO OF LEGALISM

For it is by grace you have been saved, through faith—and this is not from yourselves, it is the gift of God—not by works, so that no one can boast.
—Ephesians 2:8–9

Some of the most prominent recovery programming in the world originated from well-intentioned religious organizations. God's call to love and lead *"the least of these"* (Matthew 25:40) includes the poor in spirit—people who struggle with addiction, mental health problems, suicidal thoughts, and more. So it's no wonder that we, the church, stepped up to love like we did.

And yet when we stepped up to help people recover by sharing the gospel, we brought our baggage with us—namely the problem of religious legalism.

Religious legalism puts the law above the gospel and perpetuates the idea that God's gift of grace must be earned, or even bought in extreme cases. Legalism can show up even in the most grace-filled congregations as a byproduct of culture, tradition, or poor teaching. So it's no surprise that legalism also exists in even the best Christ-centered recovery programming. If we believe the lie that we have to earn our salvation, we will most certainly believe we have to earn our sobriety too. And while we may work out both our salvation and our sobriety with fear and trembling, initial deliverance can only be a gift from God. Because of this, those twelve steps to freedom can become lockstep in a heartbeat without deep trauma healing, authentic community, and a genuine encounter with a good Father God.

This is a huge opportunity for the church and for Christ-centered recovery by proxy. By letting go of one-size-fits-all, legalistic programming, we can embrace the simplicity of the gospel and help people transform. By releasing our stronghold on systems, processes, and rigid rules, we can learn to love and lead in the gentle way of Jesus. By all means, let's not cancel our Friday night meetings. But let's be willing to ask God, "What more would You have us do?" These critical shifts will lead to revival like we've never seen before—with identities renewed, lives redeemed, and families restored.

God, forgive me for any time I put my faith in a rule, a law, a step, or a system instead of You. Help me see what's working and not working in recovery and follow You where You lead. Amen.

February 14: LOVE OR DEATH

Place me like a seal over your heart, like a seal on your arm; for love is as strong as death, its jealousy unyielding as the grave.
—Song of Songs 8:6

Valentine's Day typically brings to mind images of flowers, candy, and all things romantic—not beating, stoning and decapitation. However, if you've ever loved and lost, or gone elbows deep into church history, you'll find the latter images are not only apt but may even be more appropriate.

Saint Valentine was a Roman priest under Emperor Claudius, a leader who infamously persecuted the church. Claudius made a decree that actually prohibited young people from getting married; he insisted unmarried men fought better in wars because they had less to lose. Valentine knew it was important to preserve God's call to marriage, so he married them in secret in the church.

Ol' Val definitely valued love over death, and he proved it by becoming a martyr. In AD 269, he was beaten, stoned, and decapitated, all because of his stand on Christian marriage. He laid his life on the line for what he believed in—love—and became known as the patron saint of lovers.

But Valentine wasn't the first to value love over death and literally die for his beliefs. He took a cue from the original perfect sacrifice, Jesus, who was willing to die so we might live and come to know His Father as our Father in heaven.

You might be thinking, *Valentine is an actual saint. Jesus is actually God. How am I supposed to love like that?* By the power of the Holy Spirit working in you and through you, Scripture says you'll do *"even greater things"* than Jesus did (John 14:12) and St. Valentine by proxy. Because of the grace you've received, you are supernaturally set up to give it away to others. Put your value in love over death, and you'll take people from death to life in Jesus's name.

God, my earthly idea of love is limited at best. Remind me of the power I carry with Your Spirit in me. Help me learn to love like You do and teach me to value love over death. Amen.

February 15: IDENTITY

My beloved is mine and I am his.
—Song of Songs 2:16

"Who do you think you are?" is a question the enemy has been asking humans since the dawn of creation. And despite our best human efforts, the world would be quick to respond for us:

+ "You're damaged goods."

+ "You're unforgivable."

+ "You're just an addict/mental case/coward/sinner, and you always will be."

These lies are poison to those of us in recovery, and deadly if we choose to swallow them. Leaning instead into the truth about our true identity—the one God gave us before the foundation of the earth—tells a different story.

It says you've been made new. It says you're loved and forgiven. It says you're a new creation and that the only label you ever need to carry is "beloved child of God." All seasons of recovery present new opportunities to come into alignment with this truth. Doing so may mean setting boundaries with people who can't or won't help you partner with the truth of your identity. It will certainly mean drawing near to God and asking Him to show you how He sees you. It can be intimidating at first because, let's be honest, somewhere along the line, you probably heard the lie that God is standing by, ready to smite you at any moment.

Hear the truth: God loves you fiercely. He thinks you're to die for. And He's standing by, waiting for you to turn back to Him, ask Him what He thinks of you, and fall into His arms of grace. Your good Father God will never ask, "Who do you think you are?" He'll say, "My beloved child, don't you know who you are?!" You're His. And He is yours.

God, how can You love me like you do!? My mind can't understand it, but my heart wants to believe it's true. I believe—help my unbelief! Show me my identity through Your eyes. Amen.

February 16: FAMILY OF ORIGIN

If anyone comes to me and does not hate father and mother, wife and children, brothers and sisters—yes, even their own life— such a person cannot be my disciple.
—Luke 14:26

There's more than one kind of family. There's the family we're born into and the family we choose. These earthly families and the experiences with each can be strong indicators of whether or not we will struggle.

Trauma in early life experiences with our family of origin—a biological or adoptive family or perhaps a social group—can leave deep wounds resulting from abuse, neglect, abandonment, and more. Even in healthy families, obsession and codependence can affect us when we put our family members before God. Life goes on, but the damage remains, often manifesting as seemingly unrelated addictions, mental health problems, and thoughts about suicide in adulthood.

As we grow and mature, we typically take a step away from our family of origin to make room for the family we choose—not just the families we marry into, but the people we do life with, including friends, mentors, colleagues, neighbors, partners, and others. When there is early life trauma, these relationships will often be less than healthy, directly mirroring or clearly compensating for how we perceived our family of origin. The problem is that even with the best of intentions, people can't bring the healing that only God can.

Thankfully, there's a third kind of family—kingdom family. It transcends any kind of earthly family with God as a good and loving Father who will never abuse, neglect, or abandon you. As you learn to embrace your identity as His beloved child, you begin to discover that He desires this relationship with *everyone*, regardless of who they are or what they've done—even your family of origin or family of choice whose actions ultimately led you on a path to discovering the Father's heart. You'll tap into a well of grace that never runs dry, and you'll want to give everyone a drink of *"living water"* (John 7:38).

Hurt people hurt people…but healed people heal people when they do it in Jesus's name. Ask the Father to redefine your idea of family today, to make *family* on earth as it is in heaven.

God, Your love is perfect. It's something I've never experienced from a human relationship. Thank You for making me part of Your family. Help me invite others in too. Amen.

February 17: AUTHENTIC RELATIONSHIPS

Be kind to one another, tenderhearted, forgiving one another,
as God in Christ forgave you.
—Ephesians 4:32 (ESV)

No one should have to walk through recovery—or life, for that matter—alone. We were created for relationship with God and with others. And while our relationship with God must take priority over every human relationship we have, we can't lock ourselves in our prayer closets and wait for the second coming. We must be intentional about community.

The problem is, community isn't always what it's cracked up to be. Simply being in the presence of another human being isn't being in relationship with them. Authentic relationships take courage because they mean going deep—beneath the superficial surface conversations. Real relationships require vulnerability, especially in a recovery context. If we can't get real with one another and ourselves, chances are we won't get real with God either.

Authentic relationships take time to cultivate. They can't be programmed. If they could, every blind date, sponsor assignment, and business partnership that worked on paper would also work in real life. It takes intentionality, grace, peace, and love to invest in one another, encourage and empower one another, and do life together.

Even the best human relationships are limited. Because we are human, we will inevitably disappoint one another at some point even with the best of intentions. When it comes to our relationship with God, we see something completely different. Ever faithful, He will never let us down. Even when we feel disappointed with God, it's because we can't understand what He's doing.

We will fail Him again and again, but He will never be disappointed in us. Because of Jesus's sacrifice for our sin, God sees us as holy, blameless, and pure—His beloved children. It's unlike any other earthly relationship we can have. But His example of grace can and should influence our earthly relationships as we put His love on display.

God, You are the most important relationship in my life. I'm so thankful for Your forgiveness. Help me extend Your grace in all my relationships, loving Your people like You do. Amen.

February 18: RIGHT HAND RELIANCE

For I am the LORD your God who takes hold of your right hand and says to you, Do not fear; I will help you.
—Isaiah 41:13

Throughout the Bible, you'll find many verses referring to the "right hand." Sometimes it's God's right hand; sometimes it's the right hand of a human such as Jacob/Israel in Genesis 48:14. Occasionally it refers to a direction or a literal *right or wrong* scenario, but more often, it's a place of security or a synonym for goodness. It's a place that we, as broken people, cannot possibly muster in our own strength or by our own right hand.

But picture this: God reaches out to you in a time of trial. He takes your hand in His and gently reminds you that you don't have to be afraid. You don't have to go it alone because He will help you. He doesn't want you to bootstrap yourself or try harder. He doesn't even want you to try to do it in your own strength. With His righteous right hand leading you, He wants you to access the power He has to carry you through.

The world will tell us that we can only rely on ourselves. Take God out of the equation and that might be true. Because we humans are human, our strength isn't perfect, and we will disappoint one another. This is why it's so important to remember where our strength really comes from—what, or more appropriately, *who* it is we can really rely on.

Lean into the Father's goodness, and you'll find His right hand holding you up, empowering you to live a transformed life—not in your own strength, but in His strength by His grace. This isn't about making Jesus your higher power. It's about making Him Lord of your life and trusting in His righteousness to make you brave. Will you reach out and take His right hand today?

God, thank You for reaching out to comfort, strengthen, and protect me. Thank You for giving me a right hand so I can remember I am created in Your image and righteous through Christ. Amen.

February 19: I SURRENDER

Submit yourselves, then, to God. Resist the devil, and he will flee from you.
—James 4:7

Surrender is a common theme in Christianity. We sing hymns and worship songs about surrender. We celebrate a testimony of personal surrender and wear it like a badge of honor. But surrender, if we're really being honest, is one of the hardest things people can do, especially in recovery.

We like to feel like we're in control. Surrender not only removes our sense of control, it exposes that we were never actually in control in the first place. It's humbling. But just as it's impossible to go forward and backward at the same time, pursuing a promised-land life of transformation is impossible if we continue to cling to the false security of an old, broken life. We must be willing to let go of it and let God deal with it however He sees fit.

Surrender isn't waving a white flag or giving up; it's the intentional process of giving over your struggles, your idols, and your past to a good Father God who will handle everything better than you ever could.

Is there any part of your life you haven't yet surrendered to God? The answer may be obvious, or you may need to think on it awhile. God is so patient and so kind, He won't make you surrender every part of your life all at once. Instead, He will continue to reveal to you new ways to surrender, come into alignment with His truth, and finally agree with who He says you are: His beloved child. He loves you far too much to leave you where you are. And in His perfect timing, He will reveal opportunities to continually surrender yourself to His love.

We die daily to our false sense of self and come alive in His presence. This is what resurrection life really looks like.

God, I admit sometimes I don't want to surrender everything to You. I give You pieces and parts of my life, and You respond by giving me Your whole heart. Help me surrender it all. Amen.

February 20: ETERNAL LIFE

Whoever finds their life will lose it,
and whoever loses their life for my sake will find it.
—Matthew 10:39

Life is fleeting, but that wasn't by design. When God created Adam and Eve in the garden of Eden, His intent for them was never death, only life in communion with Him. But sadly, they chose otherwise—as every single one of us would have—and God let them. This early-world decision forces us to face the fragile finality of life. We're dust, and to dust, we'll return. But God, in His goodness, has made a way for us to have eternal life, a life that can actually start right now.

To find eternal life—our real life, the one God intended for us all along—we must be willing to lose this one. Unless we choose to leave the old life behind, to "die to ourselves," we can't possibly step into the new life God has for us. (See Galatians 2:20.)

Much of the world—and much of the church, for that matter—would like you to think you'll never be rid of that old self, that you're damaged goods, branded and labeled forever. This is not the nature of God. God doesn't see you for what you've done; He sees you for who you are, not by the world's standards, but by the sacrifice Jesus made for you. He doesn't even remember your sin anymore; He only remembers that Jesus paid for it. And because of Christ's sacrifice, you can be in God's holy presence unashamed and untethered to that old, broken life you once led.

Eternal life for you started the moment you said *yes* to Jesus and called God "Father." The old self is dead now. You're a new creation. Man's empty praise or harsh criticisms don't even matter anymore; the only opinion that counts is God's. And in time, as you get to know more about God's nature and character, you might receive this truth and start living like you believe it.

God, it's hard to imagine life outside of the earthly one I'm living. Help me let go of this old, broken life—to die to myself and come alive again in my eternal life that starts today. Amen.

February 21: A HIGHER HIGHER POWER

Therefore God exalted him to the highest place and gave him the name that is above every name, that at the name of Jesus every knee should bow, in heaven and on earth and under the earth, and every tongue acknowledge that Jesus Christ is Lord, to the glory of God the Father.
—Philippians 2:9–11

Traditional recovery programs, secular and sacred alike, encourage participants to put their trust and reliance in a *higher power*. This is defined as "something greater than ourselves," a deity, a force, or even some higher version of self we have yet to achieve. In Christian recovery, we typically name Jesus as our higher power, assimilating Him into a man-made recovery process that continually proves to be less than effective.

Here's a sobering truth: Research shows that even Christ-centered recovery is falling short. As many as 80 percent of people who acknowledge Jesus as their higher power will still fail at recovery from earthly standards, relapsing within the first year. This certainly isn't because Jesus isn't powerful enough. It's because we don't really understand the purpose of a higher power in the first place.

For most of us, a higher power is something or someone we believe in to help us stay sober. But believing in a higher power is not the same as putting our full trust, hope, and reliance in that power so that it's in its proper place, high and exalted.

You may acknowledge Jesus as your higher power, but have you also made Him Lord of your life? Do you truly believe He can restore you to sanity? Have you really put Him in the high and exalted place He deserves in your heart and mind?

Your higher power deserves a higher place. As you go deeper into the Uncovery journey, the Father will lift you up with Him. The Bible says Jesus now sits at the right hand of the Father, and that even now, you are seated *with Him* in the heavenly places. (See Ephesians 2:6.) This means your higher power not only *exists* and is *competent* to restore you, He has scooped you up to sit in His throne room with Him as His beloved child. Higher isn't just where He is; it's where He will take you if you'll only say yes.

God, Your ways are higher and better than mine. When I put You in a place of high honor and look up to You, You meet my gaze and lift me up. Remind me You are God over it all. Amen.

February 22: POWERFUL PRAYER

Do not be anxious about anything, but in every situation, by prayer and petition, with thanksgiving, present your requests to God.
—Philippians 4:6

Nothing overcomes anxiety and depression like the power of prayer. It sounds cliché, but it's based in profound truth. The reason why prayer is so powerful may surprise you. Prayer is more than petitioning and presenting requests to God, which, by the way, He commands us to do. Prayer is meant to be quality time spent with God.

God wants to know what's on your mind, not just so He can fix things for you, but so He can meet you in the middle of this messy life and carry you through. He wants to know it all. What's bringing you joy? What's holding you back? What's tearing you down? What's breaking your heart? What do you want, need, or hope for most? Give it to Him—in thanksgiving, not in a spirit of complaining—and watch His hand move in your life.

Sometimes our struggles are so overwhelming, we can't find the words for God. And even if we found them, they would sound more like ungratefulness than thanksgiving. In times like these, the Holy Spirit can pray for you, interpreting and conveying your prayers.

For we do not know what to pray for as we ought, but the Spirit himself intercedes for us with groanings too deep for words. (Romans 8:26 ESV)

The Father knows what you're thinking before you do, but He still wants you to sit with Him, even in silence, to partner together in prayer, even when you don't know what to pray. Practicing the presence is powerful prayer. And the best part is, you don't have to get it right. The Father will meet you right where you are. He will rejoice with you and grieve with you. He will comfort your anxieties and strengthen you in times of weakness. He is there for you, always, even after you've said amen. Amen and amen, again and again, He is faithful.

God, I don't know why I make prayer so hard. I know I don't need to get it right for You; You just want to be with me. Help me sense Your presence today and lean on You in all things. Amen.

February 23: THE PERSON OF JESUS

Do not be anxious about anything, but in every situation, by prayer and petition, with thanksgiving, present your requests to God.
—Philippians 4:6

When Jesus, the Son of God, walked the earth, He most often referred to Himself as "Son of Man." It was a weird thing for God in the flesh to say, but it was absolutely true. Jesus was both fully human and fully God, but He placed emphasis on His humanity so we would trust His ability to fully empathize with our lives.

But the Son of Man identity He carried went way beyond empathy alone. Jesus emphasized His humanity to show humans what they are capable of. Jesus only ever said what the Father said and did what the Father did. (See John 5:19.) He was fully reliant on God's strength and power to perform miracles and transform hearts and minds. Jesus was a perfect example of God-ordained power and authority, which is something we carry too! The Son of Man made it plain:

Very truly I tell you, whoever believes in me will do the works I have been doing, and they will do even greater things than these, because I am going to the Father. (John 14:12)

The implications of this are huge for recovery. God doesn't just want to see you sober; He wants to see you transformed, and He will be faithful to make a way. When you feel powerless, look to the person of Jesus as your pathway to power. Look to Him, and you will see the Father. Look to Him, and you'll feel the power of the Holy Spirit in you. Live by His example, and He will not only make your path straight, He will make sure you never have to walk it alone.

God, thank You for humbling Yourself and coming to earth as a human. Thank You for the example of Jesus to show me what I am capable of in this life and that I'm never alone. Amen.

February 24: THE HOLY SPIRIT'S ALWAYS WORKING

But the Advocate, the Holy Spirit, whom the Father will send in my name, will teach you all things and will remind you of everything I have said to you.
—John 14:26

Setbacks in recovery are normal and even expected. In early seasons of sobriety, people often focus on behavior modification strategies rather than total life transformation. We work the steps. We avoid temptation by replacing bad habits. We attend meetings and go through the motions. And then, the inevitability of life happens. No matter how hard we've worked, no matter how many new coping strategies we have, when the going gets tough, we often return to what we know.

When setbacks happen, we have a decision to make. We can choose to see them as failures, or we can choose to see them as opportunities for breakthrough and growth. Even in setback, God is in control—and His Holy Spirit is always working in every circumstance, for our good and His glory. (See Romans 8:28.)

This might sound like a bunch of Christian fluff at first...until you understand that God isn't just with you, He's in you. You're one with Him. (See John 17:23.) He has taken up residence in your heart, and you are one with the Father through Jesus by the power of the Holy Spirit. Nothing can separate you from Him or His love ever again. Not even relapse.

Perhaps you're facing difficult circumstances today. Relapse, job loss, family stress, financial strain—whatever it is, God sees it all. Rest in the truth that the Holy Spirit is always working behind the scenes, in you, through you, and for you, laying a pathway forward for you and for all of God's people.

We go through what we go through so we can help people go through what we went through. The very setback we face now may become our greatest place of victory.

God, my circumstances are overwhelming, but I am overwhelmed by Your goodness. Help me see past this mess called life, to go deeper and find You always working beneath the surface. Amen.

February 25: GUIDANCE OF SCRIPTURE

All Scripture is given by inspiration of God, and is profitable for doctrine, for reproof, for correction, for instruction in righteousness, that the man of God may be complete, thoroughly equipped for every good work.
—2 Timothy 3:16–17 (NKJV)

"How do you know if you're hearing from God?" is one of the most common questions that recovery leaders hear, and a great one to be asking yourself daily. Because Jesus died and rose again to cover your sin, by the power of the Holy Spirit living in you, you now have direct access to God. You can speak to Him, and He can speak to you. You may have dreams or visions, a strong sense about something, or even hear God's audible voice. It's true! But the most common way to hear from God is through the guidance of Scripture—God's own inspired and perfect Word, the Bible.

Now, you may be thinking, *Wait! Doesn't the Bible contradict itself? How can God speak to me through something written thousands of years ago by a bunch of men?* Be encouraged. Confusion about Scripture can be overcome through a lifetime of study and authentic community to help guide you through it. In time, you'll discover the importance of context and Holy Spirit-led clarity that will uncover new truth in a passage you may have read a hundred times before. The Bible, like God, is alive and well, and the Father will use it to reveal His heart to you along your recovery journey.

Wondering if that thing you heard was actually from the Father? Ask Him to reveal it to you in Scripture. Don't throw it out if you can't find it right away; God will show you in His perfect timing. And when He speaks, listen to His instruction. God will give you grace for today and every day.

God, speak to me through Your Word. I want to hear Your voice clearly and discern Your heart and Your plans for my life. Teach me to hear Your voice so I can grow in my love for You. Amen.

February 26: GOOD FATHER GOD

*As a father has compassion on his children,
so the LORD has compassion on those who fear him.*
—Psalm 103:13

Accepting God as a good Father can be a stretch for many. It can be difficult to imagine the Father outside the constructs of our earthly fathers.

If your own father was abusive or absent, you'll have a hard time believing Father God is willing and able to be good. Conversely, even if your earthly father was present and loving, he simply can't measure up to the goodness of God as your heavenly Father.

This is why the concept of a *good Father God* is so critical to people in recovery. Far more than a mere higher power, our good Father God not only exists, He loves and extends grace to His children with a level of mercy that defies human logic. As God, He loves better than anyone else ever could. His love is perfect, and He lavishes compassion on those who fear Him. Unlike all too many earthly fathers who might elicit terror from their children, God doesn't want us to be afraid of Him. That's not what fear of the Lord is. Fearing Him is simply holding Him in reverence, acknowledging that He is God and we are not, and surrendering to His power and authority over our lives.

The best part is that when we worship and revere God as a good Father, giving Him the glory and honor that He is due, He meets us right where we are. He comes down low to dwell with us, moving in us and through us by the power of His Holy Spirit. And He lifts us up to be seated *"with him in the heavenly realms in Christ Jesus"* (Ephesians 2:6). The perfect love and intimacy He offers to us casts out all fear and teaches us who our good, good Father really is.

God, I want to believe You're a good Father. Help me put aside my ideas of what a father is and show me more of who You are—Your heart and true character. Let me fall into Your arms. Amen.

Faith shows the reality of what we hope for;
it is the evidence of things we cannot see.
—Hebrews 11:1 (NLT)

Seeing is believing. Or so the world would have you believe. This common but unfortunate phrase takes faith out of the equation, and faith is necessary for recovery and life transformation. After all, anyone can believe in what they see. This is not faith. Faith is what brings dreams to life and makes the unseen *seen* in unquestionably supernatural ways.

That kind of faith takes more than hopes and desires. It takes discipline. We were never meant to strive in our own strength. We are meant to lean into the Lord and His strength for everything—for every good work, every loving conviction, and even faith itself. When we cry out, *"I believe; help my unbelief!"* (Mark 9:24 ESV), we lean into the truth that we can't even have faith in God without God's help. Declaring faith in what we cannot yet see is a bold move of faith, but it exercises a spiritual muscle that keeps us content in any circumstance.

For example, you may have faith that God keeps His promises, even when you're still waiting on one of His promises to you. You can believe for healing and deliverance, even before you see it come or when it comes in a way you didn't expect. You can believe that a better life is actually possible, even in the early stages of recovery when you might be tempted to go back to the life you know. This is the faith that transforms lives.

So go ahead. Dare to have faith in what you can't see yet. Give your struggles and worries to God, and let Him handle them in His perfect timing. Believe He is good, that He keeps His promises, and that He will make a way toward the promised-land life you were made to live.

God, help me see the unseen through Your eyes. Help me believe for what's yet to come and stay steadfast as I wait on You. Help me believe for a promised-land life that's worth living. Amen.

For I know that good itself does not dwell in me, that is, in my sinful nature. For I have the desire to do what is good, but I cannot carry it out. For I do not do the good I want to do, but the evil I do not want to do—this I keep on doing.
—Romans 7:18–19

Step into any twelve-step program, and you'll be encouraged to admit a powerful truth: You're powerless over your struggle. It's devastating to admit, but it's true. Striving alone might get you sober, but it won't bring about the life transformation that comes with the Uncovery.

And yet, after acknowledging this key truth of powerlessness, traditional recovery insists that behavior modification is the key to lasting sobriety. If we try hard enough, say all the right words, and do all the right things, we'll change our habits and set ourselves free from our struggles with addiction, mental health, and suicidal thoughts. But in reality, true transformation requires going deeper than our surface issues to uncover and heal from the trauma that led us to struggle in the first place. This healing can't happen on our own; we need an authentic community to point us straight to Jehovah Rapha, God our Healer Himself. On our own, we can't do the good things we want to do. Paul knew it, we know it, and even Jesus knew it. (See John 5:19.)

The beauty of acknowledging God as your higher power and Lord of your life is that you don't have to recover in your own strength. You get to tap into His strength, which is made perfect in your weakness. (See 2 Corinthians 12:9.) When you acknowledge that your power really comes from the all-powerful God of the universe, you can tap into a power that never runs out. You'll have the strength you need to walk out your recovery journey and step into a truly transformed life. Rely on your good Father God and His mighty power. You will have strength for the days to come.

God, You are all-powerful. Forgive me for leaning on my own strength to heal and recover when I should be leaning into Yours. Fill me with Your power and restore me to sanity. Amen.

*My prayer is not for them alone. I pray also for those who will believe
in me through their message, that all of them may be one, Father, just as
you are in me and I am in you. May they also be in us so that the world
may believe that you have sent me.*
—John 17:20–21

Did you know Jesus wasn't a Christian? No, seriously! He lived out a perfect
Christian existence during His short time on earth. He was the Son of God
and Son of Man. But Jesus was a Jew. Christianity as a religion and a system of
belief didn't come about until after Jesus Christ's death and resurrection.

This distinction is important for modern-day believers. If you were to ask
the scribes and religious leaders of Jesus's day if He was *a good Jew*, they'd have
likely laughed in your face. Jesus wasn't one to toe a party line. He challenged
authority, fought injustice, and brought spiritual reform in a way so radical, it
got Him killed. But He never wavered. Jesus came to fulfill the law of Moses
as a perfect sacrifice for our sin so that we might all live underneath a new covenant regulation—the law of the Spirit of life. He came to set both prisoners
and captives free, regardless of how they came to be imprisoned. He came to
bring eternal living water for all who are thirsty. That well of grace still hasn't
run dry, and it never will.

Jesus wasn't a Christian. He was *the* Christ, the long-awaited Messiah who
made a way for us all to be back in right relationship with our good Father
God. All who say *yes* to Jesus's radical grace become one with Him—and one
with God the Father by proxy.

Do you believe it? Would you like to? Ask Him to show you.

*Jesus, You are my Lord and my God. Thank You for loving me when I don't
deserve it. I receive Your gift of grace. Help me align with Your heart and know I
am one with You. Amen.*

March

REPENTANCE

*Therefore, I urge you, brothers and sisters, in view of God's mercy, to
offer your bodies as a living sacrifice, holy and pleasing to God—
this is your true and proper worship.*
—Romans 12:1

March 1: REDISCOVERING SELF

But those who fail to find me harm themselves; all who hate me love death.
—Proverbs 8:36

Recovery is a journey of discovery. To experience lasting breakthrough, we must be willing to see what lies beneath our surface-level struggles and pursue life transformation over sobriety alone. March is Self-Harm Awareness Month, and we must learn to better love and lead people through the problem of self-harm.

This compulsive behavior can take many forms, including cutting, overeating or eating too little, engaging in intentionally risky or unsafe behavior, and more. Ultimately, people who struggle with self-harm cause themselves pain in order to deal with pain—painful feelings, painful memories, or painful circumstances and experiences. The problem of pain is so real that pain itself becomes the only release.

The desperation of self-harm can stem from a need to control, punish, or even connect with ourselves in a world that can leave us feeling numb. While self-harm isn't always an indication of being suicidal, it can be a way to express suicidal feelings without seeking death. For those who struggle with self-harm and those who are trying to love and lead them, we must understand the Father's heart on this issue. His heart for His children is always compassion and mercy over judgment.

We don't have to be perfect. Jesus is perfect, and God sees us through His perfect sacrifice. (See Colossians 1:22.) We don't need to be punished—Jesus paid it all on the cross. (See 1 Peter 2:24; 1 John 2:2.) We don't need to look inward for connection and purpose—God longs to reveal our oneness with Him, a supernatural connection that honors and dignifies the mind, the body, and the self. (See John 17:20–21.)

When we look for God in all the wrong places, we will struggle to find Him in His fullness. But when we seek Him with all our hearts, we will find Him. In His timing, He will reveal the truth about who He is and who you are. He will encourage healing and proper self-care worthy of the new creation you already are.

God, forgive me for the hateful ways I treat myself. I'm one with You, so I can't hate what You love. Help me learn to love and forgive myself as You've loved and forgiven me. Amen.

March 2: REAL REPENTANCE

The Lord is not slow in keeping his promise, as some understand slowness. Instead he is patient with you, not wanting anyone to perish, but everyone to come to repentance.
—2 Peter 3:9

Repentance is a loaded word with a rather dark history in the church. The idea initially came from the Greek word *metanoia*, which simply means "to change your mind." Early English Bible translations translated the word as *repent*, a word strongly tied to the idea of penance or self-punishment for sin. The problem with this concept is that it strongly implies that we must pay for sin when Jesus already bore the cost. In essence, it says Jesus's sacrifice wasn't enough.

Real *metanoia* repentance means changing your mind, aligning with God's truth, and walking toward Him and away from sin. This true repentance is absolutely necessary for believers. *"If we confess our sins, he is faithful and just to forgive us our sins and to cleanse us from all unrighteousness"* (1 John 1:9 ESV). But we humans are prone to systemizing just about everything, which creates legalistic barriers to entry for those desiring a sin-free life. Historically, our flawed theologies and doctrines have suggested God's grace can be *earned*—and even *bought* in some circles. Nothing could be further from the truth!

The gift of God's grace is just that: a gift. Trying to earn a gift dishonors the giver and misses the point entirely. Receiving God's grace gift in full leads people to real repentance. They don't just pray the sinner's prayer. They don't just quit sinning and start attending church regularly. They change their minds about who God is and who they are in Him—and they change their minds about their sins and struggles by proxy. The truly repentant will turn away from an old, broken life and pursue the promised-land life God has for them.

Have you experienced real, *metanoia* repentance? Have you confessed your sins to God and received His forgiveness? Have you changed your mind about that old life, turned from sin, and started following Jesus? Would you like to?

God, without You, sin would rule me. I'm sorry for what I've done. Thank You for Your grace gift. I receive it in full. I'm turning from my old life and stepping into the new one You have for me. Amen.

March 3: NEW BIRTH

Yet to all who did receive him, to those who believed in his name, he gave the right to become children of God—children born not of natural descent, nor of human decision or a husband's will, but born of God.
—John 1:12–13

Springtime is a wild season of resurrection, renewal, and rebirth. Depending on your geographic location, you may experience it differently. But as a general rule, we see dormant plants come back to life, higher temperatures reheating and reviving the earth, and brand new life emerging. But for believers everywhere, spring is a season to reflect on the newness of life that comes from being one with God through Jesus.

Scholars believe Jesus was crucified in the springtime somewhere around AD 33. He descended into hell for three days as a perfect sacrifice for sin that would defeat sin completely. On the third day, He came back from death to life, defeating sin once and for all so that we who believe in Him receive His gift of grace, mercy, and forgiveness.

Here's the interesting part: As we receive that gift of grace, we become one with Jesus and with the Father by the power of the Holy Spirit. This means we aren't just thankful for His sacrifice; we actively participate in it. The Bible says we were actually crucified with Jesus, and now it's no longer our old selves who live but Jesus who lives in us and gives us the power to walk free from sin. (See Galatians 2:20.) We didn't die in the traditional sense; we died to our old selves and were born again into a brand new existence.

Your oneness with God in Jesus completely reframes your identity in this world. You are no longer a sinner, but a saint! The living God lives inside you! God is birthing a new season in you, one that's no longer connected to your past identity and struggles. By grace, you're not free to sin, you're free from it—and by God's strength, you can step into the transformed life He has for you.

God, You don't just take me from death to life. You give me a completely new birth into a promised-land life of transformation! Help me see Your promise of new birth this spring. Amen.

When you fast, do not look somber as the hypocrites do, for they disfigure their faces to show others they are fasting. Truly I tell you, they have received their reward in full. But when you fast, put oil on your head and wash your face, so that it will not be obvious to others that you are fasting, but only to your Father, who is unseen; and your Father, who sees what is done in secret, will reward you.
—Matthew 6:16–18

If you grew up in church, you probably have at least a little experience with Lent, a traditional time of personal and corporate fasting during the weeks leading up to Easter Sunday. Fasting is an ancient practice, encouraged even by Jesus Himself as a way to repent of sins and draw closer to the heart of God. Unfortunately, we humans have taken Lent, laced it with an unhealthy level of legalism, and pushed it on people as an unbiblical, worth-proving practice.

The funny part is, the Bible doesn't actually say *anything* about fasting for Lent. The tradition became popular about three hundred years after Jesus's death and resurrection as people sought practical steps to prepare for baptisms, which often occurred at Eastertime. Giving up something for Lent became common in the Catholic Church and is still observed in one form or another by many Protestant denominations. All too often, when Christians fast for Lent, they let others know they are fasting and find ways to complain and talk about it during the entire experience. They focus on their sacrifice instead of the God who would seek to draw them near.

Now, nobody is saying don't fast. If abstaining from food, drink, or any other creature comfort can draw your attention to your humanity and God's deity, by all means, go for it. But before you fast, ask yourself why you're doing it. Is it because someone told you to? Is it because you don't want to be left out? Is it because you want to prove to yourself you can do it and maybe even lose a few pounds along the way? If so, consider this: fast from fasting. Wait on God to call you into such behavior and be ready to do it for nothing but the glory of His felt presence.

God, I admit I'm sometimes tempted to use fasting for my glory, not Yours. Cleanse me of my pride. Help me know what it means to seek You above all else— no boxes to check, just You. Amen.

March 5: A WILLING SACRIFICE

Follow God's example, therefore, as dearly loved children and walk in the way of love, just as Christ loved us and gave himself up for us as a fragrant offering and sacrifice to God.
—Ephesians 5:1–2

Imagine this: You're sitting in the church pew on a Sunday morning. The back doors fly open and armed gunmen corral the congregation, demanding that you denounce your faith or die. What would you say? What would you do? Would you be obedient to God and to your faith, even to the point of death?

Let's be honest. Many Christians struggle with a martyr complex, especially in the Western American church. We talk about sacrifice, what we've been willing to let go of and let God have, and what we'd be willing to sacrifice if the situation warranted, in the context of a first-world existence. While we may experience judgment, isolation, and even severe misunderstanding from nonbelievers, most of us do not know persecution, religious abuse, and abject martyrdom like the early church saints and Christians in non-Christian nations around the world.

If you want to know more about what sacrifice really looks like, look to Jesus. He lived a perfect life, free of sin. And He gave His life for you, surrendered and obedient unto death. He gave His life as a willing sacrifice for sin, and He did it for you. Call it madness or call it mercy; it's the gospel truth. So what are you willing to sacrifice for God? What are you willing to let go of and give to Him, not to earn His grace, but in response to it? God's mercy leads to true repentance, not the other way around. What would you give Him? What would you bring to Him? What would you surrender as a willing sacrifice in order to experience the joy of putting Him first?

Make no mistake: God wants you. He wants every single part of your life. He may not call you to lay your life down for your brothers and sisters like Jesus did, but He does want you to acknowledge Him as a good Father God and be willing to participate in kingdom business as His beloved child. When He calls you to a willing sacrifice, be willing to give it all.

God, surrendering to You can be so hard. It seems ridiculous, knowing what You've surrendered for me. Help me live my life as a willing sacrifice that pleases You and brings us closer. Amen.

Then Jesus said to his disciples: "Therefore I tell you, do not worry about your
life, what you will eat; or about your body, what you will wear."
—Luke 12:22

Throughout Scripture, you'll discover clear themes of generosity and abundance coming straight from the heart of the Father. Luke's gospel counts God's genuine concern for the well-being and provision of birds, plants, and every other living thing. (See Luke 12: 22–34.) He feeds the ravens. He clothes the lilies. And yet, when faced with the inevitable challenges of life and recovery, we can be tempted to worry about whether the abundant life God offers is really for us too. We wonder, *Will I have enough? Will I be okay? Can I trust God to take care of me?*

On the flip side, God's promises for our provision can sound almost irresponsible to Type A, hardworking people. By default, most of us act to benefit ourselves. In an unending struggle for control, some feel the need to earn what God longs to give us freely—spiritual, physical, and even financial provision. Is God suggesting we do nothing while believing for this provision? Certainly not! The Father longs to bless the work of our hands when they're yielded to Him. But His desire to co-labor and cocreate with us along life's journey is undeniable. Every good gift, down the last hard-earned dime, belongs to God and is available to us as His children.

Wealth and power can make unhealthy people arrogant and controlling, which is why Jesus talked about money so much in Scripture. While most religious types condemned the active pursuit of an abundant, promised-land life, Jesus teaches us to live from abundance, knowing the Father's entire kingdom is available to us here and now, on earth as it is in heaven. He even teaches us to pray this way! (See Matthew 6:9–13.) While Jesus didn't die so we could become rich or famous, He also didn't die so we would remain poor and anonymous. You can trust our good Father God to provide for you. He will make a way, even when there is no way. It's what He does.

God, forgive me for the times I don't trust in Your abundant provision and try to make my own way. Help me dream bigger with You and step into the fullness of my promised-land life. Amen.

March 7: A PROMISED-LAND LIFE

And I will bring you to the land I swore with uplifted hand to give to Abraham, to Isaac and to Jacob. I will give it to you as a possession. I am the LORD.
—Exodus 6:8

Imagine this. You're a slave in Egypt, experiencing back-breaking labor, daily beatings, and certain death for noncompliance. A deliverer shows up to tell you God is about to make good on His promise to set you free, smite your captors, and give you the land He promised to your ancestors, to own for good. And you, my friend, are so discouraged and exhausted that you don't even listen to him. Basically, you tell him, "Whatever, Moses. Get lost. I have a ton of work to do."

This is exactly how the Israelites responded when Moses accepted God's call to deliver the Israelites from four hundred years of captivity. Maybe you can relate. When slavery is all you've ever known, it can be difficult if not impossible to imagine a life of freedom. Even when that life is in plain sight, it can still seem out of reach. You can take a person out of slavery, but getting the slavery out of the person takes a total life transformation that's only possible by the power of the Holy Spirit.

The funny thing is, even when everything went down just as Moses said it would, the Israelites still struggled to believe the life they were being offered was really for them. After God brought down plagues to move Pharaoh, split the Red Sea for safe passage, and made it rain manna from the skies, they rejoiced for a little bit… but then started to grumble and even reminisce about the *good old days* back in Egyptian captivity, where they at least got their fill of meat. Their initial deliverance didn't last, and they relapsed into old ways of thinking in about two months. Because they were free but not transformed, the journey to the promised land took forty years—way longer than needed. God made good on His promise. His people did eventually inherit and inhabit the land. But some never made it at all.

Let this sobering truth ignite a fire in you. Ask the Father to show you your own potential for a promised-land life and to help others see it, too.

God, forgive me for dragging my feet on the way to the life You have for me. You've set me free. Help me learn what it means to live free in the promised-land life You have for me. Amen.

Then will the eyes of the blind be opened and the ears of the deaf unstopped.
Then will the lame leap like a deer, and the mute tongue shout for joy.
—Isaiah 35:5–6

Recovery is for everyone. Whether we come to struggle by choice or by chance, we humans are desperately in need of mental, emotional, and physical healing. And as you may have guessed, the transformative healing we really need can only from God. But in God's unfathomable wisdom, His method of healing doesn't always match our expectations.

This can be really hard for the church to accept. When we pray for healing we know is ours, and we don't witness blind eyes and deaf ears opening, literally and figuratively, we can't help but wonder why God heals the way He does. If He's really a good Father, why doesn't He heal us all, especially those people who did *nothing* to contribute to their particular struggle? Why do some wheelchair-bound people walk again while others remain seated? Why do some premature babies grow up healthy and strong, while others struggle for a lifetime? If it's not about sin or generational curses, how can we spiritually handle the cognitive dissonance that comes with these varied outcomes?

The questions go on, but the Word of God remains constant. He is Jehovah Rapha, our Healer, whether we are privileged to see it in the natural or not. When Jesus taught about the concept of eternal life, He wasn't just talking about how to go to heaven when you die so you can live forever. He was talking about tapping into the fullness of the abundant life He would die to give us all, in this life *and* the next.

March is National Developmental Disabilities Awareness Month. One day, we will see all bodies and minds made completely new as God's kingdom comes to earth as it is in heaven. But the truth is, the kingdom of God isn't just coming one day—it's already here. When Jesus taught us to pray for healing, *"On earth as it is in heaven,"* He wasn't encouraging us to wish this life away, but to begin living out our everlasting life with God *today* instead of waiting until we die. Friend, let today be the first day of the rest of your eternal life in Christ.

God, forgive me for doubting Your healing power. I know You heal, and I know one day You will bring healing for all of Your children. Help me embrace the eternal life You gave me today. Amen.

I will repay you for the years the locusts have eaten—the great locust and
the young locust, the other locusts and the locust swarm—my great army
that I sent among you.
—Joel 2:25

If Jesus walked the earth today, what do you think He would say about trauma? What would He say to someone suffering and struggling in the aftermath of abuse or neglect, violence or disaster? Would the Man who sweat blood, endured a brutal crucifixion He didn't deserve, and spent three full days in hell before rising again even acknowledge our trauma as trauma? You'd better believe it.

Jesus—Son of God, Son of Man, and friend of sinners—wants you to know just how intimately He understands the problem of pain in this world. He was despised. Rejected. He knew sorrow and pain, and He took on *our* sorrow and pain—right to the cross. Sin and death died with Him, and He rose again victorious. And He did it for you, so that you could be rescued, redeemed, and restored back into right relationship with a good Father God who is holy.

The problem of trauma in this world is what leads us down paths of unrighteousness. Addiction. Mental health problems. Thoughts of suicide. Not everyone who experiences trauma will struggle, but everyone who struggles has trauma. True recovery isn't about getting back an old broken life that drove you to struggle in the first place. It's about going deeper to identify and recover from the trauma that causes the struggle. This goes way beyond sobriety. It catapults you into transformation territory.

Trauma may be inevitable in this broken world. But that's not the end of the story. Yes, trauma can lead us to struggle, but it can also lead us to our greatest places of authority in the kingdom. Abraham nearly sacrificed his son Isaac, but later became a father of nations. (See Genesis 22:1–12; 17:4.) Joseph was sold into slavery by his brothers, but later used his power and influence to restore his family. (See Genesis 37:28; 45:8–11.) Moses was abandoned as a child, but later reclaimed his people—God's people—and delivered them to the promised land. (See Exodus 2:1–4; Deuteronomy 32:48–52.)

What might your *later* look like? Give your pain to God, and He will repay the years trauma has taken from you.

God, I surrender my trauma to You. If I hold onto it any longer, it will destroy me. But in Your strong and mighty hands, I know You'll use it to transform my life so I can help others. Amen.

March 10: CREATIVE HEALING

*In the beginning **God created** the heavens and the earth.*
—Genesis 1:1

*So **God created** mankind in his own image, in the image of God he created them; male and female he created them.*
—Genesis 1:27

Two words stand out in the Bible as critically important to understanding who God is and who we are in Him: *"God created."* He not only created everything we see, hear, smell, taste, and feel in this earthly realm, He also created the supernatural elements that can only be experienced in and through Him. And perhaps most important of all, God created us to be creators like Him.

Now, try not to overthink this. You're not God, so you're not likely to create the same things God did. But He created you with creative capabilities that aren't just meant for your enjoyment or career. He wants you to embrace the idea of getting creative in your journey toward healing from trauma.

Picture a promised-land life that you actually want to stay sober for, a personal transformation that leaves you feeling brand new and untethered to the old broken life that led you to struggle in the first place. Imagine an intimate relationship with a good Father God who loves you, forgives you, and went to hell and back again to be with you. Even if this isn't your current reality, can you imagine a future state like this? Can you fast-forward the video of your life and imagine what it could be like with God on your side?

If you can get creative with God and picture that promising future, cling to it with everything you've got. If you're having trouble picturing the transformed life that's waiting for you, ask the Father to teach you how to be creative like Him. Healing from trauma is a supernatural activity that takes creativity and imagination. You are on the verge of tapping into God's divine creative plan for your life. Ask Him for a sneak peek today.

God, sometimes I can't see past the struggles of today to a better life. Open my eyes and heart to see the future You have with me and help me take active steps to create it with You. Amen.

March 11: A MARATHON, NOT A SPRINT

Therefore, since we are surrounded by such a great cloud of witnesses, let us throw off everything that hinders and the sin that so easily entangles. And let us run with perseverance the race marked out for us.
—Hebrews 12:1

Twelve steps. Thirty days. Three months. One year. Recovery milestones and markers exist for a reason. As humans, we like process and order because it makes us feel like we know what to do to achieve success. But as is often the case for people in recovery, each journey is as unique as the person braving it.

Our preconceived notions about how long it should take to *recover* from addiction, mental health problems, or suicidal thoughts are often a far cry from reality. Many of our milestones have more to do with what insurance and pharmaceutical companies will cover, not recovery-time realities. For every instantaneous, miraculous delivery we see, there are hundreds of other people who will need to take the long road to recovery. While programming of the day might get you sober, it's probably going to take more than twelve steps to bring about the total life transformation God has for all of us.

Lockstep legalism in our recovery programming can keep struggling people stuck in cycles of seeking perfectionism and steeped in shame for not measuring up. What if relapse wasn't fatal, but an opportunity for growth? What if we were willing to go beneath the surface struggle to identify and find healing from the trauma that caused it? What if sobriety alone wasn't our endgame, but rather a promised-land life that's worth staying sober for?

The journey toward the life God has for us cannot be rushed. As a community, we need to be willing to walk out our own recovery—and love and lead other people through theirs—for as long as it takes.

God, forgive me for trying to rush what You're doing. Teach me what it means to follow Your steps in Your timing, for as long as You ask. Your ways are better, and I'm thankful for them. Amen.

His disciples asked him, "Rabbi, who sinned, this man or his parents, that he was born blind?" "Neither this man nor his parents sinned," said Jesus, "but this happened so that the works of God might be displayed in him."
—John 9:2–3

In the recovery space, there are generally two camps. The first camp, which often operates within the walls of the traditional church, believes addiction, mental health problems, and suicidal thoughts are a result of people's sin and poor choices. The second camp, which often operates within the secular medical community, believes these same struggles are purely physiological issues caused by genetics, trauma, and environment.

Admittedly, these are broad generalizations, but they help to explain the battle that has existed between the spiritual and scientific communities for hundreds if not thousands of years. Sacred groups see medical intervention and therapy as a lack of faith; scientific communities see refusal of therapy and treatment as a lack of wisdom.

So which is it? Are our struggles sin issues or physiological issues? We'd like to suggest that it's not either/or—it's both and then some. Even when people do nothing to contribute to the trauma that led them down a path of destruction, at some point, most people become willing participants in the aftermath. Even when we come from third, fourth, or fifth generation addicted families, we know from Scripture that neither our sin nor our ancestors' sin automatically results in a generational curse. The divine nature attached to our struggles only makes sense through the lens of a good Father God, who would never allow suffering that did not in some way display His power, goodness, and grace. No matter how people came to find themselves in bondage, our responsibility is to love and walk alongside souls in need.

God, forgive me for wanting to explain away struggles with sin. Forgive also the times I downplay the spiritual aspects of recovery. Move me with compassion to go deeper. Amen.

Nevertheless, I will bring health and healing to it; I will heal my people
and will let them enjoy abundant peace and security.
—Jeremiah 33:6

Being *cured* is language traditionally attached to professional medical circles, meaning complete elimination of an illness or disease. Being *healed*, on the other hand, describes something that can happen both naturally *and* supernaturally, even when no physical cure is possible. While many see addiction, mental health problems, and suicidal thoughts as defining and even permanent illnesses that require lifelong treatment, others see them as struggles that can be overcome, either by sheer will or by the power of the Holy Spirit.

So which is it? Are we trying to heal addiction, mental health problems, and suicidal thoughts or cure them? We'd like to suggest that it's both. Our struggles can be a direct result of genetic predispositions, trauma, abuse, and, yes, even our own poor and sinful choices.

But the important thing to remember, whether you're walking out your own recovery journey or loving and leading another through theirs, is that struggles don't surface because people are bad. Struggles surface because of trauma. And trauma is never, ever the victim's fault. Not everyone who experiences trauma will struggle, but everyone who struggles has trauma somewhere deep down. This is why God is calling the church to go deeper. There is a cure for trauma, deep healing to be found—and His name is Jesus.

Some struggles will require therapies, medical intervention, and even dramatic measures like incarceration and other severe consequences. Some will require fervent prayer and a whole lot of faith. Most will require both. Whether we are curing a disease or healing a literal or figurative wound, medical professionals and ministry leaders alike can do more of what they do best by leaning on one another for a more holistic, comprehensive, and collaborative approach. This is the beauty of following the Holy Spirit's lead in recovery.

God, forgive me for the times I've assumed that a cure is impossible. Your word says all things are possible, and I choose today to believe for Your healing in Your timing. Holy Spirit, come. Amen.

March 14: GOD, SAVE ME

For all those who exalt themselves will be humbled, and those who humble themselves will be exalted.
—Luke 18:14

Even the promised-land life we work toward in the Uncovery isn't our final destination. Instead, it's part of a rebirth into the eternal life we're all being invited to experience. Churchgoers might call this *getting saved*; while the sentiment is true, the methods by which we walk people through the process are at times questionable. We have them pray a sinner's prayer that isn't in the Bible, and then continue to make them feel bad about the sin for which they've been forgiven. While real repentance and a conscious decision to turn away from sin are paramount to a promised-land life, we make salvation far too complicated. It's simply the first step on a lifelong journey of transformation.

Sobriety is to recovery what salvation is to Christianity. From a practical standpoint, this means that all people who call themselves Christian are in recovery. We're all trying to get healed and whole, to get back to who the Father created us to be, to realize the abundant life that Jesus went to the cross for us to have.

When we say no to our struggles, especially for the very first time, it can create the same clean-slate euphoria we felt when we first said *no* to sin and *yes* to Jesus. Even if we were forced into rehab or bullied to the altar, initial sobriety and initial salvation remain powerful and important milestones along the Uncovery journey.

Whatever your experience was, is, or will be, know today that you are immeasurably loved and fully forgiven by God. All you need to do is receive His grace.

God, sometimes it's hard to believe I'm really saved. Show me how You see me—as holy, pure, and blameless because of Jesus—and help me rest in the safety and security of Your love. Amen.

For the wages of sin is death, but the gift of God
is eternal life in Christ Jesus our Lord.
—Romans 6:23

Scripture is clear that deliverance is not only possible, but *certain* when we lean on God's strength and Holy Spirit to guide us. But for many, the concept of deliverance is muddied with the deep desires of the human heart. This can create dissonance, where we look to deliverance stories of old, like the Israelites from Egypt, Daniel from the lions' den, Hezekiah from his deathbed, or David from King Saul. And yet our very present and ongoing struggles might tempt us to wonder if maybe God isn't in the deliverance business anymore.

We can all cling to our deliverance from sin because of what Jesus did on the cross. Sin may still be crouching at our door, but it's not in the house. It no longer has a claim on our lives and souls. It has no power over us whatsoever, unless we allow it. Coming into alignment with that truth is something that can take some time to believe, receive, and walk out in faith.

Initial deliverance of any kind—from sin, captivity, abuse, or persecution—is a necessary turning point. When the euphoria of freedom wears off, it can be easy to relapse back into old ways of thinking. Without healthy boundaries and authentic community to help with accountability, we can find ourselves back in captivity once again. It doesn't change who we are—fully known, fully loved, and fully forgiven by God. But it keeps us in a slavery mentality far longer than needed.

Have you fallen back into old ways of thinking and behaving? Grace to you. When God delivered you from sin, He did so with the full authority of the cross in mind. He didn't just cover your sin; He defeated sin, once and for all. Nothing can separate you from God and His love. Turn back to Him today in thankfulness for what He has done for you and ask Him to help you learn to walk it out in faith.

God, forgive me. You've delivered me from sin and death, and I still grow impatient about my concerns of the day. Remind me who I am in You and help me live it out faithfully. Amen.

March 16: TRUE DISCIPLESHIP

A new command I give you: Love one another. As I have loved you, so you must love one another. By this everyone will know that you are my disciples, if you love one another.
—John 13:34–35

When Jesus walked the earth, he handpicked twelve friends to do life with him: Peter, Andrew, James, John, Philip, Bartholomew, Matthew, Thomas, James, Jude or Thaddeus, Simon, and Judas.

It's worth noting that Jesus didn't call twelve guys to start a men's prayer breakfast, serve on a local church elder board, or walk through a discipleship curriculum together. He didn't vet them according to a religious standard, nor did He call them because they were in any way qualified or ready. He simply said, *"Follow me"* (Matthew 4:19), and they dropped everything to be with Him.

Of these twelve disciples, Jesus was closest to three—Peter, James, and John. Yes, even Jesus played favorites and for good reason. Jesus gave Himself *for* all, but not *to* all. Jesus was always willing to love the one right in front of Him, and when He did, each life was transformed. But He knew the benefit of pouring deeply into three people, and twelve by proxy would start a revolution in the church He was about to build. He would teach them what the love of the Farther looked like so they could go be His hands and feet for generations.

Here's the tough part about discipleship. We almost always let religion get in the way. We create boxes to check, standards to adhere to, systems to follow—and when they fail, we blame the disciple, not the discipler. This was never the way of Jesus. He so perfectly calibrated invitation and challenge with those He loved and led—and He still does it today, with each of us.

Perhaps you're living out a "Peter the rock" moment, staring your passion and purpose right in the face, or maybe you're living out a *"Get behind me, Satan!"* moment, just like Peter did right after receiving high praise from Jesus. (See Matthew 16:17–18; 22–23.) No matter where you are, know that Jesus loves you enough to meet you where you are and invite you or challenge you into His righteousness—straight into the love of a good Father God. This is true discipleship.

God, forgive me for times I've tried to earn Your love through box-checking and other man-made systems. Teach me what it means to follow You and help me lead others by example. Amen.

And surely I am with you always, to the very end of the age.
—Matthew 28:20

Saint Patrick, the patron saint of Ireland, is credited with bringing Jesus to the Irish people. Much of the rest of the world, not just people of Irish descent, know his name and use the folklore surrounding him to wear green and drink a lot of beer today. Once again, we've missed the true impact of this former slave's life and ministry—one that points us straight to God through the person of Jesus.

God is holy. And on our own, we're definitely not. This fact kept us at a distance from the Father because our unholiness couldn't withstand His overwhelming presence. The wild thing is, God wasn't okay with that separation. So He sent Jesus Christ to reveal His true character and become a perfect and final sacrifice for the sin of all people. Now, by the power of the Holy Spirit, we are one with God—*in Christ.*

St. Patrick knew this, and he wrote a powerful prayer that remains a cornerstone of the Christian faith in Ireland and beyond. Sure'n ye can wear green today for St. Patrick's Day if it helps you remember that Christ is with you always. But a better remembrance is to pray this prayer of declaration—known as St. Patrick's Breastplate—over yourself today and believe that it's true.

Christ with me,

Christ before me,

Christ behind me,

Christ in me,

Christ beneath me,

Christ above me,

Christ on my right,

Christ on my left,

Christ when I lie down,

Christ when I sit down,

Christ when I arise,

Christ in the heart of everyone who thinks of me,

Christ in the mouth of everyone who speaks of me,

Christ in every eye that sees me,

Christ in every ear that hears me.

Amen.

March 18: SIN CROUCHES

If you do what is right, will you not be accepted?
But if you do not do what is right, sin is crouching at your door;
it desires to have you, but you must rule over it.
—Genesis 4:7

Sin, in its natural state, isn't something we do. It's someone we partner with. Throughout Scripture, sin is personified as a living, breathing, moving spirit that desires to have and destroy us. When Cain was angry with Abel in Genesis 4, God reminded Cain that sin was crouching at his door. But He assured Cain if he did what was right—not killing his brother in anger—sin wouldn't rule over him.

Spoiler alert: Cain didn't listen to God. Sorry if you haven't read it yet, but it's literally in the fourth chapter of the first book of the Bible, so grab yours and get reading. Cain opened the door wide and allowed sin to enter his life. He chose offense and committed the first murder in human history.

When we align our minds, hearts, and actions with the persona of sin as Cain did, sin goes from being someone we partner with to something we do. Those actions cause us to doubt who we really are, replacing our God-given identity of *beloved child* with *sinner*. Much of the church has come to believe that being sinners is our natural state, creating an unhealthy and unbiblical view of sin as a permanent problem.

Whatever you're going through today, remember this truth: God created you good—*"very good"* (Genesis 1:31). Sin would have you believe otherwise because if you see yourself as *just a sinner*, you'll go on sinning in faith. Sinning is what sinners do. However, when Jesus died on the cross, He became a perfect sacrifice for your sins—and when He rose again, He defeated the persona of sin once and for all. Sin might still be crouching like a coward at your door, but it has no power or authority over you anymore unless you allow it.

God, forgive me for the times I've opened the door wide to let sin into my life. I want sin out of my house forever and I want You to move in permanently. Purify me and make me Your home. Amen.

March 19: SET ME ABLAZE

But who can endure the day of his coming? Who can stand when he appears? For he will be like a refiner's fire or a launderer's soap.
—Malachi 3:2

You're so much more than a sinner saved by grace. You're a saint, indwelled by the Holy Spirit, brought back into right relationship with God and an heir to His kingdom. But let's be honest. You're not perfect. Only one person ever has been perfect, and He died and rose for you and all of humankind.

And in our individual and collective humanity, God continues to something painfully beautiful: He refines us. On our own, we can't be holy enough for a holy God. But He's a good Father and wants to be with us. God made a way where there was no way by solving humanity's problem with Himself—Jesus walked the earth as God incarnate, in the flesh. When He died and rose again, He defeated sin's grip on humanity. But the enemy doesn't want you to believe that, so he continues to shame you into trying to earn the grace you've been given for free.

In this incomprehensible state of restoration, we are being actively restored, purified to even greater levels of holiness along the journey when we choose to keep our eyes on Jesus. Even in the throes of temptation, God always provides a way out. Even when we misstep, God is always there, ready to restore us and move forward. God is just, but He is also the Justifier. And the way He moves is like flame to metal, purifying it to be molded and used for His purpose on the earth.

Let's be real. Refinement can be painful. But continuing to surrender to God in this way, allowing Him to cleanse you, strengthen you, and make you righteous in His eyes, will create in you a deep hunger for the flame of His loving correction. God is for you, always. He will discipline you as a loving parent. Lean into His refining fire and align yourself with how He sees you—perfect, holy, and blameless because of what Jesus did for you.

God, thank You for making me more like You. I don't always do things perfectly, but You are always faithful to bring me back when I go astray. Purify my heart in Your fire. Amen.

March 20: HOLY, HOLY, HOLY?

Holy, holy, holy is the Lord God Almighty, who was, and is, and is to come.
—Revelation 4:8

God—the One who created the heavens and the earth, the One who always has been and always will be—is holy. Although we can never achieve the holiness of God, the more we know Him, the more He will call us to align with His holiness.

The apostle Peter, one of Jesus's favorites, made it plain: *"But just as he who called you is holy, so be holy in all you do; for it is written: 'Be holy, because I am holy'"* (1 Peter 1:15–16). Now Peter wouldn't have laid something down if we couldn't pick it up. His point was that as God's children, we can resist temptation and sin more effectively now than we could before we knew God was a good Father. Once we taste and see His goodness, we can't unsee it, and our desire for living life in a holy way will only grow.

For those in recovery, holy living transcends sober living. Getting sober is only the beginning. Living your life positioned toward the holiness of God will create a desire to not only stay sober, but be completely transformed by God's goodness. You can't be holy on your own, so stop trying. Instead, lean into the holiness of your good Father God and ask Him to teach you His ways.

God will lovingly correct you when you go astray. The world might call this your conscience, but it's really God's loving conviction of your heart. He will invite you back onto righteous paths and challenge you out of your old ways of thinking. Staying in tune to the Holy Spirit's correction can be a humbling experience, but the holiness He is calling you to is better than anything you've got going. Lean into the new creation God says you are. You're set apart, saintly, and yes, holy, not because of anything you've done, but because of what Jesus did for you!

God, make me more holy. I know I'll never be as holy as You are, but the closer I get to You, the better I am. Help me stay close to You and show me the right paths to take along the journey. Amen.

March 21: SOBER FROM WHAT?

For I am convinced that neither death nor life, neither angels nor demons, neither the present nor the future, nor any powers, neither height nor depth, nor anything else in all creation, will be able to separate us from the love of God that is in Christ Jesus our Lord.
—Romans 8:38–39

Milestones can be powerful motivators in recovery circles. Thirty days sober, a one-year chip, five solid years without a drop to drink—these are all reasons to pause, celebrate, and acknowledge God's faithfulness in giving us His power to be restored to sanity. Nevertheless, when milestones like these become programmatic success-metric markers, we set struggling people up for failure because we're going after the wrong things.

This probably goes without saying, but let's acknowledge it as truth: A *sober* person may not be living a transformed life. This is where the unfortunate label *dry drunk* came from, and the crippling state of mind is a byproduct of legalism in traditional recovery.

People often exchange one struggle for another, especially early on in recovery, making true sobriety or even abstinence incredibly difficult if not impossible to quantify or track. The answer to "Are you sober?" becomes "Sober from what?" This causes many recovery leaders to lean into legalism, with all-or-nothing, perfectionistic approaches to sobriety. And it causes people in recovery to cling to a false narrative and hide in plain sight.

Legalism in recovery doesn't work.

As you approach recovery milestones that are meaningful to you, by all means, celebrate them…but not at the expense of your *unshakable* identity in Christ. You are loved and forgiven by the Father, whether you stay sober forever or relapse on repeat. The Father will never love you more or less than He does right now. And He's less concerned with your sobriety record than He is your total life transformation.

God, I'm sorry for the times I've valued recovery markers more than Your mercy. I'm so much more to You than days, weeks, months, or years sober! I'm Your child, no matter what. Amen.

For we are God's handiwork, created in Christ Jesus to do good works,
which God prepared in advance for us to do.
—Ephesians 2:10

Scientific studies show that true, lasting recovery takes more than thirty days, six months, or even a year. In fact, for many struggling with addiction, mental health problems, and suicidal thoughts, it may take three years or more for the brain's neuropathways to rewire back to some semblance of normalcy, especially in the pleasure-reward centers.

For some, this miraculous brain healing can happen naturally in the absence of substance abuse or continued trauma, putting the full fingerprint of our God-given, divine DNA on display. For others, it can take a customized combination of therapy, medication, counseling, meetings, and other whole-life interventions, proving once again that we were all created for long-term relationship. The bottom line is the brain *can* heal, especially with multiyear abstinence.

Now, if three years sounds like a long time to have to be there for someone in a recovery capacity, consider this: Jesus walked the earth, fully Man and fully God, for thirty-three years. He only spent about *three* of those years in active ministry. God, in His wisdom, creates us to heal in the context of relationship—with Him and with others. And with His Spirit guiding us, *a whole lot* can happen in three years!

As we learn to believe for miracles *and* respect the journey with each individual we're called to love and lead, we will enter into Uncovery territory—loving without limits, honoring the divine DNA in all people. No rigid time constraints. No lofty ultimatums. No shame or condemnation. Just unconditional love for who they truly are—one with the Father.

God, forgive my impatience with Your timing. I know You are the Healer, and I know You will bring healing. I surrender to Your will and long for You to move. I'll wait on You, God. Amen.

March 23: RETHINKING RELAPSE

No temptation has overtaken you except what is common to mankind. And God is faithful; he will not let you be tempted beyond what you can bear. But when you are tempted, he will also provide a way out so that you can endure it.
—1 Corinthians 10:13

If we want to help people uncover the truth about who they really are, we must first discover the truth about who Jesus really is. As you might have guessed, this is a trial-and-error progression that requires grace, patience, and a healthy dose of humility for all involved. Unfortunately, many Christian recovery circles struggle to respond like Jesus would when people relapse—falling back into addiction, mental health problems, or suicidal thoughts after a period of freedom.

If we're honest, we'll admit the truth: relapse is an embarrassing inconvenience to us. We struggle to see the reasons why a person's "failure" matters when we have put our programs and even ourselves at the center of their stories. We care more about seeing people sober than we do about seeing them whole. Yet we are collectively called to more than that.

Sadly, most Christians don't know what to do with relapse any more than we know what to do with sin. We believe in faith to see the perfect 180-degree turns we choose to infer from Scripture—healing and deliverance, one and done. But perpetual perfection isn't really the point God was trying to make. Isn't it interesting that we rarely see the aftereffects of miraculous healing in the Bible? These people, like us, had a lot of life left to live post-healing, and chances are, they didn't walk it out perfectly. So why should those of us in recovery be expected to?

When we encounter miracles along the recovery journey, our hope is that we never go back. Relapse never dismisses the miracle. But even a miracle doesn't mean relapse isn't a possibility. Instead of seeing failure as fatal, let's choose to embrace it as a necessary part of the journey. Setbacks can in fact be setups for great success if we lean into what God is saying to us in and through them.

God, I admit I let my identity get wrapped up in how long it's been since I last relapsed into old ways of thinking and behaving. Renew my mind and remind me how forgiven I already am. Amen.

*For we know that our old self was crucified with him so that the body
ruled by sin might be done away with, that we should no longer be slaves
to sin—because anyone who has died has been set free from sin.*
—Romans 6:6–7

The idea of denying ourselves is a central theme in Scripture for good reason. On our own, we will inevitably give in to selfishness. It's part of a broken human condition that can only be remedied by embracing what Jesus did for us on the cross and leaning into the power of the Holy Spirit working in us.

As you've likely experienced, this is no small task, but the work is already done. When Jesus died on the cross, your old self—the one bound by your struggles and a slave to sin—died with Him. You died with Him, you were buried with Him, and you rose from the dead with Him, a brand new creation. None of this happened in a linear fashion. Jesus died thousands of years ago, way before you were born or had a chance to sin or struggle. But now, when you choose to receive His gift of grace today, the miracle of resurrection transcends time and space to meet you in the moment. When you say yes to Jesus, the old you dies, and you become a new creation in Him.

It's a lot to take in, we know. Even if you can wrap your mind around this reckless gift of grace, it may take your heart some time to really believe it's true. There's grace for that. This process is called *dying to self*, and it involves conscious decisions to partner with yourself as a new creation instead of believing you're still that old, broken self. Resist the urge to dig up the past. You've been miraculously transformed, whether you believe it or not. It may take a lifetime to come into agreement with the fullness of this miracle, but we encourage you to embrace this truth today. You are dead to sin and alive in Jesus Christ. That's how much your good Father God loves you!

God, forgive me for dwelling on the past instead of embracing the new creation I am. Help me resist the temptation to sin and help me die to my old self daily so I can live in You. Amen.

I have been crucified with Christ and I no longer live, but Christ lives in me. The life I now live in the body, I live by faith in the Son of God, who loved me and gave himself for me.
—Galatians 2:20

Spiritual realities rarely make rational sense in the natural. People have wrestled with the truths found in Scripture for thousands of years—one of the most mind-bending being the idea of a second birth. Jesus's secret follower Nicodemus was baffled by it (see John 3:1–9), and most of us are still puzzled today. No, you can't crawl back in your mother's belly and be born again. But Jesus didn't just die *for* you. You were crucified *with* Jesus—a supernatural convergence that transcends time, space, and reason.

If this idea is new to you, you're not alone. Yes, you have been *"crucified with Christ,"* but the original Greek word for *with* is better translated as "co-," meaning the closest possible union, not just *with* or *next to.*

When Jesus died on the cross as a perfect sacrifice for sin, *"You died, and your life is now hidden with Christ in God"* (Colossians 3:3). When He came back to life again, you rose with Him—before you were even born or had a chance to choose Him! He went before you to make a way for you to choose Him and be brought back into relationship with your good Father God. And now, when you choose to follow Jesus—who is *"the way and the truth and the life"* (John 14:6)— the Holy Spirit will guide you *"in the paths of righteousness"* (Psalm 23:3 NKJV).

Some religious types like to label this supernatural phenomenon as the *doctrine of co-crucifixion.* And while clinging to man-made doctrines over God's goodness can be problematic, this particular doctrine is critical to every component of the Christian faith. It takes away our ability to *earn* God's grace, which has already been freely given. It removes legalistic barriers to deep connection with God the Father because Jesus paid it all. It proves that the impossible is possible-for we can be simultaneously *dead* to sin and *alive* in Jesus, reborn and baptized into His death and resurrection. This is more than good news; it's *great* news! Embrace the promised-land, resurrection life He has for you today!

God, can You really be this good? Did You really choose me and make a way for me before I was even born? Thank You for Your amazing grace! Help me learn to embrace this resurrection life! Amen.

March 26: BEAUTY FROM ASHES

He has sent me to bind up the brokenhearted, to proclaim freedom for the captives and release from darkness for the prisoners…to bestow on them a crown of beauty instead of ashes, the oil of joy instead of mourning, and a garment of praise instead of a spirit of despair.
—Isaiah 61:1, 3

Every great story has an all-is-lost moment in which we don't see a way forward except through a miracle. In recovery circles, we sometimes refer to this moment as *hitting rock bottom*, a point where continuing along our current path of brokenness is more painful and scary than the discomfort of embracing change.

Perhaps you've had a moment like this, followed by a miracle that moved your recovery journey forward. Or maybe you're still waiting on this moment for yourself or someone you love or lead. One thing is certain: God loves a good *beauty from ashes* story. He wrote yours since before the foundation of the earth. While He never wrote you into harm's way, He weaved in moments of redemption to give your story power to those who would one day have ears to hear it. And He has been with you in the deepest valleys and on the highest mountaintops, guiding and directing your path for your good and His glory.

In rock-bottom, all-is-lost moments, it's critical to surround ourselves with people who have been there before and know the way forward. This is the beauty of doing recovery in the context of an authentic, Christ-centered community. When we have people to help bear our burdens together, we can see our struggles for what they are—wild opportunities for transformation and hope for the people we will one day help to set free.

We go through what we go through so we can help other people go through what we went through. This rationale may be hard to accept in the moment, but as we look back on the tapestry of life, we see evidence of it plainly. Our greatest struggles will become our greatest places of victory when we let our good Father God lead us. Healed people heal people when they do it in Jesus's name.

God, help me see beyond the darkness into what You're doing. I surrender my situation and trust that You will bless me to be a blessing. Use me and my story for my good and Your glory. Amen.

March 27: CHANGE YOUR MIND

I will give them an undivided heart and put a new spirit in them; I will remove from them their heart of stone and give them a heart of flesh.
—Ezekiel 11:19

There's an old saying that goes, "You can't change your heart, and God won't change your mind, but if you'll change your mind, God will change your heart."

This is the essence of real repentance, which simply means *to change your mind*. Paul explains this practically when he tells us, *"Set your minds on things above, not on earthly things"* (Colossians 3:2). When we are stuck in sin, struggle, and strife, it's often because we don't yet believe we can really be set free. We cling heavily to a *sinner* identity, and we keep sinning in faith. It's what makes sense.

It's the Holy Spirit's job to convict you and move your heart to repentance. You can't do it on your own, in your own strength, so it's best not to try. Instead, try partnering mentally with the truth of what God says about you: you are loved, you're forgiven, and you've been made holy because of what Jesus did for you on the cross. It's true, whether you choose to believe it or not. But making the conscious choice to believe it in your mind will ultimately help you receive it in your heart, which leads to lasting transformation. You change your mind. And God will change your heart.

Keep in mind, choosing to believe something supernatural isn't logical. It's an act of faith, a decision to believe in spite of what you see. It's a little like gravity—you can't see it, but an undeniable force keeps you grounded. Choose to believe in gravity. Choose to believe in God's goodness. Change your mind, and God will change your heart.

God, I believe. Help my unbelief! I'm changing my mind today, choosing to agree with what You say about me. Meet me here in this place and change my heart to align with Your truth. Amen.

Carry each other's burdens, and in this way you will fulfill the law of Christ.
—Galatians 6:2

Traditional Christian recovery programming can send struggling people spiraling into a vicious cycle. We get saved. We get sober. And we relapse. We get saved again. We get sober again. And we relapse again. And again, and again, and again. Dizzy and desperate, we cling to the words of those well-meaning pastors, counselors, and recovery leaders who say, "Just come to Jesus, and you'll be okay," or "…and you'll be set free," or "…and you'll never use again."

It's time for we, the church, to have a come-to-Jesus moment about these quick-fix, phony platitudes. Even when we know Jesus is the ultimate answer to every recovery question we could ever ask, it's important for us to acknowledge reality. Miraculous, instantaneous delivery from addiction, mental health problems, and suicidal thoughts is possible, and we need to go after it in faith. But it's not the norm. We'd do well to remember that God values the journey just as much as the destination. Sometimes His healing is not only progressive, but a lifelong endeavor.

Repeatedly trying to pray struggles off people can become a crutch when we refuse to partner with what God is doing in the moment. This can manifest as spiritual abuse, which leaves people who come to Jesus for help feeling even worse than they did before we prayed.

Please don't misunderstand what we're saying. If God says pray for healing, by all means, pray! But if He says to sit with those in pain, to enlist the help of medical professionals, or to extend grace long after earthly reason says is appropriate, give Him your *yes.* Break the cycle. Value transformation over sobriety. Value the healing journey as much as you do the healing itself. Trust in God's way and partner with His timing, and you'll see miracles in droves like people did in Jesus's day.

God, I'm sorry for trying to bring Your healing in my own way. Give me the sensitivity to hear Your voice, to know when to go after healing and when to wait on Your perfect timing. Amen.

Consider it pure joy, my brothers and sisters, whenever you face trials
of many kinds, because you know that the testing of your faith produces
perseverance. Let perseverance finish its work so that you may be mature
and complete, not lacking anything.
—James 1:2–4

If you've ever been to a twelve-step meeting, you've likely heard and maybe even joined in on a familiar chant to close the session: "Keep coming back! It works if you work it, so work it 'cause you're worth it!" This is an overly simplistic, somewhat self-centered mantra.

"Keep coming back" can evoke a sense of striving for some. No matter how many meetings you attend or boxes you check, you don't tap into life transformation by simply showing up. Granted, showing up—to a meeting, a counseling session, an accountability coffee date, or even time with God through Scripture and prayer—is critical. But God wants more than just your presence; He wants your participation in what He's doing.

"It works if you work it…" Until it doesn't. Lockstep legalism in our recovery programming leaves struggling people twelve-stepping their way into repeated cycles of failure. When we value the process over God's presence, we miss the point entirely. God will show up not because of our efforts, but in spite of them.

If a particular process is working for you in your current recovery season, by all means, *work it!* But if it's not working, let it go and let God provide another way.

"Work it 'cause you're worth it." Yes, you are. But not for the reasons you might think. More appropriately, our good Father God is worth it—and as His beloved child, He says you are worthy. Not because you can work to earn His favor, but because of the work Jesus did for you on the cross. You're worthy because He is worthy, just as you're holy because He is holy.

It's time to reexamine what's working and what's not working in recovery circles. Could your mantras use a makeover? Could your twelve steps use a fresh coat of grace? Could your communities use a baptism in Holy Spirit fire? Ask the Father what more He would have you do and be ready to give Him your *yes.*

God, I admit sometimes I say and do things because I think I should. But in reality, I don't know why I say and do them. Help me to only say what You're saying and do what You're doing. Amen.

March 30: STABILITY

I keep my eyes always on the LORD.
With him at my right hand, I will not be shaken.
—Psalm 16:8

Be strong. Have courage. Take heart. Stand firm. These biblical commands are easier said than done, especially when you're on shaky ground. Recovery is a journey, not a one-time event. It's never static, it's always moving, and it's rarely as stable and predictable as we'd like it to be. The wildly unstable nature of recovery is perhaps the biggest problem we, the church, seem to have with it.

Traditional recovery programming combats the surface-level behavior. Admit you have a problem, then work hard to stop it. Problem is, this approach fails to identify and deal with the trauma that created the problem in the first place. It also fails to address the systemic, cultural, and interpersonal barriers people face that keep them from healing.

The Uncovery's four-pronged approach to healing includes discipleship, community, recovery, and work therapy. It's in these four contexts that struggling people can go beneath the surface-level struggle to create a life that they want to stay sober for—and by sobriety, we mean freedom from whatever is manifesting in their life, whether it's an addiction, mental health problems, or suicidal thoughts. They need spiritual accountability from leaders and friends who have been there. They need authentic community that can surround them and share the burden. They need real recovery—a chance at a promised-land life and help removing barriers to it. They need work therapy to give them purpose, identity, and something for their idle hands to do.

With these factors in play, people in recovery can learn how to remain stable even when the world around them shakes and trembles. They won't be shaken because they're standing on the Rock of Ages, our loving God.

God, Your Word says You are my firm foundation. While the world rages around me, keep me steady and stable, focused on You and in You. Help me build a promised-land life worth living. Amen.

*But if anyone has the world's goods and sees his brother in need, yet
closes his heart against him, how does God's love abide in him?*
—1 John 3:17 (ESV)

Let's face it. Some people are hard to love. No doubt someone has already
popped into your mind. An ex. A coworker. A family member. Someone
you're trying to love and lead through recovery, or someone who's trying to
love and lead you through it.

We're all human, so we're all broken, which is why it's so good that recovery
is for everyone.

It's easy to love the lovable. Anyone can do it. But loving the unlovable takes
an extra dose of reckless grace that can only come from the Spirit of God
living in us. We don't love the unlovable because we should, or even because
we must; we love because we were first loved by God. And if we love God, we
have no choice but to love what—and who—He loves.

The Bible has a lot to say about love as a nonnegotiable, including these
verses from Paul:

> *Love is patient and kind; love does not envy or boast; it is not arrogant
> or rude. It does not insist on its own way; it is not irritable or resentful; it
> does not rejoice at wrongdoing, but rejoices with the truth. Love bears all
> things, believes all things, hopes all things, endures all things. Love never
> ends.* (1 Corinthians 13:4–8)

That's a tall order, but as followers of Jesus, it's the only way.

Loving people recklessly like Jesus did doesn't mean throwing boundaries
out the window. Enduring abuse isn't love. Making excuses isn't love. Enabling
bad behavior isn't love. But continuing to offer forgiveness? Praying for and
working toward reconciliation? Never, ever giving up on God's ability to heal
and going after it in faith? That's love.

If you're called to lead in the recovery space, learn to love the one in front
of you. No prerequisites, no strings attached. Love in the gentle way of Jesus.
Speak truth in love, honor the divine DNA in all people, and be open to God's
direction along the journey.

God, forgive me for refusing to love people well after You've loved me so well. Open my eyes to see people how You see them. Move me with compassion to love them like Jesus. Amen.

April

REFLECTION

*Let us examine our ways and test them, and let us return to the L*ORD*.*
—Lamentations 3:40

Do not get drunk on wine, which leads to debauchery. Instead,
be filled with the Spirit.
—Ephesians 5:18

You might be surprised to hear this from a couple of recovery activists, but drinking alcohol is not a sin. The Bible actually describes wine as a gift that can make life more enjoyable. (See Psalm 104:15.) It even touts alcohol's medicinal purposes. (See 1 Timothy 5:23.) Jesus Himself made wine, drank it, and led a perfect, sinless life. (See, respectively, John 2:1–10; Luke 7:34; 1 Peter 2:22.)

But let's get real. Even if alcohol is *permissible* for mature Christians in moderation (see 1 Timothy 3:8; Titus 2:2–3), we'd be kidding ourselves if we believed it was always *edifying*. The line between just enough and too much can blur rapidly, especially for those who are prone to struggle with addiction and mental health. And when drinking becomes part of a community culture, those who struggle with it can feel tempted, isolated, and alone.

As people called to love and lead in the recovery space, it's important to create safe spaces for people who struggle to be in community with you. Consider whether it's appropriate to have alcohol at events and gatherings; at the very least, have options for people you know would not or should not partake. If you balk at this, we encourage you to do some careful self-examination. Is your religious freedom to drink more important than your call to love and lead those who might struggle with it? Would Jesus sit beside a drunkard, merlot in hand, and say, "Do as I say, don't do as I do?" Not likely.

Every April, the National Council on Alcoholism and Drug Dependence (NCADD) sponsors Alcohol Awareness Month to help people understand what causes alcoholism and the treatments available for it. Substance abuse is one of the nation's biggest health problems. If you drink, consider fasting from alcohol and praying intentionally for those who struggle with it. Whether you take a day, a week, or the entire month, ask God to show you the beauty of sober-mindedness. And if you're living sober and hoping to remain that way for good, know that we're praying for you.

God, give me the wisdom to know whether alcohol can be a part of my life and the lives of those I love and lead. Keep me humble and help me have compassion for others and for myself. Amen.

"Where, O death, is your victory? Where, O death, is your sting?"
The sting of death is sin, and the power of sin is the law. But thanks be to
God! He gives us the victory through our Lord Jesus Christ.
—1 Corinthians 15:55–57

It's no secret that Christians love to talk about sin. One might even say we're obsessed with it. And while fear tactics may keep people coming back to the altar week after week—passing by the offering plate on the way there—perhaps we've missed the point entirely. Yes, we're all sinners in need of a Savior. But after Jesus, our Redeemer, finds us and makes us whole again, why on earth do we continue to identify as nothing more than *sinners saved by grace?* If we're truly saved by grace, guess what? We're not sinners anymore! At least we wouldn't be if we really believed it was true. This corporate overdose of sin-consciousness in the church is causing people to struggle much more and much longer than necessary.

Now, don't hear what we're not saying. Yes, we need to teach and preach on sin. Yes, we need to understand what sin is, and what it's not. Yes, we need to confess our sins to one another and pray for each other so we can be healed. (See James 5:16.) But in our experience, people are already *more than aware* of their sin. They're consumed by it. What they don't often know is that their sin has been defeated, and they're no longer slaves to it.

Horatio Spafford put it perfectly in the lyrics of his timeless hymn, "It Is Well with My Soul," written in 1873:

My sin – oh, the bliss of this glorious thought!
My sin, not in part but the whole,
Is nailed to His cross, and I bear it no more;
Praise the Lord, praise the Lord, O my soul!

Are you getting the magnitude of this? The sin we can't seem to shake in our own strength no longer has any power over us! Jesus defeated it! Rest in the scandal of God's grace today and know how loved and forgiven you are.

God, when I think back on my life of sin, I'm overwhelmed by Your grace to me. Thank You for forgiving me when I didn't deserve it. Help me remember how much You love and forgive me. Amen.

On hearing this, Jesus said, "It is not the healthy who need a doctor, but the sick."
—Matthew 9:12

People in recovery need an empathetic, caring, and loving community. The church should be uniquely suited to be the solution to this problem, and we've tried to be. But the same *us vs. them* mentality that keeps the church at odds with herself shows up in Christian recovery too. Case in point: Some traditions believe addiction, mental health problems, and suicidal thoughts are because of sin, while other traditions believe they are a diagnosable illness. Yup, we're going there.

Sin can certainly manifest as physical sickness. And sickness can weaken us to open the door to sin. Instead of either/or, we would like to suggest that most people struggle with both/and. Sin sickness, no matter how we come by it, is something that must be treated with trauma-informed ministry and care. If someone with a chemical imbalance receives hands-on prayer when they really need medication, we've failed them. If someone in a true spiritual crisis is encouraged to self-medicate the problem with antidepressants, we've again failed them.

Embracing God's healing through natural means, supernatural means, or a Spirit-led mix of the two is something that we, the church, must embrace. People are sick, and people are in bondage. It's time to bridge the gap between the Holy Spirit and science to bring healing in God's perfect way, in His perfect timing. Miracles can include medicine, and medicine is in fact a miracle! Embracing God's healing in whatever way it comes will help us set both captives *and* prisoners free from sickness *and* sin in the powerful name of Jesus. (See Isaiah 61:1; Romans 10:13.)

God, open my eyes to the many ways You heal. Open my heart to believe in miracles and the power of prayer. Open my mind to embrace the medicine as miraculous. Heal our sin sickness. Amen.

April 4: BONDAGE BREAKERS

Come to me, all you who are weary and burdened, and I will give you rest.
—Matthew 11:28

As recovery leaders, we're called to help broken people transform, regardless of whether the rest of the world might think they deserve their plight. Captive or prisoner, we have a responsibility to set them all free in Jesus's name. But this argument is worth a deeper look. What's the difference between a captive and a prisoner anyway?

Captives are oppressed people, held in bondage against their will. As victims, they may do nothing to contribute to the trauma that enslaves them. Prisoners are a different story. In a devastating mix of circumstances and poor choices made, sin and unlawfulness put them where they are. They may have made a choice to enter in, but they can't always make a choice to break free.

As leaders, we typically address the struggle based on its origin. In a traditional program, the perception is that the individual chose addiction, and they're forced to endure a shame-driven recovery process that continually reminds them that it's their own fault that they're in the program. So we press into that surface-level struggle as an unshakable identity that lasts years into sobriety. Most healthy people can identify with both captive and prisoner identities at some level. But regardless of how we end up in bondage to our struggles, our help comes from the same God.

Freedom is not just reserved for the captive, but for the prisoner too. Understanding the root causes of our addictions, mental health problems, and suicidal thoughts is critical to the Uncovery, but using the root cause as a weapon is not productive or redemptive. We must be willing to go beyond genetic predisposition and generational curses to explore more trauma-informed ministry tactics. This will bring about not only deliverance from bondage but a promised-land life of transformation—even for the ones we don't think deserve it. *Especially* for them. This is the grace we, the church, are called to show, the unmerited favor of a loving Father for everyone.

God, forgive me for the times I've felt like freedom is only for those who deserve it. None of us deserve it! Cleanse me of judgment so I can help set captives and prisoners free. Amen.

April 5: PRESENT PAIN, FUTURE PROMISE

I consider that our present sufferings are not worth comparing with the glory that will be revealed in us. For the creation waits in eager expectation for the children of God to be revealed.
—Romans 8:18–19

In *The Problem of Pain*, legendary author C. S. Lewis explores the reason why pain exists in a world where God is supposedly good. His take on the problem of pain comes down to this: God gave us free will. We often use that free will to inflict pain on one another. God *could* stop us, but He doesn't, which overwhelmingly suggests that pain in this temporal life has a purpose.

We don't believe that God *causes* our pain because that would be counter to His character. However, we do believe that God uses our pain to shape us into the people we were created to be. Through our suffering, we develop empathy for the suffering of those who struggle, and we're moved with compassion to be the solution we want to see in the world.

The Bible encourages us not to get caught up in the pain and suffering of this life. Why? Because our pain refines us, revealing God's glory in and through us. Is it painful? Yes. Is it worth it? Absolutely. Pain is, as C. S. Lewis insists, *evidence* of our good Father God's love for us. He writes:

> We can ignore even pleasure. But pain insists upon being attended to. God whispers to us in our pleasures, speaks in our conscience, but shouts in our pains: it is His megaphone to rouse a deaf world.[1]

God, it gives me comfort to know that You are using my pain for my good and Your glory. Comfort me when I don't understand what You're doing. Help me surrender to Your plan. Amen.

April 6: JUDGE NOT

Do not judge, or you too will be judged. For in the same way you judge others, you will be judged, and with the measure you use, it will be measured to you.
—Matthew 7:1–2

It's rather ironic that we Christians aren't typically known for our grace. We're seen by most of the unbelieving world as judgmental, bigoted, and even elitist in claiming Jesus is the only way to God the Father. And honestly, who can blame them? Truth and love are rarely present simultaneously in our conversations, and when we come to an impasse, judgment reigns. And the spirit of judgment brings out the worst in us and misrepresents the Father's heart.

---

1. C. S. Lewis, *The Problem of Pain* (New York: Macmillan Publishing Co., 1976), 93.

- Our judgment highlights our *hypocrisy*. When we judge, our own high standards may come back to haunt us.

- Our judgment manifests *deflection*. When we judge, we're suggesting others' sin bothers God more than our own.

- Our judgment fuels *self-righteousness*. When we judge, we usurp God's authority as our righteous judge and justifier.

Although we should not judge others, this doesn't mean we can't evaluate whether or not a person's decisions are wrong. Truth can only be truth, even in a postmodern world that insists truth is subjective. Anything other than absolute truth is a lie. That being said, while God's righteous judgment is perfectly just, our human judgment is terribly skewed.

Here's the really humbling part: When God sent Jesus to walk the earth, He gave Him all authority on heaven and earth. Jesus could have judged any sinner who came before Him as guilty and accountable to the Law. And yet Jesus withheld judgment. He didn't come to condemn the world, but to save it. Jesus, Son of God, Son of Man, and righteous Judge in the flesh, came to seek out and save the lost.

Are we willing to do the same? To reserve judgment for God, who is both good and just? If you're called to love and lead people in recovery, this needs to be your top priority. God's mercy triumphs over judgment every time, and we'd do well to follow suit.

God, You're the only one in a position to condemn me. But You don't. You sent Jesus to die for me, and now You see His sacrifice instead of my sin. Thank You for being my Justifier. Amen.

April 7: SHAME ON WHO

As Scripture says, "Anyone who believes in him will never be put to shame."
—Romans 10:11

There's no easy way to say this, so we'll just come right out with it: There's a whole lot of money to be made in shame.

In the last hundred years or so, we've seen the Christian church start to look more and more like a business. And while sustainable growth strategies, replicable church-planting models, expanding the reach of the gospel, and lasting financial provision are certainly of God, the ways in which we fund these activities are oftentimes not.

To be fair, the true villain here isn't the church herself. It's shame. Shame bullies people to the altar to get their slate wiped clean every Sunday. Shame keeps people coming back through fear tactics and empty promises. Shame keeps people clinging to their sin instead of the promised-land life Jesus died to give them. Shame is what keeps the church in business and deep down, we all know it.

But there is a better Way—and His name is Jesus.

Jesus gave everything so you could not only reconnect with God, but be one with Him. You get to be with Him forever. And now, the church, His bride, is wherever two or more are gathered in His name on the earth. There's nothing wrong with cathedrals and church parlors, sanctuaries and small groups, but let's be clear—the church isn't a building. The church exists in *us*, the people of God.

This is great news for people in recovery! It means you can belong before you even believe and find true healing through the Healer Himself, no strings attached. God made a Way where there was no way, and He will help you transform into the person you were created to be in the context of authentic community. Believe for it—and be it! Together, we are the church.

God, thank You for removing my shame and welcoming me into Your living and breathing church. Help me see past my assumptions and embrace Your church for who she is meant to be. Amen.

April 8: STRESSED AND BLESSED

I have told you these things, so that in me you may have peace. In this world you will have trouble. But take heart! I have overcome the world.
—John 16:33

"I'm too blessed to be stressed" is a T-shirt worthy quote, but when people say this, it's cause for deeper concern. We get the sentiment, but this memorable, bite-sized chunk of toxic Christianity keeps struggling people suffering in silence. It implies that God's blessing will remove stress from our lives, when biblical and real-world examples clearly prove otherwise. Let's look at a few.

Job? *Stressed.* Satan took everything from him, and God let it happen. But Job didn't curse God—he praised Him, even as he questioned Him. He chose humility, and God restored everything he had lost.

David? *Stressed.* On the run from murderous King Saul, David didn't retaliate. He waited on God instead of taking matters into his own hands. Saul finally fell on his own sword, and David became king.

Moses? *Stressed.* Chosen to advocate for and deliver his people from hardhearted Pharaoh—with a serious speech impediment, to boot—Moses gave God his *yes*, and God gave him Aaron to help him speak and lead.

Jesus? *Stressed.* The night before His crucifixion, He literally sweat blood, pleading with His Father to spare Him, if possible, and find another way to save the world. But He submitted to *"the joy set before him"* (Hebrews 12:2). And God raised Him up, crowning Him with glory and honor forever.

These men weren't too blessed to be stressed. The struggle was real! But even in their stress, they chose to glorify God and stay faithful to Him. And God blessed each of them. It's entirely possible to be both blessed and stressed at the same time. In fact, it's a promise in our walk with Christ! Jesus said it Himself, *"In this world you will have trouble. But take heart! I have overcome the world"* (John 16:33).

What's stressing you out today? What feels like more than you can bear? Take it to God. Let Him have it. He understands. Praise Him in the middle of the mess and receive the blessing He has for you.

God, I'm stressed! I know You understand, and I'm thankful You're willing to sit with me in my mess. I trust You, and I'll do what You want me to. Guide my steps and bless my journey. Amen.

April 9: TRAUMA TEACHES

He will cover you with his feathers, and under his wings you will find refuge; his faithfulness will be your shield and rampart. You will not fear the terror of night, nor the arrow that flies by day, nor the pestilence that stalks in the darkness, nor the plague that destroys at midday.
—Psalm 91:4–6

Traditional recovery programming has astonishingly high failure rates. Some experts say 80 percent of people in recovery will relapse within the first year. While we don't want to diminish the miracle of the 20 percent who *make it*, we can all agree that we have to do better. Lives and souls are at stake. And an 80 percent margin for error is unacceptable in any arena.

The missing element in the recovery equation is trauma. Not everyone who experiences trauma will struggle with addiction, mental health problems, or suicidal thoughts, but everyone who struggles with these afflictions has trauma as an underlying factor. This calls recovery leaders to go deeper than surface level struggles to better understand and embrace trauma-informed care and ministry.

You don't have to be a licensed clinical counselor to be trauma-informed. It's entirely possible to self-educate on the subject in a way previously reserved for elite higher education circles. Google a TED Talk by Brené Brown or Gabor Maté, and you'll learn more about trauma than you could in years of academic study. The point is, you don't have to have letters after your name to love and lead people through recovery in a trauma-informed manner. You just need to adopt a growth mindset and an open heart. God can handle the rest, better than you ever could. And His Spirit will speak to you and through you to people on the verge of breakthrough in recovery.

Trauma may be a part of our lives until God creates a new heaven and a new earth. But digging deeper with an earnest desire to learn will help us be a generation that can stop systemic trauma in its tracks through Holy Spirit-led breakthrough. We're here for it. Are you?

God, teach me more about the impacts of trauma so I can better love and lead people in recovery—including myself! Position me to be part of the systemic solution and bring healing. Amen.

April 10: SYSTEMIC CYCLES

Defend the weak and the fatherless;
uphold the cause of the poor and the oppressed.
—Psalm 82:3

Working through and overcoming deep-seated trauma in recovery requires authentic relationships and unapologetic advocacy. This is especially important when loving and leading people of color through their recovery. If you're a particularly *woke* white person, you may already be thinking about how to better show up as an advocate for people of color in the recovery space. But even if you think you're ready, you might still have some work to do.

The subtle microaggression and obvious macroaggression people of color feel is something we, the church, must learn to recognize, own, and remedy, even if we can never fully understand how it feels to walk in their shoes. If not us, then who? If not now, then when?

Whatever your walk of life, it's critically important for recovery leaders to acknowledge and address the systemic cycles that keep marginalized people oppressed and addicted. There are certainly big barriers to entry when it comes to belonging; people can scan a room and determine in about two seconds if they think they belong there. What's more, we can't deny that there are systemic issues keeping marginalized people from finding the help they need in the first place. Socioeconomic factors can keep people on the margins and out of reach from a God who desperately wants to heal them and transform their lives. What are we willing to do to ensure this stops with us?

Discrimination and marginalization because of age, gender, religion, disability, sexual orientation or identity, socioeconomic status, mental health, and addiction are issues Christian recovery leaders cannot afford to ignore or avoid. We're not advocating for some new brand of universalism that rejects the truth of God's Word. Far from it. We can—and must—have courage in our convictions.

What we need to adopt is *compassion* in our convictions. Jesus never glossed over people who were on the margins of society. It didn't matter how they got there. He welcomed them, walked with them, broke bread with them, and left them completely transformed. Are we willing to do the same?

God, open my eyes to see the systemic issues around me that are keeping people from finding You. Show me if I've contributed in any way so I can repent. Help me be Your hands and feet. Amen.

April 11: A WILLING PRISONER

I, Paul, the prisoner of Christ Jesus for the sake of you Gentiles…became a servant of this gospel by the gift of God's grace given me through the working of his power.
—Ephesians 3:1, 7

Jesus knew the Spirit of God was on Him. He said so on multiple occasions, the most memorable of which appears in Luke 4, when He quoted Isaiah. The prophet wrote:

> *The Spirit of the Sovereign* LORD *is on me, because the* LORD *has anointed me to proclaim good news to the poor. He has sent me to bind up the brokenhearted, to proclaim freedom for the captives and release from darkness for the prisoners, to proclaim the year of the* LORD's *favor and the day of vengeance of our God, to comfort all who mourn.*   (Isaiah 61:1–2)

This idea of proclaiming freedom to both captives and prisoners was shocking in Jesus's day. The Law would insist that a captive should be set free, but that a prisoner was probably getting his just deserts and should have to do his time. Jesus flipped this narrative on its head, not focusing on the rationale behind the bondage, but proclaiming freedom for all. We are meant to emulate this as we follow His lead.

After Jesus's death, resurrection, and ascension, the apostle Paul took the label of prisoner to a whole new level. He described himself as a *prisoner* of Jesus. Paul was actually in prison for preaching the gospel, but he felt indebted to Jesus because his sin was so great that only Jesus could cover it. He was a willing prisoner of Jesus, captivated by His goodness and love, surrendered to His will no matter what.

Did Paul deserve to be in bondage? By earthly law, yes. But he happily served his time and wrote some of the most compelling arguments for freedom in Christ from a jail cell. It's enough to make you wonder what you might accomplish in your weakness, where God's strength is made perfect.

God, I sometimes feel stuck, a slave to my circumstances. But if You have me here, I trust You to deliver me and use my circumstances for good. Make me a willing prisoner to Your heart. Amen.

April 12: MORAL INVENTORY

Let us examine our ways and test them, and let us return to the LORD.
—Lamentations 3:40

Step 4 is hands-down the scariest of the twelve steps in most recovery programming. It calls you to make a searching, fearless moral inventory—a list of your resentments, fears, guilt, hate, and struggles. Some traditions keep this list private, just for you, while others insist you share it with God and at least one other person. Either practice can be humbling at best. But the most terrifying part of this inventory is the power you can give it to keep you in bondage.

Many approach their inventory as a to-do list, hoping to check boxes to healing and wipe the slate clean. This legalistic approach fails often, as it can take a lifetime to find resolution to our greatest struggles. Those new to recovery often see the list and give up hope, knowing they could never be absolved of everything in their own strength.

Others mistake the inventory as a *name it and claim it* activity, lessening the reflective power of the exercise. Acknowledging the truth about our struggles ties back to step one—admitting we are powerless. However, stepping out of denial and admitting the things we've done wrong is not the same as repenting of them and seeking forgiveness.

So what's the point of a moral inventory? To count the cost of God's grace. It's good for people to know they're loved and forgiven by God, and that all they have to do is say *yes* to His grace. But the practice of examining just what He's forgiven us of—fearlessly naming the ways we've sinned and fallen short of God's glory—puts on display just how good God the Father is. Saving all of humankind from our sin cost Him everything, and He would do it again in a heartbeat, even if it were just for you. That kind of grace demands a response! Give God the glory He is due and meditate on just how good He has been to you today.

God, when my sin was great, Your love was greater. Your mercy never fails me, and it never will! Help me see just what it cost You to buy me back, and I'll never run away again. Amen.

April 13: HIDDEN SIN

Whoever conceals their sins does not prosper, but the one who confesses and renounces them finds mercy.
—Proverbs 28:13

When we confess our sin, God is faithful and just to forgive us. He cleanses us from our unrighteousness and gives us His righteousness. We know it's true. And while one half of the church would have us focus on that same sin forever, the other half likes to pretend it doesn't exist. This creates a big problem for people in recovery. God's mercy leads us to repentance, which not only means acknowledging our sin, but confessing it and receiving God's forgiveness for it in full.

Unconfessed or hidden sin is no secret to God. He knows everything we've ever done and every thought we've ever had. While it doesn't come as a surprise to Him, the magnitude of our sin often comes as a surprise to us. So why do we try to hide our sin? We would like to suggest three possible reasons.

First, it's possible that we don't yet know our sin is sin. In a world where morality is relative, what's sin to one may not be sin to another. But children of God are held to a higher standard. When God chooses to convict us of a sin, whenever it occurred, we need to be ready and willing to repent of it.

Second, it's possible that we know our sin is sin, but we'd rather not think about it or deal with it. The pain of reflecting on it is so great, it feels like we're reliving it all over again. This can push us into a cycle of shame, regret, sorrow, pain, and more shame in perpetuity. We must be willing to give our known sins over to God, confess them, and receive forgiveness.

Third, it's possible that the sin we think is ours is actually someone else's. This is often the case with abuse. Victims will carry the shame of their abuser for so long, they internalize the sin as their own, even though they had no part in it and were not at fault. They'll blame themselves and resist God's grace. We must receive grace in these situations and assume no fault or responsibility.

The closer you get to the moment of sin's inception, the closer you'll be to healing from it. When did it start? When did it become commonplace? Ask God to reveal the origin of the sin so you can see it for what it really is. Name it, confess it, and then change your mind about it being acceptable in your life. Receive God's forgiveness and rest in His unfailing love for you.

God, I don't want my sin to separate us any longer! I confess _____, _____, and _____ to You now, and I genuinely ask for Your forgiveness. I receive Your grace in full and step into freedom now in Jesus's name. Amen.

April 14: THE SIN OF UNFORGIVENESS

See to it that no one falls short of the grace of God and that no bitter root grows up to cause trouble and defile many.
—Hebrews 12:15

We know forgiveness is a good idea. Father God does it, Jesus does it, and He commands us to do the same. (See John 20:23.) So why is it so hard to forgive and be forgiven? Because it's incredibly expensive.

Anything worth doing will cost you something. Forgiving the sins against you will require you to count the cost of the sins against you and determine whether you're willing to cover them in an equal measure of grace. When we feel the cost is too great to forgive, we cling to the way the sin against us makes us feel on the inside. When internalized, the cost can go up in our minds, even if it's out of touch with reality.

What's more, forgiveness is more often a journey than a one-time event. We can extend a measure of forgiveness and later realize we hadn't fully counted the costs of the offense. This can require us to dish out even greater levels of grace—which isn't bad, but it can be confusing when we feel like we've already done the hard heart work. But lamenting it and continually surrendering it as we feel led is the key to moving on.

Here's the hardest part: Unforgiveness isn't just a bad idea, it's a straight-up sin. Forgiving offenders is assumed behavior for the children of God. *"Forgive us our debts, as we also have forgiven our debtors"* (Matthew 6:12) wasn't a suggestion. Jesus plainly said, "This is how you should pray." (See verse 9.)

If you're struggling to forgive someone, resist the temptation to run from it. Lean in. Ask God to show you how freely He has forgiven you. Receive that gift of grace and position your heart to give it away to people who have sinned against you. It'll cost you. But it will set you free.

God, I don't have the strength to forgive on my own. Help me. Give me an even greater portion of Your grace so I can give it to others and see lives transformed because of Your goodness. Amen.

April 15: WONDERFUL COUNSELOR

Where there is strife, there is pride,
but wisdom is found in those who take advice.
—Proverbs 13:10

A much-needed recalibration is taking place regarding mental health, thanks to a widespread secular push to embrace vulnerability and destigmatize therapy and medical intervention for people struggling with addiction, mental health problems, and suicidal thoughts.

Admittedly, we, the church, are late to the game on this critical shift. Secular humanists stand with arms open to hurting souls while much of the church remains guarded and in some cases gated, more of a country club for saints than a hospital for sinners. Our reluctance has created extreme dissonance as ministry leaders and laypeople alike scramble to figure out what it means for us to *"walk in the light"* (1 John 1:7) while also allowing God to work in and through medical and mental health professionals who may not exactly see Him as a good Father—if they see Him at all.

With depression, moral failure, and addiction running rampant through every rank of Christendom, it's high time for us to embrace the truth: It's okay to have Jesus and a therapist too.

Therapy and medication can help to improve a Christian's recovery journey, so why on earth would we, the church, deprive them of it? April is National Counseling Awareness Month, and this is a key season for working to break stigmas surrounding mental health and much-needed therapy for people in recovery.

God created humans for relationship. As Wonderful Counselor, He has made counselors who are wonderful. He knew we would need one another to bear our burdens together because in this fallen world we live in, they are just too heavy for any one person to carry alone. Counselors, therapists, and medical professionals can be conduits for a tangible healing experience with the Great Physician that leaves us not only cured but whole. Having Jesus and a therapist too isn't a lack of faith; it's wisdom.

God, thank You for the gift of wise counselors to offer advice and encouragement along the recovery journey. Break the stigma surrounding therapy so more people can find healing. Amen.

April 16: LAMENTATIONS

Hear my prayer, Lord; let my cry for help come to you. Do not hide your face from me when I am in distress. Turn your ear to me; when I call, answer me quickly.
—Psalm 102:1–2

Few things are more powerful than a good lament. Crying out to God in times of distress reminds us that He is near, He cares deeply, and He can take our rants with grace and strength.

If you're feeling tentative about letting God have it in this way, rest in knowing there is an entire book in the Bible devoted to laments. Contextually, Lamentations is a collection of poetic laments over the destruction of Jerusalem nearly 600 years before Jesus was born. Some scholars think Jeremiah wrote it; others say it was an anonymous author. One thing is for sure—this poet wasn't afraid to tell it like it is. With wild abandon, he beat his proverbial fists against God's chest in grief and frustration.

In the middle of the book, the fearless lamenter can't help but shift from the destruction at hand to the goodness of God. In spite of all the evidence to the contrary, the author pens this famous passage:

> Because of the LORD's great love we are not consumed, for his compassions never fail. They are new every morning; great is your faithfulness.
> (Lamentations 3:22–23)

Even in our darkest hours, when we can't comprehend what God is doing or see a way forward, acknowledging the truth about who we know Him to be can increase our faith. Although our situation may be dire, we believe Him to be the One to bring restoration.

Are you facing an injustice? Write a lament to God. Don't hold back; share your heart in a raw, real, and restorative way. He can take it. He is God, after all. And like a good Father, He will comfort, heal, and restore you for the hope-filled days ahead. This is the essence of true and lasting recovery.

God, the pain of this life feels like it might destroy me. Where are You? What are You doing? I will wait on You because you are worth it. Meet me in my pain and show me the way forward. Amen.

April 17: A NEW BOTTOM LINE

And we all, who with unveiled faces contemplate the Lord's glory, are being transformed into his image with ever-increasing glory, which comes from the Lord, who is the Spirit.
—2 Corinthians 3:18

When someone is trying to recover from addiction, mental health problems, or suicidal thoughts, going cold turkey rarely works, if ever. While we can't condone self-destructive, abusive, or illegal behaviors, we can have grace for clear and sustainable progress in someone's unique journey. This flies in the face of lockstep, legalistic programming but it's grace to people who are doing recovery for the long haul.

You may be thinking, *But I don't want anyone to struggle with anything. Won't allowing for bad behavior just enable more bad behavior?* Take a step back and see what's really going on. If a person addicted to heroin only drinks alcohol this week but doesn't shoot up, guess what? That's a win. Is it perfect? No. But real recovery values progress over perfection every time. Acknowledge the growth and honor it. And continually invite the ones you love and lead to a higher standard of living—a truly transformed life they'll love living.

The key to doing this well is clear communication and expectations. Allowing the individual to express the steps they wish to take toward a promised-land life—not just what we want for them—is liberating and empowering. When we tell them, "You'd better get sober and stay sober, or else," they're likely to rebel. But when they come to the conclusion on their own, they're more prone to try again for the right reasons. As they continually establish new bottom lines, they will continue to move toward complete freedom.

So what about you? What's your new bottom line? What measurable steps can you take toward the transformed life you want without placing unrealistic expectations on yourself? And what about the ones you love and lead? How might you invite them to establish a new bottom line that motivates them to build a life they want to stay sober for? Take it to God in prayer today. The answers He gives may surprise you—and His results will delight you.

God, sometimes my recovery journey feels overwhelming. What do You want me focused on right now? What does success look like in Your eyes? Show me Your ways; I know they're better. Amen.

April 18: EXPECTATIONS VS. EXPECTANCY

Yes, my soul, find rest in God; my hope comes from him.
—Psalm 62:5

Conflict in relationships typically stems from unmet expectations. To be fair, we often fail to clearly communicate our expectations in the first place, making it incredibly difficult for people to meet them. We typically assume past performance will predict future outcomes, that what we've experienced in the past is what we should expect going forward. This line of thinking is limited. Learning to ask for the things we need and learning to trust people to meet those needs is a vulnerable place to be, but real relationships and authentic community require a healthy level of interdependence.

The problem is, even when you clearly articulate your expectations and receive confirmation that you are heard, other people, in their humanness, will inevitably fail you sooner or later. A missed deadline, a lapse in judgment, or an all-out betrayal can leave you bitter and tempted to isolate yourself.

God says it's not good for us to be alone, but the pain of unmet expectations can tear us apart.

Take a cue from the Father when it comes to expectations. Most God-revering believers wouldn't be so bold as to say they have *expectations* of God, but they would certainly expect Him to show up, to move, and to heal. It's always best to let God determine when and how He wants to show up, because no matter how good our plans might be, His are always better.

Instead of coming to God with your list of expectations and demands, stay curious. Come to Him with your cares and concerns, and let Him lead you into right ways of thinking. Wait patiently on God, free of expectation but full of eager expectancy. And while you're at it? Give your fellow humans the benefit of the doubt. If an expectation goes unmet, clarify and try again as many times as it takes to build a truly redemptive relationship.

God, thank You for always meeting my expectations, even when You don't show up as I expect You to! You never fail me, and I rest in knowing that no matter what I face, You've got me. Amen.

April 19: LIES WE BELIEVE

When [the devil] lies, he speaks his native language,
for he is a liar and the father of lies.
—John 8:44

Believing lies, about ourselves and about God, is easier than you might think. Some lies start with a half-truth that sends you slowly spiraling into deception. Others originate with something you desperately want to be true, but it's just not. Perhaps you've been lying to yourself and others for so long, you've forgotten what the truth really is. You actually believe your own hype. You aren't the first to experience this. It's been happening since Eve believed a lie from the serpent in the garden of Eden, and humankind fell. Hard.

When the lies we believe become our source for truth, they can be hard to shake. We tell ourselves blatant lies such as:

+ God may love me, but He's mad at me.

+ I can't be close to God because of my sin.

+ People never really change, so why try?

+ I'm a sinner and I always will be.

While these lies may be rooted in some truth and even representative of some formative life experiences, they misrepresent the Father's heart and willingness to restore us to sanity.

Here's where things get complicated. God is alive—He's still speaking, still healing, and still moving us, His church, to bring His kingdom to earth. And when God decides to do a new thing, such as bringing reform in the Christ-centered recovery space, we can be tempted to dig in our heels and cling to those lies we believe to avoid much-needed change. They might sound something like this:

+ It's the way we've always done it, so it's best.

+ We must agree on every facet of religious doctrine.

+ God won't give you more than you can handle.

+ God is the same, yesterday, today, and forever, and we should be too.

+ Jesus may love recklessly, but we're not Jesus.

It can take a move of God or a life-altering experience for us to begin to question the lies we believe, to doubt our doubts about our good Father God. Death and loss, trauma and disaster, and coming to the very ends of ourselves can be powerful motivators to silence the lying voice of the enemy and adjust our frequency to hear the Father's voice.

What lies have you believed? How have they impacted your recovery journey and your ability to love and lead others? Give those lies over to God today and ask Him to fill you with His truth instead.

God, help me identify any lies I'm believing that are keeping me from hearing Your voice and doing Your will. Silence the enemy's voice and speak to me, Father. I long to hear from You. Amen.

April 20: LIVING IN THE LIGHT

But if we walk in the light, as he is in the light, we have fellowship with one another, and the blood of Jesus, his Son, purifies us from all sin.
—1 John 1:7

Imagine doing life in a community where you had no shame, no secrets, and nothing keeping you from being fully seen, fully known, and fully loved by others and by God. These authentic communities can be incredibly hard to come by, even in the church, the one place where people deserve to find a safe haven.

It's not because we haven't tried. We know we need purity, so we foster a perfectionistic purity culture. We know we need accountability, so we foster a shame-driven accountability culture. We know we need discipling, so we foster a heavy-handed discipline culture that makes people hide. We know what we need, but we are ill-equipped to fulfill that need on our own. When we try to handle these problems without the Holy Spirit leading the way, we foster religious abuse and keep people bound.

And yet, we know we are to walk in the light of God's Word. When we bring our lives into alignment with Scripture, we realize that walking in the light has nothing to do with exposure, and everything to do with vulnerability. Safe, authentic communities allow people to belong even before they behave and acknowledge sin without shame so it can be dealt with and dismissed for good.

What about your recovery communities? Can people walk in the light, free of judgment? If not, why not? Spend time in the light of God's face today. Ask Him what's working and what's not working in your recovery communities, and how you might be the change you want to see.

God, I need a safe place to recover, and I know others do too. Show me how I can help to create authentic community where people can walk unashamed in the light of Your Word. Amen

April 21: NO SECRET

For there is nothing hidden that will not be disclosed, and nothing concealed that will not be known or brought out into the open.
—Luke 8:17

Secrets can be hard to keep and even harder to share. The Bible teaches us that keeping secrets can be good or bad, but determining whether it's right or wrong takes wisdom and discernment.

Esther kept secrets. She hid her nationality so she could help save God's people. (See Esther 2:20.)

Daniel shared secrets, earned the favor of king Nebuchadnezzar, and tamed lions. (See Daniel 2:47.)

And then there was Samson, who shared a secret that got him a bad haircut and a death sentence. (See Judges 16:17–22.)

Some secrets are made to be kept. Political and military secrets, holiday gifts and surprise parties, things that would cause disappointment, pain, or serious harm if shared broadly, or that would bring greater joy on a delayed reveal. God *Himself* keeps secrets, and He does so for our good. (See Deuteronomy 29:29.) Some things are simply *"too wonderful for* [us] *to know"* (Job 42:3).

Some secrets, however, are poison to our souls. Concealing a difficult past, sweeping current sins and struggles under the rug, or making excuses for someone else's bad behavior are just a handful of examples. These secrets are no secret to God, and they will be brought into the light eventually, whether we choose to partner with it or not. God loves us too much to let them fester.

If you're in recovery or loving and leading someone through theirs, you know we all need a safe space to share secrets—not in some anonymous, confession-style tell-all, but in an environment free of judgment and condemnation. If you haven't found this community yet, perhaps you're called to create it. Take inventory of the secrets you keep. Ask the Father what needs to come into the light and partner with Him to share it with someone you can trust.

God, some of my secrets are causing me shame. I know that's not what You want for me, but I fear sharing them. Help me find a safe confidante who can hear me and help me heal. Amen.

April 22: SUBCONSCIOUS MIND

*We demolish arguments and every pretension that sets itself up against
the knowledge of God, and we take captive every thought
to make it obedient to Christ.*
—2 Corinthians 10:5

Riding a bike. Performing a dance. Playing an instrument. These seemingly automatic movements are guided by our subconscious minds—that deep inner force that allows us to be on autopilot. The fact that we can engage in behavior without really thinking about it proves that our behavior isn't as logical and rational as we'd like it to be.

For context, it's important to understand the differing levels of human consciousness.

Our conscious mind houses all of the thoughts and actions we're acutely aware of, such as the painful burn after touching a hot surface, or the fragrant scent of a white lily. We're cognizant of these things and usually in control of how we handle them in the moment.

Our subconscious mind houses the thoughts and behaviors that have become second nature to us, such as walking, driving a car, scrolling through our phones, or even reaching for a drink after a stressful day. We may be aware of the things that we're doing, but since they live in our subconscious mind, we go through the motions without giving them much thought.

Finally, our unconscious mind houses memories, past events, and experiences that we've forgotten about for the most part, by choice or by chance. For example, you probably don't remember saying your first word, even if your parents told you what it was. Similarly, you might not be able to remember early life trauma—but that doesn't mean you weren't negatively impacted by it.

Neuroscientists and psychologists work hard to understand the depths of our mind, and recovery leaders would do well to follow their lead. For people who struggle with addiction, mental health problems, and suicidal thoughts as a result of trauma, the lines can be blurred between the conscious, subconscious, and unconscious mind. Trauma-informed care professionals and ministers recognize that trauma may exist in the subconscious or unconscious mind and that uncovering it and dealing with it in the conscious mind is critical to healing.

The most powerful way to tap into the subconscious and unconscious mind is to engage in Holy Spirit-led counseling. These trauma-informed, Christ-centered therapists can help you pursue deep healing and lasting peace that passes human understanding.

God, I want to understand the trauma behind my struggles. Unlock my subconscious mind and reveal parts of my past that might be helpful in my recovery. Shine a light so I can heal. Amen.

April 23: MERCY AND GRACE

The LORD is compassionate and gracious, slow to anger, abounding in love. He will not always accuse, nor will he harbor his anger forever; he does not treat us as our sins deserve or repay us according to our iniquities. For as high as the heavens are above the earth, so great is his love for those who fear him; as far as the east is from the west, so far has he removed our transgressions from us.
—Psalm 103:8–12

Mercy and grace are similar words, but have two very different meanings, both critical to understanding the true nature and character of our good Father God. Mercy has to do with God's kindness and compassion. God is holy, and we've all sinned and fallen short of His glory. And yet God does not punish us as our sins demand and deserve. Grace, on the other hand, isn't just about withholding judgment; it's about bestowing a gift. Grace is unmerited favor—a real relationship with God and a kingdom inheritance that we surely don't deserve.

In Scripture, mercy is often equated with deliverance from oppression or judgment. God's mercy freed the Israelites from Egyptian captivity *and* spared the woman caught in the act of adultery from certain death. (See Exodus and John 8:3–11.) Certainly grace was involved in both instances, but mercy shows up as a specific subsegment of God's grace.

Grace is the game changer. God does more than just deliver us—He sustains us. He forgives us, adopts us, provides for us, clothes us in His righteousness, and sends His Spirit to dwell in us, making us one with Him—Father, Son, and Holy Spirit. Grace is an extension of His blessing to the unworthy that's so powerful, it makes the unworthy *worthy* in Him.

God owes us nothing, but offers us everything He has, including eternal life! That's a level of grace that's available to us now.

God, I'm in awe of Your mercy and grace. I need them both every day. Have mercy on me. Show me how to use Your free gift of grace to offer mercy to people who need it as much as I do. Amen.

April 24: GRACE GIVING

If you forgive anyone's sins, their sins are forgiven;
if you do not forgive them, they are not forgiven.
—John 20:23

Forgiveness is a key component to recovery. Even secular programs tout its benefits. Forgiveness frees the forgiver, even if the offender can't or won't receive it. But forgiveness doesn't just free us—it can also supernaturally free our offenders, enabling them to tap into the mercy and grace we've received.

You might be bristling now, thinking of that person you don't want to give grace to. You think forgiving them means letting them off the hook, and that grace will enable them to sit comfortably in their sins against you. Perhaps you're thinking, *God may forgive them, but I never will.*

Here's the thing: Forgiveness is price for entry into the kingdom of God. Scripture explains that we'll be forgiven to the exact measure of forgiveness we're willing to give. This isn't some grand ultimatum from God designed to bully us into releasing forgiveness. But it's a kingdom culture expectation that we give away the grace we've personally received. Do our offenders deserve it? No. Do we? No. But giving grace is, by definition, bestowing unmerited favor on someone. None of us deserve grace, but God gives it anyway. And He wants us to do the same in His name.

Trying to give grace in our own strength is pointless. Our humanness demands not only judgment, but restitution and revenge—and our attempts at grace will come with strings attached…which isn't really grace at all. This is why it's so important to partner with the Holy Spirit on our recovery journey.

As you take inventory of the offenses against you, lean into the grace you've received from God for your sins—and give it away, even to the one person you don't want to give it to. *Especially* that person. Yes, it will free you. And chances are, it will free them—opening the door to God's grace and their own recovery.

God, I know I should forgive. But I really don't want to. Help me partner with Your grace to set people free, even though they don't deserve it. I'm changing my mind, so come change my heart. Amen.

April 25: BROKEN SYSTEMS

"I have the right to do anything," you say—but not everything is beneficial. "I have the right to do anything"—but not everything is constructive. No one should seek their own good, but the good of others.
—1 Corinthians 10:23–24

In the early days of the Christian church, things were tough but simple. We took seriously our call to go and make disciples, and nobody spent time worrying about how or whether we'd be able to do it. There were no megachurches, no elaborate giving campaigns, no concrete campus expansion strategies. Our only example was the life of Jesus and the voice of the Holy Spirit. In its radically simple conviction, the early church spread like grassroots wildfire.

If we've learned anything about the remnants of the first-century church in the twenty-first century, it's that more of a good thing isn't always a good thing. This is especially true when it comes to recovery. The *big church* movement left us with outreach, discipleship, and recovery programs that not only don't work but are bleeding the church dry. Jesus never took a cookie-cutter approach, so why would we? We need less one-size-fits-all programming and more one-on-one authentic relationships, which are less systematizing and more cultivating.

Don't believe me? Take a good look around you. In case you missed it, there's a mass exodus happening in the modern church. People aren't giving up on their faith—they just want nothing to do with broken religious systems and structures that leave people bound. They also want to distance themselves from people who call themselves Christians but don't act much like Jesus at all. This is hard to hear, but we, the church, *must* be willing to hear it. If we're going to be the bride of Christ, we need to start acting like it.

The problem is corporate, but the solution starts with you. What religious systems or structures are you clinging to? Are they *truly* of God, or did man create them? Are they working? If not, are you willing to let them go? Be willing, as God leads you. This is the only way to bring reform in the recovery space, to step out of denial and embrace God's better way.

God, I want to be part of the solution in Christ-centered recovery. Help me lean into what's working, let go of what's not working, and follow You faithfully into a hope-filled future. Amen.

April 26: FORGIVING YOURSELF

Therefore, there is now no condemnation for those who are in Christ Jesus.
—Romans 8:1

As you reflect on the life that led you into recovery, you've likely had opportunities to forgive people who wronged you in one way or another, who directly contributed to the trauma that caused you to struggle. Perhaps you've tasted and seen how good forgiveness can be, but have you offered yourself a portion of grace yet?

Forgiving ourselves is the hardest thing we'll ever do. Even when we believe in and receive God's grace, sometimes we're tempted to give it away before we enjoy it ourselves. Forgiving ourselves can feel selfish and unnecessary, but it's a key part of embracing the promised-land life God has for us.

Your old sinful self is dead, and you're now a new creation. (See 2 Corinthians 5:17.) Your old self and your new self *cannot* coexist! To embrace the new, you must be willing to release the old. Like a trapeze artist flying high from one bar to the next, you must let go of one to receive the other. This is what releasing forgiveness over yourself is like. Is it scary? Yes. Is it vulnerable? Yes. Is there risk involved? Yes. But it's the only way you can have open hands and an open heart to receive the next bar, which you'll find readily available when you surrender.

If you're struggling to forgive yourself, ask God to show you how He sees you in the light of what Jesus did for you. He doesn't even *remember* your sins anymore. He sees you as perfect, holy, and blameless in Christ. This truth should not produce pride in you, but a humility that will help you admit God knows better than you do. If He says you're forgiven, who are you to say otherwise? *"If God is for us, who can be against us?"* (Romans 8:31). Not even *you!* Receive His forgiveness in full today and allow yourself to bask in His mercy and grace until you claim them as your own.

God, I believe You when You say I'm forgiven. Help me harness that grace and forgive myself for the things You've already forgiven me for. Remind me who I am in You so I can surrender. Amen.

April 27: FORGIVING GOD

How long, Lord? Will you forget me forever? How long will you hide your face from me? How long must I wrestle with my thoughts and day after day have sorrow in my heart? How long will my enemy triumph over me?
—Psalm 13:1–2

Getting hurt by people is hard. Getting hurt by what God allows is even harder. We cry out, *What?! Why?! How long?!* But we're met with what seems like deafening silence. When He doesn't answer us, or when He doesn't answer in the way we think He should, offense against God rises up in us. We put Him at arm's length, and we may even turn away from Him, wondering how He can be really good when life is so very bad.

Being angry with God isn't easy to admit. Most sermons, Bible studies, and small groups don't even raise the question because expressing frustration with God can be perceived as a lack of faith or even as blasphemous. So we suffer in silence, fueling our doubts, until we become disillusioned and disenfranchised to the point of total spiritual isolation.

It doesn't have to be this way. As a good Father, God knows there will be times His children get angry with Him. We don't always understand what God is doing or why. Quite frankly, He doesn't owe us an explanation. He's God, and we're not. And yet, in His kindness, He is willing to meet us in our pain. He hears our complaints and receives our fears, frustrations, and freak-outs with patience and love. Granted, hearing us doesn't always mean He will do what we want. God is a good Father, and His ways are better than ours. But He will sit with us in the mess, grieve with us, and show us the way forward—if we let Him.

God doesn't need your forgiveness. Even when you don't understand Him, He is all good, and He is incapable of doing anything wrong. Forgiving God is simply choosing not to be angry at Him for things you don't yet understand. It's releasing Him from your own expectations and instead remaining expectant that He will work all things for your good and His glory. Forgiving God is when you stop asking, "Why?" and instead ask, "What now, God?" This willing surrender creates intimacy with God and an enhanced ability to hear His voice, which you will need along the recovery journey.

God, I don't always understand You. But I know You're good. I forgive You. Help me see beyond my situation to where You are working behind the scenes. Help me doubt my doubts about You. Amen.

April 28: FREEDOM

It is for freedom that Christ has set us free. Stand firm, then, and do not let yourselves be burdened again by a yoke of slavery.
—Galatians 5:1

If we try to tell a newly delivered slave that they're not only free but family, it's going to take more than prayers and platitudes for them to believe it's true. The slavery mindset permeates traditional recovery culture, as we're required to identify ourselves by our struggle even years into sobriety. "Hi, my name is George, and I'm an addict" sticks around long after it ceases to be true. And the problem with this is that it perpetuates the lie that people don't really change.

Deliverance and lasting freedom are possible, but they require a mindset shift for Christ-centered recovery leaders. How can we walk in the light when we do so anonymously? How can we be free from our sins and struggles when we're under a branded label? How can we go after a new life when we keep trying to *recover* the old broken life that led us to struggle in the first place? We can and must do better.

Jesus has set us free. His grace doesn't set us free *to sin*, but *from sin*. If the *old man sinner* is truly dead, and we're alive in Christ, we, the church, need to stop trying to resurrect him! Living a true resurrection life embodies recovery as it should be—a revelation of who we really are in Christ, who we were always meant to be.

Offering freedom to others in the context of authentic community will be especially challenging if you're not living free yourself. Perhaps you've been sober for years, and you're living in a place of victory. But are there pieces of your own recovery journey that don't apply to the lives of those you love and lead? Have you embraced the unique diversity of each person's walk? And finally, are you clinging to any lies or labels that aren't helpful or edifying to you and others? Be free of them! Lay them at Jesus's feet and ask Him for a better way—His way.

God, I know I'm more than a label to You. Help me align my identity with who You say I am and invite others to see who they are in You. Help me set captives and prisoners free in Your name. Amen.

April 29: TRAUMA: AN INSIDE JOB

Cast all your anxiety on him because he cares for you.
—1 Peter 5:7

Trauma is more than just something that happens to a person on the outside. Trauma is what happens *inside* of a person as a result of what happens to them. Different circumstances impact different people in different ways for different reasons—which is why we have no room to judge what triggers trauma inside another person.

During the Vietnam War, young, able-bodied American men were taken from their homes, given a license to kill, and shipped off to fight in a war they barely understood. It's no surprise that in the face of abject confusion, trauma, and loss, many of those men became addicted to heroin while fighting overseas.

The widespread availability of the drug and our soldiers' understandable desire to escape reality birthed what *should* have been a drug epidemic in post-war America. And yet, when they came home, very few soldiers who abused heroin during their combat season remained addicted after the war. In fact, 95 percent quit cold turkey and stayed in remission.

Why? How? Because they had family, friends, and a promised-land life to come home to and stay sober for. Life certainly wasn't simple thereafter, but these men, removed from what was undoubtedly the most stress-filled situation of their lives, were better in community.

What's the lesson for today? We were never meant to do life and recovery alone. We must be willing to go deeper. Instead of asking, "Why are you addicted?" we must be brave enough to ask, "Why the pain?" and "What are you running from?"

More often than not, people encounter God through other people. Are you willing to be His hands and feet? The responsibility is huge, but it only requires one job: Faithfully representing the Father's heart.

God, I want to be Your hands and feet. Help me represent Your heart to people who need Your mercy and grace. Nudge me to go deeper and help people identify new and better ways to heal. Amen.

April 30: FIGHTING OFF THE FALSE SELF

Now if I do what I do not want to do, it is no longer I who do it,
but it is sin living in me that does it.
—Romans 7:20

Who are you really? You may think you know, but chances are, you still have more to learn. If you're walking out a recovery journey or loving and leading someone through theirs, it's important you get to know your false self and your true self.

The false self is the person you think you are, separate from God. It's your identity in the context of culture, gender, race, socioeconomic status, and other earthly factors that don't matter in the kingdom of God. It's also the identity that defines you by your struggle with labels like alcoholic, addict, abuser, or victim. Acknowledging the false self doesn't make it true, but it gives you an understanding of what the enemy's voice sounds like.

The true self is who you really are—one with God in Christ, by the power of the Holy Spirit. It's a self that says there's no lie or label that can keep you separated from the love of God, regardless of whether you're winning at life and recovery or not. Sadly, it can be hard to get to know your true self because most of the world still knows your other self and will be quick to remind you of it.

When we buy into the minor role the world expects us to play, we give the enemy an opening to cause harm and instill doubt. But when we embrace the lead role God created for us, we put His transformative goodness on display, evidenced by the promised-land life we live.

No matter the onslaught, your true self remains true. It gives you the power and authority to fight off the false self and embrace the divine DNA that runs through your veins. You are so much more than what you do. You are who God says you are—a beloved child. And when you believe this, it changes your behavior. You may spend the rest of your life coming into agreement with it, but His truth stands.

God, help me align with my true self—the person You created me to be. Shelter me from spiritual attacks that might cause me to doubt Your goodness and remind me that I'm a new creation. Amen.

May

RESTORATION

*Therefore confess your sins to each other and pray
for each other so that you may be healed.*
—James 5:16

Why, my soul, are you downcast? Why so disturbed within me?
Put your hope in God, for I will yet praise him, my Savior and my God.
—Psalm 42:11

One in five people in the U.S. struggle with their mental health, but those are only the ones we know about. There are probably more, especially in our post-pandemic world. Humans in general are resilient—and slowly but surely, many of us came out the other side of COVID-19 stronger, smarter, and more sensitive to the needs of society.

But what about those who didn't make it to the other side? We're not just talking about people who lost their lives to the coronavirus or complications from the vaccines. We're referring to people who lost their lives because of the societal impact of the lockdowns, closures, and mandates. The isolation we all faced sent addiction, relapses, mental health problems, and suicidal thoughts through the roof.

Perhaps it caused you to struggle too.

Isolation is a killer. Events and circumstances can become traumatic when we don't have people to share them with. That trauma is embedded into our memory banks as either explicit (conscious) or implicit (unconscious). Both can impact our actions and awareness.

Sharing stories of trauma with a trusted member of a safe community and having those stories received with compassion can change how they affect people moving forward. If we really want to see revival, we have to figure out how to come back together again in a post-pandemic world—physically, mentally, emotionally, and spiritually—and lean on one another again. We were never meant to operate in isolation.

Recovery in the context of authentic Christ-centered community is the answer. Aligned with the same God whom poet Francis Thompson called "The Hound of Heaven," we must never relent in our pursuit of these precious ones who are one encounter away from stepping into an abundant, promised-land life. This pursuit takes courage, strength, and sacrifice. In some cases, it may take all we have to give. But with God on our side, all things are possible.

God, make me an instrument of connection in an isolated world. Heal our land, heal our world. Show us the goodness of Your glory. Give us strength and endurance to run the race, together. Amen.

May 2: CONFESSION

*Then I acknowledged my sin to you and did not cover up my iniquity.
I said, "I will confess my transgressions to the LORD."
And you forgave the guilt of my sin.*
—Psalm 32:5

Confession is one of the most underestimated tools in our recovery toolbelt. Scripture commands it, and God is standing at the ready with healing and grace that knows no limits. Unfortunately, confession and *shame* often go hand in hand in our recovery programming. This causes struggling people, even leaders, to hide and then fall. It's hard to find a safe space to confess free of judgment in a Christian community.

While we don't exactly subscribe to the idea of a perfect clean-slate theology, confession is, in fact, good for the soul. To be fair, the church has quite a bit of baggage around confession. Confessions shared in confidence can turn to gossip quickly in well-meaning prayer chains, which perpetuates the marginalization and discrimination that comes with being seen as *unclean* in the church. This isn't the heart of God, and it shouldn't be ours either. This is why safe spaces to confess—to God and to other believers—must be available.

Once we receive God's forgiveness in full, time and wisdom can prepare us to share testimony to God's deliverance from our old way of life. This isn't to say that we must all wear our former sin on our sleeves. That's cruel! But we must indeed be ready to testify to God's goodness and His ability and willingness to set us free.

Could the story of who you once thought you were be an inspiration to others? Is God calling you to share your story to help set others free? Are you in the right season to share your victory in Jesus? The Father will nudge you when it's time. In the meantime, continue to search your heart for anything that doesn't align with God's view. Confess your sins to Him and cling to His righteousness. And be ready to help others do the same.

God, I confess that confession makes me uneasy. It's so hard to think about the ways I've wronged You when You've loved me so well. Help me be free of sin and bound to Your grace. Amen.

May 3: TALKING TO GOD

Look to the LORD and his strength; seek his face always.
— Psalm 105:4

Prayer is an undeniably powerful part of Christ-centered recovery. We pray for healing, and we pray for peace—and we believe we'll receive what we need in God's perfect timing. But prayer isn't just some powerful tool in our recovery toolbelt. Prayer is our chance to get to know the God who created us.

When we pray, we thank God for who He is, and we humbly ask for the things we want and need. But being able to talk to God as we put our lives back together is anything but transactional. We can talk to God as our good Father who loves us, forgives us, and desires deep relationship with us. (See 2 Corinthians 5:19.) We can talk to Jesus as our brother who thinks we're to die for and promises to be with us always. (See Matthew 28:20.) We can even talk to the Holy Spirit, the Person of the Trinity who's actually set up shop inside us and enables us to think, act, and be more like Jesus. (See John 14:16–17.)

Consider this also: When you pray, who do you pray to? God the Father? Jesus? The Holy Spirit? Your answer may reveal an opportunity for deeper relational growth with God. For example, if you have daddy issues, you may not feel safe praying to God as Father. If you grew up in a religious environment that didn't believe in signs, wonders, and miracles, you might feel a little off if you try to pray to the Holy Spirit. God wants you to know that He's more than you think He is, and embracing the fullness of who He is will reveal more of His deep love for you.

Prayer is a safe place to practice being present with God. Talking to Him about anything and everything in the real-time narrative of your life builds an authentic relationship with God that brings restoration into your life. You don't have to be fancy or formal. You don't need to have all the right words. Be real. Be your authentic self. That's who God knows and loves and wants to be with. Come as you are.

God, thanks for hanging out with me. I never have to pull myself together before I come to You. I'm going to keep seeking Your face, looking to You for strength. I'm at home when I'm with You. Amen.

May 4: PERSONAL ACCOUNTABILITY, PERSONAL RELATIONSHIP

The fruit of the Spirit is love, joy, peace, patience, kindness, goodness, faithfulness, gentleness, self-control.
—Galatians 5:22–23 (ESV)

There's a reason self-control is a fruit of the Spirit. Personal accountability for all believers depends on our ability, in our sound minds, to know the difference between good and evil, and choose good. In a recovery context, it's helpful to have accountability partners to turn to when things get tough. But ultimately, real recovery requires being in control of our thoughts and actions. The choice to stay sober. The choice to avoid harmful behavior. The choice to choose God when we might be tempted to choose anything but Him.

Here's the secret: Self-control is impossible to cultivate in our own strength. As a fruit of the Spirit of God, it requires a supernatural impartation. Spiritual *fruits* are gifts from God, not things we can earn or seek. The funny part is, this flies in the face of traditional recovery programming, which acknowledges our powerlessness early on, but then shifts into a self-preservation mode that's far from the higher power Himself.

Being accountable to yourself means first being accountable to God the Father. Scripture says His thoughts toward you outnumber the grains of sand in the ocean. (See Psalm 139:17–18.) This means that every time you think about God, He was *already* thinking about you. He knows your every thought, your every move…and He loves you anyway. There are no secrets in the kingdom of God, so there's no hiding from Him—or from yourself.

Personal accountability requires a personal relationship with God through Jesus by the power of the Spirit. He will not only call you to a higher, better way of living, He will strengthen and equip you to walk it out. When you succeed? Give Him the glory. When you fail? Fail forward, into His loving arms. He will meet you, restore you gently, and remind you of the life He's promised you, one you'll actually want to stay sober for.

God, I'm so tired of trying harder. I surrender my heart, mind, and will to You, acknowledging You already fully know me. Thank You for loving me. Give me Your strength in my weakness. Amen.

May 5: GENTLE RESTORATION

Brothers and sisters, if someone is caught in a sin, you who live by the Spirit should restore that person gently. But watch yourselves, or you also may be tempted.
—Galatians 6:1

Restoration is one of the most difficult concepts to grasp in Christian life. It can't be earned. In fact, it's already taken care of. All we have to do is come into agreement with the truth about it, and something supernatural happens. Apply that concept to recovery, though, and the waters get muddy. We, the church, so desperately want to cling to truth that we rarely share it in love. When someone's sins, struggles, or stumblings are inevitably exposed by a God who wants better for them, we Christians rarely respond in the gentle way of Jesus.

We're not doing it on purpose. It's all about fear. In our overzealous attempts to honor God and point struggling people to Him, we can easily forget to meet people where they are. It's funny when you think about it. Where else could we possibly meet them? In attempts to restore others, we keep them at arm's length in fear of being tempted. We let them know grace is available to them—when they get their act together, of course.

If you're called to love and lead people through recovery, be curious about the mindset and methodologies of Jesus. He rarely followed status-quo protocols. He took risks. He bucked a religious system. He loved recklessly. And He was killed for it.

You may not be called to be a martyr, but are you willing to meet struggling people where they are? Are you willing to invite them into the truth of their identity—and let the Holy Spirit do His good work? Are you willing to let Love Himself lead, knowing He is the pathway to all truth? Be willing. You may find healing for your own heart as you gently restore others. And then you'll know the truth: recovery is for everyone.

God, help me resist the urge to be heavy-handed with those I'm called to love and lead through recovery. Give me grace and move me with compassion to help others embrace Your restoration. Amen.

May 6: COMMON UNITY

How good and pleasant it is when God's people live together in unity!
—Psalm 133:1

Community is a buzzword people throw around a little too loosely. Join a church. Plug into a network. Find your tribe. Like it's that easy. Jesus knew the difficulty of this oh so well, and we believe it's one of the reasons that His public ministry was always on the move.

Even though He was surrounded by twelve apostles and a number of other disciples, only three knew Him inside and out: Peter, James, and John. As they went from city to city, they were surrounded by thousands. And yet, the Son of Man still had *"nowhere to lay his head"* (Matthew 8:20 ESV). This illustrates how hard it is to find authentic community, even for people like Jesus. He never tried to create a community inside the walls of a building. He built His church demonstrating the ways He meant for us to *be* the church.

Genuine relationships. Transformative encounters. Life together. Followers of Jesus may not have met for weekly worship sessions or Friday night meetings the way those of us in Christian recovery sometimes do. But the community they fostered was rooted in a common unity: our oneness with God, in Jesus Christ, by the power of the Holy Spirit. It transcends location, proximity, and culture with an invitation to intimacy with God and His people.

You can build authentic community by loving, leading, and doing life with the people right in front of you. Recovery also presents you with opportunities to restore broken relationships and extend grace—even when you can't continue to be with people you've hurt or those who have hurt you. Authentic community is a place where people can be fully seen, fully known, and still fully loved, by God and others. Can you see it? Will you be it?

God, I admit I've been looking for community in all the wrong places. Help me see what Your church is supposed to look like and help me demonstrate authentic community in my circles. Amen.

*We demolish arguments and every pretension that sets itself
up against the knowledge of God, and we take captive every thought to
make it obedient to Christ.*
—2 Corinthians 10:5

How are you today? No, really. Take a moment to pause, reflect, and answer honestly. Your answer doesn't define you, but it can be a strong indicator of your overall mental health. Whether you're feeling full of joy or in the depths of despair, acknowledging your current reality free of shame can create long-term pathways to healing.

This acknowledgement is the essence of lasting recovery—being true to who you are as a beloved child of a good Father God while also admitting that the struggle is sometimes still very real. When you can embrace the God-given notion that it's okay not to be okay, you give yourself permission to name the struggle, identify the trauma that's causing it, and give it to God so He can help you heal.

Perhaps you're feeling angry because your supervisor talked down to you like your father used to. This is an invitation for you to get to know your heavenly Father better. His Son went to hell and back again to lift you up. Maybe you're feeling anxious before a big interview because you're afraid to fail and disappoint your family. This is an invitation to remember that failure isn't fatal; it's an opportunity to learn, grow, and thrive in the future.

Whatever you're feeling, don't let a bad day become a bad life. Check yourself before you wreck yourself. Give yourself the grace of an honest diagnostic to help you take those thoughts and feelings captive and align with the truth about who God says you are.

God, I love how You're not afraid of my feelings. Thank You for letting me be brutally honest with You and with myself, and thank You for showing me Your better way forward. Amen.

Now the earth was formless and empty, darkness was over the surface of the deep, and the Spirit of God was hovering over the waters. And God said, "Let there be light," and there was light.
—Genesis 1:2–3

God is a God of order, not a God of chaos. At the dawn of creation, He spoke into a dark void and brought substance and order into our existence. From earth and sky to animals and humans, the natural order He gave us is undeniable. The sole reason why we can diagnose something that's in *dis-order* is because it's not operating as God originally intended.

There are dozens of scientific and spiritual reasons behind the disorders we face. Anxiety disorders. Mood disorders. Psychotic disorders. Eating disorders. Post-traumatic stress disorders. Personality disorders. And more. The root cause behind them all? Trauma.

Trauma is the ultimate disorder. We live in a fallen world, brought about by sin. Jesus died and rose again to defeat that sin, but humankind is still struggling to believe it's true. That cognitive dissonance breeds doubt, which breeds resistance, which breeds hopelessness. This was never what God intended when He created us, and His desire is to restore His natural order into our lives—breaking chains, healing wounds, and restoring hearts, minds, spirits, souls, and wills in His powerful name.

May is Borderline Personality Disorder (BPD) Awareness Month. The loneliness, fear of abandonment, and controlling behaviors that come from it all stem from trauma—early life trauma, generational trauma, and even genetic trauma. It's time we destigmatize BPD and come against the ultimate disorder—trauma—in Jesus's name.

God, thank You for bringing order out of chaos in my life. Help me continue to align with Your truth and partner with the natural order You have in mind for my life and the lives of others. Amen.

In my distress I called to the LORD; I cried to my God for help. From his temple he heard my voice; my cry came before him, into his ears.
—Psalm 18:6

One thing is certain in all of Scripture: When God's people cry out to Him in distress, He hears them. The oppressed may have no earthly helper, but God rescues those who cry out to Him for help. (See Psalm 72:12.) What a powerful truth to embrace in times of stress.

God doesn't want you to pull yourself up by your bootstraps. He doesn't love you more when you try harder, and He won't shame your lack of faith when you're struggling. He wants you to call on Him right in the middle of your distress. Let Him have it. He can take it. Be as angry or scared or sad or stressed out as you need to be—as you really are. He delights in your authenticity; He will not only listen with a compassionate ear, He will be moved with compassion in your favor. *"He will command his angels concerning you"* (Psalm 91:11), and deliver you from all your fears. (See Psalm 34:4.)

Crying out to God is a powerfully supernatural way to de-stress in distress. Let Him be your safe haven, a supernatural space to process feelings and emotions risk-free. As you process with Him, He will remind you where your help comes from and who He really is. (See Psalm 121.) In His presence, the truth of His goodness will overwhelm you with a peace that transcends your circumstances. Your heart will be softened and soothed, your gratitude for God's faithfulness will grow deeper, and your expectancy will be reignited as you wait patiently on Him. It was true for the psalmist, and it's true for us too.

Cry out to God today. He's listening. Give Him your stress, your strain, your struggle—and watch Him move mountains in your life.

God, life is so overwhelming. But I know You are so good! Deliver me from the pain and stress of this season and restore my soul. Help me remember who You are and who I am in You. Amen.

For I desire steadfast love and not sacrifice, the knowledge of God rather
than burnt offerings.
—Hosea 6:6 (ESV)

The prophet Elijah was an intense guy. One if the wildest, most zealous characters in the Old Testament, he was so fired up for God that nobody could extinguish the flame—except maybe Elijah himself. In 1 Kings 18:22–40, he contested the pagan god Baal by calling down fire from heaven and had the false prophets killed. Elijah was victorious but exhausted. And when Queen Jezebel threatened his life because of what he had done, Elijah began to experience what we now know to be burnout.

Fatigue. Fear. Frustration. Feelings of self-pity and overwhelming despair. They're so common after a major victory, aren't they? Feeling drained emotionally, physically, and spiritually causes us to crash.

High emotion, even positive emotion, is not sustainable. Eventually, we must come back down to an emotional baseline, or the pendulum swings in the opposite direction. Our bodies were made to move. Our muscles are built up through use, but overusing them can tear ligaments and cause other injuries. Our spirits are meant to be aligned with God's. When we step out of alignment and into our own strength, we open ourselves up to spiritual attacks from the enemy. This can impact our total well-being.

Elijah burned out and crashed hard. In 1 Kings 19:4, we find him huddled up under a bush and asking God to let him die. He was ready to give up! But God had plans for Elijah. He gave him rest and refreshment, restoration and renewal. And then God reignited Elijah's fire so he would burn brightly in His strength alone.

Are you feeling burned out? Step into God's perfect rest and let Him reignite your dwindling fire with His.

God, my fire grows dim. I'm exhausted, tired of fighting. Give me Your perfect rest. Restore my soul and reignite my spirit's fire with Your Holy Spirit fire. Make me burn for You alone. Amen.

Therefore I tell you, do not worry about your life, what you will eat or drink; or about your body, what you will wear. Is not life more than food, and the body more than clothes?
—Matthew 6:25

When it came to the issue of anxiety, Jesus was pretty direct. He said, *"Do not worry"* (Matthew 6:25), or *"Do not be anxious"* (ESV). These were more than suggestions; they were commands. He represented God's heart well in this area because He knew that anxiety is both unhelpful and destructive. Jesus only ever did and said what the Father was doing and saying. (See John 5:19; 8:28.)

For people who struggle with chronic anxiety, Matthew 6:25 can be especially challenging. Jesus never intended for people to hear or read His words and feel shame or condemnation for not being able to shake anxiety. He was speaking into existence the truth that we can all align our hearts with and heal. Anxiety was defeated, along with sin, when Jesus died on the cross. It has no authority over us unless we choose it—or unless we are still in bondage to it.

Coming into alignment with this truth is something most of us will spend the rest of our lives learning how to believe. For some, it requires deep trauma healing. For others, it takes mindfulness. For all of us, it requires suspending disbelief for even a moment.

When you feel anxious, take it to your Father. His consolation will bring joy to your soul (see Psalm 94:19) that transcends your circumstances.

God is never anxious. He is always in control and always available to comfort you in your moments of worry. He knows where your food, housing, clothing, and support will come from because He is the source of it all. Jehovah Jireh, your Provider, will take care of you and give you everything you need.

God, when the anxiety of life swirls, fill me with Your peace. Remind me who You are and who I am in You. Ease my worry and teach me to tap into my full kingdom inheritance now. Amen.

May 12: CO-LABORING WITH GOD

For we are co-workers in God's service; you are God's field, God's building.
—1 Corinthians 3:9

As believers, we're called to live a life of love and service that looks like the one Jesus lived. (See Ephesians 2:10.) We're not saved by the work we do, but the work we do with one another and with God really does matter. Like getting sober, getting saved is the first step on a lifelong journey. When we accept Jesus, we accept a call to co-labor with God, in Christ, by the power of the Holy Spirit. Not because we have to, but because we're one with God, and our spirit can't be at peace unless we're aligned with him.

You are called to help do God's will on earth, not because you've earned the right or are exceptional at what you do, but because He chose you and has appointed you to do incredible things in His name. You may have already sensed God's call on your life. Or maybe you're afraid to ask. Rest assured, God's will *will* be done. He doesn't just call the equipped; He equips the called, and He will equip you too.

You're being invited to go on a lifelong adventure with your good Father God, sharing the good news of His grace with the whole world. Take a moment to pray and reflect. What would God like to do with you, in you, and through you in this season? What excuses, if any, have you been leaning on instead of Him? In what areas of your life have you not yet fully surrendered to what He's asked of you? This is your moment to give Him your *yes* and step into the beautiful privilege of working with your Creator.

God, Your plans for my life seem overwhelming sometimes. Speak to me clearly so I can give You my best yes. Teach me to work alongside You with Your strength and wisdom to guide me. Amen.

May 13: RESTORE

There remains, then, a Sabbath-rest for the people of God; for anyone who enters God's rest also rests from their works, just as God did from his.
—Hebrews 4:9–10

After creation, God did a curious thing: *"He rested"* (Genesis 2:2). Not because He was tired, but because He wanted to put on display a natural rhythm intended to help His people survive and thrive. This holy, intentional rest became part of the Law as Sabbath, which was fulfilled in the person of Jesus, who was God Himself.

Jesus rested, too—partly because His humanity demanded it, but also because His Father in heaven commanded it. Jesus brought us into a deeper understanding of what Sabbath rest really is. He proved it was less about a specific day of the week or lack of activity and more about restoring and preserving a deep spiritual connection with God. The funny part is, Jesus often took this rest at times that seemed very inopportune to the disciples. When the masses were waiting on healing, even in the middle of a raging storm, Jesus never missed an opportunity to get away with His Father and take a nap!

This concept can be difficult to grasp for those of us in recovery. There is so much work to do, so much healing to find, so much vigilance required. We believe the lie that rest is for the weak, and we press hard into our journeys to the point of burnout. This is when we make ourselves vulnerable to relapse, into old ways of thinking and behaving, because we simply don't have the mental, physical, and emotional energy to stay sharp.

Take a cue from God Himself. Make rest a priority because it's important to Him. Take time to get away to be with Him today, even for just ten minutes, to rest, recharge, reconnect, and restore your soul. Be refreshed in the glory of taking intentional time away from work to be with Him.

God, forgive me for not making Your Sabbath rest a priority. Teach me Your ways. Show me opportunities in my day where I can steal away with You and get lost in Your restoring love. Amen.

May 14: REJUVENATING REST

But he said to me, "My grace is sufficient for you, for my power is made perfect in weakness." Therefore I will boast all the more gladly about my weaknesses, so that Christ's power may rest on me.
—2 Corinthians 12:9

When was the last time you found real rest? Not just sleep or a twelve-hour Netflix binge, but rest that rejuvenated your body, mind, and soul? Rest that didn't just get you back to baseline, but gave you strength for the days ahead?

Those of us in recovery can become so consumed with *working the program* that we forget real rest is actually necessary, and rejuvenation is actually possible. There's always more healing and growth available. But we were never meant to receive it all at once, nor were we ever told to keep striving without ceasing until we have it all. Quite the opposite.

God's natural rhythms of rest remind us that we can be weak and that's fine. In fact, there are times when God would strongly prefer us to be weak because it's in a place of surrender that His power can be made perfect in our lives. Paul knew it when he wrote his second letter to the church in Corinth, and his words ring true for you today. When we are weak, He is strong. (See 2 Corinthians 12:10.)

You don't have to do it all. In fact, you can't, so stop trying. Embrace the fullness of your humanity and surrender your desires to be perceived as strong, competent, and capable. Receive the fullness of God's rest, and let His power rejuvenate you and empower you for the call on your life.

God, sometimes I'm afraid to rest. I don't want to miss what You're doing or let my guard down. Help me learn to lean on Your power, provision, and protection as You rejuvenate my soul. Amen.

May 15: COMPASSION VS. CODEPENDENCE

Each one should test their own actions. Then they can take pride in themselves alone, without comparing themselves to someone else, for each one should carry their own load.
—Galatians 6:4–5

People who are called to love and lead others through recovery have their work cut out for them. Making yourself available to someone in need is critical to building the authentic recovery community we all want to see, but it can take a toll physically, mentally, emotionally, and more. Compassion fatigue is a very real concept, but only because we have yet to learn how to do community well.

No one person can be responsible for any other person's recovery. Period. Not a parent, not a spouse, not a best friend, not even a pastor or counselor. Many who are moved with compassion to help also struggle with codependency, which at its simplest level is an addiction to people. If someone we care about isn't okay, we're not okay either, so we go above and beyond, straight into burnout. Their relapse becomes our relapse. Their trauma becomes our trauma. And so on.

The fine line between compassion and codependence is worth exploring in your own life. Maybe you're the only person a struggling person feels like they confide in…and you secretly love that. Perhaps you're someone who will bail a friend out when no one else will…perhaps when no one should. Or maybe you're the one who resents your peers for not doing more to help…when you've never actually invited them in to help.

If this sounds like you, pause and reflect in prayer. Ask the Father to clarify your call. What's working? What's not working? What more, if anything, would He have you do? His answer will equip you for the call and restore your mind, body, and soul to walk with people in recovery for the long haul.

God, help me remember that You're God and I'm not. When I slip into a martyr complex as I try to help people, please show me a better way—Your Way. Help me foster healthy community. Amen.

May 16: ABLE-BODIED

Do you not know that your bodies are temples of the Holy Spirit, who is in you, whom you have received from God? You are not your own; you were bought at a price. Therefore honor God with your bodies.
—1 Corinthians 6:19–20

Bodies are funny things. We're spiritual beings, housed in temporary vessels of flesh, blood, muscle, and bone, crafted in the image and likeness of God. Why are bodies necessary to the human experience? Why do we feel, grow, and age? Why are some bodies deemed more valuable than others? And the age-old question: Did Adam and Eve have belly buttons?

The simple yet somewhat unsatisfying answer is this: We have bodies because God wanted us to. And those bodies aren't just random skin sacks, disposable upon death for a new one. Our bodies are a gift from God, meant to glorify God through good works birthed from grace alone. But we pervert this concept by thinking entirely too much or entirely too little about our own bodies and the bodies of others.

How you think about and treat your own body is a critical place to begin. Do you care for your temple by filling it with good foods and water, exercising, and avoiding substances that would harm your health? Do you think too highly of your physical appearance, or too little of it? Are you kind to your body, even in how you speak of it, as you would be to the body of a friend? This is the essence of body self-care—preserving and protecting your temple so you'll be able-bodied to carry out God's call on your life.

Consider your current season of life. How are you being called to care for your body through recovery, parenting, leadership, friendship, and more? Are you treating your body as the gift it is? Why or why not? Accept the Father's invitation today to see your body as a temple of the Most High, a place where the Holy Spirit lives.

God, forgive me for the times I think too much or too little about the body You gave me. Thank You for the gift of this temple. Help me care for it and honor it in a way that honors You. Amen.

May 17: SOUL-CARE

May God himself, the God of peace, sanctify you through and through. May your whole spirit, soul and body be kept blameless at the coming of our Lord Jesus Christ.
—1 Thessalonians 5:23

The soul is a controversial topic. What it is, where it comes from, whether it matters, and whether it's even real are common topics in post-modern culture. The true soul is a spiritual identity given by God the Father to us, His beloved children. That identity manifests in your thoughts, feelings, and emotions—an inner-being that will last for eternity.

Here's the wild part: Self-care couldn't be more acceptable and popular right now. We know treating our bodies with care and compassion will improve our health and well-being. But while our physical bodies will fade, our souls will live on forever. To tap into the fullness of our God-given identities, we must also engage in soul-care on a daily basis.

Is your soul weary? Are your anxious thoughts getting the better of you? Is your wounded past part of your current reality? Heed the words of Jesus, the restorer of your soul:

Come to me, all you who are weary and burdened, and I will give you rest.
Take my yoke upon you and learn from me, for I am gentle and humble
in heart, and you will find rest for your souls.   (Matthew 11:28–29)

The need for soul-care is dire, especially in recovery circles. Beyond spiritual practices such as prayer, meditation, and Scripture study, soul-care is necessary for trauma healing to take place. God gave us an identity, but this fallen world has warped our perspective of it, making the soul a product of both divine origin and personal experience. Ultimately, what God says about who we are is truth. But we will spend the rest of our lives trying to align our hearts, minds, souls, and wills to His truth.

God, I want my soul anchored in You. I come against lies from the enemy that say my soul is damaged goods. In Jesus's name,. restore my soul, God. Bring me back to who I am in You. Amen.

May 18: HEART-WORK

Create in me a pure heart, O God, and renew a steadfast spirit within me.
—Psalm 51:10

Your heart, figuratively speaking, is basically your second brain. Separate from the soul, which is anchored in God's truth about your identity, your heart can be easily swayed by emotion and can lead you to do things that make no logical sense, for better or for worse. Scripture says, *"The heart is deceitful above all things"* (Jeremiah 17:9), but when aligned with God's purposes, it can be a guide that leads you to better understand the heart and character of the Father.

God wants to give us the desires of our hearts. What's more, He wants our desires to be His desires, our thoughts to be His thoughts, and our plans to be His plans. When we set our minds on things above, we can come into agreement with God's will. However, this practice can fall flat when our heart-work still needs a little soul-care.

When we carry unprocessed trauma and deep wounds in need of healing, God's desires can seem unattractive at best, unfair at worst. This is when we know there is more healing to be found. If we know who we are and don't act accordingly, it's a heart issue. But when we don't know who we are and act accordingly, it's a soul issue. Both require grace upon grace, from God and from us.

What heart work might God be calling you to today? Is there any part of His truth or His call on your life that you resist, even though you know your identity is secure? Spend time with Him today and ask why. He loves to see His kids do the hard heart work that allows Him to restore souls.

God, I know Your ways are better than mine. But sometimes I struggle to desire the things You desire. Help me think and act more like a member of the kingdom family I belong to. Amen.

May 19: YOUR MIND, SET

Do not conform to the pattern of this world, but be transformed by the renewing of your mind. Then you will be able to test and approve what God's will is—his good, pleasing and perfect will.
—Romans 12:2

More so than years or life seasons, our minds establish our true age. The mind, a supernatural product of the physical brain, is continually building new roadmaps based on knowledge, experiences, and above all our willingness to stay curious. This is the difference between a fixed mindset and a growth mindset; the former leads to vicious cycling, while the latter leads to life transformation.

A *fixed mindset* assumes people never change. Our intellect, our creativity, our resilience, and even our personality are believed to be both static and given. The only way people with a fixed mindset can hope to find success is through endless striving toward lofty, set standards. This common all-or-nothing mindset is detrimental to healing and personal growth, especially for people in recovery. A *growth mindset*, on the other hand, assumes people can and do change. Failure isn't seen as fatal, but as an opportunity to stretch, grow, and course correct.

When we become rigid and set in our ways from a mindset standpoint, we age both physically and mentally. Our brain's neuropathways become hardened and worn, and our mind becomes too weary to explore a new roadmap. We literally die off, often far sooner than necessary, leaving us grumpy and ineffective for the kingdom. We must continually be transformed by the renewing of our minds so we can hear from God and align with His will.

No matter your age, stage, or season, you are His—mind, body, and spirit.

God, I want to please You and set my mind on the things You care about. Forgive me for when I resist the change You want to bring. Renew my mind and restore my youth so I can serve You. Amen.

May 20: WILL AND POWER

Father, if you are willing, take this cup from me; yet not my will,
but yours be done.
—Luke 22:42

Willpower is a powerful concept for people in recovery. Surrendering our will to the Father's will is nothing new; Jesus explained that it is part of how we're meant to pray to God in the first place: "*Your kingdom come, **your will be done**, on earth as it is in heaven*" (Matthew 6:10). But actually walking it out is much trickier than it sounds in our best moments of surrender.

Those of us in recovery have more control over our wills than we think, but we don't always understand how our wills work. A will is a part of the mind, along with reason and understanding, but it can be exhausted quickly when we fail to create life patterns to support it. We set out with a new desire for our life, but at the first test of will, we find ourselves tired, lonely, hungry, shaky, and desperate. We might expect the will to falter in extreme cases, such as when we stay up for days on end or go without food for extended periods. But the neurological premise is the same for people in recovery. Our wills are already tired, so even normal situations seem extreme.

The best part of the will is that it can be strengthened over time. By aligning with God's perfect will and plan for our lives, we can create intentional life patterns that lead us in pathways of righteousness and freedom.

Enlist the help of your heavenly Father in defining new patterns for your life that keep you away from your struggles and closer to Him.

God, search me. Bring to light any way that my will hurts me and, by proxy, hurts You. Show me what to let go of, how to let go of it, and give me a new, better pattern to follow. Amen.

The tongue has the power of life and death,
and those who love it will eat its fruit.
—Proverbs 18:21

For better or worse, there's a lot of power in your tongue. The words you speak over yourself and others can mean abundant life or certain death, which is why understanding declarations is such an important concept in recovery. Declarations put what you truly believe about yourself and others on display for agreement.

Sometimes those declarations are prophetic in nature, aligned with what our good Father God says about us in Scripture. *You're forgiven. You're worthy. Your life has value. You're so much more than what you do.* These declarations can be difficult to believe at first, but speaking them in truth builds faith.

But sometimes our declarations can be downright demonic, counter to the true heart of the Father. *You're just an addict. You're damaged goods. The world would be better without you. You're not worthy of love from God—or from anyone, for that matter.* Sadly, these demonic declarations can be the stickiest and the most challenging to come against in Jesus's name.

Those of us in recovery must declare the truth of our identity over ourselves—daily or even hourly, if that's what it takes.

Trade any old demonic declarations or limiting beliefs you've partnered with and exchange them for the hope-filled, grace-laced truth about who you are in Christ. You are beloved, accepted, safe, seen, heard, loved, forgiven, alive, and free, whether your body, soul, heart, mind, or will believe it yet or not. The power of your words can bring you from death to life in Jesus's name. Speak God's truth over yourself today and ask the Father who else might need the blessing of your words over them.

God, I want my thoughts and my words to be pleasing to You. Help me speak truth in love to myself and others and declare Your grace over lives and hearts in Jesus's name—including mine! Amen.

What a wretched man I am! Who will rescue me from this body that is subject to death?
—Romans 7:24

Most of the things we think and say about ourselves are greatly exaggerated. Just ask the apostle Paul, who tells the church in Rome that he's *"a wretched man"* in need of rescue. Before Paul became a follower of Jesus, he was Saul—a religious zealot who persecuted and murdered Christians. He was *personally* responsible for the death of the first martyr, Stephen. He was determined to do whatever it took to stop the church from growing and preventing the message of Jesus's death and resurrection from spreading.

This sounds like some pretty wretched behavior for sure. But Saul stood by his early convictions. He believed Jesus to be a liar and a fraud, and he thought God was being misrepresented. So he went right on being wretched until he had a profound encounter with Jesus on the road to Damascus. (See Acts 9:3–8.) It would have been quite the understatement for Saul to say, "I once was blind but now I see." He was given a new life and a new name, no strings of shame attached.

Why, then, did Paul refer to his healed, forgiven self as *"wretched"* when he wrote to Rome? The answer requires a bit of literary prowess—and sadly, much of the church has missed his point. Paul spoke to the church allegorically, telling the dramatic story of who he once was and who he had become. After calling himself wretched and in need of rescue, he responds immediately with the resolution: *"Thanks be to God, who delivers me through Jesus Christ our Lord!"* (Romans 7:25). He is no longer Saul, slave to sin. He is Paul, a man set free from the law of sin and death!

Resist the urge to demonstrate humility through negative self-talk. Whether you think it or say it aloud, in time, you'll believe it's true. If you think you're nothing more than a sinner, you'll keep sinning. But if you receive God's grace and speak of yourself as the forgiven and free child of God you are, you'll start thinking, acting, and believing it's true.

God, help me remember I'm a new creation. I'm no longer a slave to my sin; Jesus took care of it on the cross! Thank You for taking me from wretchedness to righteousness. Amen.

May 23: THE RIGHT TO SAY "NO"

All you need to say is simply "Yes" or "No";
anything beyond this comes from the evil one.
—Matthew 5:37

Recovery is for everyone. And as someone in recovery, it's important for you to reclaim agency and right over your own life. You live under the mercy of God the Father and yourself, which means you're not obligated to walk out your recovery journey for anyone else. This truth manifests in your God-given right to say *no*.

Jesus had a lot to say about *yes* and *no*. He loved storytelling and delivered the most powerful one-liners the world has ever received. But He wasn't one for fluff. Any extra speech or over-the-top promises indicated a higher probability that people would waver on their word, so He lovingly encouraged people to keep things simple and just say what they mean.

As we put our lives back together in recovery, the right to say *no* has to be one of the first things we claim. Otherwise, we'll be saying *yes* and *no* from unhealthy places, and when that happens, we begin to agree to things that will keep us from a promised-land life.

"No" is a complete sentence. No follow-up required. Being able to say it, to ourselves and others, is critical in creating the space and time necessary to heal from trauma. Saying no to that next drink or bump. Saying no to unreasonable or obligatory requests. Saying no to the lies of the enemy so we can say yes to God's truth. "No" becomes a powerful conduit to a promised-land life that's worth living—and worth staying sober for.

God, forgive me when I say yes to things I shouldn't. I know giving You my all will mean a hard pass on the things of this world. Help me stay vigilant and save my best yeses for You. Amen.

May 24: THE POWER OF "YES"

Above all, my brothers and sisters, do not swear—not by heaven or by
earth or by anything else. All you need to say is a simple "Yes" or "No."
—James 5:12

I (George) have a confession to make: Growing up, I used to think passages of Scripture that say, "Do not swear" were telling Jesus's followers they shouldn't cuss. In maturity, I know foul language isn't exactly becoming of Christians, but I also now know that under grace, it's possible to love Jesus and cuss a little. At least I certainly hope it is!

More interesting than oaths and George Carlin's list of things you can't say on TV, James's suggestion for what to say otherwise is pure and simple: *yes* or *no*. Not, "Yes, but…" or, "No, if…" Simply *yes* or *no*. The power to speak them clearly and plainly allows us to give our best yeses to God and say no to anything that doesn't align with His will.

The fact that God allows His children to say yes and no is astounding. Who are we to say no to the Creator of the universe? And yet, unfathomably, God in His sovereignty, power, and dominion is also a gentleman. He won't force us to say yes; He gives us free will to choose. It's a grace we don't deserve, almost as powerful as the grace that still covers us when we say no to God and yes to anything that isn't Him.

Whether you're walking out your own recovery journey or loving and leading someone through theirs, go ahead and give God your "yes to all." Position your heart to hear from Him and serve Him, whatever He may ask of you. God loves an open, willing heart, and He will empower your yes to bear great fruit for His kingdom.

God, You can have my "yes to all." Forgive me for my slow obedience. Make me quick to listen and even quicker to move when You call. I'll say no anything that keeps me from You. Amen.

May 25: HELP, ON THE WAY

I lift up my eyes to the mountains—where does my help come from? My help comes from the LORD, the Maker of heaven and earth.
—Psalm 121:1–2

Asking for help during your recovery process can be incredibly difficult. Perhaps it's because most traditional recovery programming focuses on what's known as *bootstrapping,* a military term that refers to pulling oneself up by the bootstraps and trying harder.

While bootstrapping can do wonders for resilience, it can also lead us to believe that we're on our own. For some, asking for help is basically admitting defeat, and our pride, not to mention our anonymity, keeps us in bondage to our struggles. The sad reality is, people *can* over-ask for help. Those who have been on the receiving end of this are often the ones who don't want to apply the same disregard for boundaries to someone else. But we were created for relationship. We're meant to *"carry each other's burdens"* (Galatians 6:2) and be the iron that sharpens iron (see Proverbs 27:17) when our brothers and sisters are struggling. Somewhere along our recovery journey, things are bound to go wrong. And when they inevitably do, we need to learn to be humble enough to ask for help when we really need it.

If this concept makes you cringe, practice by starting small. Ask for help with a simple task, such as holding the door, unloading the car, or even asking for prayer. Work your way up to the bigger asks—accountability, childcare, job references, and more. You will need people to walk with on your journey to a promised-land life. The best part? You might get to help others too.

Asking for help is an act of vulnerability. You may told "no" now and then, and that's all right. Respect boundaries, adjust your expectations, and remember Who your help really comes from.

God, You are my Helper. Give me courage to ask people for help in the natural. Remind me that I'm not meant to walk alone. Help me see beyond my own need for help to help others too. Amen.

May 26: INTERNAL NARRATIVES

"For my thoughts are not your thoughts, neither are your ways my ways,"
declares the LORD. "As the heavens are higher than the earth, so are my
ways higher than your ways and my thoughts than your thoughts."
—Isaiah 55:8–9

Do you ever think about how you think? Some people have verbal internal narratives in which they actually *hear* sentences in their heads. Others have abstract, nonverbal thoughts.

The funny thing is, we're typically not aware that the other type of person exists.

Similarly, we are all capable of *hearing* from God. Some of us hear in sentences. Some even hear an audible voice. Others sense feelings of His presence or a natural Spirit-led intuition. Some are even able to recognize thoughts, ideas, or desires that are so good, they *had* to come from the Father because we could never be so good on our own.

Considering whether you have a verbal internal narrative or a nonverbal one can help you hear more clearly from God. It can also help you discern voices that are clearly *not* God—your own voice, or even the voice of enemy. The voice you hear or the sense you have can impact the way you feel, so it's important to learn to determine the origin of your thoughts.

When was the last time you were certain you heard from God, verbal or nonverbal? When was the last time you heard a voice or had a thought that certainly wasn't God? Explore the verbal and nonverbal narratives you've encountered. Were they calm? Compassionate? Full of grace and love? Or were they urgent, condemning, unforgiving, and hateful? If they were any of the latter, it's time to take them captive and make them obedient to Christ.

God, thank You for making me unique and capable of hearing You in unique ways! Help me learn my own internal narratives so I can align my thoughts with Yours and dismiss the enemy's lies. Amen.

May 27: CORE BELIEFS

Anyone who believes in him will never be put to shame.
—Romans 10:11

What do you believe? Deep in the core of your being, what beliefs guide and sustain you throughout life's journey?

Most people will insist that they have core beliefs, but few can actually list them. Believers in Jesus might simplify the idea by saying, "Well, I'm Christian, so I believe what Christians believe." And yet the diversity of Scripture interpretation, epistemology, and overall theology in the church might suggest that we Christians haven't really done our homework when it comes to core beliefs.

Core beliefs are strongly held and rarely flexible axioms that cannot be shaken, even in the face of overwhelming evidence to the contrary. The beliefs might be simple—God is good; I am forgiven; recovery is possible. Or they might be complex—I'm an addict and always will be; I'm a horrible sinner, and God is mad at me; I am unlovable and unforgivable. Whatever we choose as our core beliefs, guess what? We will walk them out in faith, even if we're not aware they exist.

One of the most beautiful aspects of working with a Christian counselor or therapist is creating space to uncover and articulate your core beliefs and ask yourself if they align with God's truth. When you confront a core belief that doesn't align, you uncover an opportunity for deeper trauma healing. You can take an honest assessment of your belief systems and ask yourself if you're really walking out the abundant life Jesus died for you to have. Take time today to consider your core beliefs. Do they reflect who God says you are—who you were created to be?

God, search me. Are there any core beliefs I carry that aren't aligned with Your heart? Reveal them to me and exchange them with Your truth. Show me beliefs that make me doubt my doubts. Amen.

May 28: CORE LONGINGS

My soul yearns for you in the night; in the morning my spirit longs for you. When your judgments come upon the earth, the people of the world learn righteousness.
—Isaiah 26:9

What do you long for? Beneath material possessions, career aspirations, or relationship success, what drives those longings? It may surprise you to learn that although your specific desires may be unique, the longings those desires would potentially fulfill are the same for every individual.

All humans have innate core longings to be loved, secure, significant, accepted, understood, and purposeful. These longings were instilled by God, our Creator, as longings that only He can ultimately satisfy.

All of the accolades on earth can't compare to the satisfaction that comes with relying on the Father to help you fulfill those longings—not because of anything you've done, but because of what He has done for you. Your only response is to give Him your resounding *yes* and make Him Lord of your life.

Ask yourself honestly. Where are you searching for fulfillment of your core longings other than with God? Where are you looking for love and is it a healthy place? What makes you feel secure, and are you really? What makes you feel significant, like you matter? What makes you feel accepted, and are you really? In what ways do you feel misunderstood and why? Are you living a life that has purpose and meaning, or just letting life happen to you?

Take your answers to God. Ask Him to replace any earthly idols you've put before Him and any places where you're seeking affirmation that matters more to you than His.

God, forgive me for trying to fill my being with anything that's not You. Help me put You first always, seeking Your affirmation alone to satisfy my longings. The only important audience in my life is You. Amen.

May 29: INHERITANCE NOW

Giving joyful thanks to the Father, who has qualified you to share in the inheritance of his holy people in the kingdom of light.
—Colossians 1:12

When Jesus died on the cross, something incredible happened. We're not just talking about the resurrection, even though that was pretty miraculous. We're not just talking about Him defeating sin and death forever, although that was pretty amazing too. The wildest truth about what happened on the cross of Jesus is that when He died, we died with Him.

Now, you might be thinking, *Wait, how can that be true? Jesus died and rose again two millennia ago. I wasn't even born yet—how could I have died with Him?* Suspend disbelief for just a moment and lean into the beauty of Scripture. When Paul wrote to the church in Rome, he explained the mystery of our new union with Jesus, made possible because Jesus defeated the old law of sin and death. (See Romans 8:2.) Later, he explained:

> *Now if we are children, then we are heirs—heirs of God and co-heirs with Christ, if indeed we share in his sufferings in order that we may also share in his glory.* (Romans 8:17)

Are you catching the magnitude of Paul's words? There's not some grand inheritance that's only accessible to you when you die and go to heaven. You're seated with Christ in heavenly places right now. (See Ephesians 2:6.) You have access to the fullness of your kingdom inheritance to do the work of the Father in this world at this very moment!

Your eternal life started the moment you said yes to Jesus. It's something you literally can't mess up. God doesn't care if you've been twenty years' sober or if you relapsed yesterday; He calls you His beloved child, and your inheritance is waiting—being one with God, in Christ, by the power of the Holy Spirit. Receive His truth today and explore what your life might look like if you walked it out.

God, sometimes I don't feel worthy of You. And yet, You call me beloved, and You give me the keys to Your kingdom. Your grace amazes me! Thank You for loving me like You do. Amen.

May 30: STUMBLING BROTHERS

Do not destroy the work of God for the sake of food. All food is clean, but it is wrong for a person to eat anything that causes someone else to stumble. It is better not to eat meat or drink wine or to do anything else that will cause your brother or sister to fall.
—Romans 14:20–21

In Paul's day, newly converted Christians were coming off of generations of religious legalism. One of the most shocking cultural shifts had to do with food and drink. Paul explained to them that formerly forbidden foods were no longer *unclean* as the old law said. All food was now permissible...but not all food, drink, or behavior was edifying.

Paul's point? It wasn't really about food. Paul wanted new believers to understand that some people struggle in ways that others don't—and we need to exercise caution in loving and leading those around us.

Would you serve wine with dinner in the presence of an alcoholic family member? Would you take someone who struggled with pornography to an R-rated movie that contained nudity? Would you bring pastries or candy to share with someone who struggled with sugar addiction? If you would do any of these, it's time to repent. Even if a food, drink, or activity might not cause *you* to stumble and fall, it could mean life or death to someone else.

If you feel tempted to cling to something out of religious freedom as some kind of inalienable right, ask God to break your heart. Be willing to lay down your wine, your racy movie, your sweet treats, or whatever else keeps you from loving people like Jesus. Be willing to make safe spaces for your community to grow and thrive free from temptation. Outdo yourself by learning new ways to love and honor someone else's recovery journey.

God, help me stay sensitive to Your spirit. If something is fine for me but unsafe for someone else, make it clear and give me strength to lay it all down for my brother—even my life. Amen.

May 31: LEARN TO DISCERN

Do not be conformed to this world, but be transformed by the renewal of your mind, that by testing you may discern what is the will of God, what is good and acceptable and perfect.
—Romans 12:2 (ESV)

If you're a believer in Jesus, you're a new creation. More than an external transformation, your old self is dead, and a new, reborn self now lives—a self that has the mind of Christ. And that renewed mind is still trying to understand the transformation that's happened.

We're saved and being saved. We're perfect and being made perfect. We're renewed and being renewed. This progressive healing proves that sometimes it takes the mind a little longer than the heart to receive the full transformative power of the gospel.

Consider for a moment, why did God choose to renew our minds? To keep us from wanting to sin? To keep us under control? To keep us from bad behavior that would embarrass the church? Far from it. God renewed our minds so that we could learn to discern. Discernment is simply our ability to recognize what is of God and what is not. When we apply our renewed minds to complicated moral circumstances, we will have the mind of Christ as we love, lead, and teach people to follow God.

If you're a believer and you're still struggling, you may be wondering where your renewed mind is. You aren't the first to wonder! Just as initial salvation and initial sobriety are the first steps on lifelong journeys, it will take time to learn to access and use the God-given discernment gifts within your renewed mind.

Start small. When a thought invades that you know is wrong or contrary to what God's Word says about you, pause for a moment. Take that thought captive, name it as "not of God," and ask Jesus to take it from you. *"Take captive every thought to make it obedient to Christ"* (2 Corinthians 10:5). This spiritual practice will train your new brain to think like God thinks, not like your old dead self.

God, help me stay on high alert for any thoughts I have that don't align with Yours. I want to learn to use my renewed mind so I can hear You clearly. Give me the mind of Jesus. Amen.

June

RE**LATIONSHIP**

Humble yourselves before the Lord, and he will lift you up.
—James 4:10

June 1: ZOWEH

When Jesus spoke again to the people, he said, "I am the light of the world. Whoever follows me will never walk in darkness, but will have the light of life."
—John 8:12

In case you're wondering if we kicked off June with a big typo, think again. *Zoweh* is a word that originates from two different ancient languages: the Greek word *zoe*, which means "life," and the Hebrew word *Yahweh*, meaning "God." Zoweh is an invitation into God-life—a quality of life that's out of this world.

A Zoweh life is fully connected to God, running *with* God and running *on* God. It's a life that's sustained, protected, and provided for by Him alone. We were all made for this life and to live in the light of it. And when we walk in *"the light of life"* by following the way of Jesus, we get to tap into a life where our good Father God handles all of the arrangements. Our families, our careers, our relationships—He has a plan in mind for us.

If God planning your life gives you pause, keep in mind, He's *much* better at it than you are. His ways are always better than your ways, even in the times and seasons when you don't yet understand what He's doing. Letting the light of Jesus transform your life from the inside out will help you trust God more fully and submit to His will for you.

When you walk with Jesus, the light of the world, you'll never walk in darkness again. Open your eyes to see the goodness of His glory. Open your heart to receive the fullness of His love. Open your mind to grasp the beauty of His Zoweh, your everlasting God-life, and be transformed.

God, You are my light and life. You know the way, and You prove it time and again. Help me look to You in times of darkness and uncertainty and cling to the Zoweh only You can bring. Amen.

June 2: REDEMPTIVE FRIENDSHIPS

A friend loves at all times, and a brother is born for a time of adversity.
—Proverbs 17:17

When God created man, He knew it wasn't good for him to be alone. So He created a woman to be his perfect match, a unique soul to do life with. Now, for practical purposes, God made Adam and Eve to populate the earth with even more people, not just to create more husband-and-wife teams, but to create friendships and communities. It's not good for man to be alone (see Genesis 2:18), but this truth transcends marital relationships. Humans were created for relationship—with one another and with God Himself.

For people who struggle with addiction, mental health problems, and thoughts of suicide, friendships can be extremely complicated. When we don't feel seen, heard, or loved, by choice or by chance, it strains relationships, sometimes to the breaking point. Our struggles will inevitably impact people who share close proximity, which is why God wants to bring healing and redemption to every life and every relationship. Because human relationships, broken as they may be, are the closest earthly representation we have to our sacred covenant with God Himself.

No matter how broken a relationship may be, restoration is possible with two willing parties and the Holy Spirit in the mix. Traditional recovery programming calls participants to make amends where safe, and we must. But moreover, we must receive grace and forgiveness over our own lives so we can extend that same grace and forgiveness to others—and know how and when to ask for it when needed. This supernatural extension of grace is a reflection of God's glory.

God, it's humbling to know my struggles have negatively impacted my relationships. I can't bring restoration on my own, but I know You can. Make me humble enough to make things right. Amen.

June 3: INTO ME YOU SEE

Come near to God and he will come near to you. Wash your hands, you sinners, and purify your hearts, you double-minded.
—James 4:8

Intimacy with God is readily available to us. Right now. God has promised that He will not only be *with* us but *in* us by the power of the Holy Spirit. Nothing will ever separate us from His love. That invitation to intimacy can put our faith to the test more than just about anything else. (See James 1:2–4.)

Intimacy is the experience of knowing and being known. Intimacy with God transcends emotion, logic, and physical barriers to allow us created beings to not just know about our Creator, but to truly know Him. Because He is holy and we are not (at least not on our own), human logic insists there must be distance and separation between us and God. God hates this idea; even now, He is reconciling the whole world back to Himself. (See 2 Corinthians 5:19.)

Intimacy requires trust, and trust requires experience. If you're just getting to know God as a good Father, it might be difficult to fathom how deeply He loves you. Any perceived distance between you and God is distance that you create. God is already all-in, inviting you to see how good He really is.

God already knows everything there is to know about you. He knows everything you've ever done, everything you have ever said, and every thought you've ever had. He sees deep into your soul—and He still wants you. He calls you now, saying, "Into Me, you see." Saying yes to His call to intimacy will bring even more than His nearness. It will reveal the truth of your oneness with God, in Christ, by the power of the Holy Spirit. You're one with your Creator. He sees you, knows you, and loves you. See Him. Know Him. Love Him.

God, how could You, my Creator, want to be in intimate relationship with me? It's more than I deserve! I receive Your love. Teach me to go deeper with You, to trust You fully. I love You. Amen.

June 4: MORE LOVE

We love because he first loved us.
—1 John 4:19

As people in recovery, walking out our own journeys and walking with others through theirs, we have a call to reflect what's called Trinitarian love. This godly love triangle represents the perfect love that God the Father has for Jesus and the Holy Spirit, even though they are all one God. In the same way, Jesus loves the Father and the Spirit, and the Spirit loves Jesus and the Father. We too are meant to love God as the Trinity, Father, Son, and Holy Spirit. The God we love commands us to love our neighbor and ourselves—another godly love triangle in the natural.

When we don't love God, neighbor, and self, a cognitive dissonance sets in. We begin to see love as conditional, something that must be continually earned and can be thrown away in a heartbeat. The world's love is utterly disposable, but the love of God, Love Himself, endures forever. (See Psalm 136.) It's a patient, kind, confident, humble love that's grace-laced and hope-filled. We are meant to put this kind of love on display to a world in desperate need of God.

Here's the wild part: God can't possibly love you any more or less than He already does. He loves you in fullness, in totality, because He *is* Love. He invented it, and He loves perfectly as a distinct character trait. Now we're not God, and we will struggle to love like He does. But Scripture proves that we are made in God's image and likeness and are therefore capable of loving like Him. We won't do it perfectly, nor will we be able to do it in our own strength. But with the Spirit of the living God flowing into and through us, we can show the world there's more love available to them than they ever imagined possible. When it comes to Love Himself, He's given it all—and there's always more love to receive.

God, I only have the capacity to love because You loved me first. Loving You requires loving people in a way that's supernatural. Help me receive more love from You so I can give it away. Amen.

June 5: MORE LIFE

And my God will meet all your needs according to the riches
of his glory in Christ Jesus.
—Philippians 4:19

If you ever find yourself wanting more out of life, you just might be human. This temporal, earthly existence just can't satisfy the way the abundant life God has for us does. We may already know this, but our ambitions can sometimes deceive us and make us chase after all kinds of idols—even things that look good on the surface, but deep down are distractions from the enemy.

There is more life to be had and enjoyed, but it's not of this world. The promised-land life Jesus died to give you has nothing to do with money, fame, success, or happiness from an earthly standpoint. The kingdom life He has for you is a life of joy and peace that *"transcends all understanding"* (Philippians 4:7). The foundations of the earth may shake, but you, my friend, will not be shaken. Because you're standing firm on God's promise: an abundant, eternal life in Him.

Your need for security? Let Him be it. Your longing for love? Let Him give it. Your desire for a life of purpose? Let Him lead it. You'll find God has more to offer you than this broken world could ever muster. And in the context of eternity, aligning your desire with His will do far more for the kingdom of God than your striving ever will. You'll pray, *on earth as it is in heaven,* and you'll bring the kingdom from heaven to earth in Jesus's name. There is more. And you'll find it in Him.

God, I want more of You. I know that means less of me and less of what this world has to offer. Help me see what's You and what's not so I can help Your kingdom come and Your will be done. Amen.

June 6: MORE FREEDOM

It is for freedom that Christ has set us free. Stand firm, then, and do not let yourselves be burdened again by a yoke of slavery.
—Galatians 5:1

Here's a truth to cling to for today: Jesus set us free so we could be free. Seems like a no-brainer, but many of us still don't get it. Sin? It's defeated. Death? It's no more. Our righteousness is restored, and our future is secure. Those pesky chains were broken off by the power of the Holy Spirit. So why do we keep picking them up and putting them back on again?

Try to tell a slave that they're not only free but family, and it's going to take more than words to prove it's true. It was true for the Israelites, even after God delivered them from four hundred years of slavery. And it's still true for us today. We carry the mindset of a captive or prisoner for far longer than necessary, and it extends our journey to the promised-land life God has for us.

Renewing your mind is a process that God is willing to walk with you for as long as it takes. But you're also going to need people on this journey to remind you that you're no longer in bondage. You're free. Not because you deserve it or did anything to earn it. You're free because Jesus set you free. And He set you free *for freedom*, not bondage.

John 8:36 insists that whoever the Son sets free is *"free indeed."* Who are we to say otherwise? Receive this gift of freedom today and learn to walk it out. When that old mindset begins to creep in, telling you to pick those chains up again, don't panic. Walk the truth out in faith and remind someone else how free they are. Hurt people hurt people. Healed people heal people. And free people *free people* when they do it in Jesus's name.

God, forgive me for the times I'm tempted to pick up my chains again: I am who You say I am—free indeed! Help me walk out this freedom in faith, and let my testimony free others. Amen.

June 7: INTIMATE COMMUNITIES

Every day they continued to meet together in the temple courts. They broke bread in their homes and ate together with glad and sincere hearts, praising God and enjoying the favor of all the people. And the Lord added to their number daily those who were being saved.
—Acts 2:46–47

Small groups are the go-to, staple solution for friendship, community, and spiritual formation in the modern church. Pastors and laypeople alike cite the Acts 2 church as the model for such community. The problem with these groups is that they often forget that the early church also allowed God to add to their numbers daily by extending the gospel to nonbelievers.

Consider small groups you've been in. Were you regularly inviting people who didn't know Jesus into that space, free of agenda? Were they received immediately, knowing they belonged even if they didn't believe? Were they given space to process, ask questions, and express doubts?

More often than not, we're afraid these kinds of interactions will disrupt the Christian fellowship that small groups can bring, so we stay with a tight-knit group of people who think, act, believe, and behave just like we do.

This was never the mode of Jesus. He built a community of people around Himself that aimed to exalt God among believers and unbelievers alike. Worshipping and enjoying God mattered more than anything else, and when new people came into the mix, Jesus met them right where they were. This can only happen in a safe place where people can feel fully seen, fully heard, and fully loved. To know and be known is the essence of true intimacy in Christ-centered communities.

Whether emotional, mental, spiritual, or physical, intimacy requires authenticity. We won't get closer or go deeper with God or other people without trust. This deep, vulnerable reality transcends systematized disciple-making. It requires a move of God and a movement of His people.

Stay authentic and invite people in, so you can grow in your knowledge and love of God together.

God, help me be the kind of authentic community I want to see. Stay close to me as I grow deeper in intimate friendships with Your people. Help Your church learn to love without limits. Amen.

June 8: ONENESS

On that day you will realize that I am in my Father, and you are in me, and I am in you.
—John 14:20

The church—and the world for that matter—loves to talk about unity. We're wired for alignment of thought, deed, and a shared existence on this earth. King David wrote, *"How good and pleasant it is when God's people live together in unity!"* (Psalm 133:1). But without a God-prescribed lens through which to see it, unity becomes uniformity in a heartbeat.

The kind of unity God desires for His church has little to do with assimilation. He celebrates diversity and welcomes sinners to walk with saints so they may be changed forever by His love. What God really wants for us isn't mere unity—it's union with our fellow brothers and sisters and Him. The mystery of this union is put plainly into today's Scripture verse, but we often gloss over Jesus's words, not grasping the depth of their meaning.

Try to wrap your mind around this: Jesus is one with the Father, which makes sense if you subscribe to the theology of the Trinity. You are one with Jesus, which makes sense if you believe you were co-crucified and are now a coheir with Him. Jesus is one with you, which makes sense because of the Holy Spirit living in you. But if Jesus is one with the Father, and you are one with Him, guess what? You are also one with God the Father—you are in

Him because the Spirit and the Son are in Him, and you are in them! This is mind-blowing! Here's the fun part: This oneness is not just for you. It's for every person Jesus died to save.

When we say *yes* to Jesus, we step into that place of oneness with Him—and every other believer who ever said yes to Him. We're all one, whether we want to believe it or not. We're all one because of what Jesus did for us. (See Galatians 3:28.) Welcome to the profound mystery of oneness.

God, thank You for coming in the flesh as Jesus to die for my sins and make me one with You. I may spend the rest of my life trying to understand it, but I'm so thankful for Your reckless grace! Amen.

June 9: EXTREME CONNECTEDNESS

I am the vine; you are the branches. If you remain in me and I in you, you will bear much fruit; apart from me you can do nothing.
—John 15:5

It's no secret we were created for connection. We're hardwired for it. Connectedness with God and with others is the key to thriving. At times, this level of attunement can be elevated, as in the case of mothers and their babies, husbands and wives, and other healthy work, ministry, discipling, and friend relationships in which the connection feels entirely supernatural. This connectedness to the extreme comes with people of peace, people who are open to going deeper and opening the door to the gospel.

Now just because a connection is strong doesn't mean it won't come with challenges. New mothers struggle to soothe their babies and meet their needs. Husbands and wives may fight, even in healthy marriages. Friends, colleagues, ministry partners, and those being mentored will experience misunderstanding. And yet these extreme connections transcend circumstance and proximity.

You don't just leave when it gets hard; you lean in—knowing bumps in the road, even the big ones, can be an opportunity for deep growth and even greater trust.

Pressing in and pressing through the tough times, especially for those of us in recovery, can mean life or death to a relationship. Some relationships must come to a natural end, especially those that feel like an extreme connection for all of the wrong reasons. But whenever possible, resist the urge to disconnect from deep, intimate, healthy relationships that have room for growth.

Connectedness is the heart of recovery. For true healing to be found, you will need people of peace in your life—ones who fully see you, fully know you, and fully love you anyway. Lean into what God is doing in your relationships today and ask Him for opportunities to go deeper, even if it's for the first time.

God, I need You. And I also need people. Where my relationships are strained, bring peace and healing. Where I need to let go, help me do so. Make me a conduit of Your grace and love. Amen.

June 10: CYCLE OF GRACE

If you forgive anyone's sins, their sins are forgiven; if you do not forgive them, they are not forgiven.
—John 20:23

Grace is part of a divine cycle. We can't give away what we haven't yet received, and we need to continually receive grace from God to continue to extend it to others. We can only follow the methods and modality of Grace Himself and pray we represent His heart in our grace-giving.

This cycle of grace—receiving, giving, and receiving again so we can give again—is critical for those in recovery. As we own our part in our life's journeys, we will inevitably find places where we've fallen short. We need grace. We will certainly identify traumatic experiences that leave others in need of grace and forgiveness, and there will be times when we need to ask for forgiveness, not just from God, but from other people. Unless we have truly received God's grace, believing that we're loved and forgiven, we will have an incredibly hard time giving grace to others.

The reality is, there are eternal consequences to our ability and willingness to give grace to others. John 20:23 implies that if we do not forgive others, they are not forgiven by God. Even in the worst circumstances, this isn't something we want to partner with! Conversely, if we choose to forgive, even when people don't deserve it—*especially* when they don't deserve it—we usher in the grace of the Father to transform their lives...and ours by proxy.

Embody the characteristics of grace. Love. Forgiveness. Humility. Empathy. Wisdom. Sometimes it looks like forgiving, even when relationships can't be restored. Sometimes it looks like healthy boundaries. And sometimes it looks like wild, unreasonable, reckless reconciliation that reflects the heart of the Father.

God, I receive Your grace. Fill me with enough to let it overflow to others who need it too. Your grace saved me, and now I want to help save people in Your name, by the power of Your grace. Amen.

June 11: CYCLE OF WORKS

For God will bring every deed into judgment, including every hidden thing, whether it is good or evil.
—Ecclesiastes 12:14

Logic and wisdom tell us that since God saved us, our only response must be to make Him Lord of our lives. In doing so, we submit ourselves to what God wants, and we do whatever He asks of us. We will be moved with compassion to do good works for the kingdom, and we will see the goodness of God in the land of the living. When the works are from God, reserved for us, they are very, very good.

But here's the hard part: Contrary to what some churchgoing folk might tell you, works can also be part of a vicious cycle that's straight from the pit of hell. The works God calls us to are meant to be a response to His goodness, not a prerequisite for it. Yet in our humanness—especially our individualized, Western humanness—we can be tempted to see our works as a pathway to salvation instead of a grateful response to it. We continue to try to earn what's already been freely given to us, over and over again, by grace.

This cycle of works keeps people in recovery in perpetual victimization mode. We cling to our labels and do penance for our sins, even though God hasn't asked us to. We do good works to earn God's favor, when we already have it. And in doing so, we say we know better than God—and the sin of pride keeps us from seeing and embracing our true identity in Him.

Whatever you do, do it for God's glory—your rest or your work, running the race or standing still. Whatever you do, do it from a place of gratitude and humility, knowing you could never earn the love God so eagerly gives to you.

God, I am sorry for the times I've tried to earn Your favor by doing good things. I know You love me, and I want You to use my willingness to work for You in holy and correct ways. Show me. Amen.

June 12: GOLDEN WORDS

The soothing tongue is a tree of life, but a perverse tongue crushes the spirit.
—Proverbs 15:4

You know your words matter, but do you know just how much? The words you speak over someone in recovery have the power to change their life, for better or for worse. There are golden words that take up root in our hearts and become the core of our identities.

You've likely heard a golden word, probably from someone you trusted, that shaped your identity, for better or worse. Maybe someone told you that you were a natural leader. Or perhaps they said you would never amount to anything. Maybe they told you that you are loved by God. Or perhaps they told you that you were hell-bound. Whatever these golden words were, they really stuck—and they either showed you the heart of the Father or the black heart of the enemy.

Golden words can be complicated in church circles. Prayers, platitudes, and prophetic words can also be helpful or harmful, knowing they come through other believers, who are the most broken of conduits at best. We speak truth, but we often don't do so in love. Or we try to be loving, but in trying, we withhold a difficult truth that perhaps needs to be articulated. This is where it's so critically important to ask the Holy Spirit to help us speak and listen, so our words can be aligned with God's heart. His timing is always perfect.

Spend time with the Father today and ask Him to reveal any golden words that have been spoken over your life. Ask Him which words to cling to as part of your God-given identity and which ones you need to let go of in order to relearn who you really are, who you were created to be.

God, forgive me for letting the words of others speak louder than Yours. Help me discern what's true and what's untrue, and give me the strength to walk in the identity You gave me. Amen.

June 13: FALSE HUMILITY

Do nothing out of selfish ambition or vain conceit.
—Philippians 2:3

Pride can be our biggest downfall in recovery, but not in the way we might think. Yes, where humility is absent, pride, arrogance, and abuse of power reign. But the most common way we see pride in recovery is false humility. Thinking higher of ourselves than we ought to is rarely the problem. Instead, it's thinking, talking, and presenting ourselves as less than we truly are, less than who God created us to be. Therein lies a much bigger problem.

The first step in any sobriety-centered recovery program is to admit that we're powerless. And while we certainly are powerless on our own and in our flesh, doing recovery right isn't about rolling over; it's about assuming the power and authority we have as sons and daughters of God. Not to control our vices, but to follow the will of God for our lives. Acknowledging and embracing this power isn't pride; it's giving God the credit He is due and believing in His power to transform our hearts, minds, and lives. This can only be done in the context of authentic, healthy, Christ-centered community, where there is a deep well of spiritual power available to all.

Because we're in Christ, we are not truly powerless. We have access to the God of the universe and our full kingdom inheritance today, even if today is day one of sobriety. We have access to the collective wisdom, strength, and God-given support systems that will carry us in the natural as other people demonstrate the Father's love. We have more power than we think we do. And the recovery journey will remind us Who that power comes from.

God, purify and humble my heart. Teach me to walk out my true identity as Your beloved child, no more and no less. Help me lean into the power of Your name to heal and recover. Amen.

June 14: PRIDE MONTH

Rather, in humility value others above yourselves, not looking to your own interests but each of you to the interests of the others.
—Philippians 2:3–4

Trauma is more than just something that happens to a person on the outside. Trauma also happens *inside* a person. Different circumstances impact different people in different ways for different reasons, which is why we have no room to judge what triggers trauma inside others.

Discrimination and marginalization because of race, age, gender, religion, disability, sexual orientation or identity, socioeconomic status, mental health, and addiction are issues Christian recovery leaders cannot afford to ignore or avoid.

Case in point—June is Pride Month. And at this point, much of the LGBTQ community wants nothing to do with Jesus because of the way so-called Christians have treated them. These precious people who are walking out their own recovery journey don't need some watered-down version of the gospel that says, "Anything goes." They need people to welcome them, walk with them, break bread with them, and create space for them to have a transformative encounter with Jesus, friend of sinners.

Now, I'm not advocating for some new brand of universalism that rejects the truth of God's Word. Far from it. You can—and must—have courage in your convictions. But what we also need to adopt is *compassion* in our convictions. Jesus never glossed over people who were on the margins of society. It didn't matter how they got there. He welcomed them, walked with them, broke bread with them, and left them completely transformed.

But it's possible to be so right that we, the church, are actually *wrong* in the hate-filled, abusive ways we walk out our faith. Contrary to popular opinion, it *is* possible to stand for truth and do it in love. If it's not the truth, it's not loving. And if it's not loving, it's not the truth. Sometimes a look in the mirror is all it takes.

God, move me with compassion for people who don't yet understand who You are, and who they are by proxy. Make me a safe space and let the light of Your love shine through me. Amen.

June 15: UNION STATION

But whoever is united with the Lord is one with him in spirit.
—1 Corinthians 6:17

Union and oneness may sound similar, but they are not the same. They're both equally important, but one is about station, and the other is about being.

The mystic union we have with Jesus, forged supernaturally by His death and resurrection, reconciled our relationship with God the Father and made us coheirs with Christ. But unlike any earthly union or partnership we could enter into, our union with Christ is a kingdom family station—one that can never be earned nor broken, only received. You're in Christ. Period.

The oneness we have with God the Father is a byproduct of our union with Jesus. Here's how it works: Jesus is one with the Father, and we're in an irrevocable station of union with Jesus. Therefore, in Christ, we're also one with the Father, Son, and Holy Spirit.

The complexities of our oneness can seriously stretch the human mind. How can we be one with God and still be ourselves? We're not God, but oneness is far more than nearness or connectedness. We're talking oneness to a degree that when we recognize the divine DNA flowing in our veins, sin can no longer coexist with the holiness in our being.

However difficult you may find it to grasp the truth about your oneness with God, remember that your union with Christ comes first. From that place of deep connection and intimacy with Jesus, God will reveal who you really are—who He created you to be. The best part? He'll also show you that same divine DNA in others, people who have no idea they carry it. This is the beauty of the body of Christ. Accept your station and receive the gift of oneness that comes with it in Jesus's name.

God, show me what it means to be one with You. Remind me of my righteousness in Christ and the station I'm called to carry in union with Him. Use me to win others with Your intense love. Amen.

June 16: RECKLESS GRACE

This righteousness is given through faith in Jesus Christ to all who believe. There is no difference between Jew and Gentile, for all have sinned and fall short of the glory of God, and all are justified freely by his grace through the redemption that came by Christ Jesus.
—Romans 3:22–24

Most of the modern-day church goes to great lengths to convince people of their sin. And while being able to distinguish from what's right and wrong in God's eyes is a critical part of our faith walk, the sin-consciousness approach is limited at best. Imagine if we, the church, came at it from a different, but still completely true angle: What if we convinced people of their righteousness in Christ?

If your defense mechanisms are rising about now, take a deep breath. Sin is sin, and nobody is suggesting it isn't. But the persona of sin is a defeated foe that no longer has control over you. You've been set free by the blood of the Lamb, a perfect sacrifice to deliver you from the law of sin and death. You are a sinner no more.

Why then, even after initial salvation, do we still sin? If we've been delivered, why does the struggle still seem so real? To be frank, our obsession with sin produces a false humility that assumes we're not blood-bought children of the King, but wretches who will never get it right. We believe it's true because it's what we've been taught. And friends, we've been taught that Jesus's sacrifice wasn't enough.

You've been justified by a grace so reckless that God now sees you as innocent, not because of anything you've done, but because of what Jesus did for you. Reckless! Believe this truth and receive it in your heart today. In time, you'll learn what it looks like to walk it out on a lifelong journey of aligning your heart with God's truth. You're loved, forgiven, and free.

God, Your grace is so amazing, it almost seems reckless to me! That's how I know it's You, because Your ways are higher. Help me receive this grace and give it to others in Your name. Amen.

June 17: BELIEVING IS SEEING

Then Jesus told him, "Because you have seen me, you have believed;
blessed are those who have not seen and yet have believed."
—John 20:29

"Seeing is believing" is a common cliché that has both biblical and practical roots. When you see something for the first time, it's quite impossible to unsee it. To go back to a world where the new revelation doesn't exist would be almost impossible. And yet, how many people have we seen have a teary-eyed moment of repentance, with God or with another person, only to turn around and commit the same grievous acts that got them into the hot seat to begin with?

The fact is, seeing isn't believing after all. Especially in matters of faith and our belief in God as a good Father, Jesus as our Savior, and the Holy Spirit as a constant friend, believing is what enables us to see in the first place.

Jesus loved to heal blind eyes, but clear earthly sight and vision were never His end game for us. He was thrilled when people saw Him for who He was—a healed, whole, and resurrected King—and then believed. But there was a special place in His heart for those who believed even though they didn't see the miracle of His resurrection firsthand. He knew that's how it would be for the rest of us, and He celebrated their example because He knew we would need it.

Believing is seeing. Try it if you don't believe me. Suspend belief for just a moment and dare to doubt your doubts. If God really is a good Father, what does that mean for you? If Jesus really did pay it all, why are you still trying to pony up? If the Holy Spirit lives in you and helps you walk in righteousness, how can evil coexist? The conclusions you come to will not only bolster your faith but open your eyes to see what was hidden until you dared to believe.

God, I believe! Help my unbelief! I'm choosing to lean into who I know You are, even when I can't see it yet. Help me encourage this faith in others as I learn to walk it out with You. Amen.

June 18: RECEIVE IT

Until now you have not asked for anything in my name. Ask and you will receive, and your joy will be complete.
—John 16:24

We ask God for all kinds of things. Healing. Deliverance. Clarity. Peace. Grace. We ask, and we know that at some level, God will be faithful to deliver according to the riches of our inheritance. His Word says so. And cognitively, we can't dispute it. The dissonance comes when we ask God for the things we need, and He delivers—yet we fail to receive the gift in full.

It's a little like tracking the delivery of a purchase we've placed online. We make our request known to a retailer and follow the delivery play-by-play. Our smartphone lights up saying, "Your Amazon package has arrived!" But we open the door to find the front step bare. The package isn't by the garage or by the back door, nor has our neighbor seen it. We asked, and they delivered... but we aren't able to receive what we asked for because the package isn't where we think it's supposed to be.

Spoiler alert: It's in the mailbox. You're welcome. But the frustration, confusion, and even anger we experience until we find it there can cause us to question a retailer's integrity—and in the case of prayer, God's goodness. The promised process was clear: Ask, receive, and then find complete joy. What gives? We believed it was coming, so where is it? Why can't we receive?

Lean into the Father's heart today. Ask Him what answers He has given you that you have yet to receive. Whether they're hiding in plain sight or at some level you don't realize, you can't find joy in what you don't yet have. Receive His gift of grace over your life today and watch the blessings pile up on your doorstep. There's always more.

God, help me see where You're moving—where You've answered my prayers and I've missed Your creativity in giving me good gifts. I love You, Father, and I trust You to deliver. Amen.

June 19: RELEASING GRACE

But because of his great love for us, God, who is rich in mercy, made us alive with Christ even when we were dead in transgressions— it is by grace you have been saved.
—Ephesians 2:4–5

You can't give away what you don't have. And when it comes to grace, you'll have a hard time giving it to others if you can't receive it yourself. This is a critical element for long-term recovery, where we go to great lengths to self-examine and forgive ourselves while also finding the supernatural strength to forgive others.

Most of us struggle with one or the other—forgiving ourselves or forgiving others. But our capacity for one actually increases our capacity for the other in a God-ordained cycle sparked by Grace Himself. We can only love because He first loved us. So it's only natural that we can only forgive because He first forgave us. Yes, you read that right. He didn't forgive because you first repented perfectly. He didn't forgive because you deserved it. He forgave you because it's who He is. And your identity as a blood-bought, battle-fought, beloved and forgiven saint is because of who you are in Him. The same is true for every person Jesus died for.

If you're struggling to forgive others, chances are you haven't received God's gift of grace and forgiven yourself. If you're struggling to forgive yourself, chances are it's because you assume God's grace has already run out. Receive this truth: God's grace is a renewable resource! He never gets tired of giving it, and you will never tire of receiving it once you've tasted and seen how good it really is. And once you taste it? You'll spend the rest of your life giving it to others.

God, I receive Your gift of grace. I know I am loved and forgiven. Teach me to walk in this truth. Help me release that same grace over others and bring freedom and joy in Your mighty name. Amen.

June 20: GRACE UPON GRACE

Then Peter came to Him and said, "Lord, how often shall my brother sin against me, and I forgive him? Up to seven times?" Jesus said to him, "I do not say to you, up to seven times, but up to seventy times seven."
—Matthew 18:21–22 (NKJV)

Peter was probably feeling pretty good about himself when he asked Jesus how many times he should forgive an offense. Rabbis of the day would have suggested three times, so Peter more than doubled the baseline expectation. Jesus corrected Peter's arrogance, as He often did, by saying he needed to be willing to forgive seventy times seven. That's 490 times!

It's possible Jesus may have been giving a nod to Daniel's infinitely complex end-time prophecy, which states that transgressions of all kinds will come to an end at the end of a 490-year period. (See Daniel 9:24.) Moreover, the point Jesus was trying to make was that we need to be willing to forgive our offenders as many times as it takes. Forgiveness and grace can and must be given, alongside healthy boundaries. God never used grace to enable bad behavior or prolong abuse, and neither should we. But if God's well of grace never runs dry, why should ours?

Scripture makes it plain: *"Out of his fullness we have all received grace in place of grace already given"* (John 1:16).

Grace upon grace upon grace. So much grace, it makes no earthly sense. This is what our good Father God gives to us, and it's the same grace we're meant to give to the rest of the world, even to the very people we don't want to forgive—especially them. Not once, not three or seven times, not even 490 times. As many times as it takes.

Forgiving them frees you, but it can also supernaturally free them by the power of the Holy Spirit living in you.

God, when I struggle to forgive, remind me how forgiven I am. Move my heart with compassion for people who aren't ready to repent. Help me show them Your kindness that leads to repentance. Amen.

June 21: OWNING IT

Rise up; this matter is in your hands.
We will support you, so take courage and do it.
—Ezra 10:4

Any recovery program that's worth its salt makes us take a look inward—to own our part in our struggles and repent of anything we've contributed to those struggles that has harmed us or others. That glimpse inside is often when people relapse or *fail out* of traditional recovery. Because without authentic community to walk with us and help us carry the load, coming face-to-face with ourselves is sometimes more than we can handle.

For those brave enough to look within, it's important to name and own our part in our struggles, but only to a level that's healthy. Some people are prone to own more than their fair share of the problem, while others are unwilling to own enough of it.

God doesn't want you owning things that aren't your fault, especially in cases of abuse. God absolutely wants you to own things that you continually make excuses for, narratives that downplay personal responsibility and blame others for your struggles. Most importantly, God wants you to see your part in it all so you can assume responsibility for your own recovery—and your own life by proxy—even if the only parts you need to own are the ways in which you may have chosen to soothe that trauma-induced pain with anything other than God.

He wants you to know that He is enough. He wants you to know there's nothing you have ever done that's beyond His forgiveness and grace. Naming it will help you own it, and owning it will help you surrender it to God. He will honor your surrender and use your humble acceptance of responsibility for your good and His glory.

God, You know me and You know my struggles better than I do. As I go deeper to uncover the trauma that led to them, show me any way I partnered with that trauma so I can repent. Amen.

June 22: FEAR OF REJECTION

If the world hates you, keep in mind that it hated me first.
—John 15:18

We were created for relationship. It's why rejection hurts so badly. Anything that brings a perceived breach in human connection is something most humans will avoid at all costs...extroverts, introverts, and everyone in between. Whether we want to admit it or not, we all have a desire to be seen, heard, loved, and accepted. And when we fear we might not be, it destroys intimacy and makes it incredibly difficult to be real with people on our recovery journeys.

This fear of rejection can come from all kinds of places. For some, it's a lack of nurturing in very early childhood. For some, it's the sting of a middle school coming-of-age trauma. For some, it's life experience—divorce, loss, betrayal, abuse, or even simple words spoken over us that keep us guarded and our would-be connections at arm's length. This is why so many traditional recovery programs remain anonymous—so people can come, share, and attempt recovery without anyone else ever knowing. This can be important in the early stages, as some carry so much shame, they'd never come otherwise.

But healing from deep trauma just can't happen in an anonymous environment. To go deep, uncover trauma, and pursue healing, we must be willing to be vulnerable, to risk rejection in order to love well, like Jesus did.

Consider your communities for a moment. Do you feel seen, heard, loved, and accepted? Do you work to help others feel the same way? Do you listen more than you talk and demonstrate compassion for people like Jesus did? Be the community you want to see. Make rejection a thing of the past by welcoming people in with open arms.

God, make me "Jesus with skin on" for people who are struggling. Help me have the sensitivity to know when people are feeling rejected and help me know my affirmation comes from You. Amen.

June 23: NEEDED SPACE

If your brother or sister sins, go and point out their fault, just between the two of you. If they listen to you, you have won them over. But if they will not listen, take one or two others along, so that "every matter may be established by the testimony of two or three witnesses." If they still refuse to listen, tell it to the church; and if they refuse to listen even to the church, treat them as you would a pagan or a tax collector.
—Matthew 18:15–17

When our relationships are strained, it's almost always about unmet expectations. Whether we've stated those expectations clearly or expected people to read our minds, we can't escape conflict. It's normal, it's human, and it's rarely as insurmountable as we might think.

Scripture is pretty clear about how to handle conflict. Settle the matter one-to-one whenever possible, just between the two of you. In a perfect world, we would see eye to eye every time. But in the real world, we sometimes stand at an impasse. We need the help of safe, authentic community to help us resolve our conflict. If involving a third party or even the church doesn't work, Scripture says we're to treat them as we would pagans or tax collectors, who were the worst possible sinners in Jesus's day.

When relationship strains escalate to the point of needing space from the community at large, boundaries are not only necessary but redemptive. Sometimes relationships need a little space to breathe, a time to be silent and apart. This space allows us to hear more clearly from God about the situation and begin to see the person as separate from the offense they've caused you.

But here's the wild part: Treating your unrepentant offenders as pagans and tax collectors might not play out the way you think it will. Jesus never excommunicated sinners; He met them where they were. He broke bread with them and spoke truth to them, so that His grace left them completely transformed.

In time, God can and will move your heart toward restoration and forgiveness, even when full reconciliation isn't possible. This supernatural grace to you and through you puts the kingdom of God on display.

God, give me wisdom to know when I need space from a relationship. You're better at softening hearts and moving people to repentance than I am, and I trust You to restore our brokenness. Amen.

June 24: TOO MUCH TOO FAST

Do nothing out of selfish ambition or vain conceit. Rather, in humility value others above yourselves, not looking to your own interests but each of you to the interests of the others.
—Philippians 2:3–4

Addiction is the opposite of connection. So one might assume that connection—deep, vulnerable connection—is the surefire antithesis of addiction. It's a little more complicated than that. Nothing dooms a relationship faster than intimacy overload. We give away too much of ourselves too fast, over-promising and eventually under-delivering.

This is a common problem for people who struggle with addiction and mental health. We're so desperate for real human connection that we dive straight into the deep end with new people, baring our souls in the first week, and then we're left with little else to say. The same is true in romantic relationships, where physical intimacy can confuse healthy intimacy with a false sense of connection.

When we only see relationships through a lens of brokenness, they cause pain. But when we see relationships through God's lens of grace—to us and to others—we receive healing. Healthy relationships have healthy boundaries. They build and go deeper over time.

As you walk with God on your journey to a promised-land life, look to His example of love for healthy relationships. Be authentic with people, and they will reciprocate, which builds trust. Trust makes way for vulnerability, and vulnerability in relationships opens the door to recovery breakthrough in due time. This is the power of Christ-centered community to heal trauma. And it's available to you in Jesus's name.

God, help me look to You for intimacy first so I can learn how to build healthier relationships. Help me keep pace with what You're doing, never running ahead or lagging behind. Amen.

June 25: WORKING THROUGH TRAUMA

Then they cried to the LORD in their trouble, and he saved them from their distress. He brought them out of darkness, the utter darkness, and broke away their chains.
—Psalm 107:13–14

Trauma is more than what happens to us. It's also what happens on the inside. We've all experienced traumatic events, and yet we struggle at varying levels—and sometimes not at all. But when trauma impacts our well-being, working through it in the context of healthy community is essential.

When most people think of trauma, they think of past trauma—something that happened a long time ago, such as repressed abuse or neglect from childhood. Bullying, betrayal, discrimination, and marginalization also shape who we think we are. We often grow so close to the trauma that we can no longer see it clearly; all that remains is the surface-level struggles it caused.

It's also possible to have present trauma, something you're going through currently, often as part of a shared experience—a violent car accident, a school shooting, a terrorist attack, an online scam, or even the fall of a leader you admire. We're quick to dismiss the pain that rises from these situations, but we were designed to walk through them together.

In a perfect world, we would all work through our trauma immediately. Studies show that the quicker we are to deal with it, the longer our healing will last. But when trauma is complex, multifaceted, and even lifelong, we must embrace the idea of a journey to find true healing.

If you're struggling, find people who are willing to go deeper with you. You'll discover the power of community to heal. If you're called to love and lead, be willing to go deeper than you ever have before. You might discover there's always more healing to be found, even for you.

God, help me see my trauma for what it is. Help me process shared trauma with others to find deeper levels of healing. Invite me to work through it all in Your perfect timing. Amen.

June 26: TOTAL HEALING

Heal me, LORD, and I will be healed; save me and I will be saved, for you are the one I praise.
—Jeremiah 17:14

Sobriety isn't the endgame in recovery. It's just the first step in a lifelong journey toward a promised-land life. We might not realize this because sobriety is the predominant metric most traditional programs track. It makes sense because it's a pass or fail legalistic marker. That being said, when the endgame in recovery programming is to *stay sober*, research shows that people will inevitably go back to what they know.

When you begin to see recovery for what it really is—healing from trauma that causes addictions, mental health problems, and thoughts about suicide—you'll realize that someone may be trying to recover from a host of different struggles, some of which may be causing other struggles. The response to, "Are you sober?" effectively becomes, "Sober from what?" The sobriety metric alone disqualifies people who may actually be making real progress daily.

The truth is, you can be sober and stuck. Conversely, those who struggle to maintain sobriety can actually be more healed than those who are sober by definition. Total healing from trauma goes beyond mere sobriety into transformation territory. It's a journey you can only take with Jesus. Does God want you sober? Of course He does. He wants you healed and whole, free of anything you'd be tempted to put before Him. But He values transformation over sobriety every time—and His grace covers you as you learn to walk into the promised-land life He has for you.

God, put people in my life who will hold me accountable in all areas, not just in my sobriety. Transform my heart and mind and lead me into a life I actually want to stay sober for. Amen.

Jesus looked at them and said, "With man this is impossible, but with God all things are possible."
—Matthew 19:26

The recovery system doesn't always work the way we think it should. If it did, we'd all be delivered in twelve steps flat, never looking back. But some of us need a level of Holy Spirit intervention and Christ-centered community that even the best systems and programming can't offer. We can get sober without Jesus, but we'll be hard-pressed to tap into true transformation in our own strength.

Enter in the *higher power* of traditional recovery. We come to believe a power greater than ourselves can restore us to sanity, but we often assume that higher power is just some better version of ourselves. We prove it by striving to walk out our recovery in our own strength. When we inevitably fall, we turn around and blame that power for not showing up like we think it should.

Let's be clear: As a Christian, your higher power is a good Father God, who is fully accessible to you because of what His Son Jesus did on the cross. His Spirit now lives inside of you, and He has given you power and authority in this world. Embracing this reality not only requires *acknowledgement* of a higher power, it means realizing you've been made one with Him and are meant to be in a deep relationship with Him. God's giving you access, right now, to the keys to His kingdom, which means supernatural restoration of your life and relationships. Healing is not only possible but probable when you follow His leading instead of striving to do it on your own.

If you're in recovery, you've already admitted you're powerless against your struggles. It's time to reclaim your power—the power given to you by God in Christ by the power of the Holy Spirit. If it sounds impossible, remember that with God, all things are possible.

God, help me realize what I carry—the power and authority You've given me to heal my life and relationships. Teach me Your ways and let me be a supernatural light in a natural world. Amen.

When Jesus saw him lying there and learned that he had been in this
condition for a long time, he asked him, "Do you want to get well?"
—John 5:6

Throughout Scripture, Jesus asks people more than three hundred questions. He Himself is asked nearly two hundred questions, but only directly answers three of them. (See Matthew 22:36–37; Luke 11:1; John 18:37.) Jesus believed that we all carry answers to the real problem, not the surface-level struggle we see.

If you too want to lead people into life transformation, the question you really need to ask is, "Why are they bound in the first place?" People struggling with addiction, mental health problems, and suicidal thoughts will usually tell you exactly how they ended up there if you're willing to ask the right questions and listen more than you talk. Instead of telling people why *you* think they relapsed, try asking *them*. They may respond initially with a flippant complaint or say, "I don't know." But give them time to retrace their steps and talk about what was going on in their life and how they felt about it. Deep down, they know what the real problem is—but they may need you to help them get to the bottom of it.

Instead of shaming them back to step zero, be curious and growth-minded. Asking questions like, "How long has it been since your last relapse?" can provide insight to the whole life's journey. Asking, "What's your new bottom line?" helps them take ownership of their recovery and set realistic expectations for themselves.

When we better understand the origin of their struggles, we can better understand how to show compassion and help them build a promised-land life worth staying sober for. What's more, we can identify systemic change opportunities to prevent future generations from falling into the same traps.

God, when I'm walking with someone through their struggle, help me be slow to speak, slow to judge, and quick to listen. Help me be curious enough to ask questions that bring healing. Amen.

Truly I tell you, whatever you bind on earth will be bound in heaven,
and whatever you loose on earth will be loosed in heaven.
—Matthew 18:18

Conflict is a certainty in life and relationships, especially in the context of recovery culture. Our goal isn't to avoid conflict in relationships, but to handle conflict faithfully and create opportunities for restoration.

When conflict inevitably arises, handle it in the gentle but firm way of Jesus. In Matthew 18, He gives us clear directions for addressing conflict, offense, and sin in our communities. Address the issue one-on-one with your brother or sister. If they hear you, you've won them and earned their trust. (See verse 15.) If they don't listen, try bringing one or two community members to listen and address the issue again. (See verse 16.) If they still won't listen, bring them to your community so others can help you better understand and communicate. (See verse 17.)

If your brother or sister is repentant and willing to recommit to community standards—with your help, of course—they can stay. If they are unrepentant and unwilling to recommit, they must leave. Not to punish them, but to preserve the safe community space people need to be vulnerable and heal. When we lose someone in our communities in this way, we're to treat them just like Jesus treated pagans and tax collectors. We're to *love them*—lavishly.

Establishing a version of these conflict standards in your community and in each and every new relationship will help you set clear expectations and help others meet them. Once they know conflict is okay, relationships can grow and thrive in Jesus's name.

God, thank You for giving me directions on handling conflict. Help me embrace the nuances of these critical conversations and help me love people like You do, especially in conflict. Amen.

June 30: REAL RESTORATION

Restore to me the joy of your salvation and grant me a willing spirit, to
sustain me.
—Psalm 51:12

Real restoration starts with God, not self. When we try to navigate conflict, forgive someone, or even ask for forgiveness in our own strength, especially when we're in recovery, we end up sabotaging our relationships in the long run. That's because grace in the flesh isn't really grace at all; there will almost always be strings, resentments, and ultimatums involved.

God's grace looks nothing like that. As Love Himself, God is the originator of the idea of restoration, which means being brought back into right relationship. We can only love because the Father loved us first. We can only have faith because Jesus enables it. And we can only find real restoration by leaning on Him as Restorer, the One who makes us able to bring restoration to our relationships in the first place.

Real restoration isn't a feeling. It's a choice to align with God's best for your life and the lives of others. Instead of trying to seek or fabricate restoration by trying harder, ask God to fill you with His grace today. Ask Him to remind you how loved and forgiven you already are in Him. Ask Him about His heart for restoration and His love for your offenders. It will move you with compassion to give His grace gift away.

When you rest in this truth, peace, forgiveness, and joy will flow out of you and into your relationships, putting God's grace to you and through you on display.

God, make me an ambassador of Your grace. Help me stop trying to forgive in my own strength. Without You, I can't! Stay by my side as I bring restoration and reconciliation in Your name. Amen.

July

REDEMPTION

If we confess our sins, he is faithful and just and will forgive us our sins and purify us from all unrighteousness.
—1 John 1:9

July 1: TRULY AWARE

There is neither Jew nor Gentile, neither slave nor free, nor is there male and female, for you are all one in Christ Jesus.
—Galatians 3:28

Being privileged enough to work through and overcome deep-seated trauma requires authentic relationships and unapologetic advocacy. Believe it or not, this is harder for some people than others.

The subtle microaggression and obvious macroaggression people of color feel is something we, the church, must learn to recognize, own, and remedy, even if we can never fully understand how it feels to walk in their shoes. If not us, then who? If not now, then when?

If this line of thinking tweaks you a little bit, take a deep breath. Feel no shame or condemnation, and open your heart and mind to God's message at hand. Whoever you are, wherever you come from, whatever experiences you bring to the table, hear the truth: We're all one in Christ. Race, position, and gender don't assign value in the kingdom; they bring collective wisdom to the kingdom. When we learn to embrace all people, we will see the full expression of Christ, the bridegroom, in His bride, the church.

Do you feel the Father's nudge to go deeper with Him, to walk in the shoes of people who don't look, think, act, vote, or behave like you? You wouldn't be the first. July is Minority Mental Health Awareness Month, a time for us all to consider our privileges and what we might be called to do to lift others up. You are uniquely suited to be truly aware of the life situations of others. And your Father will be with you as you do.

God, forgive me if I've been oblivious to—or contributed to—discrimination or marginalization in my communities. Help me see Your people as You do and own my part. Amen.

July 2: CHAINS BROKEN

For there is no difference between Jew and Gentile—the same Lord is Lord of all and richly blesses all who call on him.
—Romans 10:12

It's been more than 150 years since slavery was outlawed in the United States. But unfortunately, systemic chains of oppression still exist, especially for people of color. This reality transfers into the recovery space, where black and Hispanic people are less likely than white people to complete traditional, publicly funded treatment programs, often for financial reasons.[2]

This is one of many reasons why recovery is the civil rights movement of our generation. The ways in which we come to the ends of ourselves do not discriminate. But our one-size-fits-all recovery programming leaves too many people needing far more than twelve steps to build a life worth staying sober for.

Because of what Jesus did on the cross, defeating sin, shame and death forever, the chains on our lives are already broken. We're free whether we realize it or not. Coming into agreement with this truth can be more difficult for people who carry trauma. The temptation to pick up our broken chains and carry them as part of our core identity is strong. As people in recovery and people loving and leading others through it, we must not only name this phenomenon when we see it, we must help set captives and prisoners free in Jesus's name.

Take a moment today to ask the Father, "Am I still carrying any chains that You already broke? Am I allowing or encouraging others to do the same?" He will reveal to you opportunities to surrender those chains to Him and deliver others by the power of the Spirit living in you.

God, make me an instrument of freedom in the recovery space. Help me drop my chains and live free to show others what a promised-land life looks like. Set people free in Your mighty name. Amen.

July 3: MACROAGGRESSION

But if you show favoritism,
you sin and are convicted by the law as lawbreakers.
—James 2:9

If you're a particularly *woke* white person, you may already be thinking about how to better show up as an advocate for people of color. But even if you think you're ready, you might still have some work to do.

---

2. Brendan Saloner and Benjamin Lê Cook, "Blacks And Hispanics Are Less Likely Than Whites To Complete Addiction Treatment, Largely Due To Socioeconomic Factors," *Health Affairs* vol. 32, no. 1, January 2013, www.ncbi.nlm.nih.gov/pmc/articles/PMC3570982.

People I (George) love and do active ministry with in the Christian community still cringe when they hear terms like *white privilege* and aggressively combat the phrase *black lives matter* with the response, "All lives matter."

Macroaggressions are deliberate, blatantly damaging acts of discrimination on a systemic level that hurt certain groups at the individual level. Historic macroaggressions include the forced relocation of Japanese-Americans into internment camps during World War II and the Tuskegee study in which black men were intentionally misled and denied standard treatment for syphilis. Today, we see macroaggression when employers reject job applicants whose names *sound funny*, those expressing hatred for all Chinese because of COVID-19, or corporations that intentionally jack up prices at stores in *certain neighborhoods*.

The obvious macroaggression people of color feel is something we, the church, must learn to recognize, own, and remedy, even if we can never fully understand how it feels to walk in their shoes. If not us, then who? If not now, then when?

Perhaps you've felt the sting of racism yourself. Perhaps you've struggled with racist tendencies, or enabled systemic racism with silence. Friend, there is grace for you today. Lean into the Father's heart, and He will show you the diverse beauty of creation—and how there are no mistakes in His kingdom. Receive His heart for the brokenhearted and be an instrument of peace, restoration, and racial reconciliation in your communities.

God, thank You for Your grace. I confess I don't see all people as equal, even when I think I do. Show me Your heart for Your sons and daughters and give me the compassion of Jesus. Amen.

July 4: MICROAGGRESSION

But now in Christ Jesus you who once were far away have been brought near by the blood of Christ.
—Ephesians 2:13

You've probably had to wear a bandage in your life. The question is, did it come close to the color of your skin? Your answer may help you understand the concept of racial microaggression. Historically, nearly all adhesive bandages were peach-colored, reminding people of color that they're different with every wound.

After widespread racial unrest in 2020, Band-Aid® Brand Adhesive Bandages announced that it would expand its predominantly pink-hued product line to produce a range of bandages that "embrace the beauty of diverse skin." Progress is progress, and the company did the right thing—and the smart thing. But it's still hard to believe it took as long as it did.

Even after years of intentional progress and honest effort, we, the church, still struggle to recognize racial trauma and show appropriate compassion in the communities we're called to serve. And we could be losing generations of would-be believers because of it. What will it take for us to look and act more like Jesus? When will the sons and daughters of God rise up and be His hands and feet for justice?

It starts with you. It starts today. Ask the Father of all humankind to open your eyes and open your heart to see systemic racial microaggression for what it is. If you've contributed to it, this is a chance to repent. If you've received it, this is a chance to forgive. Feel no condemnation—yet receive the Spirit's loving conviction, allowing God to break your heart for what breaks His.

God, expand my mind and my world. Help me look up to You and outside myself to see and feel the pain of others so I can bring compassionate, Christlike solutions in Your name. Amen.

July 5: SLAVES AND MASTERS

Slaves, obey your earthly masters with respect and fear, and with sincerity of heart, just as you would obey Christ.
—Ephesians 6:5

For generations, the Christian church used Scripture to justify slavery. Let that sink in for a moment. We, the church, used the Word of God to balance religion with an institution that systemically valued the life and freedom of one created being over another. It's hard to think of anything quite so anti-Christ. And yet history proves that we Christians don't always look much like our Christ. Meditating on this reality is not meant to be an exercise in shame, but one of compassion and growth.

When we read passages that seem to justify injustice, we must be willing to go deeper, to explore not only the content, but the context. *"Earthly masters"* (Ephesians 6:5) may have referred to actual slave masters of the day, some of whom may have been just in the eyes of their leaders and the law at the time. But while some passages are *descriptive*, explaining the situation and context for what specific people groups were experiencing, they are not necessarily *prescriptive*—for example, justifying slavery's existence by mere mention of it in historical content. A deep dive into any discrimination or marginalization the church has ever participated in—such as women's rights and Christ-centered recovery—uncovers many times we've assumed wrongly about God's intentions for His people.

When we encounter the aftermath of any un-Christlike behavior among Christians, we can remember the truth: as believers, we're *bondservants* or slaves *only* to Jesus Christ. Not because He has enslaved us or demands it, but because He paid a great debt for our sins, so out of our love and gratitude to Him, we make Him Lord of our lives. We belong to Him—and He belongs to us. This transcends any earthly understanding of slaves and masters. We're not just slaves; we're family. What's more, we're one with the God of the universe.

That kind of grace will move you to lay down your life for the sake of the gospel—and for your brothers and sisters who struggle to believe it's true.

God, strip any incorrect context from me that values one life over another. Humble me. Remind me who You are, and who I am in You. Make me an ambassador for freedom in Your name. Amen.

July 6: EXPLICIT BIAS

I charge you, in the sight of God and Christ Jesus and the elect angels, to keep these instructions without partiality, and to do nothing out of favoritism.
—1 Timothy 5:21

It's completely human to have preferences. It's part of how we were created in God's image. God's *favor* rests on His beloveds, as evidenced by the example of Jesus and His disciples. Yet Scripture is clear that God does not show *favoritism*, which is a form of explicit bias. (See Romans 2:11.) When we're aware that we give unfair, preferential treatment to one person or group, especially at the *expense* of another, we aren't imitating our Father, but partnering with practices that will inevitably bring about discrimination.

Explicit bias can take shape as macroaggression when people make public declarations of their prejudices against marginalized groups. Racist or sexist comments are two examples. When these words are spoken or even *tolerated*—especially in places where marginalized groups are supposed to find safe-haven support, such as the church—the divisive impact has the power to destroy communities and cultures. And in the absence of safe, authentic community, struggles with addiction, mental health problems, and suicidal thoughts reign.

Favoritism is not of the Father's kingdom. But even the sin of favoritism is typically rooted in systemic trauma. If you struggle with a race, a gender, a social class, or something completely different, it's likely because your experiences and/or your upbringing shaped a worldview that either demonstrated or tolerated such behavior.

Align yourself with God's truth today. Receive the scriptural truth that we are all one in Christ Jesus—even those brothers and sisters you might be tempted to marginalize. Ask the Father to break your heart for them and strip you of any pride that might keep you in a false construct of superiority. Go low with God and rest with Him in humility until you reemerge ready to help all people receive the Father's goodness as a fellow coheir to the kingdom of God.

God, convict my heart of any person or group that I consider inferior. I repent of anything I've done or failed to do that has kept Your beloveds down. Help me lift them up. Amen.

July 7: IMPLICIT BIAS

For we were all baptized by one Spirit so as to form one body—whether Jews or Gentiles, slave or free—and we were all given the one Spirit to drink.
—1 Corinthians 12:13

Explicit obvious racism isn't easy to combat, but it can be done. A far more challenging issue comes with what's known as implicit bias—favoritism we harbor but aren't even consciously aware of that often manifests as microaggression or careless actions or statements that might seem harmless to white people, but can be perceived as aggressive by people of color.

If you're already feeling a little tweaked, let's go deeper. Many white Christians cringe at the concept of *white privilege*, insisting they've done nothing to contribute to or perpetuate discrimination and marginalization in their communities. Even worse, some particularly *woke* white people are eager to step into conversations about racism, but slow to educate themselves about the systemic impact of generations of oppression. Many of us are either unable or unwilling to listen to learn.

Of course, this concept applies to any marginalized group, but since July is Minority Mental Health Awareness Month, it's worth acknowledging the hard truth: the church doesn't do a great job when it comes to talking about mental health. And we do an especially poor job talking about it with people of color in our communities, who already have a hard time talking about mental health with other people of color. We've failed to be the safe space where all members of the body of Christ can feel safe, heard, and loved unconditionally.

The subtle microaggression people of color feel is something that we, the church, must learn to recognize, own, and remedy. It starts by becoming aware of our own implicit biases and creating thought patterns and behaviors that will help us stay accountable to fairness, equity, and oneness—for all.

Overcoming biases is not something you can strive for. God won't change your mind, but if you change your mind, God will change your heart.

God, do I have biases that I'm not aware of? How can I love people more like You do by putting myself in their shoes and listening to learn? Purify my heart and teach me Your ways. Amen.

July 8: MARGINALIZATION

Defend the weak and the fatherless;
uphold the cause of the poor and oppressed.
—Psalm 82:3

Every human since the dawn of creation was designed for relationship. Far more than mere proximity, we were created with a core longing to not only be in community but to *belong*. Jesus, the friend of sinners of all kinds, shook the establishment by inviting marginalized social outcasts to dine with Him, receive His healing, and bask in the joy of His love. The "unclean" couldn't defile Him—but He could cleanse them of all unrighteousness in an instant.

Jesus's willingness to combat marginalization in His day earned Him a reputation that ultimately got Him killed. But He always moved with intention—seeking to save the lost, even at the expense of those who never went astray in traditional ways. Sadly, more than two thousand years later, we, the church, have become widely known by how we alienate, marginalize, and exclude rather than by our love. I dare say we're not doing it on purpose... except for when we are. And deep down, we know when we are, don't we?

Coming against marginalization in the church and in the world will take a corporate alignment with God's truth on the matter. But that group alignment starts with individual hearts—with *your* heart. Ask yourself honestly, how are you showing the love of Christ to people on the fringes of society? How are you breaking down barriers to entry and belonging in your communities? What more could you do to make your home, your workplace, your small group, or your church truly welcoming to those who have been, in one way or another, labeled *unwelcome*? And finally, how might you advocate for marginalized people in the communities you serve? Ask God to reveal His heart for advocacy to you and be moved with compassion to open doors for the forgotten ones who are loved by Jesus.

God, I can be so wrapped up in my own world sometimes. Show me where to advocate for the marginalized in my communities. Move me with boldness to seek Your justice and equality for all. Amen.

July 9: DISCRIMINATION

Do you not believe that I am in the Father and the Father is in me? The words that I say to you I do not speak on my own authority, but the Father who dwells in me does his works.
—John 14:10 (ESV)

Discrimination. Marginalization. *Dehumanization*. How do we discern what's what? Marginalization, or the powerless being pushed to the margins of society, is the downstream impact of discrimination, which is the unjust or prejudicial treatment of people based on race, gender, socioeconomic status, or even political or denominational affiliations.

Are you catching the magnitude of this?

How we treat people impacts their ability to live life in the context of a healthy community. When we discriminate by putting our explicit or implicit biases on display in macro- and microaggressive ways, we strip people of their God-given power and push them to the sidelines. In some cases, we dismiss their God-given right to coexist.

We, the church, have our work cut out for us in this area. In an era when the secular world is proclaiming freedom to captives and prisoners and demanding unity in all aspects of human existence, we are missing an opportunity to focus on union—our oneness in Christ. If Jesus is in the Father (see John 14:10), and we are in Christ (see Galatians 2:20), we must then be where Christ is.

Yep—you're one with God, in Christ, by the power of the Holy Spirit, whether you choose to believe it's true or not. And guess what? You're *also* one with everyone else who is in Christ, regardless of race, gender, socioeconomic status, or political or denominational affiliations! (See Galatians 3:28.)

If this doesn't cause us to reassess our priorities and consciously choose to stand against discrimination in all its forms, I'm not sure what will.

God, forgive me for tolerating or contributing to Christian cultures that discriminate against others. Remind me of my oneness with You and others and release Your grace to and through me. Amen.

July 10: MISOGYNY

Who can find a virtuous and capable wife? She is more precious than rubies.
—Proverbs 31:10 (NLT)

The Word of God—the Holy Bible, Scripture, the Canon, or whatever you prefer to call it—is inspired by God. His Word is inerrant, free of mistakes. Yes, even in those places where the text seems to contradict itself. And yet, even with the best of intentions, the Bible's original writers, its translators throughout the generations, its teachers in churches, seminaries, living rooms, and secret, hidden places across the globe are in fact quite *errant*, especially when it comes to women.

To dig beneath the surface of what many consider to be outright misogyny in Scripture, culture and context are critically important. For the original writers of God's Word, women were an afterthought. Jesus welcomed and empowered them as equals in ministry and overall human worth, but the eyewitness writers of such encounters often left the women nameless, so that they would be remembered as "the woman" for generations. What's more, certain passages of Scripture—taken wildly out of context and used as weapons in modern day—keep far too many would-be female evangelists silent.

Misogyny, or the hatred of women, may be *biblical* (as in, it's in the Bible), but it is still anti-Christ. Any discrimination, marginalization, or perpetual *less than* perceptions of women—especially women of color, who face a unique set of challenges—are not only counterculture, they're counter-kingdom.

Search your heart. If you're a man, what are you doing to honor your sisters in Christ? If you're a woman, how do you see your own value—by what man says, or by what God says? Align your thoughts with the Father and ask Him to reveal any misogynistic tendency in you so you can be set free of it.

God, You honor women. You empower Your daughters to do great things for Your kingdom. Reveal to me any ways I might be partnering with a spirit that seeks to oppress them. Amen.

July 11: BIGOTRY

But woe to you, scribes and Pharisees, hypocrites! For you shut the kingdom of heaven in people's faces. For you neither enter yourselves nor allow those who would enter to go in.
—Matthew 23:13 (ESV)

Throughout the Gospels, Jesus was known for showing grace, mercy, and compassion to all He met. But in one particular instance, His grace looked a little more like tough love—even heavy-handed discipline. When Jesus spoke to Pharisees, religious leaders, and scribes who were bound to legalism, He didn't mince words.

To be clear, Jesus wasn't discriminating against a group of rabbis and scribes. He was rebuking the sin of legalism inside them, which values the letter of the Law over the Spirit of the law. In an old covenant world, where following rules was the only way to earn your *in* with God, these professional box-checkers were no doubt trying to honor God. But when rules and regulations triumph over progress and transformation, a pharisaical spirit soon takes over, blinding us to God's mercy over judgment. (See James 2:12–13.)

The Pharisees weren't the originators of bigotry, but they were a historically significant byproduct example of it. Unreasonable attachment to a particular belief system, opinion, or faction over God's truth manifests as prejudice, hatred, and systemic abuse. Jesus took His most high-challenge approach with these Jewish leaders, not just because of the oppression they perpetuated, but because of His deep love for them and desire to see them find freedom too.

Have you partnered with a legalistic, pharisaical, bigoted spirit in your faith and recovery journey? Have you clung to a set of ideals that might sound like it's of God, but really isn't? Do you cling to the twelve steps so tightly, you won't allow the Holy Spirit to intervene? Ask God to reveal His love for you and others and receive His invitation to choose mercy over judgment in all cases.

God, I admit I like to know I'm right. It makes me feel safe and sometimes even important. Help me look to You for safety and significance and strengthen my obedience to Your leading. Amen.

July 12: REDEMPTION

For this reason Christ is the mediator of a new covenant,
that those who are called may receive the promised eternal inheritance—
now that he has died as a ransom to set them free from the sins
committed under the first covenant.
—Hebrews 9:15

Of the many powerful words in Scripture, this month's theme, *redemption*, is by far one of the most misunderstood. In earthly terms, we understand redemption as the paying of a debt to regain a possession, something that's been lost. This definition only scratches the surface of what redemption really means from a kingdom perspective. Because let's be honest, if all Jesus did was *buy you off* for God, then you're nothing more than a disposable commodity. That is not the heart of a good Father God.

No, God had far more in mind with His perfectly transcendent kingdom view of redemption. It goes beyond the forgiveness of sins and actually justifies you. Read that last part carefully now. It justifies *you*, not your sin. His redemption separates you so completely from your sins that regardless of your past or future track record, if you are in Christ, you're innocent. Brand new, perfect, and spotless in God's eyes. Not by anything you've done to earn it or do to strive to keep it! Only by the blood of Jesus, your Savior, friend, and Bridegroom.

Lean into your justified self today. Ask God for a revelation of His love for you—a love that doesn't just look past your flaws, but obliterates them completely. You are seen as perfect, holy, and blameless before the Father. It doesn't matter if you've been walking in wholeness for years or if you relapsed last night. Sin is a defeated foe; it no longer has a hold on you unless you allow it. You're fully forgiven and free to bask in the holiness Christ purchased for you on the cross—a gift that will never, ever stop giving.

God, Your grace is so amazing! How can You love me like you do? I may never understand, but I'll spend the rest of my life trying. Thank You for setting me free. Help me learn to walk in freedom. Amen.

July 13: PREACHERS GONNA PREACH

Not many of you should become teachers, my fellow believers, because you know that we who teach will be judged more strictly.
—James 3:1

Those called to teach and preach the gospel of Jesus in a recovery context are blessed indeed, but the burden of shepherding the flock comes with great responsibility. As leaders, we're never expected to walk out faith life and leadership perfectly. However, as James insists, when we accept the call to love and lead people toward a promised-land life, we will stand before God one day to account for how we did it.

The complexity of this truth lies squarely in our humanness. God does not call the qualified; He commissions the willing and qualifies them along the way. This trial-by-fire leadership is the essence of recovery. The more we start to believe we are *worthy* of leadership, the more we need to acknowledge our humanness and lean into humility. We love and lead by the grace of our good Father God—and we depend upon His strength to stand the tests of time.

Sadly, in recent years, we've seen so many prominent global Christian faith leaders fall from grace. Some struggled with abuse of power, covered by their own ministry teams. Some succumbed to their own struggles, struggles they likely carried silently, hoping no one would ever find out. Others were too afraid to admit that life didn't feel worth living—and some put those words to action and died by suicide. Friends, we no longer have the luxury of lifting our leaders onto pedestals so high they're untouchable. Recovery is for everyone, and the ways in which we come to the ends of ourselves do not discriminate.

Accepting the call to preach the good news to our communities and the world and shepherd flocks as the Father leads is a must. But we, the church, need to create safe-haven spaces for our leaders to get and stay healthy—mentally, emotionally, and spiritually. Even leaders need to be loved and led, and we can all accept responsibility for making sure they are equipped for the unique recovery journeys ahead.

God, bless my leaders, the ones surrounding my community in an effort to love and lead like You do. Help me support, encourage, and lift them up so they can bless far more in Your name. Amen.

July 14: CONFIRMATION BIAS

The one who states his case first seems right,
until the other comes and examines him.
—Proverbs 18:17 (ESV)

Your words have power. They can bring life, or they can bring death. (See Proverbs 18:21.) But perhaps even more dangerous than the words you speak aloud are the voices inside your head—the ones that specialize in assumption. For better or worse, what you assume of people creates bias. Whether those biases are explicit and obvious or implicit and hidden, they shape the lens through which you see the world.

For example, if a news network airs a story about a black man robbing a grocery store in the inner city, someone with implicit biases against people of color might be tempted to affirm their belief that all black people are dangerous criminals. Here's another example: suppose a jealous husband who struggles with his own self-worth sees his wife laughing with one of the softball dads. This may affirm his belief that all women are cheaters and can't be trusted.

When our biases are confirmed in such ways, it's called *confirmation bias*. We feed off of seeing our assumptions manifest and often seek out new "evidence" to confirm what we've already decided is true, even if it's not. Confirmation bias adds no value or wisdom to any situation, but it somehow validates our broken desire to be right at the expense of being redemptive.

Real redemption means asking ourselves in humility, "What else might be true?" Yes, some black men are dangerous criminals, but not all. Yes, some women are untrustworthy cheaters, but not all. When we choose to let go of our assumptions, we allow room for the Holy Spirit to reveal a deeper, more redemptive truth. This is the essence of recovery, and it can bring about the kind of redemptive healing that manifests relationship reconciliation.

God, challenge my assumptions about the world, about Your people, and about You. Give me Your eyes to see situations with supernatural clarity and grace when I ask, "What else might be true?" Amen.

July 15: INCLUSION

Therefore welcome one another as Christ has welcomed you,
for the glory of God.
Romans 15:7 (esv)

If we really want to celebrate diversity in the recovery space, inclusion is a natural next step. Now, we're not talking about policies or lockstep organizational practices, although those are well and good and above all necessary. The inclusion we're speaking of embodies the mind of Christ—not including people because we *have* to, but because we *want* to.

Today's youth are being raised in ideologies of inclusion. To be fair, some of those ideologies are rooted in Christlike values, others not so much. But teaching not only the next generation, but ourselves to be includers means teaching ourselves to identify and call out the divine DNA in all people.

Not everyone is a Christian, but every human is made in the image of God and carries some aspect of His character, whether they realize it or not. Our job as followers of Christ and leaders in the recovery space is to speak to not only the gifts but the Gift Giver as an invitation for people to encounter God as a good Father. Let us respect their journey and God's timing, and leave the door wide open for the Holy Spirit to do His thing. Inclusion answers the deep cry for belonging in all our hearts. If we're honest, we'll admit some people have been more welcome in the church than others.

Whether you've always known you were *in*, or you've never once felt that way, today is the day where you learn the truth: You belong in God's house. There's plenty of room. He's prepared a banquet for you so that you can invite your "enemies" to the table and taste and see just how good He is. You're not just welcome—you belong here. Before you believe. Before you behave. Before you know who you are or who God is. You have a seat at His table. Come and dine.

God, thank You for including me at Your table. I don't deserve it, but I guess that's the point! Help me make room for others to be included too, especially if they aren't sure they're really welcome. Amen.

July 16: COMPASSION

And when Jesus went out He saw a great multitude; and He was moved with compassion for them, and healed their sick.
—Matthew 14:14 (NKJV)

One thing's for sure about Jesus: He was (and still is) a compassionate guy. When He walked the earth, our Savior was moved with compassion to perform miracles, advocate for the marginalized, and stand up for the oppressed. He could have done these things in pursuit of earthly power and authority, but instead He only did what the Father was doing and said what the Father was saying. (See John 12:49.) He didn't care about His own reputation; He only cared about setting people free from their struggles and suffering.

This compassionate mindset got Jesus into big trouble with religious authorities, who chastised Him for healing on the Sabbath and keeping questionable company. But Jesus was unwavering in His approach because He came to call sinners, not the righteous. (See Luke 5:32.) Jesus was a good Jew, and He not only understood and honored the Law, He fulfilled it. He was not subject to it, but Lord over it. This radical assertion of grace put Jesus in a precarious and ultimately deadly situation, but He would not be moved.

As ambassadors for Jesus, we're meant to move from the same Spirit-led compassion Jesus did—not because it's trendy, socially responsible, or even because we think we should. We're meant to allow God's grace to flow to us and through us, moving us with compassion for the least of these, especially those we might be tempted to erase from the fabric of society.

Who do you see as a modern-day leper? Those bound by addiction? Those who struggle with their mental health? Those entertaining thoughts of suicide? Ask God to break your heart for what breaks His, and He will take you at your word.

God, move me with compassion in my community to love the least of these. Help me show others how good You really are so they can experience the same redemption You've given me. Amen.

July 17: EMPATHY

Jesus wept.
—John 11:35

Knowing Jesus was moved with compassion to heal, support, and fight for people might make us think He merely pitied them. And while having Jesus sympathize with our struggles could never be a bad thing, it's a shallow representation of the level of empathy He really carried.

Sympathy is a compassionate response. We see the plight of others, and we feel sorry for them, often to the point of helping them out in some way. Empathy is different. Empathy is a deep level of understanding where one can share the feelings and emotions of others as if the struggle is their very own. It's when we literally and figuratively *feel for* people at a level where their struggle becomes our struggle—and in some respects, our responsibility.

When Jesus's friend Lazarus died, Lazarus's sisters, Mary and Martha, were overcome with grief. Jesus empathized with their pain so deeply that the Son of God and Son of Man actually wept. He too became overcome with grief, even knowing what He was about to do. He didn't try to talk Mary and Martha out of their pain, nor fix the situation by quickly reviving his deceased friend. He sat with them in their grief and made it His own. In doing so, He demonstrated God's high regard and value for human emotion, something He not only created but instilled in us as part of His shared character.

In His humanity, Jesus wept. In His divinity, He raised Lazarus from the dead. Fully God and fully Man, He is still able to empathize with our situations and bring us from death to life. Who knows what miracles we might see if we were willing to sit with people in their grief, bearing one another's burdens together and grieving with those who mourn? (See Galatians 6:2; Romans 12:15.)

God, teach me to empathize with struggling people. Help me resist the urge to fix or distract from pain and teach me to sit in the mess, feeling every bit of Your great love for them. Amen.

July 18: ADVOCACY

Speak up for those who cannot speak for themselves,
for the rights of all who are destitute. Speak up and judge fairly;
defend the rights of the poor and needy.
—Proverbs 31:8–9

If you're called to love and lead in the recovery space, you will be moved with compassion to advocate for people who struggle. Whether they entered into the bondage of addiction, mental health problems, or suicidal thoughts by choice or by chance, our role as Spirit-filled believers is to set captives and prisoners free and to come against powers and principalities that would seek to keep them bound.

Recovery is the civil rights movement of our generation. The stigmas that surround those who struggle perpetuate false identity labels that keep people bound. The most important thing an advocate can do is speak up and speak out against discrimination, marginalization, and injustice of any kind toward people walking out a recovery journey.

By challenging the assumption that people in recovery are unstable or even dangerous, we can create opportunities for them to meaningfully contribute at home, at work, and in their communities, actively building the promised-land life God wants for them. Some people will never be able to do this on their own no matter how hard they try because of the systemic barriers to entry that society has built to keep them on the margins.

When we come against these systemic barriers with a grace-laced, proactive approach, we can destigmatize the struggle by letting the whole world know that recovery isn't for *those people*—it's for *everyone*. I believe the church is uniquely suited to facilitate this conversation—and in doing so, we may reposition the bride of Christ to be an inclusive and empowering entity for change in the world.

God, give me a voice to speak out and speak up for people in recovery. Help the world see who they really are in You and help invite them into the promised-land life You have for them. Amen.

July 19: PATRONAGE

My dear children, I write this to you so that you will not sin.
But if anybody does sin, we have an advocate with the Father—
Jesus Christ, the Righteous One.
—1 John 2:1

An advocate is a patron—a special guardian, protector, or supporter. Patronage in Scripture implies we're to go far beyond *following the money* to judge one's fruit. When it comes to recovery, it's important to be aware of where investments of time, talents, influence, and treasure really go. To understand biblical patronage, we must look first to Jesus, a patron who speaks on our behalf to the Father, asking Him to look not on our sin but on His righteousness in us.

Patronage is more than throwing a few bucks in the offering plate after a moving sermon or testimony. It's more than donating gently used clothes to charity or volunteering at a soup kitchen. These things are not wrong, but true Christlike patronage comes from a place of relationship. It's more than an investment in a cause; it's an investment in a person or group of people that provides support, encouragement, and opportunities they simply would not have on their own. It's motivated by love, not notoriety or influence. It's selfless.

Perhaps you're already stepping up as a patron in the recovery space. God love you. Offering practical, ongoing support through groups and people who are doing good work for the kingdom is vital. But are you doing it from a place of authentic relationship? Do you actually know the people whose lives you're changing? Do you spend time with them, leading and loving them unconditionally, or is there a part of you that believes *someone else* should do it?

Ask the Father what He thinks about this. Ask Him if there's any place He would have you go deeper into patronage by personally sponsoring or mentoring an individual or a group. Jesus and His disciples had many patrons…but Jesus left us an example of patronage that's out of this world.

God, my time, talent, and treasure are yours. Where would You have me invest them to help bring Your kingdom? Where might I authentically provide patronage to people in recovery? Show me. Amen.

July 20: WHAT MORE WOULD YOU HAVE ME DO?

So he, trembling and astonished, said,
"Lord, what do You want me to do?" Then the Lord said to him,
"Arise and go into the city, and you will be told what you must do."
—Acts 9:6 (NKJV)

When you come alongside someone through their recovery journey, keep a ballpark estimate of three years in mind. If that sounds like a long time to have to be there for someone in a recovery capacity, consider this: Jesus walked the earth, fully Man and fully God, for thirty-three years. He only spent about three of those years in active ministry.

In those three years, He preached truth to thousands, had a city-to-city following of seventy or so, and kept close company with twelve disciples *"whom he also designated apostles"* (Luke 6:13). He gave His whole heart, the same heart required for recovery ministry, to three of those twelve—Peter, James, and John—preparing them for more responsibility than the others. Jesus never hesitated to meet struggling strangers in the moment. But more often than not, He would train up and rely on the rest of the church to continue the journey with the individual.

Our point is this: No one person can take responsibility for the physical, mental, and emotional health of the entire world. Even Jesus didn't try to do this, and you shouldn't either. But you can journey with one, two, or maybe even three people for as long as it takes. You could pour into the lives of twelve people and put a life worth emulating on display for seventy. You may never preach to the masses, but your voice and your testimony speak volumes.

If we can take any insight from the life and ministry of Jesus, the Man, it's that a whole lot can happen in three years! The best part is that Jesus promised us we will do even greater things than He did in His three years of ministry because of the power of the Holy Spirit in us. (See John 14:12–14.) This your invitation to ask God the Father, "What more would You have me do?" The answer He gives may shock you.

Lord, test my patience. Help me walk with people for as long as it takes, trusting Your timing to bring healing and breakthrough. Thank You for releasing Your grace to me and through me. Amen.

July 21: WHAT'S WORKING?

Let us not become weary in doing good, for at the proper time we will reap a harvest if we do not give up.
—Galatians 6:9

Change in the church and in Christ-centered recovery can be hard to come by. Very little has changed since Alcoholics Anonymous created the first faith-based safe space for people to pursue healing in the 1930s. We've named Jesus as our Higher Power and perhaps chosen less offensive labels to identify with, but our programming remains largely the same.

That's why, in a deliberate play on words, we're encouraging recovery leaders to go deeper than ever before—to uncover opportunities for growth that aren't necessarily part of any packaged curriculum.

Our goal isn't to replace the word *recovery*, but to expand upon the concept and look at it differently. The Uncovery isn't a program, so there is no new model for others to adopt and follow. It's a shift in mindset, not method.

If you're a traditional recovery leader or someone working a traditional program, this is good news because it means there's no need to scrap everything and start over. You know your calling, and you know what your community needs. If Friday night, twelve-step meetings in the church parlor are working for your community, by all means, don't stop! Just be honest with yourself. Ask the Father what your success metrics need to be and perform an objective review of your ministry efforts using both quantitative and qualitative measures. If they're working, you'll know.

This is your invitation to embrace what's working, let go of what's not, and be open to new ideas and solutions that could make all the difference to the ones you love and lead.

God, You know my heart. I want to see people set free, and I want to love and lead them well through their recovery journey. Show me what's working and open my heart to more. Amen.

July 22: WHAT'S NOT WORKING?

Submit yourselves therefore to God. Resist the devil,
and he will flee from you.
—James 4:7 (ESV)

When you take an honest assessment of your recovery ministry or your own recovery journey, it's important to stay sensitive to the Holy Spirit's leading. Perhaps you have strategies and tactics that are performing very well, while others are not. It's in this vulnerable place that you must humble yourself before God and ask Him to reveal aspects of recovery you may need to release, surrendering them to Him. Now, if you've been in recovery circles for any length of time, you know this will be a challenge.

Our adamant cry, "It works if you work it!" is well and good...until what once worked for us stops working, or doesn't provide the same benefit to others.

For example, a high-profile executive struggling with alcohol abuse might need a safe, anonymous space to begin to pursue healing without colleagues learning of his struggle. And yet, a young mother struggling with postpartum depression and anxiety might desperately need a recovery community where she can be fully known and fully loved, even after the meeting is over. Each recovery journey is as unique as the person braving it, which is why no one-size-fits-all recovery programming will work for everyone.

It takes humility to acknowledge what's no longer working for your community. Perhaps anonymity isn't providing the deep relational connection your people need to heal. Perhaps labels like *alcoholic, addict,* and *codependent* are keeping your people in perpetual cycles of sin and shame. Perhaps twelve steps are too much or not enough for the ways in which your community struggles. If something isn't working, let it go. Surrender it to God, submitting yourself to His leading, which never looks like box-checking legalism.

God, help me let go of what's not working in my community. The way we've always done it isn't always best, but Your way is. Humble me so I can help bring redemption to people who struggle. Amen.

July 23: WHOLE-LIFE RECOVERY

Let all that I am praise the LORD; with my whole heart,
I will praise his holy name.
—Psalm 103:1 (NLT)

God cares about every facet of our lives, not just our sobriety. The total transformation we're going after is founded upon a person's whole life, including spiritual discipleship, recovery, community, work therapy, and more. By exploring and diving deep into each of these areas, we can provide a unique prescription for healing and wholeness that creates pathways to a promised-land life. The Uncovery's multifaceted, relational approach looks at the fullness of the individual, not just the struggles from which they're attempting to recover.

Sober living is a great start, but it's not the end in recovery. Getting to the root of addictions, mental health problems, and suicidal thoughts requires a deliberately comprehensive approach. This means honoring the whole person by removing labels and helping them walk through deeper-layer struggles as they come up along the journey. It's about learning new patterns of living to move beyond sobriety toward a transformed life. That life is more than meetings; it needs to include healthy community interactions, a purposeful work life, and intentional spiritual discipleship from people who understand that recovery goes hand in hand with the gospel.

Recovery is a promised-land life that God intended for you before the foundation of the world. He knew you even before He formed you, and He knew exactly what it would take to fulfill His purposes in your life. He holds every part of your life in His hands, and even now, He welcomes you to pursue wholeness His way. This is the essence of real recovery, and it's meant not only for you, but for all of God's beloved children.

God, thank You for elevating the recovery conversation. What parts of my own whole-life recovery am I neglecting? What am I neglecting in the lives of those I love and lead? Show me. Amen.

July 24: REBIRTH

Jesus replied, "Very truly I tell you, no one can see the kingdom of God unless they are born again."
—John 3:3

When Jesus explained the total life transformation that comes with salvation to Nicodemus, the religious leader was perplexed. Being *"born again"* isn't about going back to your mother's womb and coming into the world in the same way you did the first time. Instead, it's a total life transformation, a rebirth into a brand-new life, reborn by the Holy Spirit.

Real recovery is the essence of being born again. Stepping into Uncovery territory means you're not trying to recover the old, broken life that led you to struggle in the first place—you're going after a new one. It's not a second, third, or seventy-seventh chance; it's a completely new life, free of the old one you once knew.

When people in recovery experience this Spirit-led rebirth, they begin to see their life through a new covenant lens. They experience hope again or possibly for the first time ever. They learn to dream with God, knowing anything is possible with Him. They experience the opportunity and favor that bring newness into all aspects of life, family, work, community, and recovery. Rebirth puts the full redemptive power of Jesus's sacrifice on display and allows us to visualize, build, and step into a promised-land life.

Have you truly experienced this rebirth? Have you invited others to experience it? How might newness of life in the Spirit change the way you do recovery forever? The kingdom of God is here—all you need to do is believe it, receive it in full, and share it with the ones you love and lead.

God, help me grasp the concept of rebirth—for myself and others. Give me eyes to see Your kingdom coming and show me how I can be a part of it. Your gospel is new life, and I receive it! Amen.

July 25: WALKING OUT A NEW LIFE

Therefore, as you received Christ Jesus the Lord, so walk in him.
—Colossians 2:6 (ESV)

When you choose to invite Jesus into your recovery journey, He will show you what it means to walk out the new life He has for you. Whether you're pursuing healing from your own struggles, or loving and leading people through theirs, He will show you the straight and narrow way forward.

This pathway to freedom is available to all, but few walk it—and even fewer actually enter into the promised-land life Jesus died for them to have. To walk out a new life in Christ, we must begin by visualizing a life we actually want to live and stay sober for. For many people in recovery, they've never experienced such a life, so it's hard to imagine it could ever exist. This is why the community element is so critically important to the recovery journey. We all need safe spaces and safe people to help us identify and heal from the trauma that causes us to struggle. Only by surrounding ourselves with authentic, grace-filled people can we be invited into new ways of thinking and new ways of seeing the world.

When you choose to live your new life for Jesus, you'll never walk alone. In fact, when the going gets tough, He'll not only walk with you, He'll carry you through. This is your invitation to learn what it really means to walk with Him. He wants you to match Him step by step, not getting too far ahead of Him or lagging behind. He will lead you into a promised-land life where you will have the joy and privilege of following and being with Him forever.

God, I know I can trust You to lead me into a better life than I could have imagined. Help me when the road gets rough and doubt creeps in. Take my hand and lead me step by step. Amen.

July 26: DELIVERANCE

See, I am doing a new thing! Now it springs up; do you not perceive it? I am making a way in the wilderness and streams in the wasteland.
—Isaiah 43:19

When it comes to life and recovery, initial salvation and initial sobriety are powerful moments of deliverance. We were once one way, and we suddenly and supernaturally became another way, all by the Spirit's power. Although people can be transformed in a moment from slave to free, embracing that newfound freedom almost always takes some getting used to. Why? We may believe that Jesus has set us free...but when life happens, we quickly forget.

When we remove perfectionist, works-based rules and regulations in Christ-centered recovery, we create space for progressive transformation. Deliverance leads to freedom, which makes room for sustainable yet nonlinear transformation. This is the solid ground needed to cultivate a promised-land life that bears the fruits of the Spirit in recovery. Love, joy, peace, patience, kindness, goodness, faithfulness, gentleness, and self-control (see Galatians 5:22–23) are byproducts of recovery, not prerequisites! Adopting a growth mindset helps people in recovery *taste and see that the Lord is good"* (Psalm 34:8), even when they're not sure how to do it yet.

For recovery leaders, this might mean developing sustainable strategies for walking with people past initial salvation and sobriety with a grace-laced gospel approach. For those walking their own journey, it might mean receiving God's grace over your current season and embracing your righteousness in Christ. One thing is certain: God values the journey just as much as initial deliverance, if not more. That's why Jesus invites us to follow Him.

God, thank You for setting me free from sin and struggle. Forgive me when I forget all that You've done, or when I lose my lens to see You at work in the lives of others. Help me see You more clearly. Amen.

July 27: JUSTIFIED

Know that a person is not justified by the works of the law,
but by faith in Jesus Christ.
—Galatians 2:16

In the eyes of God, Jesus, the friend of sinners, did more for you on the cross than you could ever do for yourself. He didn't just redeem you, paying the debt of your sins and wiping your slate clean forever. He *justified* you, making it just as if you'd never sinned, roughly 2,000 years before you ever even had the chance to sin.

Now, the concept of justification by faith is widely misunderstood. By earthly definitions, justification means proving someone or something to be right or reasonable. Looking back on your sins, no one could say your thoughts and deeds were right *or* reasonable. Justification is not about justifying sin. It's about separating you from your sin so completely that you are declared innocent in the eyes of the Father.

If the word *innocent* sounds a little theologically controversial to you, suspend disbelief for a moment. Christ's death and resurrection was the beginning of a new covenant in His shed blood—a covenant that *completely* fulfilled the Law of Moses with its many rules and precepts for holiness. God knew that His gift of the Law wouldn't be enough to make us holy by striving, so He sent Jesus to make us, His church, His beautiful, spotless bride. That's not just an invitation to the corporate church, but to each one of us—*to you.* You are *"without stain or wrinkle or any other blemish, but holy and blameless"* (Ephesians 5:27). That's how God sees *you* because of what Jesus did. He's forgiven and forgotten your sin completely

Is this an invitation to keep on sinning? Far from it! It's an invitation to receive justification over your life by faith, not works. This spiritual alignment with the Father's heart will help you resist sin and embrace your own promised-land life.

God, it's hard to accept my innocence, knowing all the things I've done wrong. But by Your grace, I receive Your gift of justification. Help me learn to walk in my innocence and offer it to others. Amen.

July 28: PROMISED-LAND LIFE

If the LORD delights in us, he will bring us into this land and give it to us, a land that flows with milk and honey.
—Numbers 14:8 (ESV)

Throughout the generations, God fought to get His people to return to Him. He made the Law, but we could not (and often would not) follow it faithfully. He destroyed evil by water in the flood and by fire at Sodom and Gomorrah, but more sin manifested. God finally decided to destroy our sin for us—by becoming sin in and through the shed blood of Jesus. Now that sin has been defeated, the Father wants us to know how loved, forgiven, and free we already are so we can step into the fullness of the promised-land life He has for all of us.

This is radical reconciliation. Who could honestly say *no* to such a miraculously transformed life? Sadly, we all do at times. We may receive the healing, forgiveness, and favor that come from being children of God, but over the long-haul journey of recovery, relapse into old ways of thinking and behaving is not only possible, but probable.

If it only took the Israelites, God's chosen people, two months to relapse and rebel against Moses and Aaron (see Exodus 16:3), why do we assume we would be immune? What's more, the Israelites experienced a miraculous delivery from bondage, complete with plagues and a split-open sea. We are likely to think that kind of display would have strengthened their faith and caused them to never doubt.

It's quite possible that the Israelites wandered in the desert for longer than they really needed to. But whether your recovery journey takes forty years, forty days, or forty seconds, the promised-land life God has for you is already available to you now. In this moment, He is working behind the scenes for your good and His glory. And in His perfect timing, He'll bring you all the way home.

God, I know Your plans for me are good. Stay by my side through the wilderness and help me stay vigilant. I'm ready to step into the new life You've promised me. Help me see it and enter in. Amen.

July 29: FREE PEOPLE FREE PEOPLE

*Live as free people, but do not use your freedom as
a cover-up for evil; live as God's slaves.*
—1 Peter 2:16

If hurt people hurt people, helped people help people. Most recovery program leaders come by their positions honestly, not out of obligation or with an agenda. Recovery leaders are just people like you and me. Usually, they've struggled with addiction, mental health problems, or suicidal thoughts themselves, but they've discovered at least some tangible level of freedom. They want to help others taste the freedom they've found.

That's beautiful. But even as fellow travelers on a journey, our paths to transformation are unique. Each and every roadblock is a critical part of what will one day be a living testimony. The Uncovery takes recovery leaders beyond the role of *helper* to identity-driven liberator.

So ask yourself, are you walking in the fullness of your freedom right now, in a way that others could recognize and emulate? This gut-check inquiry is not intended to shame you, but to encourage an honest assessment of the level of freedom you've found. Are there any parts of your life that you have not yet surrendered to God? Is there anything left in your heart or mind that you'd be ashamed to admit to a trusted friend, to God, or to yourself? In what areas do you need to experience breakthrough so you can help to set others free? God will show you, and He will equip you fully for His call on your life.

Free people free people when they do it in Jesus's name. You're no longer a slave to sin and struggle; you're a slave to freedom—to God Himself! And when you truly receive His gift of freedom, you'll want to spend the rest of your life giving away it to others.

God, use me. Show me any part of my life or my recovery journey that You want me to surrender to You. Give me courage to change, leaning into Your strength alone to sustain me as I go. Amen.

July 30: TESTIMONY

*They triumphed over him [the accuser] by
the blood of the Lamb and by the word of their testimony;
they did not love their lives so much as to shrink from death.*
—Revelation 12:11

If you've been in recovery circles for any length of time, you've probably heard inspiring testimonies from people who were delivered from bondage *straight* into a promised-land life. They may have said something like, "I met Jesus, and I never touched the stuff again!" One meeting with Jesus was all it took. And they all lived happily ever after. The end.

We sit on the edge of our seats and soak up these testimonies but wonder why they're the exception instead of the rule in our own experiences.

Now, I (George) certainly believe God *can* and *does* heal addiction and mental health problems instantaneously and miraculously. Scripture proves it, and I've seen and personally experienced it, so you'd better believe I'm *believing for it.* But I also believe God values the recovery journey as much if not more than the moment of deliverance. It's like falling in love—it looks different for every person and every relationship, in every stage. It's always miraculous but never formulaic. It takes us by surprise, makes us want to go deeper, and always reveals our God-given identity.

Consider your own life's testimony. Has it been a miraculous, wildfire success story, or are you learning to trust even through times of trial? Did you experience miraculous, instantaneous healing and delivery, or are you still trusting God in and through your struggle? Whoever you are, wherever you're from, and whatever your story, you are uniquely positioned to bring hope to someone meant to walk a similar path. You will overcome by the blood of the Lamb and the word of your testimony—a reckless love story that has the power to change the world.

God, sometimes I wonder if my story really matters. But if it could bring hope and encouragement to anyone, give me the courage to share it whenever and wherever You lead me. Amen.

July 31: ONE SHEEP

Suppose one of you has a hundred sheep and loses one of them.
Doesn't he leave the ninety-nine in the open country and go after the lost
sheep until he finds it? And when he finds it,
he joyfully puts it on his shoulders and goes home.
—Luke 15:4–6

It's no secret that a good shepherd would leave ninety-nine sheep on a hillside to go after one little lost lamb. If we, the church, are going to learn how to be a hospital for sinners who need a Savior instead of an elitist country club for saints, we need to embrace what's working—and let go of what's not working—in Holy Spirit-led recovery.

As both shepherds and sheep, it's important we remember the intrinsic divine DNA in every person we meet along the recovery journey. Some will walk the straight and narrow, checking boxes, following steps, and remaining sober and faithful through it all. Others will wonder and wander, struggling with contentment and rebelling against God's gifts of freedom. Whether we remain in the Father's house or make our beds in a pigsty, we are no more or less loved by God. And as people called to love and lead in the recovery space, we too must learn to love unconditionally—seeking and saving the lost and welcoming them home again like a little lost lamb.

This mindset shift will bring much-needed reform to the Christian church, not only for the obvious least of these, but for those of us who are hiding in plain sight. What's more, the fruit of this reform will spill outside the walls of the church into our communities in a way that sparks revival and brings every last lost sheep home. Will you be a part of it?

God, even at my worst, You're always pursuing me. You never give up on me, even when I run and rebel. I know I can never repay Your kindness, so help me carry it forward to others in recovery. Amen.

August

REGRETS

Do to others as you would have them do to you.
—Luke 6:31

He is the propitiation for our sins, and not for ours only but also for the
sins of the whole world.
—1 John 2:2 (ESV)

When we say, "Recovery is for everyone," we're not trying to be inclusionary or cute. Countless people who have experienced physical, emotional, or psychological trauma find themselves in need of recovery. They didn't ask for their current disorder, they didn't want it, and, in many cases, they did nothing to contribute to it. They are operating as a product of it, not the cause of it.

Even worse, some struggling people either don't remember or won't acknowledge the trauma that lies beneath their struggles, often because either they or the people around them don't consider it to be *legitimate* trauma. Problem is, trauma isn't what happens to you; it's what happens inside you because of what happens to you. Trauma impacts different people in different ways at different times and for different reasons, so we have little room to judge what's legitimate—for others and ourselves.

Trauma is trauma—and at some point, many of us willingly partner with the spirit of that trauma in sin. That sin turns to unshakeable regret that can linger long into our promised-land lives unless those of us in recovery convince people not of their sin, but of their righteousness in Christ. We, the church, have failed to recognize this, and we are causing our brothers and sisters to not only stumble, but to straight-up sin because we have more faith in their ability to sin than in God's ability to heal.

In the context of safe and authentic community, we cannot only identify past trauma and heal from it, but we can own any ways in which we may have partnered with it from an identity perspective. For example, you may have no fault in abuse against you—but clinging to and perpetuating a victim mentality is something you can own and repent of, reclaiming your innocence and eliminating not only your sin, but the sins against you. Owning your part isn't taking blame—it's freeing yourself of any attachment to the offense.

God, help me look objectively at trauma in my life and own my part in it, if any. Free me of shame and condemnation that's not mine to carry, and help me align my heart and mind with Yours. Amen.

August 2: REFLECTIONS

As in water face reflects face, so the heart of man reflects the man.
—Proverbs 27:19

When you look in the mirror, who do you see? Beyond your physical characteristics, beyond the familiarity of brushing, flossing, and doing your daily routine, when you see your reflection, what kind of emotions does it elicit? Do you see yourself for all of your shortcomings—your less than ideal physical traits, your past sins, or your deepest, darkest secrets? Or do you see yourself for who you really are: a beloved child of God, made pure, innocent, and holy in His eyes? Do you come face-to-face with your regrets, or do you marvel at the new creation you really are?

Your answers to these questions will indicate whether you're in bondage to shame or walking in freedom. Wherever you find yourself, feel no condemnation, but allow the Holy Spirit to speak His truth to you. Perhaps you fear no one will ever accept you if they know who you really are. Perhaps you can't even look at your own face, thinking of all the harm you've caused others. Perhaps you feel like an abject failure, and the sight of your face brings you grief. If so, ask God to reveal to you who He sees when He looks at you.

He sees *you*—the same beloved child He was thinking of before He created the world. He sees Christ *in you*, the hope of glory, not your war-torn past. He sees you, His chosen, His anointed—one who will move mountains in His name. Ask the Father to show you how He sees you, and you'll never look at your reflection the same way again.

God, how do You see me? I see a mess, but I know You see more. Show me who You are and who I am in You—and help me invite others to see Your divine DNA in themselves. Amen.

August 3: ADDICTION

So then, let us not be like others, who are asleep, but let us be awake and sober. For those who sleep, sleep at night, and those who get drunk, get drunk at night. But since we belong to the day, let us be sober, putting on faith and love as a breastplate, and the hope of salvation as a helmet.
—1 Thessalonians 5:6–8

Addictions don't always show up in the way that we think they would. They can be chemical or behavioral, chosen or thrust upon you. Alcohol, drugs, sex, food, codependency, gambling, gaming, social media, shopping, offenses, exercise, politics—the list of potential addictions is endless. While struggling with sugar cravings might not seem to be as destructive as craving heroin or pornography, the neurological premise is the same.

In and of themselves, addictions are not the actual struggle those of us in recovery face. The real culprit is always trauma, often manifested in struggles with our mental health, worn on the surface as an addiction to a substance like drugs or alcohol, compulsive behaviors, or obsession. We are *all* struggling with something. Some of us have better coping mechanisms than others, but that doesn't make us any better or worse than anyone else. And if we continue to combat only the surface-level struggle through legalism and behavior modification strategies, we will perpetuate cycles of addiction in the recovery space.

When we find ourselves addicted, we often ask, "How do we get sober?" It's not a bad question, and most who ask it are genuine. But the real question we need to be asking is, "What's causing us to struggle in the first place?" We need to focus on the answer to this question to heal from the trauma that keeps us bound. Only when we're healed of these things can we find lasting sobriety and a truly transformed life.

God, You know me, and You know my struggles. Help me dig deeper into the reasons behind my addictions. Show me any trauma that's keeping me bound and deliver me. Amen.

August 4: "ACCIDENTAL" OVERDOSE

For I am convinced that neither death nor life, neither angels nor demons, neither the present nor the future, nor any powers, neither height nor depth, nor anything else in all creation, will be able to separate us from the love of God that is in Christ Jesus our Lord.
—Romans 8:38–39

The isolation humankind has faced in recent years has sent addiction and relapses, mental health problems, and suicidal thoughts through the roof. More than 100,000 people in the United States died of drug overdoses between May 2020 and April 2021—a 28.5 percent increase from the same period in

2019–2020.[3] The monthly toll spiked to an unheard-of 9,362 overdose-related deaths in May 2020[4] when most of the known world was on lockdown during the COVID-19 pandemic.

The scariest part about these numbers—and the part that will be hardest to prove by preliminary facts and data—is that *any number* of these deaths by overdose could have been intentional. Suicide rates didn't spike as many of us had feared, but these unprecedented levels of death by overdose may have actually been misclassified suicides.

Why aren't we studying the commonalities of death by suicide and death by accidental overdose? Some say it can't be done. We say it *must* be done. And we, the church, desperately need the scientific community's help with this so we can help people struggling with addiction and mental health problems avoid an easy-out on life itself.

Bottom line? Isolation is a killer. Events and circumstances can become trauma when we don't have people to share them with. That trauma is embedded into our memory banks as either explicit (conscious) or implicit (unconscious), and both can impact our actions and awareness. Sharing stories of trauma with a trusted member of a safe community and having those stories received with compassion can change how they impact people moving forward. If we really want to see revival, we have to figure out how to come back together again in a post-pandemic world—physically, mentally, emotionally, and spiritually—and lean on one another again. We were never meant to operate in isolation.

God, give us eyes to see desperation for what it is. Give us the courage to explore the unexplorable—to see connections between drug overdose and suicide and offer Your better way. Amen.

August 5: FIGHTING THE RIGHT BATTLES

The LORD will fight for you; you need only to be still.
—Exodus 14:14

3. "Drug Overdose Deaths in the U.S. Top 100,000 Annually," Centers for Disease Control and Prevention, November 17, 2021, www.cdc.gov/nchs/pressroom/nchs_press_releases/2021/20211117.htm.
4. Jesse C. Baumgartner and David C. Radley, "The Spike in Drug Overdose Deaths During the COVID-19 Pandemic and Policy Options to Move Forward," The Commonwealth Fund, March 25, 2021, www.commonwealthfund.org/blog/2021/spike-drug-overdose-deaths-during-covid-19-pandemic-and-policy-options-move-forward.

There's no mistaking it. God has promised us a promised-land life of freedom, abundance, and intimacy with Him. Whatever side of the Jordan we're on, we must continually ask ourselves if the battles we're consecrating ourselves for are actually the battles God has called us to.

When you're fighting a battle that's not for the promised land, you'll have a hard time reaching it, let alone mustering the courage to cross over into it. Aim low, and you may hit your target, but with zero transformative satisfaction. Aim high, and you might not hit your target or build a perfect life, but you might shoot for the moon and land on a beautiful star, a place that feels more like home than the moon would anyway.

When Joshua marched around the walls of Jericho seven times and let out a righteous shout with his army, he looked like a fool. (See Joshua 6:15–20.) Here he was, about to head into the biggest battle the Israelites had faced in the promised land thus far, in a manner that made zero worldly sense. If I (George) had been Joshua (and thank God I wasn't), I'd have been more interested in picking less embarrassing fights—or at least fighting the Lord's battles in a way that didn't look so insane to everyone watching.

Writing from a jail cell in Rome while awaiting possible execution, Paul told the church in Philippi, *"Rejoice in the Lord always. I will say it again: Rejoice!"* (Philippians 4:4). He may have sounded like a fool to them. Seriously, who does that? Who sends a letter of hope from a place with no hope? But the joy that had consumed Paul because of the good news of the gospel transcended his bondage and sparked widespread early-church revival from the most unexpected of places.

God, help me discern whether I'm fighting the battles You're calling me to. Keep my thoughts aligned with Yours and help me not to rely on my own experiences and understanding. Amen.

August 6: WHAT ELSE MIGHT BE TRUE?

A fool takes no pleasure in understanding, but only in expressing his opinion.
—Proverbs 18:2 (ESV)

Even when there is a moment of miraculous healing in a recovery journey, we fall short when we expect the recipient to walk out a perfect existence after the mountaintop moment. Truth is, after such a high, just about everything pales in comparison. People can easily forget who they really are and fall back into old ways of thinking and behaving. There is bound to be a valley following every mountaintop. But without valleys, there would be no mountaintops to reach in the first place.

When people in Christian recovery relapse, leaders typically blame it on a faith issue, a sin issue, or both. While the Uncovery implores us to get to the real reasons why relapse happened, it's even more important not to jump to spiritual conclusions. Yes, there may be a faith issue. Yes, there may be a sin issue. But there may also be a medical issue, a community issue, or an identity issue. When we're tempted to snap to judgment, we must lay aside our cynicism and ask ourselves instead, "What else might be true?"

This open-minded, openhearted approach gut checks our intentions and positions us for deep and honest conversations with people who relapse. In that condemnation-free environment, they can be free to open up and uncover the real reason why they relapsed. And when they find the true cause, they can name it and deal with it, making future relapses less likely.

While we certainly don't want to dismiss or welcome relapse, we can change the way we respond when it occurs. Instead of resetting our *days sober* counters back to zero and shaming people into false repentance, we can offer individualized, person-centered care. Instead of handing down punitive measures and threats, we can invite them to participate in the Uncovery and find healing in all the right places. Relapse may be an important and even necessary part of their journey—and we need to learn to love them well through it.

God, challenge my assumptions. Show me places where I've come to incorrect conclusions about people and open my heart to search for and receive truth. Help me see them as You see them. Amen.

August 7: TAKING THOUGHTS CAPTIVE

*We demolish arguments and every pretension that sets itself
up against the knowledge of God, and we take captive every thought
to make it obedient to Christ.*
—2 Corinthians 10:5

Self-awareness is key to walking out your recovery journey, not to mention helping people walk through theirs. Even in our places of victory in Christ, the enemy still speaks, with his obnoxious voice calling into question what God really said. His tactics haven't changed much since he did it to Eve in the garden of Eden. He is a defeated foe, but many of us give him far too much credit and attention in this area.

Paul's letter to the Corinthians speaks of taking our thoughts captive. Anything that's not of God, we must learn to identify, name, and capture before it does any more damage. The problem is, if we take thoughts captive and store them in a birdcage in our minds, they can't leave, but they remain there, really loud, continuing to scream whispers of death. We know they're locked up, so we assume they're harmless. But we all too often miss the critical step of making those pesky, pervasive thoughts *obedient* to Christ.

Making a thought obedient to Christ takes surrender. In battle, it might equate to a prisoner exchange. Even when you have the enemy bound, you may have no use for him, but holding on to him adds no value and may in fact do you harm. Surrendering your prisoner to Jesus, having Him take the enemy and give him his due justice, frees you and glorifies God. Talk about a win-win!

What thoughts are you keeping captive in the birdcage of your brain right now? What lies are you believing? What shame can't you shake? What thoughts continue to consume you, even in a promised-land life? Give them to God now and let Him deal with them.

God, You know my every thought. Show me what lies are living uninvited in my mind and help me surrender them to You. Step in as righteous Judge and give the enemy what he deserves. Amen.

August 8: EXTENDING GRACE

For it is by grace you have been saved, through faith—and this is not from yourselves, it is the gift of God—not by works, so that no one can boast.
—Ephesians 2:8–9

Grace is a controversial topic in Christian recovery. Let's be honest—it's a controversial topic in the whole church! There are about as many interpretations of how God chooses to extend grace as there are people in need of it.

Based on biblical truth and the life of Jesus, we are convinced that God initiates grace that moves people to repentance, not the other way around. This keeps our mission clear. If we can help broken people know how loved and forgiven they already are, it's much easier for them to receive the Father's grace by faith and step into their life's true calling.

Extending God's grace to others can feel a little *greasy* sometimes. Forgiving the unforgivable, giving second, third, and seventy-seventh chances, and calling people *innocent* when they're clearly not can challenge our admittedly broken theological ideologies. The reckless grace of God always seems a little greasy until you need it—and then, you realize it's unmerited favor that nobody can earn or deserve.

That kind of grace demands a response, not only to make Jesus Lord of your life, but to be an ambassador of His grace in this world. You are fully loved, fully forgiven—forever. And wildly enough, so are *all* of us, even people you don't think deserve it. *Especially* them.

Our role as recovery leaders is to invite people into safe spaces where they can learn just how loved and forgiven they already are, and be moved with gratitude to not only receive this gift, but give it to others. This radical extension of grace has the power to change the church for generations to come.

God, Your grace to me is more than I can contain. Help me release that same grace in the overflow of Your love for me, extending mercy, forgiveness, and love to all I meet. Amen.

August 9: GRACE IN THE MOMENT

Be kind and compassionate to one another, forgiving each other, just as in Christ God forgave you.
—Ephesians 4:32

Nothing will make you question God's grace more than your daily, stuck-in-the-moment offenses. A waiter who messes up your lunch order. A coworker who steamrolls you in a strategy session. A child who tests your very last limit. Exasperated, you may think to yourself, *God may forgive you, but I don't have to.* Therein lies the most destructive line of thinking that's ever plagued the human race.

"Who can forgive sins but God alone?" (Mark 2:7). It's a question many have asked, but the most memorable instance comes from a scribe who observed Jesus forgiving the sins of a paralyzed man *before* healing his physical body. The healing itself was controversial enough, but forgiving sins? Who did this guy think He was?

Here's the best part: Whatever Jesus did on earth, you have the power and authority to do too. (See John 14:12.) How is it that we entertain thoughts of healing the sick and even raising the dead, but somehow, releasing grace and forgiveness seems blasphemous?

Grace may be the most powerful tool we Christians have in our toolbelt. For all intents and purposes, it's still new with tags on for most of us.

Get it out. Use it. See what happens. Chances are, you'll see a level of transformation that reinforces God's grace in your own life—to the point where you can't help but give it away.

God, when people get under my skin, help me see them as You do. Help me ask, "What else might be true?" and learn what it looks like to release Your grace and unmerited favor in the moment. Amen.

August 10: GRACE FOR A LIFETIME

For he chose us in him before the creation of the world to be holy and blameless in his sight. In love he predestined us for adoption to sonship through Jesus Christ, in accordance with his pleasure and will—to the praise of his glorious grace, which he has freely given us in the One he loves.
—Ephesians 1:4–6

Extending grace in the moment can become a practice that keeps us going day to day, week to week, month to month, and year to year. But grace for a lifetime is something that can only come from God. To learn to walk in this radical grace life, we must first understand that we were chosen to walk it out since before time as we know it began.

Before you could be known, God knew you. He knew everything about you. Your strengths, talents, and even your potential came straight from Him. He also knew the ways you'd struggle and need His grace—a grace He was ready, willing, and *eager* to lavish on you. He knew, in your humanness, that you wouldn't do this life perfectly. So He created a way for you to be holy not by your works, but by your faith in His Son, Jesus. He chose you—and He anointed you to help identify and raise up His chosen ones who don't yet know who they are.

Grace is a lifestyle. Once you tap into a little bit of it, up springs a well that overflows in every interaction you have. You start to see people for who they really are—not broken sinners, but saints, indwelled by the Holy Spirit, whether they believe it or not. This grace compels you to act with honor in every human interaction, sometimes to the amazement of the people who receive your grace. Jesus shocked people with a grace that always went first. Will you follow suit and make the first move in Jesus's name?

God, help me initiate with grace, not just daily but as a way of life. Temper my responses in love and give me opportunities to release Your forgiveness to a world in need. Amen.

August 11: WHICH LAW?

Therefore, there is now no condemnation for those who are in Christ Jesus, because through Christ Jesus the law of the Spirit who gives life has set you free from the law of sin and death.
—Romans 8:1–2

Make no mistake: God is holy, and on our own, we're not. We might be tempted to believe this reality *repulses* God and that's why He gave us the Law of Moses, a long list of rules and regulations to keep us holy enough to stand before Him. Until we sinned, and then we had to sacrifice a goat or a bull to get square again. Ironically, the only people who could keep holy enough to encounter God in the temple were priests. So needless to say, we humans kept God at a distance for a very long time.

But God didn't give His people the Law because He thought they could keep it in their own strength. He gave it to them because He knew they *wouldn't* be able to keep it in their own strength, and that it would point the Israelites—and *us* by proxy—to our need for a Savior.

Since Jesus died and rose again, we've been living under a new covenant in His shed blood. Forget goats and bulls. Jesus's blood was so pure, so holy, and so perfect of a sacrifice that no other would ever be needed again. His blood covered sin in its entirety, past, present, and future. On the cross, Christ's work was finished. He said so Himself. (See John 19:30.)

For modern-day believers, this means we are no longer subject to the Law of Moses because it was *fulfilled* in the person of Jesus. Does this mean we throw out the original Law and all of its precepts? No. But we know now, beyond a shadow of a doubt, that we are holy by the grace of a good Father God, not by obedience to the letter of the Law. Friend, you are now subject to the Law of the Spirit of life. You are legally obligated to walk in freedom!

God, thank You for making a way when there was no way for me to be holy on my own. I submit myself to Your new covenant law. Teach me to walk in freedom according to Your plan. Amen.

August 12: GENERATIONAL CURSES

The one who sins is the one who will die. The child will not share the guilt of the parent, nor will the parent share the guilt of the child. The righteousness of the righteous will be credited to them, and the wickedness of the wicked will be charged against them.
—Ezekiel 18:20

The church is known for creating buzzwords and phrases that keep people in bondage, sometimes for generations at a time. One of the most prominent is the generational curse, a familial predisposition toward a particular sin, trauma, or perpetual torment or abuse. While we are absolutely a product of our upbringing, for better or for worse, the church has assumed this phenomenon as an inevitability, assuming sin and death are somehow passed down through the generations.

This becomes especially painful in recovery ministry, where people with addictions, mental health problems, and suicidal thoughts often assume them because a parent or family member struggled with the same. While sin can be demonstrated and even taught in a way that passes to generation after generation, the curse is something we choose to believe in and receive.

When Jesus healed the man who was born blind, the disciples asked Him, *"Who sinned, this man or his parents?"* (John 9:2). Based on the Jewish teachings, they assumed his blindness was due to his sin or a generational curse. But Jesus corrected them: *"Neither this man nor his parents sinned...but this* happened so that the works of God might be displayed in him" (verse 3). The progressive healing left the man unrecognizable to his neighbors, who only knew him as a blind beggar.

If, like the disciples, you're still asking whether addiction, mental health problems, or suicidal thoughts are caused by personal sin, brought about by the sin actions of another, or just appear seemingly at random, you're asking the wrong questions. It's time to invite people into the new creation they really are in Christ.

God, forgive me when I've assumed earthly family ties are stronger than the ties of Your kingdom family. Let us be a generation that casts off the shackles of the previous generations and lives free. Amen.

August 13: GENERATIONAL GRACE

> He remembers his covenant forever, the promise he made,
> for a thousand generations.
> —Psalm 105:8

In John 9:2–5, Jesus cleared up any confusion when it came to generational curses. They're not really a thing...unless you choose to make them one. This can change the way you see your past. You've been fully redeemed of and justified from your past; it doesn't even exist anymore in the eyes of God. This unfathomable grace has been on display for at least the last 2,000 years or so—and likely even longer when you begin to see how the old covenant did nothing but point to Jesus, the coming Messiah.

In Deuteronomy, long before Jesus walked the earth, Moses penned words that weakened the veil between us and a Holy God:

> *Know therefore that the LORD your God is God, the faithful God who keeps covenant and steadfast love with those who love him and keep his commandments, to a thousand generations.* (Deuteronomy 7:9 ESV)

If one thing has passed through the generations, it's not a curse—it's God's grace. Even when we falter, He remains faithful, ready and willing to lavish His grace upon us, time and again. By all earthly standards, we should have exasperated Him by now. But generation to generation, God's grace seems to be getting better and better as He reveals deeper and deeper facets of His character.

Accept the fact that God might be even better than you think He is, and He'll prove it to you in love.

God, You're so good—even better than I can imagine. Show me where Your grace has been in my family tree and help me align with Your grace today. Generational curses stop with me. Amen.

August 14: GRACE IN THE GARDEN

What is this you have done?
—Genesis 3:13

From Genesis all the way through Revelation, God is on a mission, reconciling the whole world back to Himself. (See 2 Corinthians 5:19.) It starts in the garden of Eden just after Adam and Eve ate of the Tree of Knowledge of Good and Evil, bringing sin into the perfect world God had made for them.

Instead of responding in anger, as many well-meaning preachers would retell the tale, God responds with the heart of a good and loving Father eager to know who convinced His children they weren't already like Him. He asks, *"Who told you that you were naked?"* (Genesis 3:11). Adam blamed Eve, Eve blamed the serpent, and nobody claimed any responsibility whatsoever. Brokenhearted, God made garments for Adam and Eve, clothed them, and ushered them out of the garden. Had they continued to eat from the garden's Tree of Life, they would have been doomed to an eternal state of sin.

Throughout the generations, God fought to get His people to return to Him. He made the Law, but they couldn't or wouldn't follow it faithfully. He destroyed evil by water in the flood and by fire at Sodom and Gomorrah, but more sin manifested. God finally decided to destroy our sin for us—by becoming sin in and through the shed blood of His Son, Jesus.

Now that sin has been defeated, the Father wants us to know how loved, forgiven, and free we already are so we can step into the fullness of the promised-land life He has for all of us. This is radical reconciliation.

God, give me a clearer glimpse of Your heart for Adam and Eve in the garden. Show me Your love and compassion for them and help me receive it from You when I go astray. Amen.

August 15: GOOD FOR YOU

I, even I, am he who blots out your transgressions, for my own sake,
and remembers your sins no more.
—Isaiah 43:25

Our sovereign God is all powerful—"*the Alpha and the Omega, the First and the Last, the Beginning and the End*" (Revelation 22:13). He does whatever He wants. But when you take a deeper look at what He really wants, it has little to do with Him, and everything to do with us.

When it comes to forgiveness, God comes off rather reckless from an earthly standpoint. He blots out or erases our transgressions and forgets them completely. Why would He do this? Wouldn't it be better to keep a list of transgressions in some permanent record database of wrongs so He can perform a quick search come judgment day? Nope. Scripture says He forgives and forgets, not for our sake, but for His own sake. He's displaying the kind of forgiveness we're meant to extend to others. We may never be able to fully forget the sins against us, but by the grace of God, releasing grace and forgiveness to others can heal our own wounded souls.

Who is in a position to condemn us? Only Jesus. But He doesn't condemn. He initiates with grace that moves His people to repentance, not the other way around. Imagine if we too forgave others before they repented or showed any remorse whatsoever—not for their sakes but our own. I believe we'd see healing on unprecedented levels, not only for the forgivers, but also for those who are forgiven.

God, by Your grace, I know I can forgive. Help me learn what it means to forgive and forget. Show me deeper healing that comes with forgiveness and make me a conduit of Your grace. Amen.

August 16: GOOD FOR THEM

And when you stand praying, if you hold anything against anyone, for-
give them, so that your Father in heaven may forgive you your sins.
—Mark 11:25

Forgiveness is a blessing that begets further blessing, a gift from God that quite literally keeps on giving. God's grace to us and through us has the power to free us from bondage. And what do free people do? They free other people, often by releasing grace and forgiveness to the very people they never thought they could.

When you forgive an offense against you, it does more than free you. It shifts the atmosphere, removing the burden of sin between you and your brother or sister. When you forgive, not out of obligation but out of gratitude for the grace you've received, your offender may sense a Spirit-led shift that brings him or her to repentance. You may not even need to tell your offender that you forgive them face-to-face, especially in cases of abuse. But following the Spirit's lead, you can harness the power to forgive the unforgivable and make a way for the Holy Spirit to do His thing.

Matthew 6:14 says, *"For if you forgive other people when they sin against you, your heavenly Father will also forgive you."* The assumption here is forgiveness. God won't force you to extend it, but if you do, you'll receive the same level of grace and forgiveness. Do the healing. Forgive and forget. And watch God move.

God, it's hard to imagine forgiving the mounting offenses against me. But if it's what You want, it's what I want. Show me how. Move me with compassion toward genuine forgiveness. Amen.

August 17: NEUROPLASTICITY

"For who has understood the mind of the Lord so as to instruct him?"
But we have the mind of Christ.
—1 Corinthians 2:16 (ESV)

The brain is a miraculous thing. It's a wonder to me that anyone could consider this three-pound, highly adaptive organ with a hundred billion neurons and not see the fingerprint of God on each person. The brain can't feel pain, but it can be damaged. The tiniest chemical shift in serotonin can cause a splitting headache. Add in stress, trauma, disease, disorders, and nonorganic chemical compounds like drugs and alcohol, and the brain's neurotransmitters and neurological pathways can become quite literally rewired, causing long-term reduced cognitive function.

The brain's ability to adapt and change like this, for better or for worse, is known as neuroplasticity. The longer the addiction, mental health problem, or suicidal thoughts continue, the more deeply ingrained they can become, making traditional recovery far more difficult. By the grace of God, medical research has proven that the human brain has the ability to rewire its own neurological pathways. Yes, the brain can actually *unlearn* addictive, disordered behavior and reset itself.

Mindfulness and meditation have been proven to help reduce the risk of relapse, which can be a permanent struggle even for people back in a place of health. And new studies of the structural changes that occur in an addicted brain are even now helping scientists and medical professionals develop new treatments, medications, and therapies. Acknowledging and celebrating these breakthroughs does no harm to the Christian church, and it might even increase our ability to share the gospel.

God, if You created my brain with the capacity to heal itself, I know You can heal my heart too. Help me stay sober and alert so I can experience the transformative power of neuroplasticity. Amen.

August 18: GRACE REFLECTIONS

I do not set aside the grace of God, for if righteousness could be gained through the law, Christ died for nothing!
—Galatians 2:21

Living in the light of grace—a life that casts off shame and regret and replaces it with Christ's righteousness—can get a little too comfortable over time. While God never tires of lavishing His grace on us, and we must never tire of receiving it, we can at times forget just how far God has carried us along the recovery journey. We don't do it on purpose; we're human, and we're easily distracted. When our miracles begin to feel a little stale, like they did for the Israelites in the wilderness, it's important to testify to God's goodness and again remember His grace, mercy, and unfailing love toward us through the years.

Pause and reflect on His grace in your life. Give yourself no limits—look for His grace in any season of your life, even before you entered recovery. Where was He in your youth? Where was He in your worst moment? How has He redeemed your story? What miracles can you testify to? If you're struggling to remember, ask God to help you recall His faithfulness throughout the generations, to you and through you.

God, You are so faithful. Thank You for always being there, even at my darkest. Thank You for giving me grace and transforming my life. Help me remember and continue to see Your faithfulness. Amen.

August 19: WHEN SYSTEMS FAIL US

He has brought down rulers from their thrones but has lifted up the humble.
He has filled the hungry with good things but has sent the rich away empty.
—Luke 1:52–53

As humans, we love systems. These logical pathways programmed to produce a specific outcome give us a sense of peace and security. In some spaces, systems are beautiful and life-giving. Hospital, justice, school, and even faith systems provide organized frameworks for people to serve, collaborate, love, and lead. Our God is a God of order; we gravitate to systems because He created us that way.

But for those of us who knowingly or unknowingly struggle with control, systems can feed a very dangerous monster, especially when the man-made systems we so heavily rely on break down. Hospitals face caregiver shortages. Parents lose custody on a technicality. Overworked teachers go on strike. Religious leaders fall from the pedestals we put them on.

In recovery, systems designed to heal can sometimes perpetuate the struggle. Twelve-step, thirty-day, or six-month programs may get you sober, but they may not equip you for real life. Eighteen-year-old kids go to prison for marijuana possession and don't know how to build a promised-land life with a criminal record. New laws and social programs create career paths for people struggling with addiction, mental health problems, and suicidal thoughts, but they're still treated as *other* in the workplace from day one.

Man-made systems will eventually fail. Necessary as our systems and programs may be, it's important that we never cling to them too tightly. As culture changes, so must our methods. We must be willing to let go of systems that no longer serve us and our communities, and reform broken systems that need God to breathe new life into them.

Be bold. Challenge the status quo. Strip the concept that, "We've always done it that way" from your vocabulary, and ask the Father, "What more would You have me do?"

God, I wish there were easy answers when it comes to reforming recovery. But if reform was easy, I suppose we wouldn't invite You into it. Open my heart. Strengthen me. Make me bold. Amen.

August 20: GETTING WHAT YOU WANT

Take delight in the LORD, and he will give you the desires of your heart.
—Psalm 37:4

Scripture is clear that God wants to give us the things our hearts desire. King David's words ring true today, especially in the light of the new covenant, where intimacy with God is available to everyone.

Removed from context, today's Scripture might lead us to believe that God is a weak parent who gives His bratty kids whatever they want as long as they delight in Him. But the next verses sober us quickly: *"Commit your way to the LORD; trust in him and he will do this: He will make your righteous reward shine like the dawn, your vindication like the noonday sun"* (Psalm 37:5–6). When we ask God for our heart's desires, are we at the same time committing our ways to His, aligning our desires with His desires?

God is a good Father. The gifts He gives His beloved children are always going to be for our good and His glory, even if they're not exactly what we think we want. Conversely, sometimes He will go ahead and give us what we ask for—and we ultimately find the gift just doesn't satisfy like the Gift Giver. This is why people who have everything can still want more, and why some who have nothing feel rich and abundant in the Holy Spirit.

God hears our pleas. We can beg, "God, if You'll just give me *this*, I know I'll finally be happy," or "God, if You'll give me *this*, I promise I'll do *this*." But ultimately, He wants the desire of our hearts to simply be more of Him.

When we ask for this, He always delivers, and we experience joy that transcends fleeting happiness. Unlikely theologian Mick Jagger may have said it best: "You can't always get what you want but if you try sometime you'll find you get what you need."[5]

---

5. The Rolling Stones, "You Can't Always Get What You Want" on *Let It Bleed* (Decca, 1969).

God, You already know my heart's desires. I'm letting go of the things I want to first receive what I need—more of You. Align my heart with Yours and teach me to want what You want. Amen.

August 21: KNOWING WHAT YOU WANT

"What do you want me to do for you?" Jesus asked him.
The blind man said, "Rabbi, I want to see."
—Mark 10:51

Blind Bartimaeus. It's an unfortunate label for a man who would eventually see. Even in Scripture, our human tendency to categorize is put on full display. The paralytic. The adulterous woman. The demon-possessed man. Even after healing and deliverance, they were still largely known by the people for their struggles and not their true identity.

But our friend Bart is one of the few recipients of healing that the Gospels actually name—and here's why: He understands *exactly* who Jesus is. Bartimaeus calls Him *"Son of David"* (Mark 10:47), which is the first public declaration of Jesus's messiahship. He responds to Jesus in faith, much to the chagrin of the people surrounding him who would have preferred that he keep quiet. As a blind beggar, he drops his cloak, probably his only worldly possession, jumps to his feet, and goes to Jesus. Bart knows *exactly* what he wants—he wants to see, so he can follow Christ on the road.

Like Bart, many of us have impediments that would keep us from following Jesus. Struggles with addiction, mental health, and suicidal thoughts can make the journey difficult if not impossible for some. This is why those of us in recovery are called to love and lead. Addressing surface-level struggles is a start, but we are meant to show struggling people exactly who Jesus is, so they can ask for what they want boldly—not just because it would be nice, but because they need deliverance in order to follow Him.

In what ways can you remove barriers to Jesus for those who struggle? In what ways do you need to clarify what *you* really want, and why you really want it? Recovery is a journey—and we can rely on Jesus to equip us with everything we need to follow Him.

God, I admit that sometimes I think I know what I want, but the reasons why are all about me, not about You. Father, You know best. Help me know what I need and teach me to want that. Amen.

August 22: THERAPEUTIC HEALING

Nevertheless, I will bring health and healing to it; I will heal my people and will let them enjoy abundant peace and security.
—Jeremiah 33:6

The word *healing* means different things to different people in the church. Being *cured* is language traditionally attached to professional medical circles, meaning complete elimination of an illness or disease. Being *healed*, on the other hand, describes something that can happen both naturally *and* supernaturally, even when no physical cure is possible. While many see addiction, mental health problems, and suicidal thoughts as defining and even permanent illnesses that require lifelong treatment, others see them as struggles that can be overcome, either by sheer will or by the power of the Holy Spirit.

Some of our struggles will require therapies and medical intervention. Some will require fervent prayer and a whole lot of faith. Most will require both. Those of us in recovery need Christian community—church gatherings, small groups, meetings, discipling relationships, and friendships. But we may also need counselors, therapists, and medical professionals who can be conduits for a tangible healing experience with the Great Physician that leaves us not only cured but whole. Having Jesus and a therapist too isn't a lack of faith, it's wisdom. God can reveal powerful truths about our identity in counseling that can heal parts of our lives we didn't even know were broken.

Healing and curing are both of God. They put His goodness on display and create a hope-filled wonder about His character and our identity. He is a good Father who wants good healing and curing things for us, His children and coheirs to the kingdom with Jesus. Our full inheritance is available to us right now.

God, what do You say about therapeutic healing, in my life and the lives of those I love and lead? Show me any barriers to healing that I've created and break them down with Your truth. Amen.

Repent, then, and turn to God, so that your sins may be wiped out,
that times of refreshing may come from the Lord.
—Acts 3:19

Confession is a hot-button topic in many Christian circles and for good reason. Beyond bearing our souls and confessing to everything we've ever done wrong—in perpetuity—we don't really understand the point of confession other than it's what we *should* do.

Confession is ultimately a display of repentance, which the church has unfortunately tied in translation to the old English word *penance*. However, the Greek word *metanoia* translated for this verse does not literally mean penance, remorse, punishment, regret, or any other shame-filled response. *Metanoia* simply means to change your mind.

If repentance isn't what we think it is, we probably don't have a full understanding of confession either. Yes, the English word *confession* can mean to admit guilt, similar to how someone might confess to committing a crime in a legal environment. It's no different in a legalistic church environment, where striving to keep your proverbial slate wiped clean is often valued over receiving and walking in God's grace. But if real, *metanoia* repentance simply means to change your mind, real confession simply means to declare with your lips what God says about you—that you're loved, forgiven, and free.

Now, don't hear what I'm *not* saying. If you have secret sin in your life, by all means, share it with a trusted member of your community and ask them to pray for you and hold you accountable. But don't think for a moment that a confession of guilt gives you the keys to the kingdom. Access to your inheritance comes from a confession of Jesus as Lord of your life and receiving His grace in full.

God, I confess that You are bigger than any sin I could ever commit. I receive Your grace over my life. Teach me to walk in it, knowing that You have set me free from sin's grasp. Amen.

God made him who had no sin to be sin for us, so that in him we might
become the righteousness of God.
—2 Corinthians 5:21

Only one man has ever lived a truly sinless life: Jesus, the Son of God. Jesus didn't keep Himself free of sin by striving; He simply knew that the authority of God that He carried on the earth could not coexist with sin, nor could He be a perfect sacrifice to fulfill the Law of Moses and defeat sin once and for all.

Was Jesus tempted? You bet He was. He was fully God, yet fully human, so He understands exactly what the temptation to sin feels like. And yet even in His humanness, He held fast against every scheme Satan threw at Him, putting on display for us the very real possibility of living a sinless life.

Now, Jesus is God, and we are not. However, Jesus set a high standard of perfection for us as His followers, not because we can achieve it on our own, but to prove that we can't do it without Him. *"If we claim to be without sin, we deceive ourselves and the truth is not in us"* (1 John 1:8). And yet because of Christ's example and perfect sacrifice for our past, present, and future sins, we can in fact be perfect, holy, and blameless in God's eyes. We've been justified. We've been set free from sin. We're innocent—as long as we continue to believe we are.

> *No temptation has overtaken you except what is common to mankind.*
> *And God is faithful; he will not let you be tempted beyond what you can*
> *bear. But when you are tempted, he will also provide a way out so that you*
> *can endure it.* (1 Corinthians 10:13)

Do you believe this? If you really do, a sinless life is in fact within your reach. Feel no shame or condemnation—no human has ever walked it out before except Jesus. But when you answer His call to follow Him, say what He says and do what He does. Align your heart with His, and you won't have to flee from sin—sin will flee from you.

God, remind me how forgiven I am. Show me pathways to a sinless life. I won't walk it out perfectly, but that was never Your plan. Give me a revelation of grace that sends Satan running. Amen.

May God himself, the God of peace,
sanctify you through and through. May your whole spirit,
soul and body be kept blameless at the coming of our Lord Jesus Christ.
—1 Thessalonians 5:23

The connection between spirit, soul, and body in recovery is undeniable. It's a God-given, even Trinitarian example of the interconnectedness of our created self. Scripture calls for our spirit, our soul (or mind), and our body to be *"kept blameless"* for when Jesus comes back—not by our own strength, but by God Himself, who alone has the power to sanctify us.

Despite scriptural evidence to its intrinsic and holy value, we humans often downplay the importance of the body, carelessly using biblical one-liners about cutting off a hand or plucking out an eye if it causes us to sin. (See Matthew 5:29–30.) It's possible that these passages—used as weapons out of context—may have been part of the origin of self-harm, a compulsive behavior that's closely linked to suicidal thoughts. Was Jesus being dramatic, ironic, or facetious? No. But when He delivered some of these challenging words during His famous Sermon on the Mount, He was not yet speaking plainly to His disciples or the crowds. (See John 16:29–33.) Instead, He was inviting them to question why they believe what they believe—and to hold themselves to an even higher, more beautiful standard than the Law required. Not in their own strength, but in His.

Your spirit, mind, and body are all of great importance to God. Your body is a temple—indwelled by the Holy Spirit, precious and meant to be cared for in this realm. Our physical bodies came from dust and will one day return to it. But while the breath of God still fills our lungs and while His blood still flows through our veins, our body remains holy and precious in God's sight. Keep and steward yours as the holy vessel it is.

God, thank You for consecrating my body, making it holy and pleasing to You and worthy of my respect. Help me care for my spirit, soul, and body as a connected unit designed to glorify You. Amen.

Brothers and sisters, I do not consider myself yet to have taken hold of it.
But one thing I do: Forgetting what is behind and straining toward what
is ahead, I press on toward the goal to win the prize for which God has
called me heavenward in Christ Jesus.
—Philippians 3:13–14

Acknowledging pain of the past and sharing regret and remorse over the things we've done and the things done to us is a critical part of healing and recovery. Reliving past scenarios in the safety and comfort of authentic community can unearth the traumas that lead us to struggle. Once we find them, the healing process can begin. Problem is, we often hold onto those past traumas for longer than we need to.

When Paul wrote to the church in Philippi, he admitted he was still very much a work in progress. (See Philippians 3:12.) He might not have had the modern language for it, but even Paul himself was in recovery. As a fellow traveler just a few steps ahead on the journey, he explained to the church the importance of pressing on—unapologetically leaving the regrets of the past in the past and chasing after Jesus. While we may never be able to forget the sins of our past as God the Father does, we can choose whether or not they will rule our present and our future.

Finally, brothers and sisters, whatever is true, whatever is noble, whatever
is right, whatever is pure, whatever is lovely, whatever is admirable—if
anything is excellent or praiseworthy—think about such things.
(Philippians 4:8)

If your past doesn't elicit any of these characteristics, resist the urge to dwell there. It's not about entering into denial—far from it. It's just refusing to give mental and emotional energy to something that is no longer true about you now that you're in Christ. Receive God's grace in full, and you'll begin to see your past as a springboard to your kingdom calling. We go through what we go through so we can help others do the same.

God, You've redeemed my past. Take and use it however You want. I release it
to You now, leaving it at Your feet. Set my thoughts on the present, where my past
is in the past and I'm in You. Amen.

August 27: A NEW CREATION

*And we all, who with unveiled faces contemplate the Lord's glory, are
being transformed into his image with ever-increasing glory, which comes
from the Lord, who is the Spirit.*
—2 Corinthians 3:18

God's Word says you are a new creation in Christ. (See 2 Corinthians 5:17.) It does not say you need to *become* a new creation, or even *be* a new creation, but that you already *are* a new creation. The old you is gone, and the new you is here; the only work you have to do is to believe it's true and learn to rest in that truth.

This is a huge opportunity for people in traditional recovery and the ones who love and lead them. Instead of going after surface-level struggles with labeling and behavior modification strategies, we can invite struggling people to embrace their new identity as beloved children of God. Instead of, "Hi, my name is John, and I'm an addict," what if we said, "Hi, my name is John, and I'm a new creation in Christ—my past addictions are overcome by the blood of the Lamb and the word of my testimony."

Admittedly, it might make our group meetings a little longer, but do you see the critical shift?

Even in the middle of our struggles, in the throes of full-on addiction, mental health problems, and suicidal thoughts, claiming our true identity not only makes us doubt our doubts, it makes us start to believe what God says about us. Declaring our righteousness in Christ over the lie of a label is the key to breakthrough in recovery.

Start by applying this simple tactic to your own recovery journey. How might you introduce yourself at a meeting or in another recovery context in a way that would align your mind and heart with who God says you are?

"Hi, my name is _____, and I'm a new creation in Christ—my past _____ is/are overcome by the blood of the Lamb and the word of my testimony."

God, it's funny to be in this already/not yet space where I'm made new and You're making me new. Thank You for all You've done, and thank You that You're not finished with me yet. Amen.

August 28: RENEWING THE MIND

Therefore we do not lose heart. Though outwardly we are wasting away,
yet inwardly we are being renewed day by day.
—2 Corinthians 4:16

Things aren't always what they seem. Even when we have eyes to see and ears to hear, we can struggle with discernment when we rely too much on our natural flesh to make it happen.

Your body is a gift from God, a holy vessel you are meant to respect and steward well. But your body is a temporary dwelling. It wasn't made to last, but to return back to dust. Coming face-to-face with this reality can lead people to believe that battle scars, imperfections, and even aging hands might somehow disqualify us from God's plan.

Nowhere in Scripture does God command us to renew our bodies. And it's a good thing too. The mind, a soul-connected manifestation of the physical brain, can continually change and come into alignment with God, even after our physical bodies fail us. Renewing the mind comes by spending time with God in His Word and allowing it to transform how we see ourselves—spirit, mind, and body.

Can allowing God to renew your mind impact you physically? Sure it can. Studies show that a positive mindset can actually produce anti-inflammatory healing properties that can expedite and enhance healing and fight disease. This is why it's so important to fix your eyes not only on what you can see, but also the unseen spiritual elements that heal you from mental and physical trauma and deliver you from your surface-level struggles for good. Renewing the mind is a transformation only God can do. But choosing to receive and grow through this renewal is entirely up to you.

God, I receive Your renewal. Cleanse my mind from any thoughts that are not of You, especially thoughts that tell me I'm too old, too broken, or too damaged to do Your work. I'm all yours. Amen.

August 29: EPIGENETIC ATTACHMENTS

But we were gentle among you,
like a nursing mother taking care of her own children.
—1 Thessalonians 2:7 (ESV)

Epigenetic studies have proven that there is no addiction gene, but that life experience affects patterns of gene expression in the brain. When certain genes go dormant, they impact the way we attach or detach from people, in social engagement or self-defense. The wild thing is, these gene expressions are developed in early childhood. If we're lacking in nature or nurture, it can increase our propensity toward addiction, compulsive behaviors, and struggles with our mental health because we never really learn to self-soothe as God intended.

The beautiful thing is that over time and under trauma-informed care, the brain can heal. These dormant genes can be reawakened through long-term sobriety, therapy, and spiritual development in the context of healthy community. We were created for relationship with God and each other. Even lab rats will forego food and addictive chemical compounds when given the option of community. We can't travel back in time to nurture people in stages of early childhood development, but we can help them identify and heal from trauma, learn to self-soothe without substances and dissociative behaviors, and receive nature and nurture, even in adulthood, that can quite literally rewire the brain.

Discoveries such as these should foster compassion and grace for each person's unique recovery journey, including our own. Let us be moved with compassion to remove systemic issues keeping the next generation in a cycle of epigenetic detachment, setting them free from struggle in the name of Jesus.

God, help me see beneath the surface to better understand how early trauma impacts our struggles. Give me compassion for others and myself and use me to bring breakthrough. Amen.

August 30: ADDICTION VS. COMPULSION

Not only so, but we also glory in our sufferings, because we know that suffering produces perseverance; perseverance, character; and character, hope.
—Romans 5:3–4

Even in recovery circles, people wrongly use the words *addiction* and *compulsion* interchangeably. Addiction is a dependence on a particular substance or behavior. Compulsion is an intense urge to do something. While a compulsion can sometimes lead to an addictive behavior, they are not the same.

We must learn to understand and embrace this concept if we want to get to the heart of the Uncovery. While the compulsions of addictive behaviors may lead to a sense of *pleasure* in the brain, compulsion without addiction provides no cognitive satisfaction whatsoever, only temporary relief that breeds shame and anxiety. Someone who struggles with alcohol addiction might answer the compulsion to drink more and more to feel pleasure or avoid pain. Someone stuck in an obsessive compulsion such as self-harm feels a release of tension, but no pleasure. Compulsions often cause great distress when carried out, whereas addictions will make people use more and more to gain pleasure at any cost.

The two struggles need vastly different treatment, counsel, support, and intercession as part of comprehensive trauma-informed care and ministry teams. God doesn't rank our struggles any more than He ranks our sins, but all struggles are not equal.

If you or someone you love and lead is struggling with an addiction or compulsion, be ready to partner with medical, spiritual, and community support teams to better serve them on their recovery journey.

God, there are so many nuances to the struggles we face. I have so much to learn, but I'm here for it. Fill me and use me to help people find tailored healing opportunities for a promised-land life. Amen.

August 31: OVERDOSE AWARENESS

And the prayer offered in faith will make the sick person well; the Lord will raise them up. If they have sinned, they will be forgiven. Therefore, confess your sins to each other and pray for each other so that you may be healed. The prayer of a righteous person is powerful and effective.
—James 5:15–16

If you love and lead people in recovery from addiction, overdose is always top of mind. Relapse after relapse, you wonder if this one will be the last—not because they break free from their struggle, but because this time, the addiction consumed their life to the point of death. We know the Bible says not to be worried or afraid, but a heightened awareness in this area is something we all must face.

The sobering reality is that not all deaths by overdose are accidental. The correlating symptoms between death by suicide and death by overdose are right in front of us, yet few will commit to studying the intrinsic links. From a ministry standpoint, we need to know where people are on the journey—their current struggles, their hopes and dreams, and the opportunities (or lack thereof) tying them to their purpose. When we begin to suspect that they're sober but not yet transformed, the telltale signs of impending relapse may be more dire than we ever thought possible.

Today, on International Overdose Awareness Day, we pause to honor those who have died from an overdose and reflect on the grief of those they left behind. Overdose is the leading cause of death for people ages eighteen to forty-five in America today. Many continue to live with the stigma associated with having a close family or friend die from an overdose.

On this day of shared grief, receive God's invitation to go deeper with the ones you love and lead. Do you feel His gentle nudge to reach out to someone who is struggling? Who comes to mind as someone who might need your help today? To whom can you provide a listening ear, a warm embrace, and a judgment-free safe place? Whoever comes to mind, reach out now. You won't regret it.

God, bring to mind anyone who might be in trouble right now—someone at the end of their rope who could use a friend. Help me be Your hands and feet. Spirit, lead me where I can serve today. Amen.

September

RECONCILIATION

Therefore, if you are offering your gift at the altar and there remember that your brother or sister has something against you, leave your gift there in front of the altar. First go and be reconciled to them; then come and offer your gift.
—Matthew 5:23–24

Therefore, if you are offering your gift at the altar and there remember
that your brother or sister has something against you, leave your gift
there in front of the altar. First go and be reconciled to them;
then come and offer your gift.
—Matthew 5:23–24

"Go and be reconciled." Jesus makes it sound so easy, doesn't He? When Jesus speaks this powerful phrase in His Sermon on the Mount, He is saying that reconciliation is a critical component for worship of God—in essence, don't bother with altar sacrifices if you know your brother has something against you. The reality is, when there's something between us and a brother or sister in Christ—and we know deep down that we need to own our part in it—asking for grace and forgiveness can be a humbling and even terrifying experience.

Part of why asking for grace is so scary is an underlying but very real fear of rejection. We know that when we confess our sins to God, *"he is faithful and just and will forgive us our sins and purify us from all unrighteousness"* (1 John 1:9). After all, He's God—and He's always good. But other people, especially the ones we've personally wronged, might not be so forgiving. Knowing they might reject our apology and refuse to extend grace keeps us in a shame spiral. We hide, make excuses, and find ways to push the blame back on them, the unforgiving ones.

Unforgiveness is a human problem, but it's no excuse not to go after reconciliation, even at the risk of rejection. Asking for grace when you've wronged someone isn't asking for a pass, or asking them to acknowledge that what you did was okay. Instead, it's an acknowledgement of your sins against them, an expression of genuine remorse, and a request for grace that can ultimately lead to some form of reconciliation, even if not in the moment. How will we ever receive this kind of grace if we don't ask for it? And even if they refuse our request, what have we lost beyond our pride?

Ask God to bring to mind anyone who may be holding something against you. Humble yourself and ask God what grace and reconciliation might look like. Follow His lead and lean into your role as a grace conduit in this earthly realm.

God, it's by Your grace that I have a desire for reconciliation. Help me own my part in the offenses against me and in my offenses against others. Humble my heart and give me Your courage. Amen.

September 2: NATIONAL RECOVERY MONTH

The LORD is my rock, my fortress and my deliverer; my God is my rock, in whom I take refuge, my shield and the horn of my salvation, my stronghold.
—Psalm 18:2

If you're walking out your own recovery journey or loving and leading others through theirs, every month is recovery month. But for the rest of the nation, September is a time when secular and faith-based recovery leaders alike celebrate new evidence-based treatment and recovery practices, as well as the people walking through and leading them. This includes not only addiction recovery but recovery from mental health struggles and suicidal thoughts too.

Now, we're not saying let's jump on every recovery bandwagon out there and dilute our message that real recovery isn't possible without Jesus. Far from it. But this is a key time for spiritual and scientific leaders to come together with a unified purpose—to see more people set free, for good.

Engaging in dialogue with people outside your typical recovery circles can not only help you learn, but also extend an olive branch of peace, bringing an end to the us vs. them mentality between Spirit and science. Who knows—you might even get to share the gospel!

This Recovery Month, refuse to be silent. Consider your spheres of influence, small as they may be, and ask the Father what you can learn, do, and share to go deeper into Uncovery territory. What barriers are you facing that could use wisdom and insight? What successes are you celebrating? What breakthroughs have you experienced that are changing the way you do recovery? Finally, ask yourself and the people around you what's working, what's not working, and what more God is asking you to do. Be a conduit of grace and reconciliation this Recovery Month and speak up for the powerless in your communities.

God, what do You want me focused on this month—a prime time when the entire nation is thinking about recovery differently? Make me a voice of hope, healing, and change in Your name. Amen.

The righteous person may have many troubles, but the LORD delivers him
from them all; he protects all his bones, not one of them will be broken.
—Psalm 34:19–20

September isn't just Recovery Month; it's also Suicide Prevention Month. You may be thinking, *Two recovery months in one month? Isn't that a bit much?* You tell me.

According to the National Institute of Mental Health, nearly 46,000 people in the U.S. died by suicide in 2020. It was the second leading cause of death among individuals between the ages of ten to fourteen and twenty-five to thirty-four, the third leading cause of death among individuals between the ages of fifteen to twenty-four, and the fourth leading cause of death among those aged thirty-five to forty-four. There were nearly twice as many suicides (45,979) in the United States as there were homicides (24,576).[6] Things didn't get better in 2021, where we saw more than 48,000 deaths by suicide.[7] If that doesn't break your heart, we don't know what will.

The Uncovery's intentional, three-part framework focuses on addiction, mental health problems, *and* suicidal thoughts because of the underlying, unifying cause of them all—trauma. Yes, suicidal thoughts may be related to a mental health problem. They may also be linked to an addiction, just as addiction and mental health problems often go hand in hand. We like to categorize our issues into neat, tidy little boxes instead of exploring the interconnectedness of the human condition. That's why we need an entire month, if not longer, to focus and expand our thinking on this critical topic.

The church is not talking enough about mental health and suicide. Suicide is often the result of unresolved addiction and mental health problems, and loved ones rarely know how to help or how to cope after a suicide. If we know lives and souls are at stake when it comes to suicide, why aren't we, the church, talking and doing something about it?

---

6. "Suicide is a Leading Cause of Death in the United States," National Institute of Mental Health, May 2023, www.nimh.nih.gov/health/statistics/suicide.
7. "Suicide Data and Statistics," Centers for Disease Control and Prevention, August 10, 2023, www.cdc.gov/suicide/suicide-data-statistics.html.

God, I may not save thousands, but break my heart and move me with compassion for people contemplating suicide who are right in front of me. Let me shine a light on Your abundant life. Amen.

September 4: MADE FOR EACH OTHER

The LORD God said, "It is not good for the man to be alone.
I will make a helper suitable for him."
—Genesis 2:18

We were created for relationship. But when God said, *"It is not good for the man to be alone,"* He had far more than a wife in mind for Adam. He was expressing a part of His own never-alone nature as Father, Son, and Holy Spirit. He told Adam and Eve to be fruitful and multiply, to fill the earth with people who were made for relationship with Him and one another.

Flash forward millennia to modern day, and our need for community has only grown stronger. In a postmodern, individualistic, Western society, we've unknowingly been trained to isolate. The Internet and social media have all but replaced authentic community, and we've become convinced that real relationships can thrive in an all-online environment. In some cases, we have no choice and think it's better to connect online than not at all. But after long periods of isolation, isolation becomes what we know—and what we crave.

It's still not good for man to be alone. That's why God gave us the gift of Himself and one another. Did He *need* to do this? No. But He wanted to... because even God couldn't bear the thought of not being with us for all eternity. We were made for each other—and for the Father's delight.

Consider your own recovery journey. Where are you actively engaged in healthy, safe, authentic community? Who are those people, and how are they helping you be your best? Conversely, in what areas do you find yourself isolating and avoiding people? What people, activities, and other influences do you need to release to create space for healthy community? Your people are waiting—God made them just for you. Go find them.

God, sometimes it's easier to isolate than to be in community. I've been alone too long, and I know others are lonely, too. Help me find my people—people who will lead me back to You. Amen.

September 5: COMMUNITY HEALS TRAUMA

Praise be to the God and Father of our Lord Jesus Christ, the Father of compassion and the God of all comfort, who comforts us in all our troubles, so that we can comfort those in any trouble with the comfort we ourselves receive from God.
—2 Corinthians 1:3–4

No one individual can be responsible for any other individual's recovery. When I (George) tried it, I failed. Perhaps you have too.

But we, the church, can take *collective* responsibility for the pathways we create toward promised-land lives for people in recovery—if we can learn how to come together, *"brought to complete unity"* (John 17:23), as Jesus prayed we would.

Authentic community is the all-too-often missing piece in the recovery puzzle. While Friday night meetings and weekend service projects present opportunities to build real friendships, they can also be a breeding ground for triggers and codependency. We need to relearn what it means to do life together in an atmosphere of transparency, vulnerability, and unconditional love that leaves no one behind.

The kind of safe-haven community where we can identify and heal from trauma transcends the proximity principle. If we are a product of the handful of people we spend the most time with, it's important to intentionally surround ourselves with those who want the same things we want. We'll be in varying stages of healing with struggles that are unique to us, but we can journey together toward a promised-land life, helping each other along the way. People in recovery need a more empathetic, caring, and loving community. We, the church, are uniquely positioned to be the solution and lead by example.

Beyond the church, God is moving individual hearts and minds to align with His heart and mind on this—and if you picked up this devotional today, friend, He's talking to you.

God, surround me with safe people on my recovery journey who will point me straight back to You. I can't find lasting recovery on my own and I'm ready to go deeper in community with You. Amen.

September 6: DIGGING UP GRACE

With joy you will draw water from the wells of salvation.
—Isaiah 12:3

Rethinking the way you see and do recovery will require you to go deeper than ever before. Whether you're walking out your own struggles with addiction, mental health, or suicidal thoughts, or helping someone else through theirs, stepping into Uncovery territory means digging beneath the surface-level struggles to reveal the trauma that caused them in the first place.

If we don't know something exists, we can't pursue healing from it, right? Coming face-to-face with the real reasons why we struggle is the essence of stepping out of denial and into the light.

The problem is, digging deeper to unearth trauma is about as hard and painful as it sounds. The deeper we dig, the more grace we will need. At times, God will have us stop, rest, heal, and recalibrate because no one can face a lifetime of trauma all at once. But in His perfect timing and with a few shovel-ready friends surrounding us on the dig, God will bring to light what He knows we are ready to heal from.

The rightful desire to be healed and whole can tempt us to rush our way through our recovery journey. This almost always ends in heartache, and sometimes sends us right back to where we started from. God can—and does—heal instantaneously, miraculously, and completely, but sometimes He doesn't because we have something more to learn along the way.

Keep digging, friend. Following God's lead with every new opportunity for healing, you will tap into a well of grace that never runs dry.

God, give me the strength to go deeper into recovery. Bring to light what You want me to see and work on with You—today, tomorrow, and every day. Guard my heart with Your grace as I go. Amen.

September 7: HUMILITY FIRST

Humble yourselves before the Lord, and he will lift you up.
—James 4:10

If we want to help people uncover the truth about who they really are, we must first discover the truth about who Jesus really is. As you might have guessed, this is a trial-and-error process that requires grace, patience, and a healthy dose of humility for all involved. Unfortunately, many Christian recovery circles struggle to harness these attributes when people relapse—falling back into addiction, mental health problems, or suicidal thoughts after a period of freedom.

If we're honest, we'll admit the truth: relapse is an embarrassing inconvenience to us. We struggle to see the reasons why a person's "failure" matters when we have put our programs and even ourselves at the center of their stories. We care more about seeing people sober than we do about seeing them whole. We're more interested in checking boxes than checking our intentions.

We are collectively called to more than that.

Think back to the last time you relapsed, whether it was twenty years ago or twenty minutes ago. Who was Jesus to you in that moment? Who was the Father and who was the Holy Spirit in your mind? Your answers will be a strong indication of how you likely saw yourself—as a reflection of the image of God you perceived, right or wrong. An incorrect or obstructed view of God will always result in an incorrect or obstructed view of yourself, which is why we must have grace and space for relapse along every recovery journey. It's not about *if* it happens; it's about being prepared when it does. Positioning yourself as a fellow traveler on the journey will give you the humility needed to set people free in Jesus's name.

God, forgive me for seeing relapse as an inconvenience or an embarrassment. Their journey with You isn't about me. Soften my heart to receive people who are ready to start again with You. Amen.

September 8: PSYCHOSOCIAL DEVELOPMENT

For this very reason, make every effort to add to your faith goodness; and to goodness, knowledge; and to knowledge, self-control; and to self-control, perseverance; and to perseverance, godliness; and to godliness, mutual affection; and to mutual affection, love.
—2 Peter 1:5–7

Erik Homburger Erikson was a German-American developmental psychologist and psychoanalyst known for his theory on the psychological development of human beings. He coined the term *identity crisis* and spurred conversations that we, the church, are just beginning to enter into. Erickson never even earned a university degree, but served as a professor at Harvard, the University of California, Berkeley, and Yale. Talk about *favor*.

Erikson's theory of personality includes life stages and the virtues developed within each stage that result in a healthy personality. His work expanded upon psychologists such as Sigmund Freud through a unique, Messianic Jewish lens. In the days that follow, we'll unpack each stage of Erikson's theory to identify aspects of traditional recovery that are in need of much-needed reform.

The virtues Erikson identified in each life stage include:

1. Hope: basic trust vs. basic mistrust

2. Will: autonomy vs. shame

3. Purpose: initiative vs. guilt

4. Competence: industry vs. inferiority

5. Fidelity: identity vs. role confusion

6. Love: intimacy vs. isolation

7. Care: generativity vs. stagnation

8. Wisdom: ego integrity vs. despair

Spoiler alert: There's an additional ninth stage we'll get into on September 17 that will blow your mind.

Erikson's life stages are linear for an individual, but cyclical for society, making them a perfect, Christlike lens through which we can see modern recovery for what it really is.

On first glance, which of the eight stages we've mentioned stand out to you? Which tensions and values feel exceptionally relevant to your season of life and place in your recovery journey? Saddle up, friend. We're going deeper into Uncovery territory together.

God, with You there's always more to learn. Open my mind and my heart to hear what You have to say to me through this research. Tweak my methods and my theology if necessary. I trust You. Amen.

September 9: HOPE: TRUST VS. MISTRUST

Can a mother forget her nursing child? Can she feel no love for the child
she has borne? But even if that were possible, I would not forget you!
—Isaiah 49:15 (NLT)

The first stage in Erik Erikson's psychosocial development theory starts at birth and continues until about eighteen months of age. In these early developmental stages, babies don't yet understand the world, and they look to a primary caregiver for consistency and stability. If they receive consistent, trustworthy care, they will have an easier time trusting others and expanding into new relationships. If not, social anxiety may develop due to lack of control and confidence in the world around them.

Success in this stage will lead children to the virtue of hope, knowing that even when new crises arise, they will have people to surround and support them through it all. But when consistency in nurturing care is not met, it can lead children into fear—mistrust in relationships, anxiety, and insecurity that can be detrimental from a community standpoint.

Consider your own life's journey. Did you build trust with a consistent caregiver in infancy? How did your very early-life experiences shape your own views of the world? Which of your struggles seem connected to your *hope season*, and which ones don't?

God, remembering my infancy is pretty tough! If there's something You want me
to know, please reveal it to me. Help me understand where I came from, so I can
know where I'm going. Amen.

September 10: WILL: AUTONOMY VS. SHAME AND DOUBT

Start children off on the way they should go,
and even when they are old they will not turn from it.
—Proverbs 22:6

The second stage in Erik Erikson's theory spans from eighteen months to three years of age. In these formative toddler years, children are trying to assert control over their physical bodies to develop a healthy sense of independence. If that independence is celebrated and encouraged, they will grow in confidence and security to help them navigate life. But when they're criticized, controlled, or shut down completely, they become overly dependent upon others for basic tasks and question their ability to survive, which breeds shame.

Success in this stage will lead children to the virtue of the will; when kids are encouraged and supported in their independence, they grow in confidence and survival instinct. When affirmation over developmentally appropriate independence is not given, it cripples self-esteem, creating a sense of perpetual doubt in all abilities, regardless of progress or natural gifting.

Consider your own life's journey. Were you supported and encouraged during your toddler years, or were you a victim of helicopter parenting? Did your parents encourage you to learn to dress yourself and perform small tasks, or did they do it for you? Which of your struggles seem connected to your *will season*, and which ones don't?

God, where did my self-doubt come from? If there's something You want me to know about my will season, show me. Help me understand where I came from, so I can know where I'm going. Amen.

September 11: PURPOSE: INITIATIVE VS. GUILT

Children are a gift from the LORD; they are a reward from him.
—Psalm 127:3 (NLT)

In the third stage in Erik Erikson's psychosocial development theory, children between ages three and five are learning to assert themselves more often through play and social interaction. In these rapid-development years, kids may come off as aggressive, but it's entirely age-appropriate and should be handled with care. As they learn to interact with school friends, play is critical for learning social constructs and determining appropriate behavior. If the natural tendency toward discovery through play is hindered or snuffed out through criticism or control, children will feel guilt for being a nuisance—and will often either lash out or shut down.

Success in this stage will lead children to the virtue of purpose; when kids can learn healthy boundaries while having fun along the way, they thrive in a fear-free environment. Conversely, too much guilt over an increased assertion of independence or asking too many questions can stifle creativity and make kids slow to interact with others.

Consider your own life's journey. Were you free to play, ask questions, and even make mistakes if it led to growth, or were you chastised for being a nuisance? Did your parents or guardian encourage creative play, or were you parked in front of the TV and left to your own devices? Which of your struggles seem connected to your *purpose season*, and which ones don't?

God, You're so patient with me. If there's something You want me to know about this purpose season, let me see it through Your eyes. Help me understand where I came from, so I can know where I'm going. Amen.

September 12: COMPETENCY: INDUSTRY VS. INFERIORITY

The LORD your God is with you, the Mighty Warrior who saves.
He will take great delight in you; in his love he will no longer rebuke you,
but will rejoice over you with singing.
—Zephaniah 3:17

Erik Erikson's fourth stage of psychosocial development spans ages six through eleven. In this self-actualizing season, kids are acutely aware of peer and authority opinions of them and use those assessments to shape their self-esteem. Winning approval and recognition by demonstrating competencies is the goal, which leads to a sense of healthy, reasonable pride. But if they feel they haven't earned such approval and no parents or teachers affirm their initiative, they will be more likely to doubt their own abilities and less likely to achieve their potential.

Success in this stage will lead children to the virtue of competence—a healthy balance between confidence and humility that leaves them feeling affirmed and significant without fueling pride. Too little or too much affirmation can skew children's perception of their own abilities, leading them to believe they're better or worse off than they really are.

Consider your own life's journey. Were your developing skills affirmed by parents, teachers, and classmates, or did you feel *less than*? Did you enjoy the act of learning and growing in a classroom environment, or did it become competitive? Which of your struggles seem connected to your *competence season*, and which ones don't?

God, You've always delighted in me. If there's something You want me to know about this competence season, reveal it. Help me understand where I came from, so I can know where I'm going. Amen.

September 13: FIDELITY: IDENTITY VS. ROLE CONFUSION

Before I formed you in the womb I knew you, and before you were born I consecrated you; I appointed you a prophet to the nations.
—Jeremiah 1:5 (ESV)

The fifth stage in Erik Erikson's psychosocial development theory includes adolescence, ages twelve to eighteen. In this searching season, teens are desperately trying to figure out who they are through intense exploration of beliefs, values, and life goals. This transition season from childhood to adulthood is critically important as adolescents try to determine where they belong in society. The desire to fit in is paramount—and when they don't, they may fixate on differences in occupational and sexual desire rather than an integrated sense of self.

Success in this stage will lead children to the virtue of fidelity—being able to commit one's self to others on the basis of accepting others, even when there may be ideological differences. For the first time ever, teens will try to assign identity to themselves, which may or may not be rooted in God's truth based on their adolescent experiences.

Consider your own life's journey. Did you have healthy, authentic relationships in your teen years? Did you explore your beliefs and identity—and for better or worse, what did you learn? Which of your struggles seem connected to your *fidelity season*, and which ones don't?

God, You're always faithful. If there's something You want me to know about this fidelity season, bring it to light. Help me understand where I came from, so I can know where I'm going. Amen.

September 14: LOVE: INTIMACY VS. ISOLATION

The LORD appeared to him from far away. I have loved you with an everlasting love; therefore I have continued my faithfulness to you.
—Jeremiah 31:3 (ESV)

The sixth stage in Erik Erikson's psychosocial development theory spans young adulthood, ages eighteen through forty. In this intensely relational season, young adults are focused on building intimate, loving, long-term relationships with other people beyond their family members. Finding these relationships can lead to the authentic, Christ-centered community we need to recover, heal, and thrive. Missing out on them can perpetuate the trauma of isolation that can lead to addiction, mental health problems, and suicidal thoughts.

Success in this stage will lead young adults to the virtue of love—an intimate, authentic kind of love that transcends sexual desire and fosters deep, meaningful relationships. Failure to develop these healthy relationships can result in intimacy and commitment issues, isolation, loneliness, and depression.

Consider your own life's journey. When you reached young adulthood, were you able to foster healthy, intimate relationships with other people? What heartache did you face—and for better or worse, what did you learn from it? Which of your struggles seem connected to your *love season*, and which ones don't? If you haven't yet reached young adulthood, whose story might help you better understand this season?

God, You loved me first. If there's something You want me to know about this love season, show me. Help me understand where I came from, so I can know where I'm going. Amen.

September 15: CARE: GENERATIVITY VS. STAGNATION

Forget the former things; do not dwell on the past. See, I am doing a new thing! Now it springs up; do you not perceive it? I am making a way in the wilderness and streams in the wasteland.
—Isaiah 43:18–19

Erik Erikson's seventh stage spans middle adulthood, ages forty to sixty-five. In this season, middle-aged adults are beginning to contemplate the idea of legacy—they want to find ways to leave their mark and know that they mattered. This season can lead people to generate, create, or care for things that will outlive them. Failure to leave a mark or contribute to something of lasting value to future generations can cause stagnation, or a sense of being *stuck* in life.

Success in this stage will lead middle-aged adults to the virtue of care—a pay-it-forward mentality that's focused on loving and leading others well. Failing to find ways to contribute can make people feel unproductive and even insignificant, causing disconnect from their community and society as a whole.

Consider your own life's journey. If you have reached middle adulthood, were you able to make your mark by loving and leading others well? Could you translate and share wisdom from your own life experiences in relevant ways, or did you feel ignored? Which of your struggles seem connected to your *care season*, and which ones don't? If you haven't yet reached middle-aged adulthood, whose story might help you better understand this season?

God, my significance comes from You alone. If there's something You want me to know about this care season, help me see it. Help me understand where I came from, so I can know where I'm going. Amen.

September 16: WISDOM: EGO INTEGRITY VS. DESPAIR

I provide water in the wilderness and streams in the wasteland,
to give drink to my people, my chosen, the people I formed
for myself that they may proclaim my praise.
—Isaiah 43:20–21

The eighth stage in Erik Erikson's psychosocial development theory spans from approximately age sixty-five through end of life. In this autumn season of life, senior adults enter into a highly contemplative stage in which they can rest in their accomplishments and enjoy a successful, happy life. This is ego integrity. But when seniors reflect on their lives and are not satisfied with their accomplishments or perceived impact, it can cause bitterness, frustration, and even despair.

Success in this stage will lead senior adults to the virtue of wisdom, enabling them to reflect on a life well lived and accept death without fear. Conversely, seniors who feel they haven't accomplished what they were created to do may look back on their life with sorrow. Most healthy seniors will balance the scales between both ego integrity and despair, operating in complete honesty about their past successes and failures.

Consider your own life's journey. If you've reached senior adulthood, are you satisfied overall with your life accomplishments and influence? Can you celebrate a life well lived, or do you fear death? Which of your struggles seem connected to your *wisdom season*, and which ones don't? If you haven't yet reached senior adulthood, whose story might help you better understand this season?

God, all wisdom resides in You. If there's something You want me to know about this wisdom season, reveal it. Help me understand where I came from, so I can know where I'm going. Amen.

September 17: REFLECTION: PSYCHOSOCIAL CRISES

Moses was a hundred and twenty years old when he died,
yet his eyes were not weak nor his strength gone.
—Deuteronomy 34:7

Joan Erikson, Erik Erikson's wife and research partner, added a ninth stage to her husband's psychosocial development theory, with a unique twist: the elderly will revisit each life stage again, with the comparative quotients reversed.

1. Basic mistrust challenges long-standing trust when elders mistrust their own capabilities. Hope is at stake.

2. Shame and doubt challenge autonomy when elders doubt whether they have control over their own bodies. Will is at stake.

3. Guilt challenges initiative when elders question their independence with things like living on their own and driving. Purpose is at stake.

4. Inferiority challenges industry when elders feel belittled, like a small child in a very old body. Competence is at stake.

5. Identity confusion challenges identity when elders no longer feel secure in their former status and roles. Fidelity is at stake.

6. Isolation challenges intimacy when elders lose spouses and loved ones and struggle to connect with others. Love is at stake.

7. Stagnation challenges generativity when elders have fewer responsibilities and creative outlets. Care is at stake.

8. Despair and disgust challenge integrity when elders struggle with healthy introspection and write people off. Wisdom is at stake.

Chances are, you haven't entered Joan Erikson's ninth stage—and if you have and you're reading this devotional, *God love you!* How does it make you feel to know that each virtue you embrace will one day be challenged? What have you learned about each life stage season that could help you or those you love and lead in recovery? What more would God have you do? Are you willing?

God, all wisdom resides in You. If there's something You want me to know about this reflection season, reveal it. Help me understand where I came from, so I can know where I'm going. Amen.

September 18: RECEIVING GOD'S GRACE

Let us then approach God's throne of grace with confidence, so that we may receive mercy and find grace to help us in our time of need.
—Hebrews 4:16

God's grace sounds entirely too good to be true, which is why so many of us struggle to receive it. Grace, God's unmerited favor, was actually released over all of humankind when Jesus died on the cross and rose again, defeating sin and death forever. In that single sacrificial act, He took care of every sin that we would ever commit. All we need to do in return is believe it and receive it. Scandalous, right?

For God so loved the world that he gave his one and only Son, that whoever believes in him shall not perish but have eternal life. (John 3:16)

Jesus took His own words pretty literally when the thief being crucified next to Him was promised paradise with his simple request that Jesus remember him. (See Luke 23:42–43.) Zero repentance. Zero baptisms. Exactly zero sinner's prayers prayed. If it sounds a little unfair, it's because it is. The gospel has never been fair. If it were, the wages of sin would still be death, and we'd all be doomed. (See Romans 6:23.) But instead, Jesus—a Man who never sinned—*became sin* for us so He could defeat it. Not because we deserved it, but because He loved us *that* much.

What do we do with a love like that? We might question it, checking for attached strings, complex legal clauses, and other fine print. Keep looking—you won't find it. Receiving God's grace is an act of faith—believing Jesus is exactly who He says He is, and that the Father might be better than we ever imagined. Receiving God's mercy, grace, and forgiveness is a supernatural act of trust in Him and His goodness. And the best part is, we don't have to understand it. All we need to do is say *yes*. This is radical reconciliation.

God, it's hard to receive something I know I don't deserve. But I know refusing Your grace is refusing You. So I'm saying yes, even though I don't yet fully understand. Teach me. Amen

September 19: GRACE GIVERS

Finally, all of you, have unity of mind, sympathy, brotherly love,
a tender heart, and a humble mind.
—1 Peter 3:8 (ESV)

When you approach a brother or sister who has something against you with a heart for reconciliation, the only thing more awkward than them *not* forgiving you is *forgiving* you. Yes, this is what you wanted. Yes, this is what you felt compelled by God to do. Yes, you know it's right, it's good, it's fine. So why does it feel so weird?

Whether it's from God or from another person, grace is still unmerited favor. You're asking for something you don't deserve—forgiveness, with a desire for restored relationship. Now, if that forgiveness comes with strings attached—I'll forgive you *if*… I'll forgive you *but*… I'll forgive you *when*…—it's not actually grace at all. Perhaps you've experienced forgiveness like this before. The real grace givers follow suit with Jesus, no strings, just an invitation into a sinless life.

Thank God there's grace to cover our grace-giving! We're not God, so none of us will walk in grace for long without our humanity showing every now and then. That said, when forgiveness is given to you, receive it at face value. Whether the earthly grace giver knows what they're releasing over you or not, your heavenly Grace Giver knows—and He will transform you both in the grace-giving process.

God, help me overcome my fear of disingenuous grace. Keep me anchored in Your love and Your grace, which knows no limits. Help me live in peace with everyone to the best of my ability. Amen.

September 20: CONTAGIOUS GRACE

For from his fullness we have all received, grace upon grace.
—John 1:16

"Grace upon grace" isn't just a platitude. God's grace is quite catching. Its contagious nature is a Holy Spirit phenomenon, something that makes absolutely no sense in the natural, but there it is before you, undeniable.

When you receive grace—unmerited favor in spite of your sin—a funny thing happens. It starts to grow, rising in your heart like bread dough that's been mixed, pounded, risen, and formed until it's ready to be placed in the oven. As it expands, it has to go somewhere—and before you know it, it's out of the oven, and you start giving slices of that warm, fresh, nourishing grace to people you never thought you'd give it to. People who annoy you. People who offend you. Sometimes even people who deliberately cause you harm. You begin to see them through God's eyes, and the grace within you releases to them in the overflow of your being. When that grace hits them, should they choose to receive it, the cycle repeats. Grace upon grace upon grace upon grace.

Whenever you feel your grace running out, there's more to be had. God never gets tired of giving you grace, and He wants to see it spread faster than disease. And if this concept of contagious grace offends you, watch out! Grace will get you in the end.

God, inject my soul with Your contagious grace. Let it pass to me and through me, especially to the people I'd hesitate to give it to—the ones who might need it even more than I do. Amen.

How long, LORD? Will you forget me forever? How long will you hide your
face from me? How long must I wrestle with my thoughts and day after
day have sorrow in my heart? How long will my enemy triumph over me?
—Psalm 13:1–2

Disappointment with God is an inevitable part of life and recovery. There will be times when we don't understand His ways. He let us down. He didn't do what we thought He should. And our relationship with Him is strained. Whether it's a major blow or a bunch of tiny things that just don't go our way, it's quite possible—and quite human—to wrestle with God and be angry with Him.

If you think what we're saying borders on blasphemy, you've clearly never been through trauma that might cause you to question everything. Needing God's forgiveness is vital to your salvation and overall well-being, but He doesn't *need* your forgiveness. Regardless of our ability to understand this, He is God, He is good, and He hasn't wronged you. Ever. It's counter to His character.

Forgiveness is a funny thing. It's less for the one you need to forgive and more for your own heart. A simple definition of forgive is "to decide not to be angry anymore." That's the kind of pure, holy, restorative forgiveness that your heavenly Father would love to receive from you, not because He needs it, but because it demonstrates your willingness to enter back into relationship with Him.

So ask yourself, are you holding any offenses against God? If you're angry, tell Him. Beat your fists on His chest in frustration and cry hot, angry tears if you must. He can take it. He'll hold you and love you through it, and when you're through, He'll accept your grace offering to Him, for your good and His glory.

God, how can I stay mad at You? I don't always understand what You're doing, but You always prove Yourself faithful. I'm not angry anymore. Forgive me for doubting You in my anger. Amen.

September 22: DEATH AND LIFE

Jesus answered, "I am the way and the truth and the life. No one comes to the Father except through me."
—John 14:6

Jesus came to earth as God in the flesh to give you abundant life—a promised-land life worth living and staying sober for. He Himself was and is the way, the truth, and the life—our only way to be reconciled with our good Father God. But are you really living the abundant life Jesus died for you to have? Are you putting down roots in the promised land, or settling just outside the border because there might be giants there?

The truth is, the promised-land life God has for you is already yours. You can choose to receive it or not. Build camp outside the borders, and you'll be no less loved and forgiven. Your golden ticket to heaven is secure. But you'll be missing out on the beautiful privilege of growing in intimacy with God in this abundant life. If you believe in your heart and confess with your lips that Jesus is Lord, you will be saved. (See Romans 10:9.) But God wants to do more than just rescue you. He wants to do more than deliver you from your bondage. He wants to walk with you on a journey of discovery that will show you who you really are in Him, and who you were always meant to be.

Take it or leave it. But life in Christ means going where He goes, staying where He stays, and moving when He moves. You may believe in Him, even love Him, but will you follow Him? Will you make Him Lord of your life? Will you enjoy Him forever and share His goodness with others? Are you willing? Be willing, friend. You don't want to miss this.

God, help me step into the fullness of the abundant life Your Son Jesus died for me to have. Forgive my slow obedience. Show me where to go and what to do next. I'm Yours. Amen.

September 23: RADICAL RECONCILIATION

All this is from God, who reconciled us to himself through Christ and gave us the ministry of reconciliation.
—2 Corinthians 5:18

Throughout the generations, God fought to get His people to return to Him. He made the Law, but we couldn't or wouldn't foll ow it faithfully. He finally decided to destroy our sin for us—by becoming sin in and through the shed blood of Jesus. Now that sin has been defeated, our good Father God wants us to know how loved, forgiven, and free we already are so we can step into the fullness of the promised-land life He has for all of us. This is radical reconciliation.

The recovery space should be no different—and yet, we remain divided. With both sacred and secular camps clinging to their convictions, we've come to see one another as *the other* at best and *the enemy* at worst. For example, the rigid, competitive dichotomy between spiritual and scientific results in major missed opportunities for those who feel a call to help people struggling with addiction, mental health problems, and suicidal thoughts. We're more interested in being right than being effective.

The key to breakthrough in recovery on all sides lies just beyond the walls we've built.

Co-laboring with people of different belief systems does not have to compromise our own convictions. When we approach one another with open hearts and willing hands, we witness true breakthrough.

God, I know I sometimes have difficulty seeing people as You see them and loving them as You love them. Teach me and guide me to be Your hands and heart to bring true reconciliation. Amen.

September 24: YOUNGER SELF REFLECTIONS

The hearts of the wise make their mouths prudent,
and their lips promote instruction.
—Proverbs 16:23

If you could write a letter to your younger self, what would you say? What battles have you fought, what knowledge have you gained, and what wisdom have you gleaned that could have helped you avoid pain and loss? Chances are, even knowing what you know now, you wouldn't be able to find the words to keep trauma from happening. At best, you might have perspective on coping strategies and the safe vs. unsafe company you may have once kept. Regardless, reflecting back on your younger self will bring to light the way you really feel about the person you used to be.

Are you angry with your younger self? Would your letter be full of high-challenge commands and "you know better" statements? Would your younger self have listened to you if they'd had the chance? Are you filled with compassion for your younger self? Were you abused, neglected, marginalized, or exploited? Would your letter highlight a way out, a way forward, or a way back home?

As you reflect on your childhood trauma and the things that led you to struggle, you may feel the need to forgive your younger self. For being naive, for lacking patience, for thinking you knew everything. You may also find yourself wishing you could somehow ask your former self for forgiveness—after all, you were the one who walked the journey in front of them. But grace to you, beloved one—that same journey is the one that led you to where you are today. You're one with God. And if your younger self knew it, even now, it could change everything.

God, help me look back on my younger self and see how loved and forgiven I was, even then. I am not ashamed of my past, and I'm not ashamed of Your gospel. I'm proud of my story in You. Amen.

September 25: RECONCILING DAD

And he will turn the hearts of the fathers to the children, and the hearts of the children to their fathers, lest I come and strike the earth with a curse.
—Malachi 4:6 (NKJV)

Most people in recovery are struggling with daddy issues. It can be incredibly hard to see God as a good Father when our earthly fathers aren't good. Not all dads are bad dads, but even the best of them fail us. Some dads leave. Some dads abuse. Some dads neglect. Some dads obsess. Some are too strong, some are too weak, some are too much, and others not enough. The higher the pedestal we put them on, the harder they fall. Because some dads don't know how to be dads at all.

God is in the reconciliation business, and He's starting by reconciling the very concept of dad. He is a Father to the fatherless, even to those of us who had fathers who weren't perfect like He is. And the beautiful thing is, He's also a Father to those fathers who never nailed it as fathers. He says to us all, "*Call me Abba.*" Whatever your father couldn't or wouldn't be, He is.

Let God father you long enough, and He'll give you a supernatural grace for your earthly dad. Whether he was a great guy, a total jerk, or not there at all, your good Father God can help you find something small to honor in your earthly dad.

We're called to honor our father and mother not by excusing bad behavior, but as the ones who gave us life—a life that eventually led us to Jesus, our way to the real Father.

God, help me see my earthly father through Your eyes and honor him in whatever way You want me to. Thank You for being a Father to the fatherless—and a perfect Abba Father to me. Amen.

September 26: FORGIVING YOURSELF

*And I tell you that you are Peter, and on this rock I will build my church,
and the gates of Hades will not overcome it.*
—Matthew 16:18

Forgiving yourself is the hardest thing you'll ever do. Far more complex than receiving grace from God and others and giving that same grace to people who don't deserve it, forgiving yourself can feel so…selfish. You may give Jesus your *yes* to grace and do your best to honor Him in word and deed, but deep down, you still think, *God may forgive me, but I can never forgive myself for what I've done.*

Yet forgiving yourself is a key part of receiving forgiveness from God and others. The forgiveness you receive and the guilt you continue to carry simply cannot coexist. God has removed your sins from you *"as far as the east is from the west"* (Psalm 103:12)—meaning your sin is now as far away from your newfound righteousness as something can possibly be. You may not feel it yet. But feelings can be deceptive when they're not rooted in truth. God says you're forgiven, and to say otherwise is to call Him a liar.

If that last line cut you to the core, good. It was not meant to shame you or bully you into some form of self-forgiveness that's under coercion or disingenuous, but to call out your own false humility. Refusing to forgive yourself is refusing to do and say what the Father does. Align with His truth today. When you receive forgiveness from God and others, let it supernaturally permeate your soul to the point where you actually begin to see yourself the way God sees you. Don't see it yet? Ask Him to show you.

God, I struggle to forgive myself for the things I've done. But if You say I'm forgiven, I must be! I choose to believe You and I receive Your grace in full. Help me learn to give it to myself. Amen.

September 27: COMMUNITY RESTORATION

And we urge you, brothers and sisters, warn those who are idle and disruptive, encourage the disheartened, help the weak, be patient with everyone.
—1 Thessalonians 5:14

Breakdown in community—including family units, church groups, recovery organizations, and other places where we do every part of life with people—can be as difficult to spot as it is to restore. Offense spreads like wildfire over something as simple as dishes in the sink, but it's never really about the dishes. There's always something deeper to uncover.

Building authentic community requires trust. And while trust is something that ideally should be given, not earned, people in your communities will have varying levels of trust on the way in. As leaders, we can set the example by letting people know they belong with us before they ever behave, or even know what to believe. Trust builds when people feel fully seen, fully known, and fully loved. In the absence of those things, we can make pleasantries and even co-labor together, but a long-standing lack of trust will cause breakdown every time.

Whether you're addressing long-term toxic community restoration or running triage after a blatant community crisis, God's grace is the solution. Does grace mean throwing out rules and boundaries and refusing to hold people accountable? Of course not! But it might mean loving them radically, even when they break every rule and boundary in the book. We're to restore our brothers and sisters gently when they go astray, and to treat them like pagans and tax collectors when they aren't receptive to counsel. And how did Jesus treat pagans and tax collectors? He loved them *fiercely* and went after them like little lost sheep. And when He found them, He said, *"Follow me."*

God, give me eyes to see how breakdowns in my community might be a sign of a bigger problem. Humble me, keeping me open to change, and guide me as I love and lead. Amen.

September 28: RESTORATION, NOT RECONCILIATION

If anyone will not welcome you or listen to your words, leave that home
or town and shake the dust off your feet.
—Matthew 10:14

God's heart is for restoration. And when we align our heart with His, ours will be too. But especially in extreme cases of betrayal and abuse, giving grace and forgiveness to someone might bring about restoration in both your hearts—but full-on reconciliation may not be wise or even possible, at least not right away.

You've likely seen it before. Domestic abuse victims go back to their abusers. Betrayed wives go back to unrepentant, cheating husbands. Molested children own their abuse and glorify their abuser. Parents enable addicted grown children with endless ways out and financial resources. These toxic, boundaryless relationships will only breed more pain without a radical encounter with the Holy Spirit. In some cases, even when grace and forgiveness are released, continuing such relationships will do more harm than good.

Does this mean we simply cut off everyone who won't see things our way? No. But heed the words of Jesus. If your offenders hear your words of forgiveness but do not truly receive them, they will not be transformed. In fact, they may even redouble their efforts to manipulate and control you, putting you back within the confines of that toxic relationship. But anyone who seeks to come between God and the ones He loves will experience His wrath—and God will do whatever is necessary to help you choose safety, wholeness, and freedom every time.

Consider a relationship in your life where restoration might not bring about reconciliation. Release grace and forgiveness to the one who has wronged you, and then release them to the Father. Keep healthy boundaries in place until God asks you to remove them. And in this time, plead with God for a change of heart on their part that may one day lead to reconciliation, in this life or the next.

God, give me wisdom to know when reconciling a relationship is a bad idea. Help me love and forgive anyway, but keep me safely protected under Your wings as You deal with their heart and mind. Amen.

September 29: DESPISED AND REJECTED

He was despised and rejected by mankind, a man of suffering, and familiar with pain. Like one from whom people hide their faces he was despised, and we held him in low esteem.
—Isaiah 53:3

There will come times on our faith and recovery journey when we feel the sting of rejection. It happens to all of us, but knowing this does not make it any easier.

Job offers are rescinded when employers discover a history of addiction. Friends end relationships because it's too hard to deal with your mental health struggles. A mentor releases you when they don't know how to handle your thoughts about suicide.

The stigma of recovery is very real—and the rejections we experience are not only painful to us, they're heartbreaking to Jesus. Although He never needed recovery in the way we do, Jesus knew what it was like to feel not only rejected, but hated. (See Isaiah 53:3.) He was fully God, but also all Man, so He had the capacity to be tempted by and struggle with anything and everything we do. He never gave in to sin, but we can imagine the sting of rejection He felt when we, the ones He died for, misunderstood Him so badly.

We're convinced this is why Jesus spent so much of His downtime in solitude just being with His Father. (See Mark 1:35.) There could be long lines of people waiting for His healing touch, but Jesus would forsake even miracles to be alone with God. This frustrated people, especially His disciples, but it pleased God, and it strengthened Jesus for the journey ahead.

When you are despised and rejected like Jesus was, do what He did. Find a place to get alone with God and let Him show you how much He loves and accepts you.

God, it's awful feeling so misunderstood. I take comfort knowing You understand. Help me follow Christ's example and always put You first above other things. Amen.

I pray that out of his glorious riches he may strengthen you with power through his Spirit in your inner being.
—Ephesians 3:16

As summer winds down and you settle into your fall routines, you may already be reflecting on this year and thinking about next year. Before the holiday season kicks into high gear—often with a host of temptations and potential recovery pitfalls—pause for a moment to set your intentions by creating a *rule of life*. This ancient practice is far more than some flippant New Year's resolution, a renewed commitment, or a program to stay sober, lose weight, or exercise more. It's about making an agreement with God about what you will and will not welcome into your life.

A rule of life is a concrete plan to keep God at the center of all you do. Your reason for doing so has nothing to do with personal gain, and everything to do with your love for Him. Each rule must be written as a declaration, not as a visionary or aspirational statement. For example, instead of saying, "I am going to sleep at least eight hours every night," declare with present-tense authority the things you need to make God a priority, such as, "I sleep eight hours a night, from 11 p.m. to 7 a.m., so I can be fresh and clear to commune with God."

These rules of life are not meant to be legalistic boxes to check. We have enough of those already, and they're not helping. But being true to our *why* and in tune with our desire for God, we will be more likely to choose to follow rules that set us up for more fruitful time with Him.

What rule of life would you like to create? It doesn't have to be about sleep—it can be about work, health, finances, growth, or a particular aspect of your recovery journey. With God's leading, see if you can create just one rule of life today. When you taste the benefits of healthy personal boundaries, you'll want to go deeper and create more.

God, what areas of my life are keeping me from being with You and putting You at the center of my life? What rule of life can I create and adopt today to put You first? I'm listening. Amen.

October

REASSESSMENT

So, if you think you are standing firm, be careful that you don't fall!
—1 Corinthians 10:12

Everyone ought to examine themselves before they eat
of the bread and drink from the cup.
—1 Corinthians 11:28

Change is in the air. Cooler temperatures, shifts in season, and the fullness of a hurried fall frenzy are in full swing. In times like this, it can feel like life is just happening to you rather than you showing up and making conscious daily decisions to run the race before you.

This all-too-common way of thinking is why October is a month of reassessment—a time to examine ourselves with God, find any wrong or troubling ways in us, reassess our journeys, and fuel up for the next leg.

When Paul wrote to the church in Corinth on this topic, it was in the context of communion. Not just communing with God one-on-one, but sharing in communion with other believers as an act of worship. Paul was a powerful grace teacher, but he didn't mince words when it came to holding the church accountable and making sure they understood the magnitude of any religious act. After all, they'd spent plenty of time worshipping Greek gods before they met Jesus; religion and following rules was their specialty. Paul knew they would be prone to going through the motions of sacred communion without thinking about it too much.

God's with you all the time. It's impossible for Him *not* to be with you because you're one with Him. But in an intentional act of worship, especially communion in a corporate setting, Paul encourages the Corinthians and all believers by proxy to *"examine themselves"* (1 Corinthians 11:28)—just as Jesus did when He told us to pursue reconciliation before making an offering. (See Matthew 5:23–24.)

Before your next act of public or private worship, search yourself. Are you keeping God at arm's length about anything? Are you eager to go through the motions because you're just not *feeling it*? God's got your back—and He'll purify your heart in His presence.

God, search me. Show me any wrong, broken, hateful, or fearful way in me. Bring it into the light so I can repent and come back home to Your arms in true and proper worship. Amen.

October 2: FEELING OFF?

Search me, God, and know my heart; test me and know my anxious thoughts.
See if there is any offensive way in me, and lead me in the way everlasting.
—Psalm 139:23–24

When you can sense something's *off* between you and God in your recovery journey, it may be time to go deeper. When all issues are on the table, when you're repented and been reminded of your righteousness, when you know how loved and forgiven you really are, but you still feel off? It may be time for a different kind of assessment.

October is National Depression and Mental Health Screening Month. While not everyone who struggles is clinically depressed or has mental health issues, it's important to be cognizant about when the bad days, thoughts, and encounters outnumber the good ones, causing us to lash out or isolate. Intense worry, intense fear, and intense thoughts and behaviors are the telltale signs of depression or another underlying mental health struggle that's rising to the surface.

Seeking help is a sign of strength and hope. Under the care of therapists and counselors, you can receive a diagnosis (if applicable) and explore the trauma that leads you to struggle. Medication and rest may be necessary, and that's okay. It can be hard to see who God is and who you are in Him when you can't tell the grass from the gravel on your recovery journey. God will restore you and heal your heart and mind with His kindness.

God, thank You for giving me space to explore aspects of my mental health with no condemnation. Show Yourself to me. I want to see You. Heal my mind and my heart. Amen.

October 3: WALK WITH ME

Therefore each of you must put off falsehood and speak truthfully to your neighbor, for we are all members of one body.
—Ephesians 4:25

When we walk in authentic community, we surround ourselves with at least a handful of people who fully see us, fully know us, and fully love us anyway. These are the priceless ones who get to speak into our lives, holding us accountable throughout our journey to a promised-land life. The dilemma is this: we, the church, hate conflict even more than we hate sin in our midst. So when we see a brother or sister stumble, we say nothing…or, when confronted, we dance around the issue, trying not to make waves or end the relationship.

There is just no room for this attitude in a Christ-centered recovery context. If *"iron sharpens iron"* (Proverbs 27:17), the iron we use to sharpen one another is bound to be sharp. Even loving and gentle correction can cut like a knife, especially when we know the person holding us accountable is right.

Those of us who struggle—and that's everyone—need to be very direct in the way we ask for accountability. It sounds less like, "I'm struggling; can you pray for me?" and looks more like, "I'm struggling with impure thoughts about a woman who is not my wife. I feel weak, and I need accountability so I don't sin. Will you walk with me until I overcome it? I'm ashamed, but I can't do this alone."

We're meant to do more than confess our sins to one another and pray for one another in community. We're meant to bear one another's burdens—and even one another!—when the situation warrants. Let's go beyond holding each other accountable to a sin nature and hold each other accountable to our destiny.

If you need accountability or have been asked to give it, be ready to value people over your relationship with them every time.

God, forgive me for the accountability I asked for without meaning it. Forgive me also for the accountability I promised to offer, but didn't. Break my heart for people and make me bold. Amen.

October 4: ONGOING THERAPY

Where there is strife, there is pride,
but wisdom is found in those who take advice.
—Proverbs 13:10

In recovery circles, we don't often hear someone say, "I've arrived." Trained counselors know that when they do hear this, it can actually be a cause for concern. This confidence can leave faithful twelve-steppers and box-checkers feeling invincible...until life inevitably gets in the way. That's because life, even a transformed one, can be ridiculously hard. Thankfully, even the promised-land life we work toward in the Uncovery isn't our final destination. Instead, it's part of a rebirth into the eternal life we're all being invited to experience.

Sobriety is to recovery what salvation is to Christianity. From a practical standpoint, this means that all people who call themselves Christian are in recovery. We're all trying to get healed and whole, to get back to who the Father created us to be, to realize the abundant life that Jesus went to the cross for us to have. This isn't a once-and-done revelation. It will take years for our hearts to catch up with our heads or vice versa. And getting there may take ongoing therapy.

What's more, the Uncovery is a journey, not a destination. As you walk it out, you may find victory over one surface-level struggle just as a new one starts to reveal itself. Trauma can be tricky, and it will take more than a few counseling sessions to bring it to light, let alone to begin dealing with it and healing from it. This is why continued reassessment is so relevant. With God, there's always more healing to be found.

Could you or someone you love and lead benefit from therapy? Ask the Father what more He might have you do to show compassion to yourself and others by destigmatizing therapy and opening doors to deep, lasting healing in Jesus's name.

God, in my weakness, I admit counseling and therapy seem beneath me. I feel like we should be able to heal on our own, but that's not how You made us. Help me grow deeper in this area. Amen.

October 5: NEED FOR PURPOSE

Great are your purposes and mighty are your deeds. Your eyes are open to the ways of all mankind.
—Jeremiah 32:19

People in recovery need a purpose, and work can be an important reason to stay sober. Helping people find and keep jobs they enjoy doing builds dignity, responsibility, knowledge, and experience. And if we can't help them find jobs, why not create them? Startups and microbusinesses can provide income opportunities and entrepreneurial training for people in recovery who want and need to work in a safe, supportive environment.

We need to see recovery from a new angle, one that's more inclusive and in-depth. We need to dig down deep, exploring the sources of our struggles. If we can work to destigmatize being in recovery, people struggling with addiction, mental health problems, and suicidal thoughts can come out of hiding and get the help they need.

Sober Truth Project primarily seeks to educate, empower, and advocate for two distinct groups:

1. People in recovery from addiction, mental health problems, and suicidal thoughts.

2. People called to love and lead people in recovery from addiction, mental health problems, and suicidal thoughts.

And believe it or not, most people find themselves in at least one if not both of these groups when recovery touches their lives. When a colleague has a nervous breakdown. When a family member dies by suicide. When we come face-to-face with our own vices. It's only through these places of encounter that people develop a desire to go deeper and do more.

Recovery is for everyone. Because at its core, recovery is the gospel.

God, help me to find my purpose in this life and help those I love and lead to find their purpose too. I know that Your plans for us are always good. Help us to listen and follow You. Amen.

October 6: LOVING OUR "ENEMIES"

You have heard that it was said, "Love your neighbor and hate your enemy." But I tell you, love your enemies and pray for those who persecute you.
—Matthew 5:43–44

Loving our enemies is more than mere emotion. Love means not only honoring them through disagreement, but leaning in hard to also honor what they bring to the table. We need to honor people trying to love and lead in recovery, despite denominational, religious, and cultural differences. Coming together to care by fostering authentic and safe relationships with them is our only hope of bridging the gap.

You may be asking, "How do we engage in a conversation like that with a medical doctor who rejects Jesus? With a dry drunk more addicted to meetings than anything else? With a family that's lost everything, including relationships, marriages, and even loved ones' lives?"

The answer is simple, but it's not easy. With humility. You can position your heart to learn all you can. You can ask open-ended questions and resist the urge to fix, correct, or brag. You can offer insight, perspective, support, and love where you can. You can invite others to offer insight, perspective, support, and love where they can.

By all means, be honest and unapologetic about your own beliefs and mission. But lay your agenda aside and treat your potential co-laborers as the beloved children of God they are—even if they don't know it yet.

Only through authentic and safe relationships like these can real breakthrough come. And only in this way could we ever hope for the opportunity to share the truth about the hope we have in God.

God, help me to see all people as my brothers and sisters, as Your beloved children. Help me to build authentic relationships with them, no matter what our differences. Amen.

October 7: FAITH AND FACT

Consequently, faith comes from hearing the message, and the message is heard through the word about Christ.
—Romans 10:17

Faith is not a leap in the dark. Genuine faith is based on divine evidence revealed in God's Word. (See Hebrews 11:1.) How can we be confident in the dark without light and experience to guide us? How can we see the unseen without learning to sense its presence? If we can't even have faith on our own (see Romans 10:17), why do we bully ourselves into thinking we can have faith in times of doubt and fear? This works-based mentality is why recovery programs fail; we shepherd others to believe that they alone are responsible for the healing to be found.

Authentic Christ-centered recovery testimonies all contain one thing you can't find anywhere else: a supernatural faith encounter with a good Father God. A phone call at the perfect time. A crisis-turned-catalyst life event. A moment that changed everything, when you knew it was God, and you could never deny that it wasn't. Once you encounter God in a supernatural way, you begin to see Him everywhere. This is the essence of faith. Not just bootstrap believing in what you can't see, but being so sure that something or Someone is there that you begin to doubt your doubts.

While we're not to test God (see Matthew 4:7), He often responds to desperate cries in desperate times. Getting into God's Word will soften your heart for a supernatural faith encounter that changes the trajectory of your journey toward a promised-land life. Where do you need God to intervene? Cry out and seek powerful scriptural testimony of similar deliverance. He will show you evidence of His ability and willingness to intervene—and build your faith by proxy.

God, I'm desperate for You. Show me a sign that You're there. Reveal Yourself to me in Your Word. Enhance my physical and spiritual senses so I can sense Your presence wherever I go. Amen.

October 8: CONTROL FREAK

*In their hearts humans plan their course, but the L*ORD *establishes their steps.*
—Proverbs 16:9

Self-control is a fruit of the Spirit (see Galatians 5:23)—one we all need to make it through this recovery journey into a promised-land life worth living. In Paul's running list of spiritual fruits, self-control is mentioned last, not because it's the least of the fruits but perhaps so that we would remember it and heed it. Realizing our powerlessness in the natural is key to realizing the power and authority we carry in Christ, our true Higher Power. In Him alone, *"we live and move and have our being"* (Acts 17:28)—and in Him alone can we harness the self-control we need to stay His course.

In our longing for and attention to harnessing self-control, a funny thing can happen. The control intended for us and our own lives spills over into the lives of others—and not in a *"my cup overflows"* (Psalm 23:5) kind of way. We try to control others because it makes us feel safe, like we can be in control of ourselves. And when we eventually discover that we *cannot* control others, we quite literally and figuratively lose our minds in the chaos of it all.

Surrendering to God's sovereign control is key to naming our own control issues and giving them over to God. When we do so, we realize we were never really in control at all—not even of ourselves. God's Holy Spirit living in us gives us the power to harness personal accountability and offer accountability to others. And thankfully, His Spirit is much better at control than we are! It's always for our good, His glory, and the kingdom He continually invites us into.

Let go of anything that's keeping you from it today.

God, hold me accountable to the self-control only You can provide. I know I can't control what others do, and I can't always even control what I do, but You can. Help me, Lord. Amen.

October 9: LETTING GO

A time to search and a time to give up,
a time to keep and a time to throw away.
—Ecclesiastes 3:6

Our perceived control over our lives, situations, and others is an illusion. Accepting this truth is one thing but *letting go* of this perceived control is something else entirely. Most traditional recovery programming encourages participants to admit their powerlessness, nearly to a fault. On our own and in our flesh, we are powerless and out of control. But in Christ, we carry His power and authority when we surrender to God's control.

The problem with this notion is that even when it makes sense, it's incredibly difficult to walk out in faith because deep down, we don't have all the evidence yet. We still wonder about God's true nature and character. Is He an all-powerful Sovereign? Is He a good Father God?

Bad things happen to good people. Healing doesn't always come like we think it should. War, famine, disease, death—even if we believe God is really in control, we may wonder if He's *really* good. And if we believe He's really good, we may wonder if He's *really* in control. And when we question either, we may relapse back into old ways of thinking. We think that maybe we'd do a better job than God, and that our recovery is really all up to us.

Take heart. You aren't the first to ponder these things. Curiosity, wonder, frustration, and even anger with God is all over Scripture, even by the Father's noted favorites. Jesus Himself fell on His face before Father the night before His impending crucifixion, crying, *"My Father, if it is possible, may this cup be taken from me. Yet not as I will, but as you will"* (Matthew 26:39).

Jesus's surrender to the Father's will was a testament to His unshakable faith. In His humanness, Jesus didn't exactly *love* the Father's plan. But He surrendered to God's will because Jesus knew the Father to be both sovereign and good, even through doubt and fear in the natural world and His present circumstance. Jesus endured pain and death…but also resurrection and glory, all because He was willing to let go.

Are you willing?

God, letting go of control terrifies me, even if I never really had it in the first place. Help me let go and surrender to Your good and sovereign will like Jesus did, for my good and Your glory. Amen.

October 10: ROLES WE PLAY

Follow God's example, therefore, as dearly loved children and walk in the way of love, just as Christ loved us and gave himself up for us as a fragrant offering and sacrifice to God.
—Ephesians 5:1–2

Humans were designed to fulfill a range of roles at different times, in different seasons, and under different circumstances. Employee. Provider. Caregiver. Spouse. Parent. Friend. Mentor. The list goes on. Recovery requires us to reassess our current life roles to determine whether we are merely playing them, living them out to the fullest with help from a good Father God, or letting them become idols, labels, or stumbling blocks that we need to surrender to God.

Being in recovery doesn't mean you automatically get to quit your job, divorce your spouse, or abandon your child because the situation feels unmanageable. The promised-land life just doesn't work that way, and deep down, you know it. But it could mean leaving a toxic work environment. It could mean ending an abusive relationship. It could mean allowing your children to stay with family until you can get healthy. Your role as provider, caregiver, friend, or mentor may need to take a backseat until you can first embrace your most important role as a *beloved child* of God.

Without this confidence of being fully known and fully loved by your heavenly Father, you will have a hard time loving, leading, and serving others in any capacity, even the places where you rightfully want and need to serve. God is faithful and will restore the years the locusts have eaten. (See Joel 2:25.) But in this critically important time of reassessment, every role you've ever had—and every role you ever will assume—must be laid out on the table for careful and honest examination.

Which roles in your life are in need of reassessment? What's working, what's not working, and what else might God have you do, even if it's just for a little while? Listen to His voice and He will guide your path.

God, help me walk in Your love first—before I ever try to earn love or affirmation from others. Help me assume only the roles You have for me in this season of reassessment, nothing else. Amen.

October 11: THINK BEFORE YOU ACT

For it is God who works in you both to will and to do for His good pleasure.
—Philippians 2:13 (NKJV)

If you've followed Jesus for any length of time, you've likely heard platitudes, adages, and not-so-subtle suggestions to stop striving and lean instead on God's strength in all things. While the sentiment is pure and good, Scripture also encourages us to adopt a spirit of self-control. *"Better a patient person than a warrior, one with self-control than one who takes a city,"* implores Proverbs 16:32. This puts at least some of the responsibility for our actions squarely on our shoulders as believers, especially those of us in recovery.

Walking in the spiritual fruit of self-control requires us to adopt a practice called self-regulation, a learned ability to control our thoughts, feelings, and actions as we pursue long-term goals. Self-regulation can be especially helpful from an emotional standpoint because it helps us to identify disruptive thoughts that are from the enemy and even ourselves so that we might take them captive and make them obedient to Christ. (See 2 Corinthians 10:5.)

Your ability to self-regulate started in early childhood, when you ideally learned how to process uncomfortable feelings without throwing a tantrum. Your success in these early years can be an indicator for healthy emotional intelligence in adult life. Failure in these areas can lead to far greater tragedy than a tantrum in adulthood. When a child does not feel safe and secure, they cannot possibly learn to self-soothe or self-regulate.

And yet God always makes a way. Regardless of your experience, you can harness the power of cognitive reframing to teach yourself and the ones you love and lead how to self-regulate. The brain can heal itself by learning new thought patterns, reassessing former and current life situations with an earnest challenge to our worst assumptions about what else might be true. Exploring this powerful question with God can help you learn to pause, reflect, and self-regulate as you wait on God's timing before you act.

God, make me slow to anger and quick to understand. Soothe my broken heart and mind and help me see situations for what they are before I take actions that could harm me or others. Amen.

October 12: INTROSPECTION

Let us examine our ways and test them, and let us return to the LORD.
—Lamentations 3:40

Do you ever pause to consider the real reasons why you think and feel the way you do? If not, it's likely you're not yet making much progress on your recovery journey.

More than mere reflection, introspection is God's invitation to separate sin from self as we objectively examine the content of our hearts and minds. In doing so, we can go deeper—into Uncovery territory—to unearth the trauma that's leading us to struggle with addiction, mental health problems, and thoughts about suicide.

The only problem with introspection is that we will typically only apply it to our own circumstances. We might explore the deep reasons why we feel the way we do—and when we find the truth, we accept it and learn from it. But we are often slow to accept the introspective findings of others about themselves and quick to judge their surface-level behaviors. This can be devastating—and even deadly—when it comes to recovery, as far too many of us are ill-equipped to provide trauma-informed ministry and care.

Adopting introspection as a spiritual practice is vital to our recovery journey. Encouraging others in recovery to do the same will make a grand difference in helping them build a promised-land life. But for every believer called to love and lead people toward freedom in Jesus's name, we must be able and willing to go beneath the surface-level struggle and help others embrace introspection that leads to healing and growth. This is what it looks like to be the hands and feet of Jesus.

God, sometimes when I go deeper, I'm quick to judge myself and others. Help me stay objective, to see sin for what it is—an attack from the enemy, who You have already defeated. Amen.

October 13: COMFORTER

Comfort, comfort my people, says your God. Speak tenderly to Jerusalem, and proclaim to her that her hard service has been completed, that her sin has been paid for, that she has received from the LORD's hand double for all her sins.
—Isaiah 40:1–2

For people in recovery, anxious thoughts can be pervasive. Even when we trade our unhealthy coping mechanisms for healthier ones, it can take quite some time for things to feel safe physically, emotionally, and spiritually.

While we're meant to walk out our recovery journeys in community, there will be times when it's just you and God. And in those precious, intimate times with Him, He will be faithful to show up as your Comforter.

The God of all comfort knows exactly what it takes to soothe a troubled mind. Partnering with His comfort takes humility, intentionality, and a willingness to follow the Spirit's lead in pursuing comfort even in times of isolation. Listening to worship music, practicing self-care and self-kindness, and visualizing the promised-land life you're actively building with God is a start. Ultimately you will discover that no self-soothing mechanism will comfort you like the Comforter does. He will ever be your constant shelter from the storms of life. You are always safe resting in the arms of your good Father God.

Friend, there will come a day when you will not need God as Comforter anymore. On that day, He will wipe every tear from your eyes, and you'll never again mourn because of death, pain, and struggles in this life. (See Revelation 21:4.) Soak up this precious time with the Comforter. Let Him come to you, cover you, restore you, and sustain you. Let Him shepherd and guide you into all righteousness and peace. Let Him soothe you when you don't know how to soothe yourself anymore. And in gratitude, pray and long for the day when you'll never need soothing again.

God, when my anxious thoughts threaten to take over, comfort me as only You can. Teach me to go beyond self-soothing to receive Your loving care and protection. Keep me safe in Your arms. Amen.

October 14: SEEING GOD

O LORD God of Abraham, Isaac, and Israel, our fathers,
keep this forever in the intent of the thoughts of the heart of Your people,
and fix their heart toward You.
—1 Chronicles 29:18 (NKJV)

In the earliest days of humankind, man's imagination was so corrupted by the fall that most humans either could not or would not see God for who He really is. *"Everything they thought or imagined was consistently and totally evil"* (Genesis 6:5 NLT). Our actions were straight-up wicked as well. This was never God's intent for our imaginations; He gave them to us so we could see His character and hear His voice.

Now, God isn't just a summation of what we imagine Him to be. Far from it. Because our imaginations can be off, we could easily misrepresent God in our minds to be someone He isn't. But our purest, most sanctified imaginations, aided by the inspired Word of God, can help us learn how to see God in our mind's eye. To see Him is to know Him, and to know Him is to love Him. Growing in that knowledge and love can help us hear His voice and obey His commands by the power of the Holy Spirit.

Yes, the Spirit of God lives in you! Because of this, your imagination has been redeemed alongside your soul. God is revealing Himself to you and enabling your imagination to operate with integrity more and more each day you seek Him. One day, you will see God face-to-face in the natural—no imagination required. But even today, you can catch a glimpse of the goodness of His glory this side of heaven.

God, reveal Yourself to me. I want to see You, hear You, know You, and love You more every day. Sanctify my imagination so I can see You for who You really are—a good Father God. Amen.

October 15: FRESH REVELATION

I keep asking that the God of our Lord Jesus Christ, the glorious Father, may give you the Spirit of wisdom and revelation, so that you may know him better.
—Ephesians 1:17

When the apostle Paul wrote to the church in Ephesus, he emphasized wisdom and revelation. Specifically, he prayed that *"the eyes of* [their] *heart may be enlightened"* (Ephesians 1:18). This prayer transcends earthly wisdom, which the Ephesians would have had in droves since their city was an epicenter of power and politics in biblical times. Seeing is believing, and knowledge is power—but only in the natural. The spiritual awakening Paul prayed for in this body of believers was meant to be a fresh, supernatural revelation of God's character rooted in His truth.

Skip ahead to the end of the New Testament, and it becomes clear that even if the Ephesians *did* get Paul's fresh revelation, they either couldn't or wouldn't receive it in full. In fact, the book of Revelation includes a stark warning to this same church, saying they professed Christ but did not give Him His rightful place in their hearts. (See Revelation 2:4–5.)

God can choose to reveal Himself to us in many ways, not only in Scripture but also in our hearts, in our minds, and in the helping hands of His people. When you encounter God in a fresh, new way—when He reveals something new to you about His character—give yourself time to chew, digest, and absorb the nutrients of His delicious truth. Receive His revelation in full and allow it to transform your heart and solidify your identity in Him.

God, I don't want to miss what You're trying to show me. Help me not only see it but receive it in full. Reveal Yourself to me in a fresh, new way and speak to me through Your Word. Amen.

October 16: SCRIPTURE REVELATION

Consequently, faith comes from hearing the message,
and the message is heard through the word about Christ.
—Romans 10:17

In many church circles, reading Scripture is on top of the corporate priority list, but not for the reasons you may think. Far more than a legalistic, box-checking approach to time spent earning God's favor, Scripture is the most reliable, consistent way in which God's people hear His voice. Getting in five minutes a day on your Bible app or five hours of intense study every weekend isn't really the point. After all, you can have the radio blaring in the background and not really listen. You can flip through the pages of a magazine without taking in more than a headline here and there. The point is to pore over the inspired Word of God to allow words penned millennia ago to speak to us in a fresh, relevant way for today.

The Holy Bible *New International Version* contains 727,969 words, each of them a portal through which you can tune into God's supernatural frequency of love. Passages that don't make sense today may one day guide you into deeper freedom than you thought imaginable. The most powerful kingdom revelation you can receive is not in vision, prophetic words, or even encounters of healing and deliverance. God's most common form of revelation comes through His Word—often in a passage that you've read a hundred times before that suddenly leaps off the page with stirring relevance.

You know you're really hearing from God when you can back up what you sense Him saying to you in Scripture. If it's not in His Word, it's likely not Him. And if you're not sure if it's in His Word, it's time to dig deeper and find out. Start somewhere—anywhere. Just start.

God, I admit sometimes I feel intimated by Scripture. I don't always understand it, and when I do, I struggle to receive it. Stir in me a hunger for You and Your Word. Speak to me. Amen.

October 17: PRAYER METHODS

This, then, is how you should pray: "Our Father in heaven, hallowed be your name, your kingdom come, your will be done, on earth as it is in heaven. Give us today our daily bread. And forgive us our debts, as we also have forgiven our debtors. And lead us not into temptation, but deliver us from the evil one."
—Matthew 6:9–13

When Jesus taught His disciples to pray in Matthew 6, we're not sure He ever intended us to recite the Lord's Prayer the way we do in church. There's definitely a benefit to raising our voices together and aligning with the Father's heart in a corporate setting. Memorizing this passage of Scripture is a vital part of Christian life and can help us keep our prayers on a more authentic, comprehensive track that honors God. But Jesus prayed often—and He never once prayed or led the prayer after that initial teaching.

Now, one might argue that Jesus never prayed the prayer He taught because He Himself never sinned against anyone. He would need no debts forgiven, nor would He need any transgressions wiped clean from His conscience. More importantly, we don't think He ever meant to repeat the words verbatim—He merely wanted to demonstrate how to pray authentically in all circumstances.

In a corporate setting, we're not meant to impress with fancy language or vain repetition, but to lead others as we ourselves are led by the Holy Spirit to pray. In small groups of two or more, we can invite God into intimate conversations—taking turns making our requests known, listening, and discerning together. And in personal prayer, we're meant to spend time with God as a friend, knowing that even when we can't find the words to pray, His Spirit intercedes and prays for us. (See Romans 8:26.)

Spoiler alert: There are no gold stars for prayer methods in the kingdom. Whether you're going after healing, deliverance, provision, or resurrection, be who God created you to be and encounter Him as the good Father God He is.

God, I love You and praise Your name. Help me pray in agreement with You on all things, trusting You hear me and that You will lead me in righteousness. Keep teaching me to pray, God. Amen.

October 18: JOURNALING PRAYER

Write down the revelation and make it plain on tablets so that a herald
may run with it. For the revelation awaits an appointed time; it speaks
of the end and will not prove false.
—Habakkuk 2:2–3

Writing prayers out is nothing new. People have been doing it since the beginning of time. When the people of God are willing to pray to God in writing—and let Him speak to them in writing—the Holy Spirit's power is put on display. This phenomenal act of co-creation isn't reserved for people like Moses and David, although they certainly made a lasting impact for the kingdom with their words.

God wants to speak to you and through you using creative acts of worship—namely writing. Now, you don't have to be a writer to participate in journaling prayer. You can simply put pen to paper or fingertips to keyboard and let the Holy Spirit flow. Perhaps God will give you a passage of Scripture to write out and meditate on. Maybe He'll give you a sense of what He's saying to you or a glimpse of just how good He really is. Perhaps He'll give you an original thought—something nobody has ever thought about before. Or perhaps He'll stay silent while you make your requests known to Him. He longs to hear from you, commune with you, and grieve or rejoice with you. And writing your encounters down—even bullet points will cut it!—can help you remember His faithfulness to you day by day.

There's no right or wrong way to journal. Your words may stay private, remaining as an intimate exchange between you and God alone. Your writings may be helpful in recovery to document progress and point back to God's faithfulness along your journey. But who knows? Your written words today may not only speak prophetically into your *own* life, but into the lives of the ones you love and lead. Start journaling prayer today using these prompts:

1. **What's Working?**

   Record three highlights of your day, when you felt and emulated Jesus most, and ask God to show you where He was in those moments. Pray on these moments and ask God to speak to you.

2. **What's Not Working?**

   Record three low points in your day, when you stumbled or struggled most, and ask God to show you where He was in those moments. Pray on these moments and ask God to speak to you.

3. **What More Would You Have Me Do?**

   Ask God to shine a light on how you might do tomorrow differently. What do you need more of? What do you need less of? What new thing might He be calling you to? Dream with God and let Him speak to you.

October 19: BREATH PRAYER

Then the LORD God formed a man from the dust of the ground and breathed into his nostrils the breath of life, and the man became a living being.
—Genesis 2:7

When God created Adam, He could have snapped His fingers, waved a hand, or simply said the word, and Adam would have sprung to life. But unlike all other created beings, Adam wasn't *spoken* into existence—he came alive by the very breath of God into his nostrils, a representation of His Holy Spirit in the natural. God *breathed* Adam to life—and that same divine breath still flows through the lungs of every descendant of Adam, even us.

This wildly intimate concept can be difficult to grasp outside of experience. This is why for generations, believers have used breath prayer, an ancient but easy spiritual practice that allows you to harness your God-given breath to reconnect with your Father and recenter yourself in times of anxiety.

Before you overthink this practice, start small—and start now. Close your eyes. Imagine yourself somewhere safe. Breathe deeply, in and out, becoming intensely aware of the air passing through your lips and nose and its divine origin. Then, recall a simple verse, Scripture, or helpful platitude, and breathe it—out loud or in your mind. Try one of the following breath prayers, or write your own:

Inhale: Lord Jesus, have mercy on me. Exhale: your beloved child.

Inhale: My sin was great. Exhale: your love is greater.

Inhale: Be still and know. Exhale: that He is God.

Repeat the phrase over and again, at least ten times. Then, when you're ready, slowly come back from the safe place fully equipped with God's peace.

God, thank You for being as close as my breath. Your presence is a healing balm to my anxious soul, and I'm so thankful You're willing to meet me with Your peace anytime, anywhere. Amen.

October 20: IGNATIAN PRAYER

I am the LORD your God; consecrate yourselves and be holy, because I am holy. Do not make yourselves unclean by any creature that moves along the ground.
—Leviticus 11:44

In some circles of Christianity, human imagination is frowned upon. Anything out of linear biblical context is considered risky at best and heretical at worst, leaving little room for the Holy Spirit to speak to us and through us.

However, God gave your imagination to you as a gift that reflects His own imagination. And He allows you to use it however you choose...for better or worse. Free will is a tricky thing for sure.

Enter Ignatian prayer, an ancient practice that encourages us to use our imagination to explore deeper facets of the gospel. A sanctified imagination can allow us to feel a full range of emotions, embracing our personal reactions to and feelings about Jesus and His truth. In the safety of this imagination-friendly prayer, we have permission to speak to God one-on-one about the delightful and even disturbing aspects of His Word without fear.

Friendship and intimacy with God are key to letting Him lead us in life and in recovery. This closeness requires something called consecration—allowing God to take all aspects of our lives and make them pleasing to Him. This includes our imaginations, of course!

Saint Ignatius penned a beautiful prayer that can position your heart for this kind of experience with your good Father God:

> Take, Lord, and receive all my liberty, my memory, my understanding, and my entire will, all I have and call my own. You have given all to me. To you, Lord, I return it. Everything is yours; do with it what

you will. Give me only your love and your grace, that is enough for me.

This prayer positioning takes practice. You won't walk it out perfectly, and God doesn't expect you to. All He wants is intimate friendship with you. When you meet Him in imaginative prayer, He will open your mind and show you more of who He really is.

God, align my imagination with Yours. Take it and make it something that makes You happy. I know You already love me fully—help me learn to love You even more than I already do. Amen.

October 21: WALKING WITH GOD

Do two walk together unless they have agreed to do so?
—Amos 3:3

When you're with a friend, you walk side by side, laughing, talking, and sharing your heart. You might notice your surroundings, but only to point them out to your friend. You're present, focused, and agreeing to walk together with your friend.

This is what God wants with you.

Now, walking with God may not be a literal, physical stroll down the street. Walking with God refers to a lifelong journey. Wherever you are, whatever you're doing, He wants you in constant communion with Him—by His side, laughing, talking, and sharing your heart as He does the same. While the distractions of life may try to pull you from your focused walk, He will continually invite you back in to walk with Him, even in silence, even if He has to carry you. On the mountaintop and in the valley, He will journey with you into a promised-land life.

Walking with God through recovery will require sacrifice, some clarifying *nos* and necessary endings. Habits, sins, labels, distractions, and unhealthy relationships must be left behind because they don't make for a fulfilling walk. Letting God strip you of anything that's more important to you than Him is key to your faith walk and recovery journey.

It may take time to learn what works on your walk with God—and that's okay! As you press on together, you'll see more and more of His character walked out in your journey.

God, let's go for a walk that lasts forever. Talk to me, laugh with me, and share Your heart. Stay by my side as I seek You and keep calling my name through distraction, exhaustion, and fear. Amen.

October 22: REPENT AND BELIEVE

Repent, then, and turn to God, so that your sins may be wiped out,
that times of refreshing may come from the Lord.
—Acts 3:19

When you take time for a reflective reassessment of how your recovery journey is really going, you're bound to find more opportunities to repent and believe. To repent simply means to change your mind. When you change your mind to align with God's mind, you will have to turn away from old ways of thinking and toward God. He doesn't just forgive sin, but destroys it—wiping it out completely, as if it never happened.

We humans get caught up in clean-slate Christianity, trying to maintain our God-given holiness in our own strength. When we fail, as we inevitably do, we start to believe holiness isn't even possible in the natural, so we stop trying altogether and assume God will forgive us anyway. Repentance is a beautiful invitation to look objectively at our lives and ask God, "What's working? What's not working? What more would You have me do?" As He reveals His delight in our obedience, His pain in our disobedience, and His hope for our future, we can simply say, "You're right, God. I'm choosing to believe what You believe."

Repentance is more than saying you're sorry. It's more than even *being* authentically sorry. It's more than repentant thoughts, words, and actions, although it might lead to all three. Repentance is a continual heart positioning that draws us closer to God as we reassess each new day, month, year, and season of life. Genuine repentance brings transformation when God's mercy leads us to it.

God, remind me how broken I am without You. I take You for granted, and my life is getting sloppy. Help me lean on Your mercy and rest assured that I'm Your new creation. Amen.

October 23: A NEW NARRATIVE

Listen, I tell you a mystery: We will not all sleep, but we will all be changed.
—1 Corinthians 15:51

Could the story of your life use a rewrite? Good news! Your good Father God, the Author of life itself, has full rein to rewrite your narrative in light of His grace. From a salvation standpoint, this means that when you accept Jesus and decide to follow Him, your sins aren't just forgiven—they're washed away in a process called justification. This leaves you innocent, perfect, holy, and blameless before God because of what Christ did.

This divinely inspired creative editing transcends your past sins to reframe your past trauma. What was once your greatest struggle will one day be your greatest place of victory when you let God lead you. Struggles with addiction, mental health, and suicidal thoughts can be defeated through a careful, strategic edit of your past.

We're not talking about omitting things or pretending they never happened. But we're allowing God to use them for our good and His glory in ways we could never imagine.

Your story is God's story. He's a brilliant Author, and while you're still breathing, God is still writing and rewriting. Through plot twists and all-is-lost moments, He alone knows the outcome, and He alone will redeem your story into a new narrative that inspires other believers to embrace His changes.

God, redeem the parts of my story that I struggle to understand. Show me where You were in my trauma and reveal Your glory for all to see in my story of redemption and hope. Amen.

October 24: MINDFULNESS

You will keep in perfect peace those whose minds are steadfast, because they trust in you.
—Isaiah 26:3

When was the last time you were fully present, aware of not only where you were and what you were doing but who you were in the moment? Mindfulness allows us to harness this God-given self-awareness to go deeper into recovery and help the ones we love and lead to do the same.

Sadly, many Christians equate mindfulness and even meditation with New Age practice, dismissing the truly divine state of being one with God and fully connected to oneself. Only through mindfulness can we begin to experience the Father's presence, a supernatural connection that typically transcends the senses. When He speaks through worship lyrics, comforts through a friend's warm embrace, or puts the full glory of creation on display in nature, we must stay mindful of His presence to experience the glory of being one with Him.

The goal of mindfulness is to sharpen our mental, emotional, and physical capabilities so we can overcome anxiety, thwart temptation, and *take captive every thought to make it obedient to Christ*" (2 Corinthians 10:5).

Be fully present to God, yourself, and others, resisting the urge to judge your emotions as good or bad; instead, view them as helpful and informative. Cling to the truth of your oneness with the Father, Son, and Holy Spirit so you can see life situations for what they actually are, not just what you perceive them to be through a lens of trauma. Pay attention. Live in the moment. Be kind to yourself. And breathe in deeply the love of God.

God, I want to be aware of who You are and who I am in You always. Help me stay present in the moment, mindful of Your love for me and the ones I love and lead. Show me Your glory. Amen.

October 25: BOOTSTRAPPING

Being confident of this, that he who began a good work in you will carry it on to completion until the day of Christ Jesus.
—Philippians 1:6

Pulling yourself up by your bootstraps can be beneficial in business or military strategy. In essence, bootstrapping means getting yourself into or out of a situation using only the resources at your disposal.

While we might all benefit from the idea of starting where we are, using what we have, and doing what we can, doing recovery with Jesus puts different resources at our disposal. The key to harnessing these resources is to recognize *who we are* in Christ while simultaneously acknowledging *what we carry.*

We're beloved children of a good Father God. (See Galatians 3:26.) We're coheirs to the kingdom of heaven with Jesus. (See Romans 8:17.) And we're one with God, in Christ, by the power of the Holy Spirit. (See John 14:20.)

Friend, this good news means that on this lifelong recovery journey, you have full access to far more resources than you knew! So start where you *really* are. Ask God to show you the progress you've made and give you a glimpse of the promised-land life He's leading you into. Use what you *really* have. Tap into the fullness of your kingdom inheritance and believe for healing, provision, favor, and total-life transformation. Do what you *really* can—no more, no less. And trust that in the places where you will inevitably fall short in your humanness, God can and will take it from there—faithful to finish the good work He began in you. (See Philippians 1:6.)

God, forgive me for trying to bootstrap myself, believing my recovery is all up to me. I'd be lost without You on this journey. Help me lean on You in all things and trust You to deliver me. Amen.

October 26: BEST EFFORT

But God demonstrates his own love for us in this:
While we were still sinners, Christ died for us.
—Romans 5:8

Leaning into the Father's strength is key to lasting recovery. When we acknowledge that we're power*less* on our own and power*ful* in Christ, we take meaningful strides toward a promised-land life that's worth living—and worth staying sober for. And yet, there will be times when we grow weary, resentful, or apathetic on our journey, times when we struggle to stay present and grateful, when we entertain thoughts that aren't healthy or helpful, and when we compromise on self-destructive behaviors that can lead to recovery stagnation or even relapse.

These are the times when we must ask ourselves, "Am I really giving my best effort?" Make no mistake, God can (and often does!) work miraculously in our lives when we haven't done a thing to deserve it. In fact, Jesus died for us while we were still sinners (see Romans 5:8), when we not only weren't giving our best effort, but were in all-out rebellion against Him! This kind of mercy and grace moves us to repentance. Real *metanoia* repentance requires us to align our thoughts with the Father's and make our best effort to act like the beloved children of God we are. He gave us His all when we did not deserve it. So let's give Him our all—because He deserves it!

Free of shame, reassess your current recovery reality. What's working? What's not working? What more would God have you do? What places in your life is God asking you to surrender to Him? Where is He calling you to reengage with Him on the journey, bringing Him your best effort? When He reveals it to you in love, give Him your best—your life and your all.

God, forgive me for times when I've become lazy in my recovery. I know going through the motions won't get me closer to a promised-land life. Help me give You my best effort. Amen.

October 27: FAILURE ISN'T FATAL

But he said to me, "My grace is sufficient for you, for my power is made perfect in weakness." Therefore I will boast all the more gladly about my weaknesses, so that Christ's power may rest on me.
—2 Corinthians 12:9

No matter how committed we are to walking out a faithful recovery journey, we won't do it perfectly. No one does. This truth can be problematic when we're working the steps and tracking days, weeks, months, or even years sober, because the metrics many recovery leaders use to determine our recovery progress demand perfection. Relapse is normal, especially in the first three years of recovery. And if we shift the way we think about recovery, we might even find our failures to be helpful indicators of where God is ready to bring more healing in our lives.

It can be difficult for us to embrace a growth mindset in recovery—one where failure isn't seen as fatal, but as an opportunity to stretch, grow, and course-correct—because people are dying, and we are desperate. In fact, struggles with addiction, mental health, and suicidal thoughts can be deadly, especially when those who struggle are given all-or-nothing ultimatums on their recovery journey.

While we certainly don't want the ones we love and lead to fail, we must embrace the idea that God's strength is perfect in our weakness. (See 2

Corinthians 12:9.) He meets us where we are, even in our worst moments of failure, and makes a way for our freedom.

Free people free people when they do it in Jesus's name, and the word of your testimony truly matters. Your time spent in the valley is a precursor to your unique calling in this life—to seek, save, love, and lead the lost to Jesus.

God, show me times in my life where failure wasn't fatal. Help me give myself grace along the journey and teach me when I stumble and fall. Your loving correction strengthens my soul. Amen.

October 28: LIFE IN OVERFLOW

And to know this love that surpasses knowledge—that you may be filled to the measure of all the fullness of God.
—Ephesians 3:19

Scripture makes it plain that we are meant to be vessels for God to use to hold His treasure—"*jars of clay to show that this all-surpassing power is from God and not from us*" (2 Corinthians 4:7). Of course, this assumes that we are being actively filled with the things of God and not the things of the world. What is holy can't coexist with what's not holy, so we will have a hard time being filled to *the fullness of God* when we don't create space for Him.

Staying full of God is as simple as walking out the grace-laced principles in the Uncovery every day. It means being intentional about filling our eyes, ears, mouths, minds, and hearts with what's true, noble, right, pure, lovely, admirable, excellent, and praiseworthy (see Philippians 4:8)—and doing our best to avoid what's not. What we focus on expands, and when we focus on the things of God, He will fill us with even more of Himself to the point of overflowing.

Life in overflow looks like carrying so much of God's love, mercy, and grace that some of it will inevitably splash out onto the people around you. They'll be delightfully confused about the promised-land life you lead, and they'll become desperate for more of what you carry. God is not a finite resource; there is always more of Him for His children to access. May you live a life so full of God that you're literally bursting at the seams.

God, fill me up. Rinse out of me anything I'm carrying that's not of You and fill my empty places with Your love. Seal my heart from this world and make me a conduit of Your grace today. Amen.

October 29: GROWING AND KNOWING

For now we see only a reflection as in a mirror; then we shall see face to face.
Now I know in part; then I shall know fully, even as I am fully known.
—1 Corinthians 13:12

As believers, we're called to grow in our knowledge and love of Jesus and make Him known in our communities and the world. This growth is twofold, personal and corporate, providing for healing and recovery for us and for the ones we're called to love and lead. This growth can be both literal and figurative, but it must start with a shift in mindset—a shift to valuing progress over perfection, brave daily choices over milestone chips, and total life transformation over mere sobriety.

Adopting a growth mindset can help you see circumstances for what they really are and learn from them. Unlike a fixed mindset, this shame-free approach reinforces the truth that people really can (and do!) change and teaches us to recognize and value that change in ourselves and others. Adopting this mindset keeps you hungry to learn, willing to pivot, and eager to give, knowing there is no scarcity in the Father's kingdom.

Moreover, when it comes to knowing God, there's always more to learn. You may never know Him fully in this life for it's impossible for us to comprehend the sheer vastness of His being. But He will know you fully and love you fully no matter what, and He will always be willing to give you more and more of Himself.

God, keep me growing. Give me Your living water and bright morning light to cultivate in me a mind fixed on growing and knowing You more, free of shame and full of Your glory. Amen.

October 30: EMBRACING THE JOURNEY

Let us run with perseverance the race marked out for us, fixing our eyes
on Jesus, the pioneer and perfecter of faith.
—Hebrews 12:1–2

Seasons of reassessment require embracing recovery as a lifelong journey, not a one-time event. This may sound simple, but as each new season comes and goes, we can lose sight of why we entered recovery in the first place. We can be slow to remember God's faithfulness in our lives up to this point. We can be quick to forget that even though we've come a long way, we may still have far to go.

It's as true in life as it is in recovery—you never really *arrive*. And if you think you have, it can actually be cause for great concern. This false confidence can leave faithful twelve-steppers and box-checkers feeling invincible...until life inevitably gets in the way. That's because life, even a transformed one, can be ridiculously hard.

Thankfully, even the promised-land life we work toward in the Uncovery isn't our final destination. Instead, it's part of a rebirth into the eternal life we're all being invited to experience.

Whether you're ten days' clean or twenty years' sober, pause and reflect on the recovery journey you're taking with God. Rejoice in how far you've come, even if you aren't sure where to go next. Be present in the moment, right where you are, and take an honest assessment of your progress and efforts. Then put one foot in front of the other and keep going, letting God alone guide you and staying with Him all the way. Friend, there will be a time when this precious journey comes to an end. Savor every moment in the race set before you— until you come face-to-face with Jesus.

God, help me stay steadfast on my recovery journey. I know it will last my whole life, but there are times when I grow impatient. Help me remember how good You are and how good You'll be. Amen.

October 31: TRANSFORMED AND TRANSFORMING

Not that I have already obtained all this, or have already arrived at my goal, but I press on to take hold of that for which Christ Jesus took hold of me.
—Philippians 3:12

What's done is done...unless it's not, or unless we believe it's not. Paul's letters speak often of the concept of spiritual perfection, and Jesus told us, *"Be perfect, therefore, as your heavenly Father is perfect"* (Matthew 5:48). And yet Jesus was the only human to ever live a perfect life. What gives? If we know we won't walk out our life and recovery perfectly, why would Scripture command us to do so?

Jesus and Paul were calling out a significant truth in the lives of every believer. When Jesus died on the cross, He became sin and defeated it, once and for all. He covered your sin—past, present, and future—and now presents you perfect, holy, and blameless before God. Not because of anything you've done, but because of what He did for you on the cross. When He became a perfect sacrifice for your sin, you were co-crucified with Him; you were transformed completely more than 2,000 years before you were born. This reality transcends time, space, and human effort. That's the magnitude of the grace you've been given.

For you, this reality means your status before God is *perfect*, and your life is continually being perfected, coming into agreement with what God already says about you. It means you're transformed into a new creation and yet actively being transformed into the person God created you to be. This certainly doesn't dismiss personal accountability, but it's proof positive that the grace over your life has you so locked in to the love of God that no mistake you could ever make could possibly separate you from Him and His love.

You're perfect and transformed because of what Christ did for you. And if you actually received it? You might start living like you believe it's true.

God, show me how You see me. Reveal the divine DNA You gave me and help me tune my thoughts and actions to the frequency of Your heart. I am who and what You say I am. Amen.

November

RE**CONNECTION**

Let the word of Christ dwell in you richly.
—Colossians 3:16 (ESV)

November 1: DEEP WOUNDS

"He himself bore our sins" in his body on the cross, so that we might die to sins and live for righteousness; "by his wounds you have been healed."
—1 Peter 2:24

When we seek healing, especially in recovery, we're often focused on the surface-level struggle. We pray in earnest for the addiction to vanish, for the mental health problem to fix itself, and for thoughts about suicide or self-harm to cease. These aren't incorrect prayers, and those who pray them do so in earnest. But even if we can find instantaneous, miraculous healing from such struggles, the deep wounds beneath them can still fester and rot in our spirit, causing the struggles to resurface or manifest in new and perhaps even more damaging ways.

Going deeper into the Uncovery means uncovering and healing from deep wounds—the trauma that caused us to struggle in the first place. Deep healing has the power to defeat surface-level struggles from the inside out in Jesus's name. Going deep can be difficult, especially when we're lacking safe, authentic community. But the church is uniquely positioned to be a safe-haven triage for those in need of a full spiritual excavation.

The beautiful part about deep wounds is that they can heal when you acknowledge them. God will definitely pull you out of your comfort zone, but He is kind and gentle in how He reveals opportunities for deeper healing. He won't shame you into it, nor will He beg. But in His perfect timing, He will reveal what's really going on beneath your surface-level struggle and help you heal from it all for good.

Where do you sense God showing you that there's more beneath the surface struggle? What pieces of your past feel too painful to process, and what do you need God to show you that you need to name and heal from? Ask Him. Open your heart, mind, and soul to a healing forged deep in His wells of grace.

God, You know me so well. You know what I've been through, even the things I don't want to think about. Help me face what lies beneath my surface-level struggle and find deeper healing. Amen.

Heal me, LORD, and I will be healed; save me and I will be saved,
for you are the one I praise.
—Jeremiah 17:14

Inner healing can seem hard to come by, especially since many of the deep wounds we carry are the result of trauma that happened many years ago. The further we get from the pain, the more difficult these memories can be to recall and face head-on. We may even try to bypass healing altogether, acting as if the trauma never happened. We may look healed and whole on the surface, but inside, we're concealing a cancer on our souls.

Good thing for us, God stands outside of time. He's omnipresent, which means He always has been, always is, and always will be—and He is not bound to the present like we are. When we pursue inner healing, our spirit can travel back to the time when the trauma took place, and we can observe it safely and objectively. While we may feel emotion regarding the pictures in our mind's eye, we can also have the out-of-body capability to see where God was in our moment of trauma.

Was He weeping with you? Comforting you? Protecting you from something far worse? Was He full of righteous anger against the trauma—and even in that moment creating a way forward for that place of trauma to become your greatest place of victory?

You won't know unless you go. And the best part is, you don't have to go alone. Work with a counselor, pastor, prayer team leader, or trusted friend to process your trauma in prayer to pursue deep inner healing. This precious process closes past story loops in your mind, which can set you free from struggles today.

God, take me back to the places I don't want to relive. Help me see them as parts of my story that You've brought me through. Show me where You were then, and where You are now. Amen.

November 3: RECONNECTING WITH GOD

The Lord is with you when you are with him. If you seek him, he will be
found by you, but if you forsake him, he will forsake you.
—2 Chronicles 15:2

Somewhere along the line, likely in an Old Testament, out-of-context reference, many of us have come to believe that our sin keeps us separate from God. (See Isaiah 59:2.) Sadly, this was once true—under the old covenant law. Gladly, we live under a new covenant in the shed blood of Jesus, which insists that nothing can separate us from the love of God, not even our sin! (See Romans 8:31–39.) This is exceptionally good news because it means that the God of the universe is standing by, eagerly waiting for us to turn to Him in worship, prayer, and the intimacy of His presence.

When we struggle and sin—and yes, we all do—it can be tempting to believe that God turns His back on us, ashamed of our unholy actions. *This is a lie from the pit of hell.* In fact, God doesn't even see your sin; He only sees Jesus's righteousness. He sees us as holy because He is holy—and we are one with Him. It doesn't matter how badly or how often we blow it; He never gets tired of lavishing grace on us and drawing us back to Himself.

If you're convinced God isn't there or that He doesn't care, suspend disbelief for just a moment. What if it's your perception alone? What if God is eagerly waiting like a good Father for you, His beloved prodigal, to come home? He longs to reconnect with you, and it's His desire that you never believe that you need to leave again. There is no distance and no separation between you. You are one with the Father by the power of the Spirit.

God, I miss You. I felt like You were at a distance, but I now realize it was me keeping You at arm's length all along. Draw near to me, and I'll draw near to You. Never let me go. Amen.

November 4: RECONCILING FORGIVENESS

For if their rejection brought reconciliation to the world, what will their
acceptance be but life from the dead?
—Romans 11:15

Forgiveness doesn't always bring about reconciliation, especially in cases of severe abuse. But the supernatural power of God's grace can bring about restoration and reconciliation in relationships that are too reckless to rekindle by all earthly standards. The adulterous spouse. The abusive parent. The exploiting coworker. The betraying friend. Reconciliation isn't probable, but it is possible when you have two willing parties and the Holy Spirit in the mix.

Real reconciliation is something only God can bring. We can't forgive in our own strength, love in our own strength, or even *have faith* in our own strength—so why would we be able to single-handedly bring about the profound heart change that allows for reconciliation? Only God can transform a heart. And He does, sometimes in surprising or shocking ways.

Seeking reconciliation can be difficult. Wanting to seek reconciliation can be even harder. Receiving God's grace and releasing it over your offenders is your first step. Only by coming into agreement with what He says about you and your offender can you hope to be moved with compassion to reconcile a relationship. And only by that same supernatural grace can your offender's heart also be moved to the real *metanoia* repentance that heals, transforms, and restores.

Start with you. Are you open to reconciliation if it's what God wants? If not, why not? Take your laments to Him and let Him do a work of grace in you that's so profound, you simply have to give it away.

God, give me a heart for reconciliation. Forgiveness is the price of entry, but I want to want what You want—to let Your love heal and restore where I think it's impossible. Show me, Lord. Amen.

November 5: KEEPING WITH REPENTANCE

Produce fruit in keeping with repentance.
—Matthew 3:8

True *metanoia* repentance simply means to change our mind, to turn away from our sin and toward God. Repentance is a powerful connection point with God that can create deep intimacy with Him along our recovery journey. But just like recovery, repentance isn't a one-time event. If we truly change our mind about our sin, we must not only turn from it, but make conscious, ongoing choices not to turn back to it. We must keep on choosing Jesus over our sin, or we've missed the whole point of repentance.

If this sounds a little unrealistic, take heart. God won't love you any more or any less if you sin or don't sin. That's not how His grace works. Continually turning from sin is an ongoing part of your lifelong recovery journey. You won't do it perfectly, but you will need to do it. And the more you choose to turn toward Jesus, the less you'll want to turn back to sin. You'll get caught up in the beauty of His gaze, lost in His glory, now dead to the sin that once captivated you.

Keeping with repentance by continually choosing to turn from sin builds spiritual resilience and produces the fruit of righteousness. This fruit is born in freedom that can only come from God. Are you tempted today? Turn to God. Are you struggling with sins of your past? Turn to God. Are you lost, confused, and ready to break? Turn to Him. Let Him change your heart so you can change your mind, making it easier to turn to Him.

God, I'm choosing You again. I know I've done it so many times before, and I choose You still. Help me rest in the light of Your face and resist the sin You've defeated. You're so much better. Amen.

November 6: TRADING LIES FOR TRUTH

"You will not certainly die," the serpent said to the woman.
"For God knows that when you eat from it your eyes will be opened,
and you will be like God, knowing good and evil."
—Genesis 3:4–5

We humans have been believing lies since the fall in the garden of Eden—the first being the serpent's manipulative scheme to bring sin into the world through Eve. Eve knew better; she knew if she touched the forbidden fruit, she would die, because God told her so. When the serpent insisted she wouldn't, instead of going to God for clarification, she partnered with doubt and did her own thing. Adam didn't do any better, and none of us likely would have either.

While it's true that gaining the knowledge of good and evil didn't instantly kill Eve, this knowledge opened the floodgates to sin and death in the world God created. Not only did Eve eventually die, all of humankind was sentenced to death too. Yet though our bodies may wither and die in the natural, our spirits will live on forever in the eternal life Jesus died for us to have. God is so much bigger than any lie we could ever believe. Even when we fail, He can and will redeem every part of our lives.

What lies are you believing right now? Is the enemy instilling doubt? Are your own ways more attractive than God's? Take a lesson from Eve. When something feels counter to the Father's heart and character, leaving you wondering if He's really good, take your questions to Him instead of sinning in rebellion. *"Sin is crouching at your door"* (Genesis 4:7), but you don't have to open it. In fact, you can command sin to go in Jesus's powerful name because the Holy Spirit lives in you.

God, You alone are my source for truth. When I don't understand Your ways and feel tempted to believe a lie, show me what is true. Deliver me from sin and death to eternal life in Jesus's name. Amen.

November 7: HURT THAT HEALS

Consider it pure joy, my brothers and sisters, whenever you face trials of many kinds, because you know that the testing of your faith produces perseverance.
James 1:2–3

Pain is an unavoidable problem in this life, and it does not discriminate. God is not the originator of our pain. It's not in His character. But even in His sovereignty, He allows pain because He knows it can drive purpose when we let Him into it.

It can be quite a stretch to see the connection between pain and trauma, healing and growth. The healing process is all about connecting our past to our future, understanding that if we don't acknowledge and heal from past pain, we will stay stuck—unable or unwilling to step into the promised-land life God has for us. When we walk in intimacy with God, we open ourselves up to align our thoughts with His. He will often bring to mind deep wounds and repressed trauma that's holding us back from deeper levels of healing and greater measures of freedom. Yes, it hurts, but the refining fire of God will cleanse your deep wounds and purify your heart and mind to see your trauma as an opportunity to grow and one day serve others.

Hurt people hurt people, and healed people heal people. Decide today if you will stay hurt or receive healing. You can't heal from what you don't or won't acknowledge as part of your life's journey—and God loves you too much to leave you stranded and stagnant. So go ahead. Lean into the pain. Find a safe space and a safe person to process the hurt and find healing. And let the Father's grace turn your trauma into an epic victory in Jesus's name.

God, my pain is so real—I don't want to go back there. But I have to be where You are. I'll follow You into my painful memories for my good and Your glory. Hold me fast. Amen.

November 8: THREE-IN-ONE HEALING

May the grace of the Lord Jesus Christ, and the love of God, and the fellowship of the Holy Spirit be with you all.
—2 Corinthians 13:14

When you pray, who is your go-to member of the Trinity? Father, Son, or Holy Spirit? Do you know why?

When believers learn to pray for healing, they are typically taught to pray for or declare healing in Jesus's name, saying, for example, "Jesus, we pray for Your healing," or "I declare total healing in Jesus's name." This is certainly not incorrect, but for some believers, this approach can perpetuate Trinitarian theology issues that we barely understand.

For Christians to be Christian, we must agree on the doctrine of the Trinity. We believe in one God, represented in three persons—God the Father; God the Son, Jesus; and God the Holy Spirit. Father, Son, and Spirit are all God, but the Father is not Jesus, Jesus is not the Holy Spirit, and the Holy Spirit is not the Father. A mind-bender to be sure. Jesus tends to feel like the more relatable of the three, since He is human and understands our plight. God the Father seemed a little angry in the Old Testament, so some steer clear of Him. Others all but dismiss the Holy Spirit in the context of modern faith. This travesty demonstrates an opportunity for the church to embrace a three-in-one approach to prayer and healing.

Sozo is a Greek word meaning wholeness. It's also a spiritual prayer practice and broad global ministry that engages all three persons of the Trinity to pursue healing in all facets of your life—body, mind, and spirit. Working with experienced ministry leaders, you'll ask Father, Son and Holy Spirit to reveal lies you're believing, opportunities for healing, unforgiveness in your heart, sins you need to let go of, and more. Going after three-in-one healing is not only the key to lasting recovery, but your fastest way to connect to the heart of God.

God—Father, Son, and Holy Spirit—show me the fullness of who You really are as my Healer. Help me embrace all facets of Your character and get to know You more each day. Amen.

November 9: YOU ONLY KNOW WHAT YOU KNOW

If we claim to be without sin, we deceive ourselves and the truth is not in us.
—1 John 1:8

When you're loving and leading people through the early stages of recovery, they're usually painfully aware of their sins. They're in crisis mode, so all they can see is the struggle. This acute awareness actually helps them identify lies they may be believing. This can build a great deal of momentum that can lead to transformation.

The awareness problem compounds when people have been in recovery for many years. They're not acutely aware of their problems because they've conquered so many. They can become lazy, apathetic, and even step back into new places of denial about their life and recovery journey. Even worse, those who have never walked through recovery may still be in need of it—but the longer they resist it, the worse their struggles may become. Arrogance sets in; they not only keep themselves from healing, but they become a barrier to healing for others.

We only know what we know. And until we know it, there is grace to cover our ignorance.

However, when God chooses to reveal something new to you along this journey of life, you will consistently come to points where you can never go back to *before* you knew the truth. When He reveals the struggle of a loved one that you had a hand in. When he reveals a sin in your life you had grown numb to. When he hands down a fresh revelation of His grace that changes the way you see everything and everyone. It is in these times that you'll experience the essence of real recovery.

At the risk of sounding like a broken record, we'll say it again: Recovery is for everyone.

God, show me my blind spots. Let me encounter situations and people who challenge my assumptions and inspire my faith in Your healing power. I want to know You more. Amen.

November 10: THE SPIRIT/BODY CONNECTION

Have mercy on me, LORD, for I am faint; heal me, LORD,
for my bones are in agony.
—Psalm 6:2

Bridging the gap between Spirit and science is a critical element of the Uncovery—and not just because it's the right thing to do in community. Many physical ailments we carry are manifestations of spiritual struggles. The simple act of talking with a trusted friend or counselor can actually reduce inflammation in the body, so it's not a far stretch to understand how unresolved emotional trauma can cause diagnosable physical ailments, including cancer.[8]

If spiritual and emotional trauma can cause physical disease, spiritual and emotional healing can combat it. This may be why God sometimes addresses a spiritual issue first when we go after healing in prayer—not to shame us for a lack of faith, but to deal with the real culprit causing our physical ailments. When God doesn't heal like we think He should, He's often positioning us to experience healing His way. And as grace would have it, He starts with the heart.

Are you weary? Do your bones and flesh cry out in agony? Have you prayed without ceasing until your words became groans? Call on God, your Healer, to reveal His plan for your healing. His ways aren't always easy, but they are always best, even when you don't understand what He's doing. Especially then. Let the Father reveal the divine mind/body connection you carry and show you the vast depths of healing He has in store for you.

God, could my physical struggles be a lingering part of my past trauma? Show me how to pray. I'm willing to go deeper with You, to stop disease at the source with deep soul healing. Amen.

---

8. Dr. Wendy Nickerson, "Psycho-Oncology: How Unresolved Emotional Trauma Can Cause Cancer," Nickerson Institute of Integrative Health Training,www.nickersoninstitute. com/blog/psycho-oncology-how-unresolved-emotional-trauma-can-cause-cancer.

Bear with each other and forgive one another if any of you has a grievance against someone. Forgive as the Lord forgave you.
—Colossians 3:13

Forgiveness is always a good idea, even when that forgiveness doesn't mean reconciliation or even direct contact. Forgiveness doesn't just free your offender of an obligation to you; it frees you from the attachment to your own offenses. No matter how deep your wounds are, any counselor worth their salt will help you identify people you need to forgive.

You may be thinking, *I'm all squared up! I've already forgiven the people who sinned against me, so there's nothing more I need to do.* If so, you're about to learn just how contagious forgiveness really is. Once you start giving grace, you'll keep on giving it. You'll even look for fresh opportunities to extend grace, perhaps even to people you've already forgiven.

But here's the wild part: There may be a handful of people whom you obviously need to forgive on your journey, such as someone who abused or betrayed you. But what about the offenses that were so subtle, you may not have yet acknowledged the identity damage they really caused? The teacher who gave backhanded compliments. The coach who pushed too hard. The pastor who didn't have his own theology straight. The parent who couldn't really parent because they weren't parented either. Dig down deep, and you may even find yourself resenting God—and although He doesn't need your forgiveness, He wants you released from the misperceptions you've had about Him and His character.

Lean in with the Father—and, ideally, a trusted counselor too—to explore the myriad of contributors to your deep wounds. Have you fully forgiven them? Have you counted the costs of the sins against you and released them of obligation completely? If not, or if you're not sure, it's okay. Follow the Spirit's leading and tap into a well of grace that never runs dry.

God, who am I missing? Is there anyone I'm holding onto offense with who I need to forgive? Your grace over my life is so profound. Help me find even more people to give it away to. Amen.

November 12: GENERATIONAL TIES

Honor your father and your mother, so that you may live long in the
land the LORD your God is giving you.
—Exodus 20:12

For better or worse, family members have the greatest propensity to hurt you. Since the bulk of trauma that causes struggles with addiction, mental health, and suicidal thoughts starts in early life, the care or carelessness you received from your father, mother, or guardian can leave you with deep wounds that can sometimes carry through the generations as part of a broken family culture.

For example, a grandmother's abusive alcoholism may cause a mother to be anxious and overbearing with her own children, ushering them into a lifetime of codependence or rebellion. It was never meant to be this way, but ever since Cain killed Abel (see Genesis 4:8), family drama has remained a constant for people in need of recovery. While there may be nothing you can do to erase the sins and struggles of your parents, grandparents, and other close relatives, you can break unhealthy generational ties in your own life.

It starts with honor. In the kingdom of God, honor isn't just something deserved—it's often bestowed. Honor is a gift of grace that has the power to invite people to embrace their true identity, even if they're not yet fully walking it out. Perhaps your mother was overbearing, but you never missed a meal growing up. Perhaps your father was absent, but had a strong work ethic and provided for your family. Even in cases of abandonment or abuse, finding something to honor—military service, overcoming difficult times, or even doing the best they could—can move you with Christ's compassion toward forgiveness.

God, what unhealthy generational ties am I holding onto in offense? Are there family wounds that need healing or family members I need to forgive? Make me an instrument of peace in my family. Amen.

November 13: RENOUNCING SIN

"The Lord knows those who are his," and, "Everyone who confesses the
name of the Lord must turn away from wickedness."
—2 Timothy 2:19

Scripture makes it clear that if we confess our sin, God is faithful to forgive it, every time. (See 1 John 1:9.) And while confession is as simple as coming into agreement with what God says about something, naming and understanding the nature of sin is critical to faith and recovery. After all, if we don't recognize sin as sin, we can't possibly confess it or turn from it. Even more importantly, we can't formally renounce that sin and stop it in our lives.

Christian recovery programming typically comes with a hefty helping of sin consciousness, dripping with shame and regret. Participants are bullied into all-or-nothing behavior modification strategies that glorify spiritual warfare over the divine romance between you and God. If you make a vow of marriage covenant, you don't don a shock collar that punishes you each time you look at the opposite sex—you simply renounce all other lovers, past, present, and future, and shift your gaze to the one you love. *"My beloved is mine and I am his"* (Song of Songs 2:16) means renouncing anyone or anything that keeps you from Him.

This formal declaration that you have abandoned sin will be an ongoing journey. You won't walk it out perfectly, nor will you be able to renounce all of your sin all at once. But God's grace is patient. As the Holy Spirit reveals more opportunities to let go of sin and self and cling instead to your good Father God, renouncing and releasing your own sin will keep your own path straight on your way to a promised-land life and inspire others in recovery to do the same.

God, reveal any sin in my life that's keeping me from walking with You. I renounce it now, leaving space only for You in my life. Help me stay centered on Your path of grace. Amen.

November 14: PEACE MISUNDERSTOOD

You will keep in perfect peace those whose minds are steadfast,
because they trust in you.
—Isaiah 26:3

The Word of God promises us that God's peace isn't a finite resource. There's always more peace where our last bit of it came from—Peace Himself. The only problem with God's peace is that it doesn't always look like we think it should. From an earthly standpoint, we think peace means freedom from disturbance, or even tranquility. We think of peace as the antithesis of war, when nation won't rise up against nation or brother against brother anymore. But God's peace doesn't always work like that. His peace has the power to deliver us from our circumstances, but moreover, His peace is meant to transcend our circumstances, guarding our hearts and minds along the journey.

Even though we can't fully understand how God's peace works (see Philippians 4:7), we can learn to lean into it in times of trouble. Instead of complaining, we can rejoice in the Lord always. Instead of lashing out, we can be gentle and kind like Jesus. Instead of partnering with anxiety, we can make our requests known to God in every circumstance. These subtle alignments put the power of God's peace on display in the midst of struggle and suffering, allowing the joy of the Lord to be fully recognized and revealed in us.

Tapping into the deep well of God's peace is difficult if not impossible when you're not actively walking with Him. He doesn't want to be a God you only call on in times of crisis—He wants to give you His peace in all things. In Him, you already have all you need. When you receive this truth, you not only become authentically grateful for all He has given you, you develop a desire to help others see His beauty, even in this broken life. May His baffling peace surround you today and always.

God, help me see where I take Your gift of perfect peace for granted. Help me always look to You because You're the source of my help. Give me Your wisdom to see You in all circumstances. Amen.

November 15: GRATITUDE

Sacrifice thank offerings to God, fulfill your vows to the Most High, and call on me in the day of trouble; I will deliver you, and you will honor me.
—Psalm 50:14–15

Gratitude is an often overlooked spiritual practice in recovery. With so much focus on our struggles, it can be difficult to keep a glass-half-full mindset, let alone intentionally focus on the positives in our walk with God. We're convinced this is why Scripture so often refers to prayers of thanksgiving and gratitude as *sacrifices*. To set our thoughts on the things we're grateful for means intentionally shifting our thoughts away from the things we might otherwise be tempted to complain about and wallow in. This is no small task.

Your time with God will be greatly enriched when you lead with gratitude. Recognizing Him for who He is and who you are in Him will automatically position your heart toward thankfulness. Standing in awe of His goodness, your prayers and petitions over very real struggles will no longer feel like vain complaints or unanswered rants. Instead, they will feel like a much-needed soul alignment with the heart of God—an alignment that will fill you with hope, awe, and wonder as you wait in eager expectation of what He can and will do.

If gratitude still feels like a forced concept, start with simple journaling prayer. In a notebook, on your smartphone, or in the margins of this devotional, write down three things you can thank God for today. They can be simple, such as, "Thank You for loving me," or specific ones like, "Thank You for the job interview." Thank Him for people, places, and unexpected gifts and encounters. Whether small or great, present these *thank offerings* to God first, before you make your requests known to Him. Then watch Him move powerfully in your life as your gratitude list grows.

God, I'm thankful for _____, _____, and _____. Help me remember Your faithfulness and find even more to be thankful for. Manifest Your goodness in my life, Lord. Amen.

November 16: CONNECTING WITH GOD

So Moses thought, "I will go over and see this strange sight—why the bush does not burn up." When the LORD saw that he had gone over to look, God called to him from within the bush, "Moses! Moses!"
—Exodus 3:3–4

When was the last time you encountered God in a burning bush? Never? You're not alone.

Scripture shares powerful moments of God's people connecting with Him in truly miraculous, undeniable ways, but we don't see or hear many stories like this in the present day. It's not because God doesn't communicate that way anymore. It's because we've replaced our expectations for a genuine spiritual experience with religious activity. Today's church—and today's Christ-centered recovery programming—prefers box checking to burning bushes ninety-nine times out of a hundred.

While we would never suggest that we throw out our Bibles, ditch our devotionals, and skip small groups and recovery meetings in search of a burning bush, we see great opportunity for God's people—especially those of us in recovery—to be open to and eager for more.

When it comes to connecting with God, are you really connecting or just going through the motions? When you read your Bible, are you allowing God's Spirit to speak through it, or consuming it like a textbook? When you spend time in fellowship and communion with other believers, are you seeking God together or trying to force community in inauthentic ways?

Feeling disconnected from God is a human mental construct. There truly is no distance or separation between you and God. Any you perceive is on your end. Turn your face toward Him. Rather than going through the motions, go after a genuine encounter with your good Father God. He may not light a bush on fire like He did for Moses, but He will draw you nearer to Him until you realize you're one with Him.

God, I want more of You than what my own religious efforts have to offer. Show me a side of Yourself I can't deny. Powerfully reveal Your heart to me when I least expect it. I long to see You. Amen.

November 17: THORNS OF RESENTMENT

And the God of all grace, who called you to his eternal glory in Christ,
after you have suffered a little while, will himself restore you and make
you strong, firm and steadfast.
—1 Peter 5:10

Going through the motions with God is a dangerous business. When it feels like we follow every command, check every box, and do everything our pastors, counselors, or friends suggest, and we still don't see any spiritual fruit, a different fruit—rather, a thorny weed—can take root: resentment.

Resenting God puts us at a perceived distance from Him. He certainly doesn't go anywhere, but we turn our faces from Him and squirm, writhing madly and trying to escape the palm of His hand. Or worse, we tune Him out altogether, avoiding the hard and even awkward conversations we desperately need to have with Him.

Your resentment doesn't stir anger in Him like you might think—it moves Him with love and compassion for you. Like any good parent, He won't force your patience, presence, or desire to understand. And He will love you ceaselessly, into and through every consequence you bring through your rebellion.

You *will* suffer in this life. (See John 16:33.) It's part of being in a broken world with a deep, collective need for Christ. Be willing to ask yourself if any of your suffering is self-inflicted or even chosen. Is your present struggle something that honors God and draws you closer to Him, or does it foster fits of religiosity, rebellion, and resentment? Does your life bear fruits of love, joy, peace, patience, kindness, goodness, gentleness, faithfulness, and self-control? Or are they choking on thorns of resentment before the blooms can fall?

Tend the garden of your heart with your Father. His skilled and loving hands can help you overcome resentment as you're overcome with His goodness.

God, I feel choked up. I'm doing everything I'm supposed to do, and I'm frustrated that I haven't seen You move. Give me patience to wait on You and clear thorns of resentment from my heart. Amen.

November 18: TRUE FAITH

And at three in the afternoon Jesus cried out in a loud voice, "Eloi, Eloi, lema sabachthani?" (which means "My God, my God, why have you forsaken me?")
—Mark 15:34

Having faith is easy...until it's not. The realities of the broken lives we live and the broken world we live in can leave us in moments and even seasons of doubt in which if we're honest, we'll admit that we don't really know if God is good all the time. Shame would have us believe that these doubts are the opposite of faith, but nothing could be further from the truth. Naming our moments of frustration, confusion, and disappointment with God creates honest, vulnerable times when God meets us in the middle of our messes to show us more about His character.

True faith may, in essence, be believing in what you can't see. (See Hebrews 11:1.) For example, you can't see air, but you know it's there. You may see evidence of it when your breath clouds up on a cool morning or feel deep gusts on an afternoon walk through the park. But chances are, you don't think of air much at all—until you don't have access to it. Faith manifests in this way when it comes to God. He's always there, but in tough times, it can be hard to see Him, feel Him, or connect with Him in the ways you're used to.

When times of trial inevitably cause doubt, don't hesitate to take that doubt straight to God. Even Jesus acknowledged the pain of this human doubt during His darkest moment on the cross, when He asked why God had forsaken Him. (See Mark 15:34.) God didn't forsake Jesus forever—in fact, He *was* Jesus incarnate. He heard His Son's lament, but knew deliverance wasn't what was best. God had a better plan for Jesus, and He has a better plan for you and me too. True faith means choosing to believe despite all evidence to the contrary.

God, I'm riddled with doubt. Show me evidence of where You are and what You're doing. Even if I don't understand, I just need You to remind me that You're there. Help my unbelief. Amen.

November 19: REDISCOVERING FATHER GOD

I will be a Father to you, and you will be my sons and daughters,
says the Lord Almighty.
—2 Corinthians 6:18

Seeing God as Father, head of the Trinity and Creator of all humankind, might seem like Christianity 101. But with our wild and weary systemic and generational daddy issues, we Christians have come to see the term *Father* as more of an author and originator than a loving, caring, involved parent. How quickly we forget that God always finishes what He starts—and calls it good. Even us.

Even if our earthly fathers were loving, caring, and involved, seeing God in an intimate *Abba Father* role can feel like quite a stretch. We read Scripture, sing songs, and pray prayers that affirm His nearness, but being *"under his wings"* (Psalm 91:4) both literally and figuratively can be an abstract concept.

When was the last time God gave you a hug? When did He play ball in the yard with you, or invite you to sit on His knee for story time? Thoughts of such encounters can be tough to reconcile in the natural, even when you believe them to be true.

It's time to rediscover God as Father. He is alive, speaking, and actively working in your life. He doesn't just want your awe, reverence, and worship; He wants your love, your delight, and every part of your heart. The God of the universe not only created you and knows you, He has made Himself known to you so that you can walk in intimate, loving, reciprocal relationship with Him. No earthly father could ever love you the way your good Father God does—and He will never love you any more or less than He does right now. You are a child of God, adopted into the family of your Creator. Everything He has is yours—so give Him your everything.

God, teach me how to receive Your perfect Father's love. Show me who You are and who I am in You. Challenge my wrong assumptions about You and make Your true self known to me. Amen.

November 20: OUR BROTHER JESUS

For those God foreknew he also predestined to be conformed to the image of his Son, that he might be the firstborn among many brothers and sisters.
—Romans 8:29

Savior. Bridegroom. Friend. Brother. Jesus holds a lot of mind-boggling names, with brother perhaps topping the list. If we can accept God as Father and Jesus as His Son, we lay the foundation for our kingdom family tree. And if what Scripture says about Jesus being our brother is true, it means we are nothing less than children of the living God—coheirs to the kingdom with Christ.

Jesus, quite literally your spiritual big brother, made a way for you to reconnect and commune with a holy God by dying for you while you were still a sinner. This kind of love transcends flesh and blood—your divine nature revealed by new birthright. Jesus is the only begotten, biological Son of God, which means you are His adopted child by a new birthright. Being born again isn't just about dying to your old life and starting a new one; it's about receiving your kingdom inheritance this side of heaven and learning to live your life like you believe you're royalty. Jesus, your brother, is even now interceding on your behalf to the Father, making a way to Him and the promised-land life He has for you.

This world would have you believe that you are not worthy to call Jesus your brother. And without His gift of grace to you, that would be true. But now that He has defeated your past, present, and future sin, you stand innocent before God—worthy, because He is worthy. Your brother Jesus was the first-born among many brothers and sisters, including you. And once you receive this truth, you'll want to spend the rest of your days giving it away to your other brothers and sisters in this world, even the ones who don't know who they are yet. Especially them.

God, what sweet grace could make Jesus my brother and You my Father? How could You love me so lavishly? Thank You for choosing me to be part of Your royal family. I owe You everything. Amen.

November 21: HEY, HOLY SPIRIT

And hope does not put us to shame, because God's love has been poured out into our hearts through the Holy Spirit, who has been given to us.
—Romans 5:5

Although the concepts can be difficult to grasp, Christian believers generally acknowledge God as Father and Jesus as brother. These core tenets of our faith make sense from a familial standpoint, even if our earthly families failed to represent our kingdom family. And yet the most often overlooked element of the Trinity is the Holy Spirit—the God who lives in us. The shocking mystical nature of the Holy Spirit defies comprehension even more so than the miracles of creation or Jesus's resurrection because they require an intensely personal experience with God.

The Holy Spirit manifests in our lives as the most nurturing, intimate person of the Trinity. The Spirit's gentle, almost motherly presence showcases God as Comforter in a radically personal way. More than an all-powerful Creator, more than a kinsman-redeemer brother, the Holy Spirit, our Helper, makes it possible for us to be one with God in Christ, by His power. The Spirit is not the Father or Jesus Christ, but the Spirit is all God, dwelling in us as His holy temples.

The God of the universe decided to set up shop within us, His created vessels. It makes absolutely no sense, but this truth positions us not only for fullness of life but as conduits for grace. As God's Spirit speaks to you and through you, your unfolding story can and will be a blessing to the ones you love, lead, and walk with through recovery. He will continually remind you just how precious you really are.

God, what a privilege it is to carry Your Spirit. Help me be attuned to You—living in me—so I can learn what it means to walk out an abundant life as Your beloved child for all to witness. Amen.

November 22: THOUGHTS ON THANKSGIVING

I will praise God's name in song and glorify him with thanksgiving.
—Psalm 69:30

Families and friends across the United States will gather in the coming days to roast turkey, eat pie, and be thankful. This holiday season can be equal parts blessing and curse for people in recovery, as relational strain can reach new heights, while temptation toward overindulgence and stress can take a toll on our mental health. With so much to be thankful for, what's to be done when the thoughts of Thanksgiving make us feel anything but thankful?

Turn your thoughts to God's goodness. Remember how far He has brought you and ponder the promised-land life He is helping you build. Praise Him even in the swirl of activity and pressure surrounding the holiday and elevate your thoughts to experience a deeper connection with Him.

God isn't terribly interested in our ultra-secularized national holidays, but He is passionate about blessing us to be a blessing, even to the ones who might otherwise bring us the most stress.

So walk humbly. Connect deeply. Listen quickly and respond slowly. Set boundaries—and go ahead and break them if God asks you to. Stay in step with your good Father God and remember that His good gifts transcend your circumstances, today and every day. Wherever you are, wherever you've been, and wherever God is calling you, pause right now and acknowledge God's blessings over your life.

God, I'm so thankful. I'm humbled by Your gifts of grace and mercy to me as well as the rich blessings You give me each day. Help me remember Your goodness and give thanks always. Amen.

November 23: A SERVANT HEART

You, my brothers and sisters, were called to be free. But do not use your freedom to indulge the flesh; rather, serve one another humbly in love.
—Galatians 5:13

Freedom is something worth celebrating. We were once slaves to sin. And now, because of what Jesus did, we are free people who are meant to free people in Jesus's name. It was for freedom that we were set free—a state Jesus invited us into while we were still sinners. This grace-laced, unmerited gift makes us free indeed, but it also demands a response.

Jesus walked the earth a free Man. Fully God and fully human, He had the freedom to choose whatever He wanted. But He didn't ascend to earthly power, riches, or pleasure. He humbled Himself, becoming obedient to God even to the point of His own death on a cross. From a Western perspective, this sure doesn't sound like freedom. But Jesus was, in fact, free to choose. And He chose to become a sacrifice for sin—for us and for all who would believe in Him. God Himself put a servant's heart on display in the natural, giving us the opportunity to claim our freedom in Him and follow His lead.

Jesus lived a life worthy of emulating. His servant heart is meant to be our heart positioning too—not out of obligation, but out of a desire to recognize, celebrate, and honor who He is and who we are in Him. Jesus set us free *from* sin, not *to* sin, which is why we humble ourselves and make Him Lord of our lives. Paul described being a willing slave to Christ (see Romans 1:1), which in essence means that serving Jesus was the most freeing thing he ever knew in this life.

That same freedom exists for you today. Your servant's heart, like Jesus's, will set even more people free.

God, make me a servant, moved with compassion by Your love. Remind me how good You've been and how much my freedom cost—and help me spend the rest of my days honoring it. Amen.

November 24: WHY, GOD?

Though he slay me, yet will I hope in him; I will surely defend my ways to his face.
—Job 13:15

No matter how hard we try, there will be times when we just don't understand God. Getting to know a God who can't be fully known can be frustrating to our finite human brains, especially in times of crisis. Deep down, we know Jesus meant it when He said, *"In this world you will have trouble"* (John 16:33). But deep down, we've also believed the lie that if we follow Him faithfully, we *won't* have trouble. When the inevitabilities of life arise on our journey toward a promised-land life, we cry out, "Why, God?"

If you've *been there, done that*, take heart in knowing that you're definitely not the first person to ask. Whether the answer to your *why* is already obvious or something that won't be revealed this side of heaven, God's silence on such matters can be frustrating—even devastating.

We belong to an omnipotent, omnipresent God who loves hearing our questions. They're important to Him, as evidenced by Scriptures that are full of pressing inquiries from God's favorites. Sometimes we get answers. Sometimes we don't. But no answer we could get from Him would satisfy the way His presence alone does. This is why He sometimes sits with us in the silent dissonance of life, meeting us and grieving with us in the moment.

Your *why* can bring you closer than ever to the heart of God, closer to understanding His ways and His character. When you sense the answers you seek aren't coming or might not be helpful anyway, align your heart with God's. Instead of asking, "Why, God?" try an open and expectant, "What now, God?" In these tender, earnest moments of surrender to God's perfect will and plan, He can provide something far more satisfying than the answers you seek.

God, I know You hold all the answers. But You don't owe me answers. Show me what I'm meant to know and nothing else. Deep down, I know Your ways are better than Your answers when I wonder "why." Amen.

November 25: THE HEALING JOURNEY

When he saw them, he said, "Go, show yourselves to the priests." And as they went, they were cleansed.
—Luke 17:14

Healing doesn't always happen like we think it should. That's why God maintains His role as Jehovah Rapha, our Healer, and any healing we do as

His people can only be done in Jesus's name. And it's a good thing, too. We Christians can become overly dependent on box-checking, legalistic healing strategies measured through quotas, and human efforts, celebrating our own perceived achievements instead of giving all glory to God.

Our recovery journey will be filled with wild opportunities for physical, mental, and emotional healing for us and the ones we love and lead. God our Healer never gets tired of healing—and Scripture commands us to lean into His power to bring healing in this earthly realm. (See Matthew 10:8.) But as finite, time-bound beings who serve an infinite, omnipresent God, we can become consumed with worry and doubt if we don't see total healing in Jesus's name when we pray for it. This can rob us of the beauty of walking out a progressive healing journey with God—the opportunity to heal as we go, progressively and on God's terms—in His timing.

From God's perspective, His healing is already yours. The more you align with His perspective, the more you'll realize your healing. But in the brief moment of eternity you spend on this earth, bound by time and clinging to God's promises, pause to consider what else He might be showing you along the healing journey. What truths do you need to relearn? What lies do you need to discard? What part of the Father's heart or character have you not yet fully embraced or experienced? Wait for it. Wait on Him. Sometimes it's in the process, in the waiting and wondering, that true healing is found.

God, I claim Your healing as my own. Help me taste and see as much of it as possible in this life, then in fullness for eternity. Your timing is always better than mine. I trust You. Amen.

November 26: THICKER THAN BLOOD

Consequently, you are no longer foreigners and strangers, but fellow citizens with God's people and also members of his household, built on the foundation of the apostles and prophets, with Christ Jesus himself as the chief cornerstone.
—Ephesians 2:19–20

It's said that blood is thicker than water, and in some cases, that may be true. There's the family you're born into—and family you choose. But there's also family that God will bring into your life in His perfect timing and for His perfect purposes, sometimes when you least expect it. Brothers and sisters in

Christ. Spiritual mothers and fathers. Fellow citizens of heaven and members of God's royal family. These people, carefully woven into the narrative fabric of your promised-land life, change you from the inside out. That's the beauty of living in God's kingdom, where Jesus's living water is *way* thicker than blood.

For those of us with difficult family origins, this blessing tastes extra sweet. When we can overcome the pain and trauma of our families of origin, we can allow our good Father God to parent us rightly through His people. Conversely, even people with supportive and healthy families can benefit from the spiritual reinforcements that come with a fellowship of believers. God created us for connection, and the power of community is key. Whoever we are, whatever we've faced, we need it.

Throughout your recovery, God will connect you with people who carry the rich blessing of context for your journey. They may not struggle in the same ways you have, but they can embrace the idea that recovery is for everyone, reminding you that you're never alone. Consider the people in your life—the family you were born into, the family you've chosen, and the family God has given you along the way. Who can you lean on today? Who may need to lean on you? Ask God to show you what family really looks like.

God, thank You for all kinds of family. Strengthen and reinforce my kingdom community so I can be blessed to be a blessing. Teach me how family can go beyond blood in Your name. Amen.

November 27: HOLIDAY BOUNDARIES

Seldom set foot in your neighbor's house—too much of you,
and they will hate you.
—Proverbs 25:17

The holiday season goes hand in hand with community as family, friends, and even acquaintances find reasons to gather. Whether it's a Thanksgiving dinner, a Christmas luncheon, or a New Year's Eve party, you may find yourself in demand—and putting others in demand as well. These holiday community expectations can leave you feeling stretched thin. At times, you may even dread get-togethers that would otherwise seem appealing.

Self-awareness is key to navigating the holidays without relapsing. And the best way to stay self-aware is to stay connected to God and to others who know you, know your story, and champion your recovery. Yes, there may be an obligatory work party or church gathering to attend. Yes, there may be people there who are not safe, or who regularly trigger you. But your willingness to let the Father go before you into these situations, level-setting intentions before your foot crosses the threshold, will keep you of sound mind and body this season.

Before RSVPing to a single event this season, take time to consider your motivations. Are you hosting a gathering because you're feeling isolated and want company, or is it out of obligation? Are you surrounding yourself with people who bring out the best in you, or those who trigger trauma and cause you to stumble? Are you allowing for adequate self-care during the hustle and bustle of things, or are you stretched so thin you might snap? Give yourself permission to set boundaries this season in whatever way God calls you.

God, lead me into safe places with safe people this season. Help me resist the urge to please people and instead lean into Your perfect rest, even when I'm feeling overwhelmed. Cover me. Amen.

November 28: FAITHFUL BOUNDARY LINES

Better is open rebuke than hidden love.
—Proverbs 27:5

Communicating boundaries is key in any relationship. It allows for intimacy and promotes deep emotional connection and authentic community with people and God. When we set intentions with the people we love and lead— what we will do, what we won't do, what's acceptable, and what's not—we teach each other how we want to be treated and equip others to love us well.

The problem with communicating faithful boundary lines is that they can often come off like a rebuke. Sharing things that make us uncomfortable with others can feel selfish to the person setting the boundary and shameful to the one receiving it, especially when healthy boundaries aren't a shared core value. For people in recovery, each step on the journey toward a promised-land life will mean establishing and reestablishing boundaries day by day, even moment by moment. Failure to do so leaves us vulnerable to relapse and damages the much-needed relationships we need to keep our momentum going strong.

Others don't have to view your boundary lines unfavorably. One way to present a new boundary line is to articulate where your comfort level stops.

For example, "I'm enjoying our friendship, but I'm not ready to date," or "I love talking with you, but I won't participate in gossip." Such statements establish positivity and preference without being harsh. In extreme cases, a direct approach may be necessary, followed by a potential consequence. For example, "If there will be exotic dancers at your bachelor party, I will have to pass," or "I'm in recovery, so I won't be attending any parties this season where alcohol will be served." These offer the clarity some people need to understand and respect a boundary.

Whether you're drawing boundary lines or trying to respect someone else's this season, stay close to the Father's heart. Relationships with clear expectations and mutual respect will create the authentic community you were created to have in this life.

God, help me be honest about what I need and don't need this season. Help me receive boundaries from others objectively and with a humble heart positioned toward honor and respect. Amen.

November 29: HOLIDAY HAZE

See to it that no one takes you captive through hollow and deceptive philosophy, which depends on human tradition and the elemental spiritual forces of this world rather than on Christ.
—Colossians 2:8

The holidays are a season of peace, hope, and joy, especially for followers of Jesus. But if we're honest, we'll admit sometimes it doesn't feel that way. Financial, relational, and logistical holiday stressors escalate quickly, making it difficult for people who struggle with addiction, mental health problems, and suicidal thoughts to stay sober. With less than clear boundaries, unrealistic expectations, holiday meeting breaks, sponsors on vacation, and dwindling budgets, friends, family, and other members of our community may not be there for us in the ways we need.

Before you wander into *holiday haze*—a murky, muddled season you'd rather escape from than participate in—pause with God to mind your mindset. People in recovery need a plan for the holiday season, and yours can equip and empower you for your most meaningful year yet. Objectively visualize the situations you may face that could cause you to struggle. A work Christmas party soaked in alcohol? An extended family gathering dripping with competitiveness and codependence? An obligatory gift exchange that doesn't fit your budget? Prepare your heart.

Ask God to give you language to handle any situation coming your way. When He suggests responses such as, "No wine for me, thanks, but I'd love a sparkling water," "I'm free for dinner, but then I'll be heading back to the hotel," or "Things are a little tight, so let's set a price limit on gifts," you'll know God is equipping and empowering your recovery in this season by covering you in His grace.

God, I may not always be able to avoid hazy holiday situations, but I know Your Spirit will guide me and give me the words to say to protect my sobriety and mental health. Stay with me. Amen.

November 30: RECONNECTING WITH HOPE

For everything that was written in the past was written to teach us,
so that through the endurance taught in the Scriptures and
the encouragement they provide we might have hope.
—Romans 15:4

Hope. Perhaps you've had it before: not just a vain want or ambitious desire, but a strong sense of expectation for what God can and will do in your life. Whether you were raised in the church or simply marveled at the vastness of the sky in your youth, you've likely found hope in something (or Someone) bigger than yourself—and trusted that you would receive what you need.

As believers, hope is woven into the fabric of our divine DNA. God has proven Himself to be faithful time and again, so we are right to hope in Him to lead and intervene, especially in times of trouble, but also in times of peace, growth, and celebration. But as November comes to a close and we step into the Advent season leading up to Christmas, hope can seem a little hard to come by if we don't know what (or Who) we're really looking for.

Rediscovering hope, especially for those of us in recovery, requires a genuine encounter with Hope Himself—in the person of a good Father God. As you discover more about Him and His character, you learn just how loved and forgiven you really are. You're not only free but family. God's not only near; He's made Himself one with you.

As you learn to receive these truths and walk in them, you begin to see the Father everywhere, working in every one of your life circumstances. Watch Him long enough, and you won't be able to deny His goodness and His ability to deliver you, transform you, and lead you into a promised-land life.

God, show Yourself to me as Hope. Help me lay down my expectations this Advent season and wait on You in eager expectancy. Remind me again of Your faithfulness and love. Amen.

December

RE**SOLUTION**

*Brothers and sisters, if someone is caught in a sin, you who live by the
Spirit should restore that person gently. But watch yourselves,
or you also may be tempted.*
—Galatians 6:1

December 1: THE ADVENT CONTINUUM

*The people walking in darkness have seen a great light; on those living in
the land of deep darkness a light has dawned.*
—Isaiah 9:2

Recovery is not a one-time event. It exists on a continuum that manifests in a journey toward a promised-land life. The same is true of Advent, an annual end-of-year season of reflection emphasizing repentance, reconciliation, and resolution that leads to renewal. Advent calls us to be intentional about fully experiencing the days leading up to Christ's birth—to look forward, celebrating His first and second coming.

But even as Advent calls us to look forward, we can't experience the season for what it is without recognizing a powerful truth. Yes, God is *for* us. Yes, God is *with* us. But there is a deeper truth: God is *in* us.

Jesus was and is God incarnate. When you received His grace and mercy poured out on the cross, you also became one with God, in Christ, by the power of the Holy Spirit. Advent is more than a celebration of the coming Christ; it celebrates that He's already here, in the flesh, living in you.

You're in Christ and Christ is in you. In your suffering. In your blessings. In your addiction. In your relationships. Through sobriety and relapse, connection and isolation, progress and setback, the living God lives in you, even when you sin, struggle, and stray. This Advent season, center your heart on your oneness with God. Look forward to Christ's coming through a new covenant lens, knowing how loved, forgiven, and restored you already are.

God, teach me to see Your first coming in Jesus as the thrill of hope it truly is. Help me not only look forward to Christmas, but to an eternity I get to spend with You that starts today. Amen.

December 2: GHOSTS OF CHRISTMAS PAST

*I, even I, am he who blots out your transgressions, for my own sake,
and remembers your sins no more.*
—Isaiah 43:25

People in recovery often carry a sordid history of holiday trauma. Seasons of overindulgence, relational warfare, and sin sickness can come back to haunt us, leaving us emotionally straddled between who we once were and the truth of who we are now in Christ. Like Ebenezer Scrooge in Charles Dickens's *A Christmas Carol*, we may experience the ghosts of our past, present, and future as a blessing or a curse, depending on our heart positioning and kingdom perspective.

Perhaps the painful memories are flooding back now. Instead of resisting them, embrace them objectively and free of shame. What comes to mind? What was at stake, what really happened, and what was the outcome? What was yours to own, and what are you burdened with that's not yours to carry? Look back on yourself with compassion, even if it really was all your fault. What did you learn? How have you changed? What grace did you find that led you here, today, to this moment? Ask God to reveal where He was and what He was doing even in those dark times. You'll rediscover Him as a God of resolution; He's faithful to finish what He starts in you. (See Philippians 1:6.)

The best part about old Scrooge's character is the total-life transformation he experiences—one that's available to you today. After his deliverance, Scrooge knew how to keep Christmas well. Dickens does not have him wallowing in perpetual shame for his past sins. Instead, he walked forward in love and light, blessed to be a blessing for the rest of his days on earth. His story, a parable of generosity if there ever was one, points us straight to the heart of the Father.

God, You've separated me from my sin "as far as the east is from the west." When holiday trauma comes back to haunt me, help me see how far You've brought me. Amen.

December 3: DANGEROUS TRADITIONS

I urge you, brothers and sisters, to watch out for those who cause divisions and put obstacles in your way that are contrary to the teaching you have learned. Keep away from them.
—Romans 16:17

When people say, "It's a tradition," it's usually a veiled way of saying, "It's how we've always done it, for better or worse." Passing something down from generation to generation during the holidays isn't always a good thing. And for people in recovery, some traditions can be dangerous—even deadly.

Heavy drinking and partying can lead to relapse and overdose. Obligatory religious services with no space for authentic worship can feel stifling. Overindulging in food, spending too much on gifts, overloading your schedule, and spending too much time with toxic relatives can put your mental health at risk as your struggles bubble up to the surface. Yet you may feel pressure to comply with tradition out of obligation or fear of losing community, relationships, and basic human connection. All of this can perpetuate your struggles and keep you in willing bondage.

This season, stay sensitive to God's leading about where to spend your time, energy, and money. If attending or hosting a holiday party with alcohol will tempt you or the ones you love and lead, find an alternative or skip it altogether. If going to Christmas service will stir up an old offense with the church, stay home and dig deep into your Bible instead. If keeping pace with family and friends on gifting is putting you into debt, consider thoughtful, nonmaterial gifts you might bestow instead. Whatever traditions have you bound, let them go to experience the fullness of a Christmas season that carries only one tradition: the love of the Father, displayed in the incarnation of Jesus Christ.

God, be the one tradition I keep this year. Help me let go of rituals, gatherings, and activities that no longer serve me or others and lean into what You might have me do instead. Amen.

December 4: YOUR FELLOW HUMANS

Glory to God in the highest heaven, and on earth peace to those on whom his favor rests.
—Luke 2:14

Peace on earth. Goodwill toward men. Christmas platitudes rooted in Scripture will be just about everywhere you look in the coming days, from holiday movies to candy commercials. But do we believers truly embody the peace and goodwill of God? Do platitudes, carols, and one-liners inspire the total life transformation that brings about a promised-land life?

In our westernized American version of Christmas, individualism reigns supreme. We've learned it's far better to receive than give—and if we're honest, we only give because it makes us look and feel like better versions of ourselves. This perversion of generosity can cause us to see others not as fellow travelers on a journey, but as resources to be used and abused. Putting others first requires both spiritual conditioning and Holy Spirit-led intervention. If we truly want to emulate the life of Jesus, we may be called to do radical things for others.

You'll know your call is authentic when you're moved with compassion instead of obligation or competition, when your gifts and sacrifices for others bring peace, not an expectation of reciprocity.

Don't wait until January to make this resolution: Love your fellow humans well. Comfort, lead, and give selflessly. Establish healthy boundaries to avoid conflict and offense. Assume the best in people—and bring out the best in them by bringing increased levels of goodwill to the table. This is the essence of community, and it's the key to lasting recovery.

God, help me consider my fellow humans over myself this Christmas season. Teach me to identify falsehood and selfishness and replace it with Your peace and goodwill to all. Amen.

December 5: SING WITH JOY

Shout for joy to the LORD, all the earth, burst into jubilant song with music.
—Psalm 98:4

Whether or not you can carry a tune, the holiday season inspires Christmas crooners and the tone-deaf alike to repeat the sounding joy. Scripture is clear on this. You're to shout with joy to the Lord (see Psalm 98:4) and rejoice with loud singing (see Ephesians 5:19) because God does the same over you! (See Zephaniah 3:17.) Your heavenly Father loves you so much, He's singing over you right now, which is why singing is such an important aspect of worship.

Perhaps you've been cranking up the Christmas tunes since the day after Halloween. Or maybe you're shifting playlists every time you hear a jingle bell. True joy transcends your mood and circumstances. True joy means exulting or celebrating God for who He is, what He's done, and what you know He will do. He doesn't care if you're not feeling it. He doesn't care whether or not you can carry a tune. He doesn't even care if you sing a sad song inspired by the book of Lamentations. Happiness is a fleeting feeling, but true joy lasts for eternity.

What song can you sing to God today? What song do you hear Him singing over you, and how can you respond? Listen for His voice in the hustle and bustle of the season. Ask Him to remind you that Joy Himself came to earth as a baby and rose up to save us all. Ask Him to remind you that Jesus paid it all—and that the oneness you now share with Him is the same oneness you share with all of humankind. *"Rejoice in the Lord always. I will say it again: Rejoice!"* (Philippians 4:4).

God, You are worthy of my praise always. On my good days and bad days, You're always working for my good. You are worthy, and I will sing with joy and thanksgiving to You. Amen.

December 6: PREACHING PEACE

He came and preached peace to you who were far away and peace to
those who were near.
—Ephesians 2:17

Jesus, the Prince of Peace, explicitly practiced and preached peace. It's why He came to earth, and it's what He offered to everyone everywhere He went—not just to the Jews, but to all people. The kind of peace Jesus preached wasn't just about making literal wars cease. He didn't come as a conquering general, nor did He supernaturally change the hearts or minds of His people's Roman oppressors. While He taught that it's best to make peace and live in peace with everyone (see Matthew 5:9), He also knew this could only be possible when humans could make peace and live in peace with God.

Now, if you're new to the Christian faith, you might be thinking, *Make peace with God? I didn't even know we were fighting!* But if you're honest with yourself, you know we're all products of a broken world.

At some point, we've all taken offense with God, even if we've never realized it or articulated it before. That offense didn't make God put us at arm's length like some well-meaning teachers might insist. Any perceived separation from God is on our end. And meanwhile, God has been reconciling the whole world to Himself—including us! (See 2 Corinthians 5:19.)

Have you made your peace with God? Is there anything between you—a perceived injustice, a misunderstanding, or a disappointment you need to share with Him? Yes, He already knows. He understands your offense better than you do. But He longs for you to bring it to Him so He can ease your mind, soothe your heart, and give you a way forward. Come to Him—and let His perfect peace give you rest.

God, I want to be at peace with You and others. Thank You for hearing my complaints and reassuring me of Your character. Preach peace to my heart so I can be a peacemaker for You. Amen.

December 7: BEING HAPPY

He who heeds the word wisely will find good,
and whoever trusts in the LORD, happy is he.
—Proverbs 16:20 (NKJV)

In this happiest season of all, it's worth noting that happiness can be a fleeting feeling. Unlike joy that transcends circumstance and peace that passes understanding, happiness is almost completely dependent upon how we humans choose to perceive what's happening around us. That said, choosing happiness can be a sign of emotional maturity and even selflessness—as long as it's not a bootstrapping attempt to be okay when we're really not okay.

Scripture doesn't say much about happiness at all. Joy, peace, and love are everywhere, but you won't even find the word *happiness* in some Bible translations. The *New King James Version* showcases the word *happy* as a direct description of people who trust in God (see Proverbs 16:20 NKJV), not because of what they receive due to God's faithfulness, but simply because they trust Him and remember His Word.

Happiness from an earthly standpoint isn't always bad, but the pursuit of happiness will never satisfy the way journeying with God will. Through peaks and valleys, joy and pain, happiness and sadness, He wants you to walk beside Him, free of earthly ambition and full of His peace. In time, you'll discover the truth: Happiness isn't a feeling, it's a choice to trust in God and not your own understanding. (See Proverbs 3:5.) Stop trying to *get happy*. Just be.

God, I trust You, so I am happy and blessed, even when I don't feel like it. I know You're good and You're worth it, no matter what I face. Teach me what healthy happiness looks like. Amen.

December 8: OVERSTIMULATED

We were under great pressure, far beyond our ability to endure, so that we despaired of life itself. Indeed, we felt we had received the sentence of death.
—2 Corinthians 1:8–9

In recovery, we may experience *too much of a good thing* a time or two. Our brains are wired in a delicate pendulum swing between pleasure and pain; too much of either one can do real damage. For some, the holiday season comes with full plates—on the table and on the calendar—and a sense of urgency to fit in *everything* before it's all over.

At first, the influx of pleasure in the season can produce reasonable amounts of dopamine and reasonable joy. Some might even call these mountaintop moments. But what goes up must inevitably come down, not because joy is bad but because our brains were created to maintain the pleasure/pain balance. The higher we climb, the harder we fall—and the harder it can be to achieve the same high again, even when we repeat the same activity. This might not be life-or-death struggle when it comes to an activity like Christmas caroling, but throw in troubles such as addiction, mental health, and thoughts of suicide, and lives can be at stake. For example, when one glass of red wine at a holiday dinner party ceases to satisfy the way it did yesterday—and yesterday's glass didn't satisfy like the day before—the pleasure/pain balance demands more and more.

But what if we weren't looking for substances or situations to satisfy? What if we leaned wholly on our good Father God to satisfy our many needs and desires with all of Himself? God's presence transcends the pleasure/pain principle—He never gets tired of giving, and there's always more to receive.

When you're at your lowest, God raises you up. And the higher you climb with Him, the further from the ground you'll be forever.

God, I'm overstimulated, struggling to find joy the way I used to. Be my joy. Fill me to overflowing with more of You. Teach me what really satisfies—Your love, a high that lasts for eternity. Amen.

When Joseph woke up, he did what the angel of the Lord had
commanded him and took Mary home as his wife.
—Matthew 1:24

When it comes to Christmas gifts, the most shocking of all time *had* to be the news Joseph received from his teenage virgin fiancée Mary—that she was pregnant by the Holy Spirit and carrying the Son of God, the Messiah, the Christ. *Surprise!* We can only imagine what this poor man must've been thinking as he received this news from his future wife, but we suspect he was scared to death.

Scripture tells us very little about Joseph, other than that he was the son of Jacob and probably a carpenter or builder of some kind. (See, respectively, Matthew 1:16; 13:55.) Most importantly, Scripture says he *"was a righteous man"* (Matthew 1:19 NLT), as evidenced in his grace-filled plan to send Mary away quietly so she wouldn't be disgraced for being pregnant before the wedding ceremony. His fiancée was carrying a child that wasn't his, and yet he still thought of her first.

Did Joseph believe Mary's story? Perhaps. Was he embarrassed or hurt by it? Possibly. Did he see himself in the coming Christ's story? Probably not. Thankfully, God intervened with a decidedly reassuring angel, and Joseph resolved to wed Mary and stay faithfully by her side, protecting her purity through it all. (See Matthew 1:20–24.)

Jesus's earthly father wasn't really his father at all. If Jesus had been Joseph's, He couldn't have been God incarnate. And He couldn't have given Joseph, and all of humankind by proxy, the most precious Christmas gift of Himself. Joseph's grace to Mary and his adoption of the Son of God put the heart of our heavenly Father on display for the whole world to see.

God, do I trust You like Joseph did? Do I believe in Jesus so much that I'd be willing to look like a fool to my peers? Teach me to have faith for Jesus and grace for Mary like Joseph did. Amen.

December 10: STICKY LOVE

How sweet are your words to my taste, sweeter than honey to my mouth!
—Psalm 119:103

Of all the words for love in the Bible, the Hebrew word *hesed* is arguably the most complex. Bible scholar Darrell L. Bock describes *hesed* as "wrapping up in itself all the positive attributes of God: love, covenant faithfulness, mercy, grace, kindness, loyalty—in short, acts of devotion and loving-kindness that go beyond the requirements of duty."[9] *Hesed* love is faithful and intensely actionable; it's a love that really lasts, which is why some call it *sticky love.*

God's sticky love gets lost in translation in and through the English Bible, replaced with words like *mercy, steadfastness,* and *loving-kindness,* but these words barely scratch the surface of this rich, decadent love that demands savoring. What's more, this sticky love embodies the sweet grace of Jesus that's so good, we just have to share it!

Yes, sticky love isn't a love you keep for yourself. You were always meant to give it away to others. And when you experience it, you'll realize there's more than enough for all. Have you tasted this love? A love that's sweeter and stickier than honey on your lips? Come taste and see for yourself just how loved you really are by your good Father God. *Hesed* is God's love in action, to you and through you to all of humankind.

It's through this love that we find the healing, restoration, reconciliation, and resolution we all seek, through the affection of Love Himself.

God, Your love is wild and perfect and all-encompassing. It really sticks—I can't even get away when I try to rebel because nothing can separate me from You! I'll stay stuck on You too, Abba. Amen.

December 11: MARY'S MAGNIFICAT

My soul magnifies the Lord, and my spirit rejoices in God my Savior, for he has looked on the humble estate of his servant.
—Luke 1:46–48 (ESV)

---

9. Avital Snow, "The Meaning of Hesed: Hebrew Word for Love," Fellowship of Israel Related Ministries, May 27, 2021, firmisrael.org/learn/the-meaning-of-hesed-hebrew-for-love.

These days, stories about pregnant teenage girls are common enough to warrant reality TV shows. Yet most of us still see teen pregnancy as less than desirable for a host of reasons—not only for the physical health of the mother and child, but for the mother's mental and emotional health as well. Flashback two thousand years ago to a teen pregnancy that ended in triumph—that of Mary and her baby, Jesus.

Scripture doesn't tell us much about Mary. She was likely around age thirteen or fourteen and Jewish, in the line of King David, making Mary and her betrothed, Joseph, very distant cousins. When an angel of the Lord told Mary she would fulfill Isaiah's prophecy by giving birth to the Messiah as a virgin, sweet young Mary took it with maturity and grace. (See Luke 1:26–37.) She was excited, even though she knew that few people would fully understand her situation—her future husband included. Her soul longed to make God's goodness known in the land of the living.

"My soul magnifies the Lord" is the first phrase in Mary's "Magnificat" song of praise to God—for being mindful of her humility and making her known throughout the generations through this wild supernatural pregnancy—unplanned by her but planned since before the foundations of the earth by God. (See Luke 1:46–56.) In the midst of stress, uncertainty, and fear, Mary chose awe, wonder, and a heart of gratitude to her Maker. She didn't have all the answers, but she knew the child she carried was the answer to any question she could ever ask.

God, how could a young girl trust You so completely? Make me like Mary. Teach me to praise You and glorify Your name, even when I'm walking through overwhelming circumstances. Amen.

December 12: INCARNATION

The true light that gives light to everyone was coming into the world.
—John 1:9

Incarnation. God in the flesh. When Jesus walked the earth, the incarnational Spirit of God was in Him, meaning Jesus wasn't just like God—He was fully God while also being fully human. This radical state of being put the oneness of the Father, Son, and Holy Spirit on display—a oneness not only reserved for the Trinity, but for all people who would believe in and receive Christ as the Messiah.

The incarnation is lost on us when it's not also embodied within us. Far from being *Jesus with skin on* to the ones we love and lead, we are meant to embody, in the flesh, the Spirit of the living God in us. Jesus, the true light, illuminates our hearts with His love so that we might shine brightly in a dark and desolate world. Jesus is *"the light of the world"* (John 8:12) and in Him, so are we. (See Matthew 5:14.) We're one with God, in Christ, by the power of the Holy Spirit—each and every one of us chosen, crowned, and beloved.

The Christmas season isn't just about remembering the incarnation, the moment when God took on flesh and entered the world to save us from sin. It's about making a conscious decision to *be* the incarnation.

People who walk in darkness need to see Christ's light shining in you and through you. So *"let your light shine before others, that they may see your good deeds and glorify your Father in heaven"* (Matthew 5:16).

God, let Your Spirit fall fresh on me this season. Help me be Your light in dark places with hands and feet eager to do Your work. Teach me the truth of my oneness with You and help me share it. Amen.

December 13: HOLIDAY RELAPSE

Peace I leave with you; my peace I give you. I do not give to you as the world gives. Do not let your hearts be troubled and do not be afraid.
—John 14:27

If there's one holiday tradition we'd all like to break, it's relapse. But in a season of overindulgence, people are bound to be triggered into struggling with our addictions, mental health problems, and yes, even thoughts of suicide. People struggling with food addiction are surrounded by tasty treats. People struggling with depression are pressured to feel *jolly*, whatever that is. People lacking in community find themselves feeling isolated and alone, wondering if their life really matters at all. It's no wonder we relapse into old ways of thinking and behaving this time of year. It's so common, it's almost expected in some cases.

But you have permission to believe for better this year—for something you may have yet to taste, but know is possible in Christ. Freedom. Freedom in setting boundaries. Freedom in saying *no*. Freedom in giving grace...to yourself and to others. Jesus set you free so you could *be* free (see Galatians 5:1)—not free *to* sin and struggle, but free *from* sin and struggle.

It's time to create new holiday traditions with God this season. What's working for you in your current holiday festivities? Keep doing those things. What's not working and causing you to struggle? Let go of these activities, no matter how much this might disappoint others. Finally, what new traditions can you try this year that will fill the void in your spirit with more of God? Take these questions to God and ask Him to reveal anything you're missing, especially if it's more of Him.

God, I give You permission to interrupt my plans this holiday season. Walking with You, step for step, I know You can keep me free from sin and struggle and help me overcome temptation. Amen.

December 14: EXPECTATIONS VS. EXPECTANCY

The Lord is good to those who wait for him, to the soul who seeks him.
—Lamentations 3:25 (esv)

We, the church, must reconsider our expectations for people in recovery. After all, recovery isn't a one-time event, a series of boxes to check, or even steps to take. It's a journey as unique as the person braving it—and we must align our hearts to better support people on their journeys. Even in letting go of some of our own unrealistic expectations, we must remain eagerly expectant of God, hopeful in the miracles that only He can bring. He's proven His faithfulness time and again, and He is ready and willing to bless those of us who are willing to wait on Him.

Far too often, we see a self-fulling prophecy come to pass in recovery—for ourselves and for the ones we love and lead. When we *expect* to fail, we likely *will* fail. When we *expect* others to fail, they likely will. But when we expect God to show up in power, He is faithful to exceed our expectations. He rarely shows up in the way we expect, or in the way we think He should. We know in part and we prophesy in part, which is why we must leave room for God to be God and act in ways that surpass our understanding.

Let God's perfect track record instill hope in your heart that He can and will intervene on your behalf. Let go of your expectations of God. He always knows best, far better than you could ever ask for or imagine. Instead, wait on Him and His timing free of expectations but filled with expectancy. Partner with Him in your prayers. When you pray, *"Your kingdom come, your will be done"* (Matthew 6:10), resolve to expect it to happen in Jesus's name.

God, I release my unrealistic expectations of myself and others, including You. Help me learn what it means to wait on You. Teach me the joy of receiving and rejoicing when You intervene. Amen.

December 15: LEADERSHIP

Keep watch over yourselves and all the flock of which the Holy Spirit has made you overseers. Be shepherds of the church of God, which he bought with his own blood.
—Acts 20:28

Recovery isn't just for the person walking through it. It's for everyone. Ask anyone on a journey toward a promised-land life, and they'll agree—we go through what we go through to help others go through what we went through. In its shocking simplicity, this reality explains the problem of pain in this life. Hurt people hurt people, but healed people heal people when they do it in Jesus's name.

As we humans exist in a broken world, we will struggle. Scripture is clear on that. But not a second of struggles will be wasted in the context of eternity. When we experience the total-life transformation that comes with embracing the Uncovery, we will ultimately be called to share the hope we've found with others.

Whether you're called to share your testimony, become a sponsor, or shepherd a whole community of people seeking Jesus in recovery, you will one day be called to love and lead others. And regardless of where you are on your own journey, you will be uniquely equipped to serve them sacrificially because you've been where they are and you know the way forward.

Some leaders are born; others are forged in the fire. True leaders partner with the heart of God, learning to see the true potential of others through a new covenant lens. Recovery leaders believe in miracles because we've experienced them firsthand. And while we may never *arrive*, we can resolve to walk with others step for step, showing them the gentle way of Jesus.

God, on my own I don't feel worthy to lead. But if You say I'm to shepherd others, I know I can and I will. Help me to love and lead like You do—gently, faithfully, and with Your grace. Amen.

December 16: SUSTAINABLE LEADERSHIP

Pride goes before destruction, a haughty spirit before a fall.
—Proverbs 16:18

Loving and leading people through recovery requires us to see their potential, which they may not yet see in themselves. Traditional recovery programming often focuses on the sin or struggle instead of what a promised-land life could look like without it. This is something that must change as new generations of Christ-centered recovery leaders emerge in the church and in the world. Yes, it will require risk. Yes, it will require humility. And it will also require a level of vigilance—over ourselves and over others—that we, the church, have yet to assume.

Stepping into recovery leadership can bring with it new levels of stress and uncertainty that feel unsettling at best. We're now not only responsible for our own journeys, but we also assume collective responsibility for the well-being of the people we love and lead. While no one person can be responsible for anyone else's journey, we must be ready and willing to call out what we see in people, for better or worse. We must be willing to declare life and freedom over them, even if they'd prefer death. We must be willing to call out thoughts and actions that aren't aligned with God and invite them back into truth. We must be willing to walk our own recovery journeys with authenticity and vulnerability while inviting others to do the same.

We can't do it alone. In our own strength, we are indeed powerless. *"But with God all things are possible"* (Matthew 19:26). We can come against the selfishness that puts us at arm's length from God and others. We can defeat our fears of failure or success, knowing that God's love isn't based on our performance. We can overcome the lies we believe about ourselves, embrace our God-given identities, and help others do the same. This is the essence of leadership.

God, help me lead with humility. Lives and souls are at stake in this kind of work, but I know You wouldn't call me to it and not see me through it. Show me the art of sustainable leadership. Amen.

December 17: TITLES ASIDE

But by the grace of God I am what I am, and his grace to me was not without effect. No, I worked harder than all of them—yet not I, but the grace of God that was with me.
—1 Corinthians 15:10

One of the most beautiful things about Christian recovery is the way struggling people are invited into leadership roles when they would be otherwise overlooked. Even in twelve-step programming, new attendees are given a job and invited into the fullness of community life early on. This means that people still in the throes of struggle can be invited to read Scripture, lead worship, facilitate small groups, and more.

While most leaders exercise caution and discernment with the volume and types of leadership roles newly recovering individuals are invited to assume, the stigma of *being ready* to take on these roles in recovery is almost nonexistent. God doesn't call the qualified; He commissions the willing and qualifies them along the way. Leadership isn't something we fight to earn but something we grow into. To people in recovery who are invited into this build-the-plane-while-you-fly-it style of leadership, it's called grace—unmerited favor that reflects the heart of the Father.

God initiates grace that moves people to repentance, not the other way around. This keeps our mission clear. If we can help broken people know how loved and forgiven they already are, it's much easier for them to receive the Father's grace by faith and step into their life's true calling.

Titles and responsibilities aside, *you* can love and lead like this—because you were first loved and led like this. You carry the heart of your good Father God.

God, help me share the good news of Your gospel to people in recovery. Make me a conduit of Your love and grace, ushering in forgiveness of sin and an open heaven for all. Amen.

Each one should test their own actions. Then they can take pride in themselves alone, without comparing themselves to someone else, for each one should carry their own load.
—Galatians 6:4–5

When new recovery leaders rise, it's the responsibility of their fellow leaders to empower and strengthen them, affirming God's call on their life. Because we never really *arrive* in recovery, we are never really *ready* to assume a leadership role. Even kingdom-driven promotion will take a bit of getting used to, which is why discipleship and accountability are important within recovery leadership ranks.

With the enhanced level of vigilance that leaders are expected to have on the long-term, collective recovery journey, we might be tempted to think we're not only called to point out our fellow travelers' potential pitfalls, but also prevent them from falling. This is a lie from the pit of hell. As difficult as it is to accept, we cannot control what others do. Let's be honest: it can be hard enough to control what *we* ourselves do. But moreover, emerging recovery leaders sometimes need to fail—to fall flat, learn humility, and lean on us, their fellow leaders, to restore them gently.

There is a fine line between empowering and enabling in leadership development. It's no different in the recovery space. As leaders, we won't walk it out perfectly, and the ones we love and lead won't either. Grace means loving people enough to hold them accountable and loving them enough to let them fall when they need to. By God's grace and with our help, they can and will get back up again.

God, help me love my fellow leaders enough to let them fall and deal with the consequences. Keep me free of judgment, but vigilant to Your truth. Strengthen my resolve to restore. Amen.

December 19: HOW THE MIGHTY FALL

So, if you think you are standing firm, be careful that you don't fall!
—1 Corinthians 10:12

The apostle Paul was quick to give the church in Corinth some warnings about Israel's history. (See 1 Corinthians 10:1–11.) He spoke to the favor of God's people and how they often chose bondage, idolatry, and immorality that in many cases led to death. He didn't do this to scare people into repentance; he did it to remind the emerging leaders in this powerhouse church just how fragile God's chosen people can be when they take their eyes off of Him.

Flash forward a couple thousand years to today, and sadly, not much has changed. In fact, we continue to witness leaders at all levels who fail morally and fall despite knowing better and even preaching against the very things they succumbed to. What goes up must come down—and when we put our leaders on too high of a pedestal, they fall harder and farther than any of us could imagine. In an era of hero worship and unprecedented Christian celebrity, we must resolve to glorify Christ only and empower God's chosen leaders with support, encouragement, and accountability.

Leaders fall. It's often not a question of if, but when. And when they fall, whether it's public or private, a tiny trip or full-on face-plant, we must learn to come around them, love them, support them, and lean into the collective learning that's being put on display. None of us will ever walk out a perfect existence, which is why resolving to embrace God's grace is so critical. Yes, there may be consequences for actions, and in most cases, there need to be. But beyond helping leaders see what they might have done differently, repent, and believe again, we can restore them gently and witness the kind of personal transformation that also transforms Christ-centered communities for the better.

God, help me learn to lead up, to love my leaders enough to hold them accountable and restore them when they fall. You're in the restoration business, and I'm partnering with You on this. Amen.

December 20: POWER AND AUTHORITY

Let everyone be subject to the governing authorities, for there is no authority except that which God has established. The authorities that exist have been established by God.
—Romans 13:1

All power and authority comes from our good Father God. He gave it to Jesus (see Matthew 28:18), and Jesus gave it to His disciples—and to us by proxy. (See Luke 9:1; 10:19.) Power and authority from an earthly standpoint—titles, roles, and positions of privilege—still come from the Father. But in God's kingdom, *"the last will be first, and the first will be last"* (Matthew 20:16), so those with power and authority must learn humility.

Some of us struggle to realize the power and authority we carry, making us weak and ineffective for the kingdom on earth. Some have a hyper-awareness of their power and authority, thus tempted to forget the source. And some of us are so used to walking in the power and authority we have, we lose our compassion for those who aren't there yet.

Consider what power and authority you carry that others may want, for better or worse. How might you humble yourself before them? How might you keep from holding any privilege over them? How can you invite them into the truth of what you carry in humility and share your kingdom inheritance? Be willing to serve sacrificially, lifting others with you as you rise. God will give you power and authority to be a great equalizer for people in recovery, in the church, and in the world.

God, thank You for giving me Your power and authority to set people free and bring the kingdom here on earth. Help me steward it in humility and invite others to step into this great destiny. Amen.

December 21: SAINT NICHOLAS, THE WONDER-WORKER

Good will come to those who are generous and lend freely,
who conduct their affairs with justice.
—Psalm 112:5

The Saint Nick we know and love at Christmastime may be a secularized children's hero, but he's not far removed from the patron Saint Nicholas, the archbishop of Myra in Lycia. This man was a wild, generous spirit who became widely known as a wonder-worker in Christ. Legend has it that he healed his mother's illness while she was giving birth to him, and as an infant, stood upright for three minutes, unassisted, during his baptism. It's said he even fasted from nursing two days a week during very early childhood to honor God and his parents.

But St. Nicholas's most noteworthy signs, wonders, and miracles came during adulthood, when he carried God's power and authority in the church. He was a radical, known for bestowing wild and generous gifts, combatting injustice, and setting captives free. Sounds familiar, right? St. Nicholas carried the heart of the Father, the hands and feet of Jesus, and the Spirit of the living God well.

This season, let God reveal His heart to you in the way He once revealed it to St. Nicholas. Whenever you see Santa Claus—in the mall, on a billboard, in a holiday movie, or on your own trimmed tree—pause to ponder all that God can do through one person fully devoted to Him in all things. You may never have cathedrals named after you like old St. Nick did, but make no mistake, you too are a saint, a wonder-worker, indwelled by the Holy Spirit of the living God. This is the greatest gift ever given.

God, with Your Spirit living in me, I know I can do wonderful things in Your name. Keep me firmly fixed on You, ready and willing to give generously, combat injustice, and set captives free. Amen.

December 22: IMAGINING THE FUTURE

Now to him who is able to do immeasurably more than all we ask or imagine, according to his power that is at work within us, to him be glory in the church and in Christ Jesus throughout all generations, for ever and ever! Amen.
—Ephesians 3:20–21

The moment you were conceived, God gave you a powerful gift of imagination—one that allows you to dream with Him, build with Him, and do far greater things than you could ever come up with on your own. This gift of imagination has many uses, not just visioning for the future, but imagining a better version of yourself within it. This goes so much deeper than New Year's resolutions. It's the intensely practical act of imagining a future in which your struggles no longer call the shots, and your identity as a beloved child of God is secure.

Can you picture it now? What does it look like? Taste like? Feel like? This future state you're imagining may feel a world away from where you are today, and that's okay. But when you imagine a specific and measurable hope for the future, you can begin to dream with God and discover what it will take to make that dream a reality. Are your dreams aligned with God's? Is your vision

His vision? Have you paused to ask Him what He has planned for you and how you might partner with Him in the days to come?

The more we lean into the Father's heart, the more we want to have a God-inspired imagination. We won't walk it out perfectly. Even if we saw Him face-to-face, we still wouldn't understand Him fully. We'd have to use our imagination to test the waters, stay sensitive to His leading, and wait to see the future He really has for us, which will be far better than anything we could ask for or imagine.

God, show me the future You have for me. Give me something new to hope for and wonder about. Help me be present today so I can experience this future tomorrow. Amen.

December 23: VISIONING WITH GOD

And afterward, I will pour out my Spirit on all people. Your sons and daughters will prophesy, your old men will dream dreams, your young men will see visions.
—Joel 2:28

We've all done it before. We have a big idea, pursue a dream, and ask God to bless it along the way. And when the endgame doesn't satisfy like we thought it would—or when the dream journey comes to a screeching halt—we stand dumbfounded, resenting God and wondering what happened.

But visioning with God is meant to be a collaborative process. It isn't necessarily an actual *vision* from God. Some of us hear from God in pictures and dreams in our mind's eye. Some of us through Scripture and strong leadings. Visioning is the act of asking God what the future He has planned for us looks like and aligning with those plans in thought and action. God certainly wants to partner with us in pursuing our dreams, but we need those dreams to be the dreams He gave us. This takes imagination, humility, patience, and resolve.

Visioning with God is a lifelong pursuit. More often than not, He will reveal part of His vision for your life but not the whole thing—because you couldn't handle it! You can trust Him to give you just enough vision to step out in faith, but not so much information that you become overwhelmed and refuse Him. He will give you exactly the vision you need, when you need it. As you respond to what God shows you and begin walking it out in faith, He will be faithful to give you the next steps.

God, be my vision. I don't want anything or anyone but You. Show me what You have in mind for my life. Help me look to my future with confidence and excitement, knowing You're in it. Amen.

December 24: AWE AND WONDER

Everyone was amazed and gave praise to God. They were filled with awe and said, "We have seen remarkable things today."
—Luke 5:26

Miracles happen. And the wild reality is, the more we see them, the more we see them. Throughout Jesus's three-year personal ministry, people who followed Him saw miracle after miracle after miracle and came to know Him as a miracle worker. And today, by the power of His Spirit living in us, we are meant to be miracle workers in His name.

When Jesus commanded us, *"Heal the sick, raise the dead, cleanse those who have leprosy, [and] drive out demons"* (Matthew 10:8), He wasn't kidding around. We're meant to do all He did and more. (See John 14:12.)

You may not have participated in any resurrections recently, but you embody the same divine Spirit Jesus did. Miracles are happening all around you—and by the power of the Holy Spirit, you will also bring struggling people from death to life in Jesus's name.

Stand in awe and wonder of God's goodness today. The God of the universe took on flesh and defeated sin so you could know Him as Father. Jesus made a way where there was no way, and the Holy Spirit has taken up residence in you—mind, body, and soul. And as if these miracles weren't enough, God is still healing, still cleansing, still resurrecting, and still liberating, not just for you but *through* you if you align yourself with Him.

Perhaps the greatest miracle of all is God's revelation of our oneness with Him—a grace-laced reality that promises He will be with you always. What amazing love!

God, teach me to see the miracles happening right in front of me. Help me be the Spirit-led miracle worker You want me to be. Show me how to walk in my oneness with You. Amen.

*For to us a child is born, to us a son is given, and the government will be
on his shoulders. And he will be called Wonderful Counselor,
Mighty God, Everlasting Father, Prince of Peace.*
—Isaiah 9:6

When God came to our rescue, He could have taken on any form. He could have come as a conquering warrior, a political leader, a Pharisee, or a king. He could have snapped His fingers and saved us in one second…but instead He sent Himself as a child. Jesus came as a little baby born in a stable to a teenage virgin, so that He could grow up and live out every single part of our shared human experience.

Recovery isn't possible without Jesus. Without the fullness of His human life on display, we would have no concrete example of a life worth emulating. He was *"tempted in every way, just as we are—yet he did not sin"* (Hebrews 4:15). He knew what it was like to struggle—and while He never became addicted, wrestled with His mental health, or contemplated suicide, He intimately understood the trauma that causes these afflictions. He became a perfect sacrifice for our sin, and in giving His life for us, He defeated sin and released us from its grasp. Now we who believe in Him live free—and our eternal life starts now.

God came as a child because He wanted us to see ourselves in Him. Had He come as God only, His sacrifice would have meant nothing to us. Had He been just a man, His sacrifice would have had no power. But as we come to know Him through Scripture and Spirit-led encounter, we appreciate and identify with His every moment—from the cradle to the grave and back again. We were with Him—co-crucified and co-raised, and one day, we will be co-glorified. He is with us forever, our Immanuel.

God, You understand me and my life better than anyone else ever could—You see me, know me, and love me. Thank You for going to such great lengths to reconcile me back to Your heart. Amen.

December 26: REAL REVIVAL

Will you not revive us again, that your people may rejoice in you?
—Psalm 85:6

The word *revival* stirs up all kinds of emotional connotations for people, some good and some bad. At some level, revival is something we all want to see. But instead of embodying revival, we rely on our trusty systems and programs that make revival a weeklong event to schedule, complete with a marketing campaign, or another mountaintop moment to strive toward in our own strength. Revival has become something we think we can bring into its fullness without the Father participating in the process at all.

Instead of being the ones to usher in revival, we think we're the ones leading it—or worse, that we somehow *are* it. The worst part is that people trying to lead corporate revival haven't even experienced personal revival. Father, have mercy on us! Even with the best of intentions, we have no idea what we're doing.

What if the revival we all want to see could be attained through the Uncovery? What if it led to multitudes coming to Jesus with a renewed excitement about the gospel and our restored relationship with the Father? What if those thousands—even millions—of people who are about to step into the fullness of their identity as the Father's beloved children are the very ones who are now struggling with addiction, mental health problems, and suicidal thoughts?

This pursuit takes courage, strength, and sacrifice. In some cases, it may take all you have to give. And when you give it all for the One who gave it all for you, you will see revival like you've never experienced it before.

God, make me an instrument of revival in the recovery space. Breathe new life into me for the journey ahead, with manna for today and milk and honey in the life You've promised me. Amen.

December 27: MENTAL MAPS

Therefore the LORD has recompensed me according to my righteousness,
according to my cleanness in His eyes.
—2 Samuel 22:25 (NKJV)

We process the world around us using mental maps—frameworks we create in our minds to help us navigate life. These maps start forming at birth and are written and rewritten by our experiences. When our maps are accurate, we feel purpose-driven and confident about where we're heading. When our maps are incorrect, we feel lost or stuck.

A growth mindset updates our mental maps in real time, just like a Google Street View car. But a fixed mindset stops editing and reading maps altogether, assuming there is no viable pathway forward, like a GPS with no signal. This is when the brain begins to deteriorate, neural pathways are broken and rerouted, and our ability to thrive wanes. People struggling with addiction, mental health problems, and thoughts of suicide are often in this desperate place of having a fixed mindset with no way forward. Recovery helps people rewrite their mental maps to see the world for what it really is and find their way in it.

Shifting to a growth mindset so you can rewrite your mental maps isn't something you can do alone. You need God, and you need community. Leaning into the One who created you, formed your brain and body, and knows every thought you've ever had takes an honest, objective assessment of your mental maps. Are you seeing the world for what it really is? Are you helping others do the same? Let your good Father God rewrite your mental maps like He's rewritten your life story—from sinner to saint, from lost to found, and from death to life in Jesus's name.

God, show me Your way. Teach me to walk confidently in paths of righteousness using the directions You've given me. Help me see the world accurately and find my place in it. Amen.

December 28: PAYING RECOVERY FORWARD

So in everything, do to others what you would have them do to you,
for this sums up the Law and the Prophets.
—Matthew 7:12

Step 12 in most anonymous twelve-step recovery programs is the most powerful discipleship tool most people in traditional recovery never use. They think, *We got sober. We checked our other eleven boxes. What more do You want from us, God?*

But the total life transformation that comes with real recovery is downright contagious—and those who experience it will not be able to keep it to themselves. Just like the good news of the gospel, *recovery is for everyone*. And those of us who receive this truth have a responsibility to carry the message to others. This can be daunting at first, especially in a context where anonymity is still a stronghold. We'll be less likely to offer help when we worry it will expose our secret struggles to the world, which is why destigmatizing struggles with addiction, mental health, and suicidal thoughts is so important. When we no longer have to carry shame over our struggles, we can free other people from shame too.

In what ways are you sharing the new, transformed life you've been given? In what ways are you testifying to the hope you've found in Jesus? In what ways might you step out in faith to surround those who struggle, living your life in the overflow of God's grace?

Healed people heal people. Freed people free people. Transformed people transform people. It's what we do. Paying recovery forward is the essence of real recovery, and it helps form the community we all need to heal from trauma.

God, don't let me keep this gift of recovery to myself. Give me boldness in testifying to Your faithfulness in my journey! Give me courage to lead others to You so they can be free like me. Amen.

December 29: INTANGIBLE TRANSFORMATION

Since you are precious and honored in my sight, and because I love you,
I will give people in exchange for you, nations in exchange for your life.
—Isaiah 43:4

The promised-land life you're journeying toward comes not by way of baseline sobriety, but by multidimensional transformation. And yet most recovery programs still focus on days, weeks, months, and years sober because personal transformation is extremely difficult to measure through hard data and numbers.

If sobriety is your only measure of success, it means you'll have to start all over again with every bump in the road. This can leave you feeling burned out, unable to recognize and celebrate the work that you've done. This is why it's important to find ways to *qualify* success in your own recovery journey beyond quantifiable means. Admittedly, numbers and data are important evidence markers—you don't need to throw them out altogether—but you are not a number. Every part of your life matters, *especially* the intangible elements of your recovery that can't be easily tracked.

Spend some time with the Father today, asking Him to reveal the intangible elements of your recovery that He wants you to measure. Don't ask yourself, "How many days sober am I?" or "Did I go to my meetings?" or "Have I accepted my struggle?" Instead ask, "Am I making progress on my journey?" or "Did I connect with my community?" or "Do I know my true identity in Christ?" The answers to these intangibles will encourage your heart and keep your momentum going strong for the journey ahead.

God, thank You for giving me tangible and intangible ways to see Your healing hand in my life and recovery journey. Remind me that I'm more than just a number—that I'm Yours. Amen.

December 30: FINISHING WELL

He who was seated on the throne said, "I am making everything new!"
Then he said, "Write this down, for these words are trustworthy and true."
—Revelation 21:5

Years come and years go while the journey toward a promised-land life continues. In the swirl of it all, it can sometimes feel like life is just happening to us. We lack intention, purpose, and resolve, which can make us feel stuck, apathetic, and depressed.

The truth is, you are not a victim of your circumstances any more. Life isn't happening *to* you; it's happening *for* you according to God's perfect will over your life. Each year, each day, each hour, each moment, and each breath have new mercies and new opportunities to align with God's heart concerning you and the ones you love and lead.

As this year comes to a close, take some intentional time away like Jesus did. (See Luke 5:16.) Reflect on the last twelve months and ask God to reveal insights on and encouragement for your ongoing recovery journey.

Find a journal and pray through these prompts: What has God showed you this year? How has He been moving in your life? What might He be calling you into next year, and how would He have you prepare your heart? What verse, word, mantra, promise, or lesson does He have for you to end this season well and start again renewed?

Finishing this year well will position your heart for what's next and equip you for a lifelong journey with God that will one day end, when He tells you, *"Well done, good and faithful servant!"* (Matthew 25:23).

God, as I reflect on this year, I'm in awe to see how You've been with me every step of the way. In good times and bad, victory and struggle, You've been there. Let's do it again, Father. Amen.

December 31: START FRESH (NOT OVER)

Because of the LORD's great love we are not consumed, for his compassions never fail. They are new every morning; great is your faithfulness. I say to myself, "The LORD is my portion; therefore I will wait for him."
—Lamentations 3:22–24

We receive new mercies every morning. It's a good thing too. We can fail a thousand times, but God's grace never fails to restore us. Recovery is a lifelong journey because recovery is life itself.

If you identify as a Christian, you're in recovery from an old, broken life that led you to struggle. But in Christ, you've been reborn into a new life—a promised-land life that's worth living and staying sober for. The best part about this promised-land life is that you're already there. You just don't know it yet. The journey toward this life that's revealed in and through the Uncovery is really a process of discovery by which you learn what's always been true. You're loved. You're forgiven. You're free. You're perfect, holy, and blameless in God's eyes. And yes, that promised-land life you've been trying so hard to get to is yours—right now. Go ahead and unpack.

As you embrace this total-life transformation, there will be days when you doubt. There will be days when you forget where you are, who you are, and Whose you are. But when circumstantial evidence tries to disprove God's truth and you lose your way, resist the urge to go back to the beginning and start all over again. Find your bearings, get back on the path, and start fresh, honoring how far you've come and how far you will go with your good Father God.

God, thank You for this promised-land life! Help me learn to embrace it and live like I'm a full-on resident in Your kingdom, a coheir who is seated with Jesus in heavenly places right now. Amen.

ABOUT THE AUTHORS

George A. Wood is an ordained minister, pastoral care counselor, recovery ministry founder, and recovery activist.

A former addict and suicide survivor, George has dedicated his life to radically grace-laced, Christ-centered recovery for people struggling with addiction, mental health problems, and suicidal thoughts.

He works tirelessly to bridge the gap between the spiritual and scientific communities to help people see recovery differently and build a new baseline for trauma-informed care.

A highly charismatic and sought-after teacher and preacher, George has become a nontraditional recovery authority by founding radically divergent ministries, including the Timothy Initiative and the Sober Truth Project.

The Timothy Initiative is a faith-based ministry and open-ended program that works with men in addiction by providing safe housing and work opportunities. The Sober Truth Project aims to reshape how the world views addiction, mental health, people with suicidal thoughts, and the roles that faith, science, and trauma play in recovery to develop a more empathetic and loving society.

George studied business management at Binghamton and Morresville State universities in New York and mental health and Christian life coaching with the American Association of Christian Counselors. A certified addiction specialist, he is an ordained pastor and pastoral care counselor ordained by Cornerstone Mission Family Church.

George currently works directly with the Sober Truth Project, speaking, consulting, and coaching in order to engage, educate, equip, and empower faith communities, churches, and leaders of all people groups. He also has a successful podcast *The Sober Truth*, which highlights the meeting of faith and recovery, bringing light and understanding to all of the topics of *The Uncovery*.

"There is a world that is hurting, lives that are being lost, and future generations that are wandering with no one to lead them home," George says. "Addiction, mental health, trauma, and suicide are terrifying topics; we all feel ill-equipped for the challenges that surround those who are suffering. We cannot continue to sidestep the challenges, and we cannot hold on to the same old procedures that have never worked just because they feel safe. We all must do better."

George lives in the inner city in Tampa, Florida, with his wife Julie and a community of brothers and sisters living out the gospel in a radical way. He has seen how the power of community can heal the trauma that causes addiction, mental health problems, and suicidal thoughts, so he is focused on mobilizing a generation of believers to go deeper into the Uncovery space.

To connect with George, visit:

www.georgeawood.com

www.youtube.com/@GeorgeWoodSoberTruth

———

Brit Eaton is a writer, teacher, spiritual director, and all-around pursuer of the kingdom of God. She helps corporate, nonprofit, and ministry leaders find the words to say to move people to action.

An eager apostle and strong advocate for nontraditional recovery and women in ministry, Brit ministers in diverse, spirit-filled environments committed to unity in the body of Christ.

In addition to this devotional, she also coauthored *The Uncovery: Understanding the Power of Community to Heal Trauma*, inspired by and developed with George Wood, and *Reckless Grace*, a book inspired by and developed with Bill Vanderbush.

Brit received a B.A. in Visual Communication from Mount Vernon Nazarene University, where she serves as an adjunct professor of business and marketing. She received her M.S. in marketing and communication, summa cum laude, from Franklin University. She also served in the U.S. Marine Corps Reserve.

Brit lives in a log home on ten wooded acres in Mount Vernon, Ohio, with her husband Mike and daughter Bella.

To connect with Brit, visit www.briteaton.com.

ABOUT THE SOBER TRUTH PROJECT

The Sober Truth Project is changing the way the world thinks about recovery, starting with the church. The ministry goes beyond traditional twelve-step programming to help struggling people not only get sober but also experience a total life transformation as they discover the truth about their identities as beloved children of a good Father God.

The ministry wants to end the message of shame that currently surrounds anyone in recovery, especially those affected by addiction, mental health struggles, or suicidal thoughts.

"Real recovery is the discovery of a person's God-given identity and learning what it means to walk in it for the rest of your life," says founder George A. Wood. Thus, recovery is for everyone.

The Sober Truth Project seeks to rebuild the message of recovery by engaging, educating, equipping, and empowering communities to develop a more empathetic and loving society that helps people realize a promised-land life.

To learn more about the Sober Truth Project, visit www.sobertruthproject.org.

Welcome to Our House!

We Have a Special Gift for You

It is our privilege and pleasure to share in your love of Christian books. We are committed to bringing you authors and books that feed, challenge, and enrich your faith.

To show our appreciation, we invite you to sign up to receive a specially selected **Reader Appreciation Gift**, with our compliments. Just go to the Web address at the bottom of this page.

God bless you as you seek a deeper walk with Him!

WHITAKER
HOUSE